30

D1611663

Tobacco Colony

Life in Early Maryland, 1650-1720

GLORIA L. MAIN

Princeton University Press, Princeton, N. J.

For My Mother and Father

Eifiona Llewelyn Lund
and
Howard Gates Lund

CONTENTS

LIST OF TABLES

List of Tables

ACKNOWLEDGMENTS

Since we all, of necessity, build on others' work, let me here bear grateful witness to the many debts accumulated while engaged on the present work.

Historians are particularly dependent on archivists and librarians for efficient access to the raw materials of their trade. Under the far-sighted tutelage of Morris Radoff, and his able successor, Edward Papenfuse, the Hall of Records of the state of Maryland has become a mecca for workers wishing to mine the rich stores of public records deposited there. Its highly trained staff and magnificent system of indexes made working at the Hall always a pleasure.

Situated high in the upper recesses of the same building are the offices of the St. Mary's City Commission, funded by the state of Maryland and assisted by grants from the National Endowment for the Humanities. Under the direction of historian Lois Green Carr, the staff of the commission have produced a stream of published and unpublished articles of extraordinarily high quality and usefulness, to which the many citations contained in my bibliography attest. Dr. Carr has also done much to advance the field of local history in general and of Maryland's colonial past in particular by freely offering aid, advice, and warm hospitality to visiting historians. Maryland's citizens can take deep pride in these two state-supported institutions and in the high caliber of their professional personnel.

The entire field of colonial and early American history bears an especial debt to another institution, one not supported directly by public monies but by the generosity of Colonial Williamsburg, Inc. and by the College of William and Mary: the Institute of Early American History and Culture. Headed first by Lester Cappon, then by Stephen Kurtz, and now led by Thad Tate, the Institute has helped to attract the cream of young historians to the field by means of its fellowship program, manuscript prizes, conference series, and, above all, by the quality and flair of its great journal, *The William and Mary Quarterly*.

I also take great pleasure in acknowledging the support for this book and its sister project in colonial Massachusetts rendered by financial grants from the American Philosophical Society and the American Council of Learned Societies. As an NEH Fellow for six months at the American Antiquarian Society, I was able to use, though not exhaust, its rich collection of published and unpublished works in early American history and genealogy. My special thanks to the staff there for providing a most congenial atmosphere for working, and to Marcus McCorison, Director, and to John Hench, Research and Publications Officer, for making it possible.

The Center for Advanced Study in the Behavioral Sciences in Stanford, California, where my husband served as a fellow during the academic year 1980-1981 made my own stay there especially fruitful by daily exposure to the conversation and formal presentations of scholars drawn from a broad variety of disciplines. The staff cheerfully gave their time and help to me even though I was not myself a fellow, enabling me to complete the revision of the manuscript for the present work.

Those individuals who have read and commented on all or part of earlier drafts of *Tobacco Colony* have my heartfelt gratitude. They are not to blame for blemishes still remaining: Lois Green Carr, Paul Clemens, Stanley Engerman, Art Goldberger, Darrett Rutman, and Lorena Walsh. Conversations or correspondence with the following scholars have proven especially worthwhile: Cary Carson, Russell Menard, John McCusker, Allan Kulikoff, A. G. Roeber, Alice Hanson Jones, and Anita Rutman. My thesis advisors at Columbia University deserve thanks for their help then and their continuing support since: Stuart Bruchey and Burton Singer.

Bill Atwood did much of the programming for this and the Massachusetts project. Polly Ceckler drew the beautiful graphs.

Every scholar, too, contracts debts to the people we live with. My three children, Jackson Jr., Eifiona, and Judson Main have given me something more besides their love, affection, and respect: many, many hours of privacy and quiet to read, write, and ponder the meaning of what my research had yielded. My greatest debt, as all who know us know well, is to my husband. Jackson Turner Main was already an accomplished typist and copy editor when I married him and a promising young historian, to boot. All of these skills have been called upon repeatedly and contributed without stint. Jack has been a good listener and a loving husband, but best of all, great fun to live with. Thanks, Jack.

LIST OF ABBREVIATIONS

≈   roughly equal to

PRIMARY SOURCES

Md.Arch.   Archives of Maryland
Inv. & Accts. Inventories and Accounts

PERIODICALS

AHR   American Historical Review
EHR   Economic History Review
JEH   Journal of Economic History
JSH   Journal of Southern History
MdHM   Maryland Historical Magazine
VMHQ   Virginia Magazine of History and Biography
WMQ   William and Mary Quarterly, 3d ser.

TOBACCO COLONY

INTRODUCTION

Besides the strange and wonderful animals and peoples inhabiting the New World, Englishmen of the seventeenth century saw lands naturally fertile, well-watered, and warmed by a sun more generous than their own. The difference in climate excited them to dreams of producing semitropical products such as wines and spices, which were then very costly and under foreign control. Not only would producing such goods themselves keep their money at home but surpluses could be sold to others, diverting precious bullion from their neighbors' pockets to their own.

When the colonizers discovered that the natives were too few and too reluctant to supply the labor power with which to work plantations, they realized that laborers, too, would have to be transported to their New World enterprises. Thus, unfree labor, white and black, came to fuel England's first empire.

The motives for colonization shifted as accumulated experience gradually taught the English the limits as well as the possibilities of the New World. The public rationale for colonizing shifted as needs dictated, but disparate goals were finally woven into a flexible fabric, capable of clothing diverse aspirations.[1] It was generally

---

[1] The literature on mercantilist thought is extensive, but the classic work is that by Eli F. Hecksher, *Mercantilism*, 2 vols., 2nd ed. (London, 1955). Charles Wilson, *Mercantilism* (London, 1958) provides a readable summary. See also Philip W. Buck, *The Politics of Mercantilism* (New York, 1942); William Cunningham, *Growth of English Industry and Commerce*, 3 vols. (Cambridge, 1921-1927), II, Part 1 on mercantilism; and Jacob Viner, *Studies in the Theory of International Trade* (New York, 1937), Chapters 1 and 2. Joyce Oldham Appleby, *Economic Thought and Ideology in Seventeenth-Century England* (Princeton, 1978) extends our understanding of mercantilist thought in England. On the relationship between England and her colonies, J[ames] F. Rees, "Mercantilism and the Colonies," in *The Old Empire from the Beginning to 1781*, vol. I of *Cambridge History of the British Empire*, edited by J[ohn] Holland Rose et al. (Cambridge, 1929), 561-602; Charles M. Andrews, *The Colonial Period of American History*, IV, *England's Commercial and Colonial Policy* (New Haven, 1938); George Louis Beer, *The Old Colonial System, 1660-1754*; Part 1, *The Establishment of the System, 1660-1688*, 2 vols. (New York, 1912) and *The Origins of the British Colonial System, 1578-1660* (New York, 1908); Lawrence A. Harper, *The English Navigation Laws: a Seventeenth-Century Experiment in Social Engineering* (New York, 1939); Curtis P. Nettels, "British Mercantilism and Economic Development of the Thirteen Colonies," *JEH*, XII (1952), 105-14; D. A. Farnie, "The Commercial Empire of the Atlantic, 1607-1783," *EHR*, 2d ser., XV (1962), 205-18; Thomas C. Barrow, *Trade and Empire:*

agreed that the presence of colonies would encourage shipping, a desirable goal since ships and mariners made up the first line of defense for the island core. With a strong fleet, Englishmen should be able to pocket the middleman's profits for their own carrying trade and for the sale of English goods abroad. Another motive—quite persuasive once it proved feasible—was the idea that colonies could put to useful work the surplus population eating up the scanty supplies of food at home. Observers complained that England was overpopulated, her people underemployed, and the poor a growing burden on the productive classes. Why not ship them off, then, and do everyone a favor? By promising them land and the opportunity to set up for themselves, colonial proprietors and English merchants succeeded in luring abroad a vast stream of humanity that washed across the shores of the American continents from Hudson's Bay in the north to the coast of Guyana in the south.

Another set of motives for supporting colonies came to prominence by the final quarter of the seventeenth century: their usefulness as markets. Rather than shipping over the dwindling supply of cheap labor, people should be put to work at home to supply expanding overseas markets for English-made goods.[2] The colonies became just as important as buyers from the mother country as they already were as suppliers, while continuing to yield a steady stream of customs revenue to a government that had grown dependent on it.

As the English came to recognize the significance and benefits of their commercial empire, they began to impose more stringent trading and marketing restrictions, which sometimes harmonized but often conflicted with the economic interests of the disparate parts of their empire.[3] The Navigation Acts and the personnel staffing the boards, committees, and enforcement agencies helped shape the course of colonial development while promoting England's interests in an armed and hostile world. Because imperial policies wrought occasional hardships in exchange for often nebulous benefits, they have tended to draw the blame for the troubles and discontents that plagued the struggling settlements in the seventeenth century.

The British Customs Service in Colonial America, 1660-1775 (Cambridge, Mass., 1967); Michael Kammen, *Empire and Interest: The American Colonies and the Politics of Mercantilism* (New York, 1970).

[2] Sir Josiah Child, *A New Discourse of Trade* (1668; London, 1718), pp. 215-16.

[3] A particularly good exposition of the economic effects of imperial organization and politics on colonial development is Richard B. Sheridan's *Sugar and Slavery: an Economic History of the British West Indies, 1623-1775* (St. Lawrence, Barbados, 1974).

The mercantilist strategies of the mother country bridled but did not seriously distort colonial development in the New World, which came to depend on the two most important export crops, tobacco and sugar. These provided the cash income that underwrote virtually the entire enterprise, even in New England, which could not have survived without the trade to the West Indies. Both crops were comparatively recent introductions to the growing consumer market at home and on the continent. Although tobacco inspired revulsion and resistance among many churchmen and their lay supporters, both it and sugar found wider popular acceptance as their prices declined.

The weight of expanding supply, however, eventually created a pressing need for additional markets, but international rivalries hampered English efforts to dispose of Chesapeake tobacco in Europe, whereas wars and privateering repeatedly disrupted the shipping lanes across the Atlantic. The vicissitudes of the markets for colonial staples not only made precarious the situations of producers, they governed the very process of settlement itself by attracting or deflecting potential emigrants and venture capital from the mother country. Good prices for sugar brought waves of new capital and slaves to Barbados, enlivening the market there for the fish and timber products of New England. Good prices for tobacco, on the other hand, attracted less capital but did invigorate the recruitment of servants among the unemployed young men crowding the port towns of home.

When the markets for both staples stagnated, as they did during the 1680s, prospective immigrants and capital flowed elsewhere or stayed at home. Pennsylvania and Carolina then welcomed the new arrivals as well as overflows from older settlements, but these events signaled the end of England's great migration, never again to be renewed at such high levels. Maryland's colonists enjoyed the benefits and suffered the ills common to all producers of agricultural staples for sale in markets that are beyond their control.[4] Its early history cannot be told apart from that of tobacco, its culture, and the mutability of its fortunes.

[4] On the so-called "staple thesis" and its application to the economy of early America, see text and notes to chapter 2 of "The Economy of British America, 1607-1790: Needs and Opportunites for Study," by John J. McCusker and Russell R. Menard, unpublished paper prepared for a Conference on the Economy of British America held at Williamsburg, Virginia, October 9-10, 1980. An earlier version of the argument appears in David W. Galenson and Russell R. Menard, "Approaches to the Analysis of Economic Growth in Colonial British America," *Historical Methods*, XIII (1980), 3-18.

Although Maryland's founder and proprietor, the first Lord Baltimore, intended the new colony to provide a haven for persecuted Roman Catholics, he also expected his grateful subjects to earn their living and his by following Virginia's example—to raise the smokers' weed. Nearly two hundred colonists debarked from the Ark and the Dove in the spring of 1634 to be welcomed by natives and provisioned by Virginians. As the Jesuit priests fanned out to preach to the Indians, the others were occupied in planting fields that had been amicably tendered in exchange for military protection against marauding tribes.

Born thus in peace and plenty, Maryland grew quickly, its population soon swelled by the influx of Quakers and Puritans harried out of Virginia by Governor Berkeley's repression of all religious dissent. Despite Maryland's "Act Concerning Religion" (1649), which granted freedom of conscience to all Christians, however, hatred and fear of Catholics caused repeated political turmoil, overthrowing the Proprietor's rule in 1654 and again in 1692. Not until the fourth Lord Baltimore, Benedict Leonard Calvert, renounced the Catholic creed did proprietary rule firmly reestablish itself in 1715. By then, however, a native-born and powerful planter class had arisen to challenge external sources of constraint.

Although religion often divided his lordship's subjects in the first century of settlement, the culture of tobacco continued as their common lot. In order for us to understand life in early Maryland, we must understand the tobacco economy, how it functioned, the demands it placed on its producers, and perhaps most important of all, the unhealthy environment of the Chesapeake tidewater lands on which it was then grown. Malaria and water-borne disease afflicted the immigrant and native-born alike. The consequences of high adult mortality included the prolongation of frontier conditions, a continuing need for fresh supplies of labor, the early break-up of families, and the orphaning of children. Capital accumulation within and across generations was interupted by the early death of fathers and remarriages of mothers. Thus, economy and demography intertwined.

Chapter One traces the growth of Maryland's population in the seventeenth century and relates its pattern to the functioning of the tobacco economy that pulsed in response to demand in England and on the Continent. When prices were good, recruitment of servants supplied white male adults to planters anxious to expand output, and swelled both immigration and exports. Two long periods of depression, 1686-1696 and 1703-1716, forced planters to turn to other means of making ends meet and witnessed the growth of population on lands that were marginal to profitable production of tobacco.

Chapter Two examines the process of development in economic terms, using probate records to trace the course of average wealth over time, and locating growth in the increasing numbers of rich men in the colony. This was partly due to the demographic changes underway, which altered the age profile of the living population as well as of the probated decedents, and resulted in a growing pool of older men with fortunes accrued over longer working lives. The growing wealth of those at the top extended inequality in an already highly stratified society, but the two depressions eroded the holdings of the middling planters and drove away the young, the poor, and the newly freed servants. How the economy of early Maryland adjusted to these depressions constitutes the bulk of the chapter's story.

The 1680s and 1690s witnessed another transition, as well, which Chapter Three addresses in detail: the shift from servant to slave in the tobacco economy. In it I argue, with Russell R. Menard, that the decision to buy slaves was essentially an economic one, arising out of considerations of supply and price.[5] Those who acquired slaves, moreover, lost interest in buying servants even after the market again reduced the price differential between them. The chapter goes on to explore the process of transition, tracing the numbers and distributions of the two kinds of laborers in successive periods, and analyzing the composition of the labor force at the plantation level. Finally, conditions of black and white servitude come under survey, and attempts are made to compare them.

Whereas these first three chapters are devoted mainly to the production side of the Maryland economy, the last four attend to the consumption side. There are chapters on housing, the standard of living of the poorer planters and their families, the life styles of middling and affluent planters, and an examination of the unspoken system of priorities among them, which one can infer from the selection of household goods found at successively higher wealth levels within the planter class. The conclusion is clear that Maryland planters, rich and poor, placed investment ahead of consumption, and lived at a level that proved spare, crude, and unself-conscious. Despite major changes in both the demographic and social structure

[5] Russell R. Menard, "From Servants to Slaves: The Transformation of the Chesapeake Labor System," *Southern Studies*, XVI (1977), 355-90.

7

of the colony, the daily life of ordinary men and women scarcely differed in 1720 from that in 1650. The material circumstances in which they lived had not altered at all.

Economic decisions made by individuals acting independently of each other often have profound implications for the larger social organism of which they form a part. The long period of expansion in the tobacco economy nurtured the settlement process and provided hope and opportunity to the thousands who emigrated. The cessation of that expansion inflicted hardship on the most recent arrivals, forcing many to try their luck elsewhere, and deprived the more affluent planters of their usual source of labor. Slaves filled their needs and reduced the demand for servants, who otherwise would have faced rather gloomy prospects after freedom. A moral dilemma was thus born out of an economic one—a familiar progression in the history of humankind.

Individual success in the tobacco colony was primarily the product of good timing and good health. If a white man survived the rigors of crossing, seasoning, and servitude, he could then begin to amass the necessary capital with which to acquire land, a wife, and then a servant. If he lived long enough and aggressively expanded his enterprise while tobacco prices were up, he could ride out the down part of the cycle and then proceed to take advantage of the next upturn. By rigorously saving and reinvesting his cash income, he could secure his own enterprise and help his children launch theirs. Fortunate indeed were the children whose father lived long enough to give them a head start.

Chapter One

TOBACCO COLONY

The Growth of Maryland's Population in the Seventeenth Century

In order to understand life in early Maryland one must begin with three facts about the residents: for most of the seventeenth century they were almost entirely immigrants, most of them were white and male, and all made their living from tobacco. Tobacco is the reason they had come—as tobacco had paid the way for at least a third of all English immigrants to the New World in the seventeenth century, including those to the British West Indies prior to 1640.[1]

The size and destinations of the emigrant stream out of the British Isles altered over the course of the century as it responded to changes in the relative attractiveness of the different regions open to settlement. In the 1630s, the prospective immigrant could choose between New England and the various islands of the British West Indies as well as the Chesapeake. After that decade, however, New England found it a struggle to earn foreign exchange and offered scant opportunity to newcomers without skills, capital, or connections. The switch to sugar and slaves on Barbados and later the other islands favored the wealthy and well connected, so the islands gradually gained the reputation of being inhospitable to the single young men of little means who made up the overwhelming majority of those leaving home.[2]

In contrast, the tobacco colonies of the Chesapeake offered, in

---

[1] H. A. Gemery, "Emigration from the British Isles to the New World, 1630-1700," *Research in Economic History*, V (1980), 179-232; Russell R. Menard, "British Migration to the Chesapeake Colonies in the Seventeenth Century," an unpublished paper presented to the Economic History Workshop, Department of Economics, University of Chicago on February 29, 1980, p. 18.

[2] Robert Carlyle Batie, "Why Sugar? Economic Cycles and the Changing of Staples on the English and French Antilles, 1624-54," *Journal of Caribbean History*, VIII (1976), 1-41.

Alfred D. Chandler argued in an early article that 30,000 people left Barbados in the thirty years after 1650, calling it the "largest population movement within the colonies during the seventeenth century." Chandler, "The Expansion of Barbados," *Journal of the Barbados Museum and Historical Society*, XIII (1946), 106-14, quoted in Sheridan, *Sugar and Slavery*, p. 133.

return for service, land that grew a crop with ready buyers, a crop that required no more than an ax and hoe and a man's strong back. As Table I-1 shows, an increasing portion of Englishmen leaving home came to the shores of the Chesapeake. Of some 9,000 servants leaving the port of Bristol in the years between 1654 and 1679, well over half headed for Maryland and Virginia.[3] After that time, however, the bright promise of the area dimmed as the opening up of Pennsylvania and the Carolinas offered, in their turn, ready access to good land and the opportunity to earn a farm of one's own in a few years' time.

For ambitious young Englishmen, economic opportunity abroad provided the attraction, but declining real wages, civil war, and social upheaval at home applied the "push." Prior to 1640, prices of farm crops in England rose faster than those for livestock. Those who bought their food—the small holder, the farm laborer, and the craftsman—found their expenditures outstripping their wages. The farmer who grew grains, however, waxed wealthy and bought more land from his smaller neighbors. Rapid growth of the population during the previous two centuries had meanwhile produced a labor force too large for the sputtering economy to absorb, with consequent crises occurring at the end of the sixteenth century and again twenty years later. Textile workers, who were already hurting

TABLE I.1
ESTIMATES OF BRITISH MIGRATION TO THE AMERICAS, 1630-1700

Years	Total Migration	To the Chesapeake	% of Total
1630-1640	41,100	9,000-10,100	21.9-24.6
1640-1650	46,100	8,100-8,900	17.6-19.3
1650-1660	58,200	16,700-18,200	28.7-31.3
1660-1670	55,200	19,500-20,900	35.3-37.9
1670-1680	53,700	21,700-23,000	40.4-42.8
1680-1690	40,200	14,600	36.3
1690-1700	44,100	15,800-16,000	35.8-36.3
Total	338,600	105,400-111,700	31.1-33.0

SOURCES: H. A. Gemery, "Emigration from the British Isles to the New World, 1630-1700: Inferences from Colonial Populations," *Research in Economic History*, V (1980), 179-231; Russell R. Menard, "British Migration to the Chesapeake Colonies in the Seventeenth Century," unpublished paper presented to the Economic History Workshop, Department of Economics, University of Chicago, February 29, 1980, Table 4. I have used Menard's modifications of Gemery's figures.

[3] Abbot Emerson Smith, *Colonists in Bondage: White Servitude and Convict Labor in America, 1607-1776* (Chapel Hill, 1947), p. 309.

10

from the inflation in food prices, now faced dislocations in the overseas markets for their product. Sometime after the mid-point of the century, however, all these "push" factors began to lose their thrust, while the "pull" of opportunity abroad also abated. Food prices at home turned downward and employment rose as the English economy picked up speed. The pool of labor began shrinking as the rate of population growth slowed, narrowing the size of the group of potential migrants, as well.[4] Simultaneously, the prices of sugar and tobacco gently skidded downward, gradually depressing the margins of profit among the planters and finally leading to general stagnation in total output after 1680.[5] By the beginning of the eighteenth century, therefore, Englishmen had virtually ceased to emigrate in any sizeable number and population in the older colonies was left to grow, or decline, on its own.[6]

The actual course of the colonies' demographic processes followed very different routes. New England, for instance, had received within the single decade of the 1630s an infusion of some twenty thousand immigrants and almost none thereafter. Yet by the year 1700, the region could claim a total white population almost four times the size of its initial immigration. In the Ches-

[4] D. C. Coleman, *The Economy of England, 1450-1750* (New York, 1977) provides a good overview. W. G. Hoskins, "Harvest Fluctuations, 1620-1759," *Agricultural History Review*, XVI (1968), 15-31, shows that the worst runs of bad harvests came in 1646-1650, 1657-1661, 1695-1698, and 1708-1711, all but the latter years of heavy immigration into the Chesapeake. See also E. H. Phelps Brown and S. V. Hopkins, "Seven Centuries of the Prices of Consumables Compared with Builders' Wage-Rates," *Economica*, XXIII (1956), 296-314; D. C. Coleman, "Labour in the English Economy of the Seventeenth Century," *EHR*, 2d ser., VIII (1956), 280-95; Barry E. Supple, *Commercial Crisis and Change in England, 1600-1642* (Cambridge, 1959), chapters 6 and 7; E. Kerridge, "The Movement of Rent, 1540-1640," *EHR*, 2d ser., VI (1953), 16-34; Elizabeth B. Schumpeter, "English Prices and Public Finance, 1660-1682," *Review of Economics and Statistics*, XX (1938), 21-37; Peter Bowden, "Agricultural Prices, Farm Profits, and Rents," in *The Agrarian History of England and Wales*, IV, edited by Joan Thirsk (Cambridge, 1967), 617-27; J. Cornwall, "Evidence of Population Mobility in the Seventeenth Century," *Bulletin of the Institute for Historical Research*, XL (1967); and his "Migration in England, 1660-1730," *Past and Present*, LXXXIII (1979), 57-90.

[5] For prices of sugar in London, see K. G. Davies, *The Royal African Company* (London, 1957), Appendix IV; for prices in Amsterdam, see his, *The North Atlantic World in the Seventeenth Century* (Minneapolis, 1974), pp. 188-90; for tobacco prices, Russell R. Menard, "Farm Prices of Maryland Tobacco, 1659-1710," *MdHM*, LXVIII (1973), 80-85, "A Note on Chesapeake Tobacco Prices, 1618-1660," *VMHB*, LXXIV (1976), 401-10, and "The Tobacco Industry in the Chesapeake Colonies, 1617-1730: an Interpretation," *Research in Economic History*, V (1980), 157-61.

[6] Coleman, *Economy of England*, pp. 15-16.

apeake, by contrast, over a hundred thousand arrived during the century, but fewer than seventy thousand whites were living there at its close.[7] This extraordinary discrepancy between the demographic experiences of the two regions can be explained by two factors: age at first marriage for women and the differences in the mortality of adults. The sex ratio among immigrants to both regions was equally lopsided in favor of males, but those women going to New England could, and did, marry far younger than those going to the Chesapeake because the latter went under indenture and had to serve four or five years before they could marry. The relative youth of New England's first white mothers, moreover, made it possible for the founding generation to continue to bear children even after their children began bearing theirs. The virtual absence there of epidemic diseases in the seventeenth century combined with relatively low ages at marriage to promote astonishingly high levels of marital fertility and unusually long lives, with a consequent rate of population growth unparalleled in Western European history before the nineteenth century.[8]

Not only did the immigrants and their children thrive in the northern clime, successive generations grew up there in the company of their grandparents. At the end of a span of time that saw the passage of as many as three sets of such patriarchs in Massachusetts, immigrants were still as numerous as native-born in Maryland, where only a handful of children had grown up in the sight of their grandparents; yet the two colonies had been founded within

[7] Menard, "British Migration," p. 9. U.S. Bureau of the Census, *Historical Statistics of the United States, Colonial Times to 1970*, Bicentennial edition, 2 parts (Washington, D.C., 1975), series Z 1-19, 1168 gives figures of 91,083 whites living in New England and 68,538 in Virginia and Maryland combined.

[8] J. Potter, "The Growth of Population in America, 1700-1860," in D. V. Glass and D.E.C. Eversley, eds., *Population in History: Essays in Historical Demography* (Chicago, 1965), pp. 631-88. For a recent review of work, see Daniel Scott Smith, "The Estimates of Early American Historical Demographers: Two Steps Forward, One Step Back, What Steps in the Future," *Historical Methods*, XII (1979), 24-38. Most useful are Philip J. Greven, Jr., *Four Generations: Population, Land and Family in Colonial Andover, Massachusetts* (Ithaca, 1970); Kenneth A. Lockridge, "The Population of Dedham, Massachusetts, 1636-1736," *EHR*, 2d ser., XIX (1966), 318-44; John Demos, "Families in Colonial Bristol, Rhode Island: An Exercise in Historical Demography," *WMQ*, XXV (1968), 40-57; Maris A. Vinovskis, "Mortality Rates and Trends in Massachusetts before 1860," *JEH*, XXXII (1972), 184-213; Susan L. Norton, "Population Growth in Colonial America: A Study of Ipswich, Massachusetts," *Population Studies*, XXV (1971), 433-52; Daniel Scott Smith, "Parental Power and Marriage Patterns: An Analysis of Historical Trends in Hingham, Massachusetts," *Journal of Marriage and the Family*, XXXV (1973), 419-28; idem, "The Demographic History of Colonial New England," *JEH*, XXXII (1972), 165-83.

a half-dozen years of each other. Indeed, such was the longevity and fertility of generations in the northern colony that it would have been possible for a woman born in 1610 with a daughter born in 1630 to have cuddled in her arms her first great-granddaughter by 1675. Furthermore, if she survived into her eighties, she might even have seen her great, great-granddaughter before the century saw its close.

If the New England colonies were exceptional in the fecundity of their people, the tidewater areas along the Atlantic coast, from the great bay of the Chesapeake down to the marshlands of Georgia, were outstanding for their morbidity.[9] Dysentery and malaria so greatly weakened their victims that typhoid fever, pneumonia,

[9] Outstanding pioneer works in colonial southern demography include Wesley Frank Craven, *Red, White, and Black: The Seventeenth-Century Virginian* (Charlottesville, 1971); Lorena S. Walsh and Russell R. Menard, "Death in the Chesapeake: Two Life Tables for Men in Early Colonial Maryland," *MdHM*, LIX (1974), 211-27; Irene W. D. Hecht, "The Virginia Muster of 1624-5 as a Source for Demographic History," *WMQ*, XXX (1973), 65-92; Edmund S. Morgan, *American Slavery, American Freedom: The Ordeal of Colonial Virginia* (New York, 1975); Darrett B. Rutman and Anita H. Rutman, "Of Agues and Fevers: Malaria in the Early Chesapeake," *WMQ*, XXXIII (1976), 31-60; idem, " 'Now-Wives and Sons-in-Law': Parental Death in a Seventeenth-Century Virginia County," in Thad W. Tate and David L. Ammerman, eds., *The Chesapeake in the Seventeenth Century: Essays on Anglo-American Society* (Chapel Hill, 1979), pp. 153-82; idem, " 'More True and Perfect Lists': The Reconstruction of Censuses for Middlesex County, Virginia, 1668-1704," *VMHB*, LXXXVIII (1980), 37-74; Russell R. Menard, "The Growth of Population in Early Colonial Maryland, 1631-1712," unpublished report prepared for the St. Mary's City Commission dated April 1972 (copy on file at Hall of Records, Annapolis); idem, "Immigrants and Their Increase: The Process of Population Growth in Early Colonial Maryland," in Aubrey C. Land, Lois Green Carr, and Edward C. Papenfuse, eds., *Law, Society, and Politics in Early Maryland* (Baltimore, 1977), pp. 88-110; Daniel Blake Smith, "Mortality and Family in the Colonial Chesapeake," *Journal of Interdisciplinary History*, VIII (1978), 403-27; Terry L. Anderson and Robert Paul Thomas, "The Growth of Population and Labor Force in the 17th-Century Chesapeake," *Explorations in Economic History*, XV (1978), 290-312; Carville V. Earle, "Environment, Disease, and Mortality in Early Virginia," in Tate and Ammerman, *Chesapeake*, pp. 96-125.

For slaves, see Russell R. Menard, "The Maryland Slave Population, 1658-1730: A Demographic Profile of Blacks in Four Counties," *WMQ*, XXXII (1975), 29-54; Allan Kulikoff, "A 'Prolifick' People: Black Population Growth in the Chesapeake Colonies, 1700-1790," *Southern Studies*, XVI (1977), 391-428; Darrett B. Rutman, Charles Wetherell, and Anita H. Rutman, "Rhythms of Life: Black and White Seasonality in the Early Chesapeake," *Journal of Interdisciplinary History*, XI (1980), 29-53.

Nothing like this imposing array of systematic and highly sophisticated works exists as yet for areas outside of the Chesapeake, but see Peter H. Wood, *Black Majority: Negroes in Colonial South Carolina from 1670 through the Stono Rebellion* (New York, 1974); J. M. Gallman, "Mortality among White Males in Colonial North Carolina," *Social Science History*, IV (1980), 295-316.

and influenza met scant resistance. A young man of twenty-one who lived through the rigors of "the seasoning" in early Maryland could expect to live another twenty or twenty-five years—no more. The average age at death among white male adults in the Chesapeake was close to forty for immigrants, significantly less than fifty for native-born, but—by contrast—close to sixty for men in New England.[10] If a man had to serve four years as a servant and then delay marriage four or five years longer while saving his wages, any children he might eventually sire would be orphaned before the eldest could reach maturity.[11] This assumes that a man succeeded in finding a wife when he sought one, and that she was young enough, and healthy enough, to give him children in the first place.

Thus, the unfree status of most of the young people making up the immigrant flow to the Chesapeake was fully as important to this drama as the unhealthy circumstances of the region. The immigrants were young, certainly, but mostly servants, and mostly male. Close to three-quarters came in bondage, and there were 274 men for every 100 women.[12] The relative scarcity of women was further compounded by the risks they faced during pregnancy, risks exacerbated by the loss of immunity to malaria engendered by the fact of pregnancy itself.[13] Those men who lived long enough did eventually marry, having waited their turn in an extended queue for those few women who survived seasoning, service, and weaker spouses. The average age at marriage for male immigrants to the Chesapeake was about thirty, but over a fourth never married at all.[14]

Most women servants were already past twenty when they arrived. After four or five years of service, they had their pick of a multitude of eager suitors, but their average age at the birth of

[10] Walsh and Menard, "Death in the Chesapeake," p. 220; D. B. Smith, "Mortality and Family," p. 415.

[11] Lorena Seeback Walsh, "Charles County, Maryland, 1658-1705: A Study of Chesapeake Social and Political Structure," (Ph.D. dissertation, Michigan State University, 1977), p. 144. Lois Green Carr and Lorena S. Walsh, "The Planter's Wife: The Experience of White Women in Seventeenth-Century Maryland," *WMQ*, XXXIV (1977), 555, reports that of 1735 adult male decedents in the counties of the lower western shore of Maryland, 72 percent died without children or with children not yet of age. Only 16 percent could be proved to have a child of age.

[12] Close to three-quarters of all immigrants to Maryland prior to 1681 were servants. Menard, "British Migration," Table 7, also reports sex ratios.

[13] Rutman and Rutman, "Of Agues and Fevers," p. 52.

[14] Walsh, "Charles County," p. 63.

their first child was well above twenty-five, with consequences for the birth rate greater than one might suppose.[15] The older a woman is when she has her first child, the longer the interval between subsequent births, and the greater danger to both herself and to her babies. The older the woman at marriage, then, the fewer children she will bear. The effects of delayed marriage on population growth and structure become dramatically clear by illustration. In a study of one colonial New England community, the average number of children born to women married before age 20 was 7.5, but for women who married after age 24, that number fell to just 4.5.[16] In circumstances such as these, forty percent of potential babies would never get born as a result of later marriages for mothers.

Thus the delay in marriage imposed by servitude, a lopsided sex ratio, and heavy adult mortality severely circumscribed the number of families that could form and the number of children that could be born. Only a third of all marriages in the early Chesapeake lasted as long as a decade, and an average of only two children were born to them.[17] Not surprisingly then, births did not exceed deaths and the population could grow only through continued immigration. A core of native-born gradually expanded in the sea of nonnatives, but they did not come to outnumber immigrants until the turn of the century or even later.[18] Among them the situation was different: as many females as males grew up, and most married quite young since they did not have to indenture themselves. The average age at marriage of native-born girls in one Maryland county was just sixteen.[19] Only when the proportion of natives grew large enough did births finally exceed deaths, at which point natural growth of the population took place.

[15] Menard, "Immigrants and Their Increase," p. 100.

[16] Susan L. Norton, "Ipswich, Massachusetts," p. 444, discussed in Carr and Walsh, "Planter's Wife," p. 552.

[17] Walsh, "Charles County," p. 67.

[18] Carr and Walsh, "Planter's Wife," p. 565 n. 76. Rutman and Rutman report that the proportion of native-born in Middlesex County, Virginia, was close to half as early as 1687; "More True and Perfect Lists," p. 63. Of that colony generally, Governor Nicholson reported to the Board of Trade in 1701, "The Country consists now most of Natives few of which have . . . been abroad in the World." Quoted in John C. Rainbolt, "The Alteration in the Relationship between Leadership and Constituents in Virginia, 1660 to 1720," *WMQ*, XXVII (1970), 431.

[19] Russell R. Menard, "The Demography of Somerset County, Maryland: A Preliminary Report," unpublished paper given at the Stony Brook Conference on Social History, June 1975.

To summarize, growth of the population in the Chesapeake colonies during the seventeenth century depended on infusions from abroad, and these had to be lured by the promise of a better life and of economic opportunity. The region competed with other colonies and with the home market for the young men and women entering the English labor force, and the price of tobacco received by the planters determined the force of their bidding. Push and pull factors altered with changing circumstances, but the fortunes of the international tobacco market played a key role in our story.

How the Tobacco Economy Functioned

Tobacco lies at the heart of Maryland history in the colony's first hundred years, not only because the ups and downs in its price orchestrated the volume and pace of immigration into the region but because every time its production expanded, the lines of settlement were extended, the numbers of colonists increased and total output was raised. Each downturn sharply constricted the incomes of the planters and eroded the capacity of freed servants to strike out on their own. Tobacco prices, therefore, provide a kind of index to the general welfare of the population as a whole as well as a guide to the course of tobacco growing over the century. Figure I-1 assembles the available data, mostly from literary sources before 1660 and from Maryland probate inventories thereafter. These point estimates are displayed on a semi-logarithmic scale and form a clear picture of protracted decline. Since the number of planter households increased over time, roughly at the rate of 3 percent a year, output multiplied as well, placing great pressure on the price of tobacco as a consequence. Its downward course could not continue indefinitely since costs must be covered or producers will quit. Freed servants would find prospects dismal and land owners would attract neither buyers nor tenants. In the short-run, however, people had to continue to grow tobacco because it was their only source of cash income. With it they could pay taxes and debts. If they postponed purchases, including new servants, they might last out the depression until prices again revived.

Prices did move up and down in a short-run pattern very similar to the behavior of agricultural prices today, and it was to these short-run fluctuations that people responded.[20] After Virginia's first boom, prices plunged and the little settlement found itself in

[20] Russell R. Menard, "Tobacco Industry," pp. 107-77.

Figure I - 1

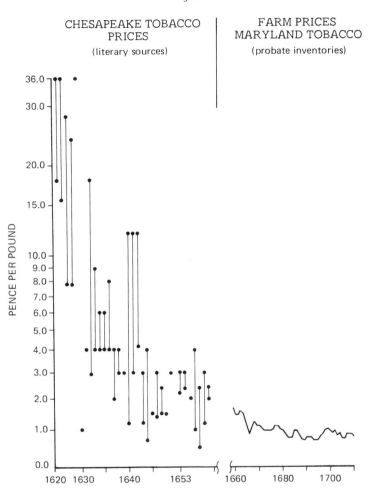

CHESAPEAKE TOBACCO
PRICES
(literary sources)

FARM PRICES
MARYLAND TOBACCO
(probate inventories)

SOURCE: See n. 23.

its first depression by the end of the 1620s, facing new competition from the first of the West Indian settlements. Prices recovered, however, as they were to do again and again over the course of the succeeding decades, and during this particular recovery Maryland and other West Indian colonies were founded to take advantage of the boom. By 1637 another depression threatened as civil troubles at home disrupted markets and shipping across the At-

17

lantic. During the 1640s, Maryland actually lost most of her earliest settlers and several of the West Indian islands found themselves in similar danger. Dutch ships came to the rescue of many and aided the switch from tobacco to sugar on Barbados, the most populous of the Caribbean colonies.[21] Tobacco prices peaked again during the years from 1648 to 1654, but slumped thereafter. The Anglo-Dutch wars and the efforts of the home government to enforce England's monopoly of major colonial staples constricted the market, beating down the prices received by the planters to a new low in 1666. Recoveries thereafter tended to be mild, brief, and to be spaced further and further apart. After 1680, prices remained generally depressed until the 1730s, the slump broken only by the interlude between the wars of King William and Queen Anne, and again when the French farmers-general began buying tobacco directly from small merchant suppliers based in England.[22]

The output of tobacco expanded in bursts of activity following each upturn in domestic prices, but did not contract very much with the downturns, since the resident population had swelled in the meanwhile. Customs figures on imports of tobacco into Great Britain offer some insight into the pattern of long-term production, although none survives for the years between 1640 and 1663, and only scattered figures are available thereafter until the annual colonial series commenced in 1697. Figure I-2 discloses that less than half a million pounds were imported from Virginia in 1630, but this figure approached sixteen million by the end of the 1660s from the two colonies combined. Imports rose to some 21 million by 1682 but fluctuated thereafter between 28 and 31 million pounds until commencing its rise after 1717. Population, meanwhile, had swelled from about 2,500 living in Virginia in 1630 to 23,000 in

[21] Batie, "Why Sugar?" p. 36.

[22] Crucial to an understanding of the evolution of international markets in which the tobacco planters competed is the work of Jacob Price, in particular *France and the Chesapeake: A History of the French Tobacco Monopoly, 1674-1791, and of Its Relationship to the British and American Tobacco Trades* (Ann Arbor, 1973). See also idem, *The Tobacco Adventure to Russia: Enterprise, Politics, and Diplomacy in the Quest for a Northern Market for English Colonial Tobacco, 1676-1722*, in *Transactions of the American Philosophical Society*, new series, LI, part I (1961); idem, "The Economic Growth of the Chesapeake and the European Market, 1697-1775," *JEH*, XXIV (1964), 496-511, and idem, "The Rise of Glasgow in the Chesapeake Tobacco Trade, 1707-1775," *WMQ*, XI (1954), 179-99. French demand was the crucial factor in pulling the Chesapeake out of its protracted doldrums. The power of its organized monopoly transformed the marketing organization of England, Scotland, and the colonies.

Figure I - 2

BRITISH IMPORTS OF CHESAPEAKE TOBACCO AND THE
TOTAL POPULATION OF MARYLAND AND VIRGINIA

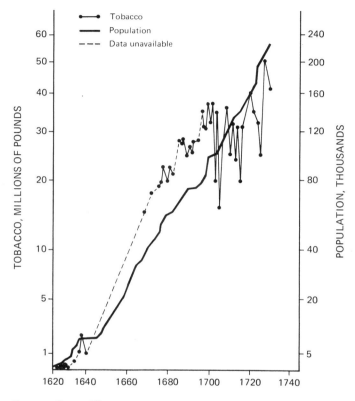

SOURCE: See n. 23.

both colonies in 1650, was double that number by 1670, and reached 100,000 sometime about the year 1700. At that point, exports per capita began to decline, reflecting not only a withdrawal of labor time from tobacco production, but a shift in the composition of the population as it moved from a high proportion of male immigrants in the labor force to a family-dominated society with larger proportions of women and children who either did not participate in tobacco production or who did so at lower levels of productivity than men.

The income of the planters gyrated in response to the fluctuating prices of their staple. By putting together tobacco prices and export data, we can calculate annual gross income from tobacco over the course of the colonial period.[23] By dividing this gross figure by the number of inhabitants or by the number of "taxables" in Maryland and Virginia, we can obtain estimates of annual income per capita and per taxable. Figure I-3 displays the results for the period 1669 through 1723. Gaps in the export data, which are actually imports of tobacco from the Chesapeake colonies into England, require us to interpolate somewhat before 1697, and the graph extends beyond 1719 so that readers will not project the temporary economic recovery beginning in 1716 beyond its actual bounds.

Two kinds of movement dominate the annual series of income from tobacco, a secular trend that bottomed out before 1716 and large year-to-year fluctuations, which are more pronounced after 1700 than before.[24] After 1680, and particularly after 1702, the

Figure I - 3

INCOME PER TAXABLE AND PER CAPITA
MARYLAND AND VIRGINIA 1669–1723

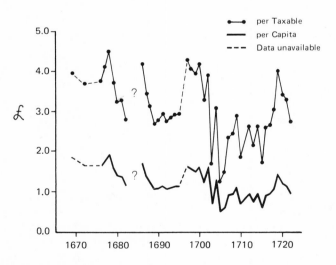

[23] Russell R. Menard, "Farm Prices of Maryland Tobacco," pp. 80-85; idem, "A Note on Chesapeake Tobacco Prices," pp. 401-10; idem, "The Tobacco Industry in the Chesapeake Colonies," pp. 157-61.

[24] Menard states, "Income per taxable from tobacco . . . fell sharply from the mid-1620s to the 1630s, and then, despite the apparent cyclical fluctuations, remained stable for about seventy years before beginning another decline just after

picture looks rather grim from the point of view of the planters. Depressions stretched longer and deeper, and recoveries were all too brief. For most of the seventeenth century, there were no ready substitutes for tobacco to obtain needed cash income. One could sell wheat and barreled pork to passing ships from New England, but before the more aggressive planters could discover reliable outlets at consistently profitable prices, the market for tobacco recovered again and put an end to such endeavors. As planters faced prolonged periods of stagnant demand for their staple, one finds evidence of more sustained efforts to exploit other sources of income and to substitute home manufactures for foreign imports.[25]

The difficulties encountered by the planters in marketing their product in the years between 1680 and 1717 arose from a combination of factors: market saturation in England itself, European competition on the Continent, and war-related disruptions of shipping. This becomes clearer when we follow the marketing process in more detail.[26] Most planters sold their crops to their neighbors or to factors and ship captains in return for clothing, tools, and other necessities. By doing so, they avoided all the costs and worries of shipping, freight charges, and customs duties, but they were at a disadvantage in the bargaining process. Planters who could afford to do so assumed these risks and costs and undertook correspondence with merchant firms in Britain, who hoped to sell their product at the best price through agents. This practice paid off principally for those raising varieties of tobacco preferred in the home market and commanding premium prices for exceptional quality. Members of the corresponding firms to whom such tobacco was consigned were expected to seek out buyers who offered the highest prices in cash or good bills of exchange. When the tobacco was sold, the

---

1700"; "Tobacco Industry," p. 122. If one fits a regression line to "farm income per taxable" from 1669-1695, the regression coefficient R^2 is $-.753$ for a line with the slope $-.07605$, intercept 4.12. If one extends that line through the year 1702, R^2 falls to $-.134$ with a slope of $-.02033$, intercept of 3.42. If one extends the line yet further, through the year 1717, R^2 rises abruptly to $-.631$ for an average slope of $-.04515$, intercept at 3.96. Thus, for the period 1669-1717, there is a strongly negative slope to the trend in income per taxable, interrupted by the good years between the wars, 1696-1702. Long-term *decline*, not stability, seems a more reasonable interpretation of Menard's carefully assembled data.

[25] Chapter Two below discusses efforts at diversification and regional growth.

[26] Price, *France and the Chesapeake*, pp. 658-60; Lewis C. Gray, "The Market Surplus Problems of Colonial Tobacco," *Agricultural History*, II (1928), pp. 1-34 and idem, *History of Agriculture in the Southern United States to 1860* (Washington, D.C., 1932), pp. 213-76.

proceeds were credited to the planter's account, to which were then debited all the costs of shipping, customs, landing, storing, and transshipping the hogsheads—costs that together multiplied the domestic price of the leaf several times over. Consumers paid, in addition, for the cutting up of the tobacco leaf for pipe smoking, for distribution charges, and for the retailer's profit. The accumulated overlays of all these intermediate costs made the grower's share a mere fraction of the retail price. Small changes in the price he received were more important to him in terms of income than they were to the consumer, to whom such differences in outlay were truly inconsequential.

Englishmen consumed far more tobacco per capita than any other Europeans in the seventeenth century, but their capacity for still more may have reached its peak as early as the middle of the century, when merchants were already reexporting large quantities to the Continent. The Dutch, who had rescued the planters by purchasing substantial portions of their crops in the years before the first Anglo-Dutch War (1653-1654) were squeezed out of the colonial market by enforcement of the Navigation Acts (1650, 1660, 1662, 1663, 1672, 1696, and 1699). As a result, the Dutch began to grow their own and to mix it with good Oronocco leaf from the Chesapeake, selling the resulting mixture with great success throughout the north of Europe in direct competition with the English. Tobacco growing spread to Germany and beyond to meet the needs generated by aggressive Dutch marketers. English merchants could not supply competing mixtures at Dutch prices because they had to pay freight costs on even the cheapest grade of Chesapeake tobacco. Thus the English found themselves selling medium-priced Oronocco to competitors who had no need for cheaper English grades and no desire for the more costly sweet-scented, which was in greatest demand in the home market. Chesapeake growers of inferior leaf found few takers for their crops except during years of scarcity.

Competition by the Dutch thus constricted the market for one type of tobacco, but aggressive selling by the Dutch also extended the market for Oronocco, the leaf produced primarily by planters of the upper peninsula of Virginia and the middle and lower western shore of Maryland. The benefits of this enlarging market were repeatedly offset by interruptions in shipping that followed in the wake of war between England and France, declared in 1689, and that continued for most of the years down to 1713. French privateers captured thousands of English vessels, including those carrying tobacco, not only disrupting trade but almost shutting it down entirely for several years in the 1690s and again from 1702 through 1706. Under such adverse circumstances, the planters could never be sure of selling their crop, and the gluts that occurred when few ships arrived drove down farm prices. Freight and insurance costs, meanwhile, tripled as a result of heavy wartime losses.

War-created shortages on the other side of the ocean stimulated the further extension of tobacco growing on the Continent. As more and more of the European demand for tobacco came to be met by European-grown leaf, prospects dimmed accordingly for a strong revival in demand for the Chesapeake product in the post-war period. Indeed, imports of tobacco into England did not grow substantially until the late 1720s, when the fashion for snuff-taking spread in France, creating a new demand for the cheaper types of tobacco.

Depressions in the tobacco market stimulated efforts in the colonies to cut costs and to organize efforts to raise prices by limiting output. Although the governments of the two colonies never succeeded in cooperating in the suppression of production, their separate efforts to improve quality came to have the same result.[27] As Russell Menard has pointed out, colonial efforts to create towns were in part designed to reduce freight charges by collecting tobacco in central places, thereby shortening the time spent in the colonies by ships and crews.[28] Increasing the sizes of the hogsheads in which the crop was packed reduced both freight charges and the amount of duties paid.[29]

---

[27] Descriptions of planters' responses to declines in tobacco prices may be found in Gray, *Agriculture*, pp. 264-66; Philip A. Bruce, *Economic History of Virginia in the Seventeenth Century* (New York, 1895), I, 381-400; Vertrees J. Wycoff, *Tobacco Regulation in Colonial Maryland* (Baltimore, 1936); Joan de Lourdes Leonard, "Operation Checkmate: The Birth and Death of a Virginia Blueprint for Progress, 1660-1676, *WMQ*, XXIV (1967), 44-74; John C. Rainbolt, *From Prescription to Persuasion: Manipulation of the Seventeenth-Century Virginia Economy* (Port Washington, N.Y., 1974); Edmund S. Morgan, *American Slavery*, pp. 185-95. Maryland legislation on tobacco controls and formation of port towns may be found in *Md.Arch.*, I, 360, 362, 408, 414-15, 446, 495; II, 150. Town acts are discussed in Lois Green Carr, " 'The Metropolis of Maryland': A Comment on Town Development along the Tobacco Coast," *MdHM*, LXIX (1974), 124-45; John C. Rainbolt, "The Absence of Towns in Seventeenth-Century Virginia," *JSH*, XXXV (1969), 343-60; John W. Reps, *Tidewater Towns: City Planning in Colonial Virginia and Maryland* (Colonial Williamsburg, 1972).

[28] Menard, "Tobacco Industry," pp. 133-34.

[29] Hogshead sizes mentioned in Maryland probate records expanded from about 250 pounds in the 1650s and early 1660s to 400 pounds at the end of the century,

Despite the vicissitudes of repeated depressions and sporadic efforts to lower costs and output, population rose, and output rose with it throughout the period of expansion that came to a halt well before the end of the seventeenth century. When the price fell below a penny per pound, on the average, and stayed below that level for several years, pressures mounted. An ever-increasing portion of the population became engaged in activities designed to reduce their outstanding obligations; cut back their purchases of imports for which the only pay was tobacco, bills of exchange, or coin; make substitutes for the imports they were no longer buying; and seek out new sources of income to purchase those necessities that they could not make for themselves. After 1680, especially, planters with the best lands and many laborers acted to diversify their crops and to undertake new enterprises. Others moved out of the tidewater entirely or to the cheapest lands, often remote from water-borne transport. For still others, no real alternative to planting tobacco existed. They needed the income to pay their debts and to hang on for another year. The response of people in this position was to increase their effort, that is, to raise *more* in order to obtain the same income.

The conditions of labor supply had meanwhile altered radically. During the first long surge of West Indian expansion between 1625 and 1654, demand for labor and capital had expanded rapidly, competing directly with the Chesapeake colonies in the process. However, Englishmen at home gradually came to resist the blandishments of the West Indian planters.[30] A number of factors began to divert prospective servants. First, the situation at home had changed for the better. The long secular inflation in food prices at last came to an end, and real wages in England began to rise. Employment, too, probably also rose as the economy began to pick up steam in the final quarter of the seventeenth century under the stimulation of war-created demand.[31] Second, working conditions in the sugar islands altered as large plantations replaced small farms. British servants began to avoid a region in which they could not buy land and from which their poverty might prevent any escape. They probably knew, as well, that the slave population on the sugar

but did not attain the extraordinary weights of Virginian casks packed with sweet-scented tobacco from which the stems had first been removed.

[30] Batie, "Why Sugar?" pp. 14-16. Chapter Three will probe more deeply into the economics of labor and the process whereby slavery established itself in Maryland.

[31] Coleman, *Economy of England.*

islands was growing very rapidly. In looks, language, customs, and condition, the African contrasted strongly with the white servant, and from the latter's point of view, to work alongside blacks would surely reduce his own status. The problem was exacerbated by the large numbers: individual whites might well feel themselves submerged in the black tide. For several reasons then, the demand for labor fed by the surge into sugar production soon encountered a rising wall of white resistance.

The continental colonies were at first the happy recipients of the overflow of capital and laborers who had been squeezed off the islands by the changeover to sugar, and of those from England whose own trajectories were deflected by the same processes. On the American continent, land would always be within physical reach of freed servants, plantations were still operated in small units, and slaves remained as yet scattered and few. Despite these advantages, however, the supply to the Chesapeake of indentured servants ultimately faltered, as well. By the final decades of the seventeenth century, Englishmen were ceasing to respond to the beckoning promise of land and economic opportunity in the New World. The precise reasons for this drying up remain as uncertain as those that first prompted the outpouring. Economics, politics, religion, and the spirit of an age all undoubtedly played their parts. In any event, the years of exploration, adventure, and emigration had come to an end for a half-century or more as Englishmen and women sought their destinies closer to home.

By staying home, however, they forced the Chesapeake planter to seek alternative sources of labor. He did not himself produce nearly enough sons to meet his requirements, as did the New Englanders in their healthier climate.[32] The planters might have tried to close the borders with Indian treaties in order to retain their freed servants as a trapped pool of cheap labor, but the opening-up of Pennsylvania to the north and Carolina to the south quickly drained settlers away, in any case. The planters could offer them land on lease for a share of the crop, and such means provided a useful option throughout the colonial period for those who owned sufficient acreage, but it did not solve the labor problem. Men with good, well-situated tobacco land preferred to farm it themselves rather than to lease. Such men, moreover, were in the best position

---

[32] On "replacement rates" (of fathers by surviving sons reaching adulthood), see Paul G. E. Clemens, *The Atlantic Economy and Colonial Maryland's Eastern Shore: From Tobacco to Grain* (Ithaca, 1980), pp. 64, 68-69. For New England, see the works by Greven, Lockridge, Demos, and Norton in note 8 above.

to undertake the long-term investment required by the only remaining alternative: slaves.

The price of slaves excluded from the market everyone who lacked sufficient capital or credit. They cost about two-and-a-half times as much as servants, and the prices of both were rising over the long run: for slaves because of continuing demand in the sugar islands and elsewhere, for servants because alternative opportunities beckoned at home, bidding up the price at which they could be enticed to emigrate to the Chesapeake—that is, the conditions or terms of their indentures.

Despite the growth in the number of planter households and in the potential demand, the relative number of servants present in the region declined by half or more after 1680. Figure I-4 shows the evidence taken from Maryland probate records: the average number of servants per estate, smoothed by means of a five-year weighted moving average, peaked in years of rising tobacco prices; but troughs deepened and lengthened in the 1690s and after 1702, showing an average of about 1.5 servants per estate before 1672, a number that gradually declined to less than .25 after 1710. The average number of slaves, on the other hand, shows a strong up-

Figure I - 4

NUMBERS OF SERVANTS AND SLAVES PER ESTATE
INVENTORIES OF SIX COUNTIES, MARYLAND
1662 – 1717 (5 year weighted moving average)

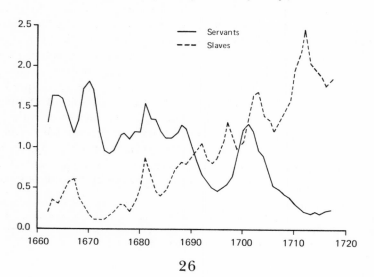

ward trend from the late 1670s to the close of the period, going from an average of .25 per estate in the earlier years to about 2.0 after 1710.

So extensive an alteration in the conditions of labor supply and employment carried serious implications for the structure of society as well as for its economy. The virtual disappearance of servants resulted in a sharp decline in the proportion of planters owning bound labor, and the creation of a despised caste whose members were owned by a relatively small class of slaveholders transformed the social structure of colonial Maryland. This process was aided still further by the emergence of a native-born generation some members of which were fortunate enough to have had healthy, long-lived, successful fathers who passed on a considerable patrimony. The gradual accretion of pools of capital encouraged the acquisition of slaves, indeed made such acquisition possible in bad times when many planters were forced to sell off their assets.[33]

The distinctive features of mature tidewater society were all in place before 1720, having emerged during years of stagnation and depression, not in times of prosperity. Succeeding chapters will take up this story, linking depression to the rise of slavery and the growth of inequality, on the one hand, and to the transition from a frontier-type population to one native-born and family-dominated, on the other.

Tobacco Culture and the Process of Settlement

Americans today like to think that most immigrants who came to this country in times past benefited from their move, both tangibly and intangibly. Overlooking for the moment the cruel exceptions of black Africans and white convicts, probably most immigrants to the colonial Chesapeake who survived the rigors of the crossing, the seasoning, and the terms of servitude did eventually succeed in improving their lot.[34]

[33] On the delayed emergence of family-based elites, see David W. Jordan, "Maryland's Privy Council, 1637-1715," in Land, Carr, and Papenfuse, eds., *Early Maryland*, pp. 65-87, and idem, "Political Stability and the Emergence of a Native Elite in Maryland," in Tate and Ammerman, eds., *Chesapeake*, pp. 243-73.

[34] On economic opportunities for freed servants, see Chapter Three below and Russell R. Menard, "From Servant to Freeholder: Status Mobility and Property Accumulation in Seventeenth-Century Maryland," *WMQ*, XXX (1973), 37-64; Lois Green Carr and Russell R. Menard, "Immigration and Opportunity: the Freedman in Early Colonial Maryland," in Tate and Ammerman, eds., *Chesapeake*, pp. 206-42.

They came from a country still predominantly agricultural, where two-thirds of the population lived at the level of bare subsistence, and where unemployment blighted the lives of virtually all who did not have their own farms. In an age when the only true security lay in owning land, and the more the better, it is little wonder that homeless men and women from the British Isles risked their lives across the seas for the promise of land and independence from landlords, bailiffs, sheriffs, and manorial courts. Despite a perennially bad press, the merchants in the ports dealing with the tobacco trade were able to recruit thousands when the demand for tobacco was high.[35] They fed and clothed their new charges and found them passage in the ships going over to load the crop.

Most settlers viewing Maryland for the first time saw their new home from the deck of a ship. Except for a layover somewhere in the West Indies to take on fresh water and provisions, passengers from England bound for the Chesapeake rode on board their vessel for some six weeks at a minimum, and often much longer. How welcome, then, must have been the sight of the capes between which they passed to enter the bright waters of the great bay ahead!

The extensive river system of the tidewater region around Chesapeake Bay was at once both the delight and the despair of Englishmen. All along the thousands of miles of its shoreline, the ship from Europe could choose to enter the mouths of any one of the broad and placid rivers that flow into the Chesapeake. Those passengers bound for Maryland passed, in turn, the mouths of the James, the York, and the Rappahannock on the western shore before encountering the wide Potomac, which formed the watery boundary in the west between Virginia and Maryland. On his first view of the Potomac, Father White exclaimed, "This is the sweetest and greatest river I have ever seene, so that the Thames is but a little finger to itt." All of the early writers stressed the immensity of the water system: "Its full of Rivers and Creeks." Ocean-going vessels found over 3,000 miles of shoreline along the bay's edge and many hundreds more up the rivers themselves. "Noe country can compare with it . . . the number of navigable rivers, creeks, and inlets, render it so convenient for exporting and importing goods into any part thereof by water carriage." Augustine Herman's beautiful map of 1673 shows individual plantation sites in Maryland, which, spaced between one-quarter to one and one half miles

---

[35] For the trade in servants, see David Galenson, "Immigration and the Colonial Labor System: An Analysis of the Length of Indenture," *Explorations in Economic History*, XIV (1977), 360-77; A. E. Smith, *Colonists in Bondage*, part one.

Map of Maryland's Tobacco Coast

Source: Hermann, *Virginia and Maryland* (London, 1673).

apart, closely follow the configuration of the water's edge, forming a paisley like pattern on the map as a result.[36]

In the beginning, relatively few passengers sought out places along the marshy coastline of the lower eastern shore of the bay, but settled, instead, on the north side of the Potomac, along the Matapan or the Patuxent. Any stretch of well-drained land readily accessible to seagoing vessels attracted the keenest attention. As the process of immigration continued over the course of the century, settlement first followed the shorelines of the bay, around the mouths of successive rivers from south to north. Colonists reached the Severn and the Gunpowder as early as 1650, long before they began to crowd the upper reaches of more southerly rivers.

The coastal plain, or tidewater, which brackets Chesapeake Bay in Maryland gradually narrows as one moves toward the northerly end. Most of the rivers that wind through this broad and nearly level area of nearly 5 million acres are sluggish, and surface drainage is often imperfect. Elevations vary between 100 and 180 feet on the western shore, but most of the eastern side lies less than 25 feet above sea level. The soils of the tidewater region are generally light and sandy in the southeast, whereas clay and fertile loams more often characterize the southern and western parts.[37] In many places, however, a layer of hardpan, which hinders drainage, lies beneath the surface. A wet spring can so delay the setting out of the young tobacco plants that the remainder of the growing season will prove insufficiently long for them to mature fully before the onset of cold weather. Thus good drainage is critical to the success of the year's crop.

A light topsoil over an impermeable clay rendered many areas particularly vulnerable to soil erosion and to a rapid stripping away of the available nutrients. Yet tobacco is a voracious crop and demands the richest soils.[38] The variability of the land itself in the

[36] "Father White's Relation," in *Narratives of Early Maryland 1633-84*, edited by Clayton Coleman Hall, 2d ed. (1904), p. 40; "Calvert's Relation of Maryland," ibid., p. 79; Hugh Jones, "Maryland in 1699; A Letter from the Rev. Hugh Jones," edited by Michael Kammen, *JSH*, XXIX (1963), 368; Earle, *Evolution of a Tidewater Settlement System*, p. 19.

[37] United States, Department of Agriculture, Soil Conservation Service in cooperation with Maryland Agricultural Experiment Station, *Soil Survey of Anne Arundel County, Maryland* (Washington, D.C., 1973); idem, *Soil Survey of Calvert County, Maryland* (Washington, D.C., 1971); idem, *Soil Survey of Charles County, Maryland* (Washington, D.C., 1974); idem, *Soil Survey of Worcester County, Maryland* (Washington, D.C., 1973).

[38] The soil surveys cited in the previous note treat soil types in terms of tobacco

tidewater, therefore, assured an uneven pattern of settlement, for in an age when most people farmed for their living, the quality of the soil, the suitability of the terrain, and the adequacy of drainage were all matters of the most critical importance. Proximity to deep-water transport, moreover, carried an equally high priority, for what did it benefit the grower to produce a fine crop if he could not get it to a buyer?[39]

THE earliest detailed descriptions of the processes involved in the production and curing of tobacco are those of Thomas Glover for Virginia in 1671 and of George Alsop for Maryland in 1656. The principal point about tobacco as a crop is that it used more labor per unit of output than any other crop grown commercially during the colonial period, except for flax and rice. As John Taylor of Caroline said in *Arator*,

> It would startle even an old planter to see an exact account of the labour devoured by an acre of tobacco, and the preparation of the crop for market. . . . He would be astonished to discover how often he had passed over the land, and the tobacco through his hands, in fallowing, hilling, cutting off hills, planting and replanting, toppings, succerings, weedings, cuttings, picking up, removing out of ground by hand, hanging, striking, stripping, stemming, and prizing.

In a similar vein, William Tatham remarked that the tobacco planter "must keep the ground constantly stirring during the whole growth of the crop."[40]

The second major point about growing tobacco is that although it demands a rich soil, men of the times did not approve the use of animal dung as fertilizer to improve less fertile soils, for they believed that dung "left its savour" in the final product.[41] Virgin-

needs, because tobacco remains the major commercial crop of the lower western shore of Maryland.

[39] George Alsop, "A Character of the Province of Maryland" (1656) in Hall, ed., *Narratives of Early Maryland*, p. 364.

[40] John Taylor, *Arator* (Baltimore, 1813; reprinted 1817), p. 232. William Tatham, *An Historical and Practical Essay on the Culture and Commerce of Tobacco* (London, 1800), reprinted in G. Melvin Herndon, *William Tatham and the Culture of Tobacco, Including a Facsimile Reprint of an Historical and Practical Essay on the Culture and Commerce of Tobacco by William Tatham* (Coral Gables, Fla., 1969), p. 17.

[41] C.T., *An Advice How to Plant Tobacco in England and How to Bring It to Colour and Perfection, to Whom It May Be Profitable, and to Whom Harmfull* (London, 1615), p. 10.

ians, said one traveler in 1648, chose land with huge "timber trees" and at least two feet of black mold, "they alledging each plant [grown] there dried and cured, will bring a pound, whereas worn land [only] five to six to a pound. Of the three upper leaves they make [especially good tobacco]. . . . The Dutch give for this double price, and the English double."[42] Such a spot would be located a year in advance, then the trees girdled so they died and their leafless limbs cast little shade. In early spring, the workers prepared the seedbed and sowed the tiny seeds kept from the previous year.[43] Delay in sowing the seed meant delay in bringing the crop to perfection before winter frosts arrived. One Maryland governor complained that his overseer, by such tardiness, had ruined the whole year's crop: "he did Neglect his Business in the Beginning of the year in drinking . . . Thereby Neglecting Sowing of Tobacco Seed and for the want of plants could not plant his Crop in a Seasonable time as other men did."[44] On the other hand, sowing could not be started too early, since the tender tobacco plants might be nipped by late frosts.[45]

After the seeds were planted, the bed was covered with oak leaves and boughs to protect the seedlings from cold, sun, and flies.[46] When the plants "be grown to the Breadth of a shilling," they were transplanted to prepared hills in other fields.[47] The replanting took place in moist weather—in May in Virginia, or in June in Maryland.[48] The "little hillocks," as Alsop called them, were placed about

[42] Edmund Plowden [Beauchamp Plantagenant], "A Description of the Province of New Albion," in Peter Force, *Tracts and Other Papers, Relating Principally to the Origin, Settlement, and Progress of the Colonies in North America, from the Discovery of the Country to the Year 1776* (Glouster, Mass., 1963), II, no. VII, 336.

[43] Thomas Glover, *An Account of Virginia*, cited in Gray, *Agriculture*, I, 215; Alsop, "Character of the Province of Maryland," p. 363. See also the description in Jonathan Carver, *A Treatise on the Culture of the Tobacco Plant; with the Manner in which it is usually cured. Adapted to Northern Climates, and Designed for the Use of the Landholders of Great Britain* (London, 1779).

[44] *Md.Arch.*, X, 219. This was Governor Stone speaking in 1653.

[45] Tatham, *Historical Essay*, in Herndon, *William Tatham*, p. 23.

[46] Bruce, *Economic History*, I, 438-39.

[47] Glover, *Account of Virginia*, cited in Gray, *Agriculture*, I, 216. "C.T." advised doing this when they were three inches high. *Advice*, p. 7.

[48] Bruce, *Economic History*, I, 439; Alsop, "Character of the Province of Maryland," p. 363. In William Byrd's diary an entry under the date May 12, 1709, states, "The people were all planting because it was a rainy day." Louis B. Wright and Marion Tinling, eds., *The Great American Gentleman: The Secret Diary of William Byrd of Westover, 1709-1712* (New York, 1963), p. 21. Court day broke up on June 25, 1650, in St. Mary's, Maryland, when "Uppon the earnest mocon of the Inhabitants to bee discharged . . . it being very like to bee plantable Weather"; *Md.Arch.*, X, 27.

four feet apart between the dead and leafless trees.[49] The soil was kept clear of weeds by continuous hoeing, and the tobacco worms were picked off. Some planters used turkeys to do this.[50]

Within a month, the plant grew to a foot high.[51] Hoeing and worming continued on a daily basis until the tobacco was nearly ripe. When the plants put out the appropriate number of leaves, they were then topped to prevent flowering and to force the existing leaves.[52] Topping is described by Tatham: "this operation, simply, is that of pinching off with the *thumbnail* the leading stem or sprout of the plant." He added, "Many of the Virginians let the thumbnail grow long, and harden it *in the candle,* for this purpose: not for the use of *gouging* out people's eyes, as some have thought fit to insinuate."[53] The lower or ground leaves were required by law to be removed; this was called "priming."[54] The topped plant put out suckers between the existing leaves, which had to be removed weekly since the law also prohibited the cultivation of these.[55]

Tobacco must be fully ripe when cut or it will not cure properly.[56] This underlines the third important point concerning the culture of tobacco: its success demands the kind of knowledge acquired only through long experience and diligent attention to detail. Failure to make a proper judgment at any one of the crucial steps in harvesting, curing, and packing might not only reduce the quality of the product but even damage it beyond salvage by inducing fermentation and ultimate spoilage.

[49] Charles McKew Parr, *The Voyages of David De Vries, Navigator and Adventurer* (New York, 1969), p. 236. De Vries was a Dutch sea captain of extensive experience who sailed into the Chesapeake late in the 1630s and again in the early 1640s. No complete translation into English of De Vries' journal exists, and Parr's is a popular retelling of De Vries's life based on a modern Dutch transcription. Partial English translations may be found in the *Collections of the New York Historical Society,* 2d ser., III, 1-129; and in *Narratives of New Netherlands,* edited by J. Franklin Jameson (New York, 1946).

[50] Harold B. Gill, Jr., "Tobacco Culture in Colonial Virginia, A Preliminary Report," prepared for Colonial Williamsburg Foundation, Inc., April 1972, p. 8.

[51] Ibid., p. 9; John Ferdinand Dalziel Smyth, *A Tour in the United States of America* (London, 1784), II, 82 quoted in Gray, *Agriculture,* I, 217.

[52] Early Virginia laws restricted the number of leaves per plant to nine. Bruce, *Economic History,* I, 308.

[53] Tatham, *Historical Essay,* in Herndon, *William Tatham,* p. 18.

[54] Gray, *Agriculture,* I, 224-25.

[55] Glover, *Account of Virginia,* cited ibid., p. 216.

[56] Tatham, *Historical Essay,* in Herndon, *William Tatham,* p. 37: "the most experienced planters acknowledge that they are more apt to err in cutting their tobacco too soon, then in deferring it too long."

The earliest technique in harvesting may have been to "pick the leaves individually when ripe, lay them in the Sun for a few hours, string them on a thread and lay them out of the wind, 10, 12, 14 days."[57] Sometime before mid-century, harvesters began cutting down the entire plant, doing so in the mornings so that the plants lay out under the sun to wilt.[58] The stalks were then carried to specially built houses where they were pegged and hung to cure in the air.[59] The walls of the tobacco houses were only partly sheathed in order to give free passage to the air, although they were roofed over to protect the drying tobacco from rain. When the tobacco had reached its appropriate texture for "striking," it was said to be "in case." At this point, it was neither too dry, so as to crumble when handled, nor too damp, which brought on rotting later. "This condition can only be distinguished by diligent attention and frequent handling."[60] In a court proceeding originating in Maryland in the year 1657, the purchaser of three hogsheads of tobacco complained that it was rotten and demanded recompense of his supplier. A witness testified, "He came accidentally into ould Little's house when he and his foulkes were Strikeing Tobacco, and this Depon[t] Sayeth that he tould ould Little that the Tobacco was not Cured, whose answer was the weather is Cold, and I must make room . . . and this Depon[t] replyed that the Tobacco would not keep."[61]

In a similar case, the complainant argued that the tobacco delivered to him was not "merchantable," because the contents of the hogsheads had been "struck" when they were in "too high case," and were therefore rotting, whereas others were frostbitten, and many ground leaves had been mixed in.[62]

The curing of the tobacco could take as long as six weeks to get it properly "in case," but allowing it to stay up too long would "burn" it.[63] If the weather did not cooperate during curing, the planter had to resort to building fires to hasten the process. This, however,

[57] C.T. in 1615, *Advice*, p. 10.

[58] Parr, *De Vries*, p. 236, mentioned in 1633 the planters cutting down the plants. Harvest took place in August in Virginia and in mid-September in Maryland. Glover, *Account of Virginia*, cited in Gray, *Agriculture*, I, 216; and Alsop, "Character of the Province of Maryland," p. 363.

[59] Bruce, *Economic History*, I, 441.

[60] Tatham, *Historical Essay*, in Herndon, *William Tatham*, p. 37.

[61] *Md.Arch.*, X, 531.

[62] Ibid., LIV, 221.

[63] Bruce, *Economic History*, I, 441.

might affect the leaf, giving it a "'smoky smell," to which many buyers objected.[64]

The plants were struck down in moist weather when the leaves were made pliable by the damp, then stripped off the stalks, bundled into "hands," and packed into hogsheads.[65] The latter process was called "prizing," and the very large casks adopted late in the century required special equipment for the purpose, including a large screw operated by levers pushed by several workers at once. Such equipment was owned only by the more well-to-do planters, who often acted as wholesalers to their lesser neighbors.[66] Shipping in bulk was an option only in years of brisk demand, when the smaller ships of England's outports plied the upper reaches of the bay and the rivers to gather up such loose tobacco.[67] Packing the hogsheads was "the most tedious part of the whole process connected with the culture of tobacco, for this is a business which must not be hurried over."[68]

The quality of the finished product, as one can now understand, must have varied markedly, not only because of the differences in soils, rainfall, or mean temperatures, but also in the degree of expertise, honesty, and good fortune with which the tobacco had been tended, cured, and packed.[69] As one observer remarked, poor tobacco "differs from the best Tobacco, as Buff does from tanned Leather . . . the best Tobacco will weigh the heaviest, and pack the closest."[70] It was recognized early that quality depended on skill: "half the virtue of the plant lies in its manipulation after the leaves are gathered."[71]

---

[64] Robert Carter defended himself to one irate purchaser, "Indeed, sometimes in funky, foggy weather, when tobacco is just upon turning, we are forced to make smothers in our houses to dry it, and this is what is practiced by the best planters in Virginia and ever was since I have been acquainted with the making of tobacco." Louis B. Wright, ed., *The Letters of Robert Carter, 1720-1727* (Chapel Hill, 1940), p. 2.

[65] Gill, "Tobacco Culture," p. 18.

[66] Gray, *Agriculture*, I, 217.

[67] Governor Francis Nicholson in W. Noel Sainsbury, et al., eds., *Calendar of State Papers, Colonial Series* (London, 1860-1939), IX, 512.

[68] Tatham, *Historical Essay*, in Herndon, *William Tatham*, p. 51.

[69] In a 1695 inventory, for instance, the crop of one Maryland planter consisted of "good," "old," and "terrible" tobacco, ranging in price from six shillings per hundredweight to just one shilling. *Inv. & Accts.*, Liber 13B, f. 8.

[70] Rev. John Clayton, "Letter to the Royal Society, May 12, 1688, Giving an Account of . . . Virginia," in Force, *Tracts*, III, 17.

[71] Quoted in Bruce, *Economic History*, I, 303. This was about the year 1630. John Lawson, writing some three-quarters of a century later, confirmed this: "all Men

The incentives to produce tobacco of the very best quality influenced primarily those planters who could afford to wait during the bargaining process and extract, thereby, the best price for their "brand."[72] Otherwise, the chief incentive was to produce quantity rather than quality, paying off debts and taxes with minimally merchantable leaf, and conserving the best quality for the highest bidder.

The hogsheads were rolled down to shipside or onto lighters, and this was hard work. No one in Virginia, commented an early Dutch visitor, lived far from deep water.[73] Some seven decades later, when population had extended into the interior, Robert Beverly complained that "the sailors . . . are put to the hardhsip of rolling most of the tobacco a mile or more to the waterside."[74] These huge barrels got heavier over the course of the century, from 300 pounds in the 1650s to 400 or more in Maryland by 1700. They were often much larger in Virginia, due to the practice there of removing the stems from their sweet-scented variety prior to packing.[75]

Labor costs were understandably high for transforming the standing plant into "merchantable leaf" packed into ocean-going containers. The case of James Turner furnishes an illustration. When he died in 1696, someone had to take care of his crops. The administrator of his estate dispatched a hand "to house his tobacco and corn," which took the man thirty working days. The estate

---

(that know Tobacco) must allow, that it is the Ordering thereof which gives a *Hogoo* to that Weed, rather than any Natural Relish it possesses, when green." John Lawson, *A New Voyage to Carolina* (Readex Microprint, orginally published 1709), p. 173.

[72] Robert Carter complained in 1720, "It troubles me not a little that Mr. Pratt should get more fore his miscellaneous stuff that comes from all parts of the country, low lands as well as high, than I do for mine that is made with my own people and upon as good and proper [. . .] as anybody can boast of." Carter, *Letters*, 2. Word missing is obscured in original.

[73] Parr, *De Vries*, p. 243.

[74] Robert Beverly, *The History and Present State of Virginia*, ed. Louis B. Wright (Charlottesville, 1947), p. 157. Rolling them a mile or so was cheaper than carting them. One account in the Maryland probate records charged an estate in Somerset County the equivalent of the contents of one hogshead for carting four! *Inv. & Accts.*, Liber 22B, f. 119.

[75] Gray, *Agriculture*, pp. 220-21; Ebenezer Cook, *The Sot-Weed Factor: Or, a Voyage to Maryland. A Satyr* (London, 1708), p. 23; *Md.Arch.*, X, 381, 462; Bruce, *Economic History*, I, 383 gives the average net weight of 189 hogsheads in York County, Virginia probate records for the years 1657-1662 as 390 pounds; Maryland probate records provide numerous observations on sizes of hogsheads: *Inv. & Accts.* Liber 1, f. 513; 3, f. 164; 13B, f. 119; 15, f. 67; 18, f. 114; 20, f. 250; 25, f. 111; 27, f. 107; 28, f. 98; 30, f. 17; 32B, ff. 121, 126, 135.

bore this charge at the rate of 20 pounds of tobacco per day, or 600 pounds total, and then an additional 40 pounds apiece for each hogshead to pack the tobacco, and finally 160 pounds for stripping it. The crop had totaled 1,740 pounds of tobacco plus three barrels of corn and two bushels of beans. If we value the corn at 100 pounds of tobacco per barrel and the beans at 50 per bushel, the total labor charges for harvest and packing, which came to 760 pounds, amounted to 36 percent of the estimated value of the total crop for the year.[76] The charges in this and in other cases for stripping and packing alone averaged about 10 percent of the crop.[77]

Getting the casks in the first place often proved a headache. A Maryland Act of 1671 required coopers to complete half the supply of hogsheads by October 10 and the remainder by December 10.[78] Planter Robert Brooke petitioned the court in suit against two coopers in 1653. They had promised to supply him with sufficient casks in October of the previous year, but by the next April, he had received only twenty-two of them, "to his great damage having at that time 2 great houses full of Tob.: the one 100 foot in length the other 90 foot in length, and both 32 foot in breadth, while long hanging much wasted and a Great part of it blown down & Spoiled, the latter End of Winter for want of Caske, and of those 22 Casks 8 of them were altogether useless falling in pieces in the Carrying home."[79]

A crop stored too long would rot. John Jeffries, a London merchant with twelve years' experience in the business, testified in 1657 before the High Court of Admiralty in England that tobacco "is a Commoditie: which with the heate of the Country in Virginia will be spoiled if it be kept after the month of March next following after the yeare it groweth."[80] When a lawsuit in 1654 delayed the shipment of some 17,000 pounds of tobacco, already packed in hogsheads and stored for two years, the overseer reported he "was forced to flinge it awaye for wante of roome to cure our crops nor could be noe longer kept by reason of the extreme stinke it yielded in the summer tyme."[81]

---

[76] *Inv. & Accts.*, Liber 15, f. 67.

[77] Citations same as in note 75 for Maryland.

[78] *Md.Arch.*, II, 288.

[79] Ibid., X, 278.

[80] Quoted in Morgan, *Slavery*, p. 174.

[81] Ibid. A Maryland act of 1727 required all tobacco to be ready for shipment by the last day of May, and one of 1735 prohibited any shipments between August 31 and November 25. Gray, *Agriculture*, I, 223.

How much could a single worker expect to produce in a year? Probably a very general but adequate estimate would be 1,500 pounds, yet a number of factors influencing the final harvest created a broad range, from 400 to well over 2,000 pounds in some cases. Early attempts by the Virginia House of Burgesses, for instance, to reduce output in order to raise the price, placed a limit on the number of plants permitted each family member to 2,000 each. Later this was reduced to 1,500 plants.[82] Since the very best land yielded a pound of tobacco, dried and cured, to each plant, and the poorest land produced only lightweight plants, taking 5 or 6 of them to make up a pound of finished leaf, 2,000 plants might yield as much as 2,000 pounds or as little as 400.[83]

The amounts of tobacco reported as crop in the earliest Maryland inventories averaged well under that maximum.[84] Improvements in techniques raised output per hand so that by 1649, one Virginia booster reported, "a man can plant two Thousand waight a yeare . . . and also sufficient Corne and Rootes, and other provisions for himselfe."[85] A French Huguenot visitor to the same colony in 1686 estimated the crop per hand in his landlord's household at 2,000 pounds of tobacco, plus 67 bushels of Indian corn, between 2 and 3 bushels of wheat, 5 bushels of beans, and 17 bushels of turnips.[86] The estimate of 2,000 pounds per hand also seems to be confirmed by a House Resolve in the Maryland Assembly meeting in 1702: "Let it be considered that 2000 # of Tob° p. year is one with another what every Labourer makes in this Province."[87]

Systematic counts of crop sizes per hand, as reported in the inventories and accounts in Maryland probate court records, yield rather lower averages, however (see Table I.2). Estimates based on these records tend to overstate actual crop sizes, moreover, because some contributions to the reported total may have come from work-

[82] Bruce, *Economic History*, I, 308.

[83] Plowden, "New Albion," in Force, *Tracts*, II, No. 7, 13 (1648). Laws, meanwhile, required men to plant two acres of corn for each laborer working in tobacco. Gray, *Agriculture*, I, 37. John Rolphe estimated in 1619 that one man could tend four acres of corn and 1,000 plants of tobacco; ibid., I, 27. Thomas Nairne of South Carolina estimated in 1710 that a Negro could clear, plant, and hoe three acres in a year; ibid., I, 326. A farmers' magazine just before the Civil War estimated that 1,000 pounds per acre was the standard of a "good" tobacco crop; ibid., I, 218.

[84] *Md.Arch.*, IV, 90, 92, 466. These are all from the late 1630s and early 1640s.

[85] "A Perfect Description of Virginia . . ." (1649), in Force, *Tracts*, II, No. 8, 4.

[86] *A Frenchman in Virginia: Being the Memoirs of a Huguenot Refugee in 1686*, translated and edited by Fairfax Harrison (n.p., 1923), p. 114.

[87] *Md.Arch.*, XXIV, 227.

TABLE I.2
CROP SIZE PER HAND IN EARLY MARYLAND (pounds)

County	1656-1683 N	Mean	1684-1696 N	Mean	1697-1704 N	Mean	1705-1712 N	Mean	1713-1719 N	Mean	Total N	% N
Anne Arundel	49	1501	38	1568	52	1662	30	1573	32	1361	201	19
Baltimore	22	1737	29	1778	28	1435	43	1605	38	1518	160	15
Calvert	35	1484	51	1549	63	1499	47	1590	63	1480	259	24
Charles	28	1626	16	1936	26	1616	41	1774	73	1820	184	17
Kent	23	1553	27	1436	17	1457	56	1582	33	1553	156	15
Somerset	5	1147	10	1122	16	1229	31	1512	37	1069	99	9
Totals	162		171		202		248		276		1059	99
Averages		1547		1585		1522		1609		1515		

SOURCE: Probate records of six counties, Maryland, in Hall of Records, Annapolis.

NOTE: In making these calculations, estates without bound laborers listed and with no wages paid in accounts of administration were treated as equal to one "hand." Negro children were rated according to the proportion their inventory value bore to that current for a prime field hand. For example: Negro boy Tom is valued at £12 and Negro man Tom is valued at £30; young Tom is credited as .40 × 1.00 hand. This procedure ignores the influence of life expectancy on price, but seems a reasonable approximation of relative productivity.

ers who had been paid off before the account was made up or from servants whose terms had expired with the completion of the crop and whose freedom dues were paid over prior to the administrators' assumption of responsibility for estate debts. Furthermore, such records disregard the possible contributions of wives and children, sources of bias for estimating productivity that became more important with the passage of time.

In order to test for such effects, one writer calculated the range in crop sizes per hand among eighteenth-century tenant farmers in Talbot County, Maryland, dividing the observations into those for unmarried tenants and those from married tenants. He found that the range for the single planter was from 1,000 to 2,100 pounds per year, while that for the married man ranged from 1,500 to 4,000 per year.[88] One must conclude from this test that a real but unacknowledged contribution of the wife raised total output in these cases. The precise amount attributable must have varied with individual circumstances, depending on the number and ages of any children present.

Despite the discrepancy between the Assembly's estimate of 2,000 pounds average per hand and a probate average of 500 pounds less, we can see that the changing makeup of the colony's population complicates the issue of just how, where, and by how much production of tobacco declined during the years from 1680 to 1730, when imports of tobacco into England did not grow, but population in the Chesapeake virtually quadrupled. Areas within the colony that were settled by high proportions of married men owning no bond labor, such as Charles County on the lower western shore after 1680, could be expected to show larger than average crop sizes per hand, as inventories of this county indeed reveal. When such data are examined in terms of the phases of the tobacco price cycle, furthermore, one discovers gains in the yields per hand during periods of lowest prices, such as 1684-1696 and 1705-1712 (see Table I.2). These gains probably resulted from enhanced efforts on the part of the poorest families and of those most deeply in debt, because their fixed obligations had to be met regardless of current prices.

When the soil became exhausted by successive crops of tobacco, the planter sowed it to corn or wheat or both, in a system that maximized the return to labor by planting wheat in the fall between

[88] Paul G. E. Clemens, "Economy and Society on Maryland's Eastern Shore, 1689-1733," in Land, Carr, and Papenfuse, eds., *Early Maryland*, p. 156.

the already weeded rows of corn.[89] The actual period of cultivation of any particular piece of land depended on its situation, but was longer for the bottom lands than it was for the sandy uplands, ranging from as many as eight years to as few as three.[90] A fifty-acre plantation would have more than half of its land in woods, about a fourth in pasture, and only an eighth or a tenth under close cultivation in any given year. These figures assume that the land was all good for farming with no waste, but most working plantations had to be a good deal larger than fifty acres to accomodate both waste area and the variety of uses. Within the confines of his plantation, however, the planter and his family would always be clearing new land while old fields returned to woods.[91] The duration of the cycle depended on the number of hands at work, as well as the quality of the land itself, since each could clear, plant, and hoe about three acres per year if he were in prime physical condition. Land that was not allowed to recover its fertility under sufficiently long fallow, estimated by one student to require at least twenty years, must be forced to bear by other means.[92] One could pen cattle on the fields intended for tobacco, but doing so invited difficulties in marketing the manured product. Rising tobacco prices, however, tended to attract new tenants into old producing areas, and these may have been content to extract one or two crops from partially restored soils before moving on. No excessive pressure was placed on the land, though, until well into the middle of the eighteenth century, when the last big boom of the colonial period started.[93]

In seventeenth-century Maryland, before the full effects of long-term population growth had manifested themselves, new purchasers sought to acquire lands of the best soils and situation as a

[89] Parr, *De Vries*, p. 236; Durand, *Frenchman in Virginia*, p. 109; Edward Miles Riley, ed., *The Journal of John Harrower, an Indentured Servant in the Colony of Virginia, 1773-1776* (Colonial Williamsburg, Inc., 1963), p. 60. One 1679 Maryland inventory referred to wheat "growing in the orchard." *Inv. & Accts.* Liber 6, f. 319.

[90] Bruce, *Economic History*, I, 461.

[91] Durand, *Frenchman in Virginia*, p. 109; Earle, *All Hallow's Parish*, p. 27. As Earle points out, this system incorporated Indian methods of husbandry and was conservationist in effect rather than wasteful; ibid., pp. 27, 30.

[92] Earle, *All Hallow's Parish*, p. 29.

[93] Edward C. Papenfuse, Jr., "Planter Behavior and Economic Opportunity in a Staple Economy," *Ag. Hist.*, XLVI (1972), 297-311, argues that soil erosion in the Tidewater region resulted from the introduction there of inappropriately deep plowing techniques associated with grain cultivation in the late colonial and early national period, and not from the soil use practices of tobacco culture based on the hoe.

matter of course, but they also sought such lands in quantities sufficient to ensure a steady supply of fresh or rested land annually, depending on the numbers of hands expected to work it. The most successful planter was not one who could make the most to the acre, but the one who could make the most to the hand.[94] Since tobacco required the best land and a great deal of labor to tend it, the planter found it cheaper to disperse the laborers in small groups to wherever the soil conditions were best.[95] To ensure an adequate supply of such soil, without incurring the heavy costs of using additional labor to obtain and apply fertilizer, men with sufficient capital purchased large tracts along the rivers and creeks. Another motive also was at work: "every man provides beforehand to take up so much at the first Patent, that his great Grandchild may be sure not to want Land." The proprietary government in Maryland sought to forestall such engrossment by requiring evidence that such lands were actually being "seated" according to certain rules defining minimum cultivation and use.[96] Large landowners circumvented the rules easily enough, and if pressed, offered leases on good terms to attract tenants to do the seating, frequently sweetening the bait by advancing the food, stock, and tools necessary to start up a new place. Many a freed servant got his start in just such a situation.

Simple economic and geographic determinants thus resulted in a scattering of the population along the watercourses, and no towns developed. Visitors, government officials, clergymen, and educated laymen were wont to decry both the universal dependence on tobacco and the lack of settled communities as fundamentally detrimental to life and morals in the new society.[97] Not only did the wide dispersal of the people over the land result in inefficient use of the land, they thought, and impose expensive delays in loading the ships, it also inhibited the growth of a domestic market for the goods and services of craftsmen and led to the neglect of the church. It certainly hindered the proper governance of the people. Spreading out weakened the colonies' ability to repel enemy attacks on an

[94] This paraphrases a comment made by James H. Hammond in the *Carolina Planter* in 1840, quoted by Gray, *Agriculture*, I, 450.

[95] Chapter Three provides instances of such dispersion drawn from Maryland inventories.

[96] Marshall Harris, *Origin of the Land Tenure System in the United States* (Ames, Iowa, 1953), pp. 216-19. As early as 1671, Lord Baltimore restricted water frontage in land patents, *Md.Arch.*, V, 95.

[97] Rainbolt, *From Prescription to Persuasion*, particularly chapters 2, 3, and 4; Carr, " 'The Metropolis of Maryland.' " See also the works cited in note 27, particularly Reps, *Tidewater Towns*, chapters 4 and 5 on the town acts of Virginia and Maryland.

ever-widening frontier. The collection of taxes and debts became more costly and unsure. Even more serious because more fundamental, the very nature of man appeared to the seventeenth-century Christian to require settled, structured communities wherein man's selfish and sinful instincts could be countered, controlled, and civilized. The pious man abhorred the "natural" man and feared a mass reversion to savagery by Englishmen who went off to live by themselves beyond the reach of their betters.

But the recalcitrance of the people frustrated the best efforts of their leaders. Individuals persisted in extending the lines of settlement in the face of repeated attempts by their governors to restrict access to land and to control the planting of tobacco. Indeed, whenever the price of tobacco sank—and it seemed always to be sinking— the inevitable and universal outcry once again encouraged lawmakers to busy themselves with new, and old, schemes for the betterment of both the economy and the society. Stinting the crop, controlling its quality, and designating ports as collection and inspection centers constituted the major items on this recurring agenda, which surfaced with all the regularity of a natural phenomenon. That it took so long to achieve in both colonies testifies to the relative weakness of such legislative efforts.

This search for order in Chesapeake society focused on control of the economy, for it seemed obvious that the source of the society's woes lay in the attachment to tobacco. The seemingly voracious demand for land and the rush to gain access to the waterside resulted from the requirements peculiar to the crop. It was bulky, yet fragile, so that the process of getting the crop into the ship's hold imposed narrow limits in physical and monetary terms. Delivering a marketable product at a price remunerative to all concerned presented continuing challenges year in and year out, for the vastness of the market made it unresponsive to individual efforts at its control.

The long-term operation of this economic system came to affect the very landscape. As the people dispersed, and as the great planters acquired reserves of untouched land, Maryland appeared half-civilized to the European eye. Extensive forests separated the straggling plantations. Some sought to clear the ground just "to let in the ayre," and imputed to the density of the big trees a major source of sickness and death.[98] The thick stands of trees alternated with

[98] John Hammond, *Leah and Rachel, or, the Two Fruitful Sisters, Virginia and Maryland; Their Present Condition, Impartially Stated and Related* . . . (1659) in Force, *Tracts*, III, No. 14; "Newes of Sir Walter Rauleigh with the True Description of Guiana,

43

abandoned and overgrown fields, all interspersed with small clearings and occasional wooden buildings, many of them quite ramshackle. To the traveler's eye, the decay and disorder clearly arose from the lazy and wasteful habits of a people engaged in raising a noxious crop—although their willful lack of care and order might well have been seen by others as due to a natural preference for leisure reinforced by the enervating effects of malarial fevers, improper diet, hot summers, and the seductive abundance of a fertile and easily worked soil. But the devotion to tobacco clearly bore the ultimate blame for a disordered landscape: "As fast as the ground is worn out with tobacco and corn, it runs up again in underwoods; and in many places of the country that which has been cleared is thicker in woods than it was before the clearing."[99]

The human consequences of a scattered settlement system were not confined to aesthetic considerations. We might well ask whether the physical isolation of planter households imposed major spiritual costs while conferring rather paltry economic benefits. Or whether the possibilities for individual freedom or for enhancement of privacy counterbalanced the loneliness, homesickness, and loss of kin. Certainly there were trials and agonies enough for the immigrant to bear, but most whites, at least, had elected to make the journey, whereas the native-born Virginians and Marylanders positively reveled in the "fresh aire" of their New World. Hartwell, Chilton, and Blair reported in 1697 with some disgust the "ingenuous" argument of one Virginian "who had never been out of the country." This fellow complained to his colleagues in the House of Burgesses, "that they might observe already, where they were thick seated, they could hardly raise any stock, or live by one another, much more, concluded he, would it be impossible for us to live when a matter of an hundred families are cooped up within the compass of half a mile of ground."[100]

The thinness of settlement precluded the cultural benefits of organized town life and severely hampered the extension of religious communion. Particularly was this the case in Maryland, where

as also a Relation of the excellent Government, and much hope of the prosperity of the Voyage. Sent from a Gentleman of his Fleet, to a most especial Friend of his in London From the River of Caliann, on the Coast of Guiana, November 17, 1617," ibid., No. 4, p. 17; Plowden, "New Albion," ibid., No. 7, p. 5; Lawson, *A New Voyage*, pp. 84-85.

[99] Henry Hartwell, James Blair, and Edward Chilton, *The Present State of Virginia and the College*, edited by Hunter Dickinson Farish (Colonial Williamsburg, 1940, 1964), p. 9.

[100] Ibid., p. 14.

official Toleration prohibited the establishment of a state-supported church until the royal assumption of the colony's government after the Glorious Revolution. Without an assured income of sufficient size, competent ministers were not tempted to emigrate to such a wilderness, and most of the people were denied the comforts of their traditional religion.

That this unmet need may have sorrowed the seventeenth-century settlers of the Chesapeake is suggested by the early successes of the Quaker missionaries there. The fervent welcome accorded the itinerant preachers of the Great Awakening of the eighteenth century testifies to the misunderstanding on the part of the so-called "better-sort" concerning the true nature of the needs of the people of those times. Perhaps circuit riders of less education and culture but more genuine compassion for their hearers might have overcome much of the disability imposed by rural dispersion a century earlier.

Horses may have proved the greatest single boon to social life in early Maryland. Despite the distances between plantations and the obstructions posed by the multitudes of streams and rivers, a man or woman on horseback could cover many miles without tiring. William Byrd's diary, for instance, records frequent trips back and forth from Westover to Williamsburg and from his home plantation to the others situated near the falls of the James, all on horseback.[101]

Although horses came to play a crucial role in Chesapeake society, they did not become plentiful and cheap until the final quarter of the seventeenth century. By then, however, almost everyone had a mount.[102] Planters of all levels of wealth owned at least one horse, most of which were worth about £ 2 each, slightly less than a third of the cash value of an average hand's crop of tobacco.[103] Perhaps the closest modern equivalent to the horse is Henry Ford's Model T or the Volkswagen beetle, but these required more upkeep, even if they matched the ten years' reliable service of a good Maryland pony.

[101] Byrd, *Secret Diary*.

[102] Horses were very scarce and expensive in the first years of settlement but proliferated so rapidly in the woods that wild horses eventually provided both fun in the chase and potential mounts for those skillful enough to catch a young one. See the delightful description of this sport in Robert Beverly's *History*, p. 312.

[103] From a sample of 606 estates of fathers of young children drawn from the probate records of six counties of Maryland, 1656-1719. Appendix A provides a full description of this sample. If the average size of a hand's tobacco crop was 1,500 pounds, this at a penny per pound came to a fraction more than £6 in current money of Maryland, roughly equal to sterling for much of this period.

The ease of travel made possible by horses and a level, stone-free soil, meant that a scattered settlement system did not necessarily impose degrees of social isolation equivalent to the physical distances involved. Every house, furthermore, served as a free motel where the visitor was warmly received and abundantly entertained. As Beverly particularly remarked, if the householder owned but a single bed, he gladly offered it to company.[104] The absence of towns ought to be viewed only as a manifestation of a system of widely distributed social and economic activities, not as evidence of the lack of such activities.[105] The nonexistence of banks, for example, did not signify an absence of financial arrangements. On the contrary, in every county an extensive network of debts was supported by legal institutions through which debtors and creditors could meet each others' needs. The regular meetings of the county courts in Maryland and Virginia not only enforced early debt settlements and thus ensured a reasonably orderly collection system, they encouraged confidence in those risking their funds or goods.[106] Furthermore, court days brought together the citizenry, providing the most important social and political entertainment in the annual calendar. The location of the court house thus served as an important nodal site of activity, if only on a periodic basis.

The primeval beauty of the relatively untouched land, the sparkling purity of its air and waters, made Maryland seem an earthly paradise to its earliest visitors, one that promised all the bounties of Eden. Those who came to live there, however, had to wrest their living by tearing and rending the land itself. Conserving labor meant scarring and slashing the landscape, abandoning used-up fields, and letting the buildings go to ruin, for it made no sense to build well or to maintain and restore structures that lost their usefulness when the planter again moved his residence to save riding time.

The centripetal forces of the tobacco economy and the opportunity to own land dispersed the people over the countryside, enforcing considerable isolation on them and greatly inhibiting the

[104] Beverly, *History*, p. 313.

[105] See the argument for this system as one of "urban process" in Joseph A. Ernst and H. Roy Merrens, " 'Camden's turrets pierce the skies!': The Urban Process in the Southern Colonies during the Eighteenth Century," *WMQ*, XXX (1973), 549-74.

[106] Tommy R. Thompson, "Debtors, Creditors, and the General Assembly in Colonial Maryland," *MdHM*, LXXII (1977), 60; A. G. Roeber, "Authority, Law, and Customs: The Ritual of Court Day in Tidewater Virginia, 1720-1750," *WMQ*, XXXVII (1980), 29-52.

development of formal social and cultural institutions. Community ties, however, could be created, and loneliness relieved, by visiting back and forth. The crudeness of the people's manners and living style were perhaps more than counterbalanced by simple abundance and genuine hospitality.

Chapter Two

ADAPTATION UNDER FIRE

Tobacco paid the immigrants' way, and its culture molded their own. How well had it treated them, then? Perhaps they would have been better off recreating the mixed economy of their homeland, living in compact communities, developing an artisan class, insulating themselves from the turbulence of a European world at war with itself. Who is to say?

The market system that they had elected put their incomes on a well-greased roller-coaster ride, their fates and fortunes a matter of luck as well as grit. Inevitably, the demand for their staple sometimes lagged, the best-situated lands became occupied, the supply of cheap labor dried up, and the long period of expansion gave way to a half-century of depressed markets broken by brief interludes of good prices. The story of how the planters succeeded in protecting their assets from eroding—how they found alternative ways to make a living and to supply themselves with things they formerly had purchased from abroad—can be discovered in the records of Maryland's county probate courts.

Before commencing a chronological account of how the planters fared, it would be wise for us to take a closer look at the documentary source on which it is based. Probate records consist primarily of inventories, wills, and accounts of administration concerning the estates left by deceased property holders. In seventeenth-century Maryland most of these were adult white males, of whom the majority but not all were heads of households. Few women and almost no single women appeared before 1700 in these records.[1] Each set of documents pertaining to an individual estate might include none, one, or several of each kind of record, but estates

---

[1] Under the property laws of England, which Maryland retained, married women could not legally dispose of property without a letter of attorney from their husbands. Since most women who survived their first spouses married again, even several times in succession, few widows appeared in the probate records until after 1700, when the demographic profile of the living population approached more familiar contours. To keep more fully comparable the record set for the entire span of time, 1656-1719, widows' estates have been excluded. Their wills and inventories deserve a separate study.

with large numbers of debts owing to, or from, the estate tend to have more accounts than others, and men who wrote wills tended to be richer, on the average, than those who did not.

Decedents, of course, tend to be older on the average than living adults, and because older men have had longer earning lives than younger men, their accumulated assets tend to be greater, as well. Since their estates are disproportionately represented in probate records, the mean wealth of probated estates tends to be higher than the mean for the living population of free adult property holders subject to probate.[2]

Not every free white adult male who died in early Maryland appears in these records, and the documentation of others remains incomplete, introducing two important and opposing sources of bias: poorer men, particularly those without land, are under-represented, whereas the total wealth of others, particularly of the richest men, is understated. Neither of these sources of bias can be directly measured, for there exists no consistent means of detecting just who, or what, is missing. Nor did either of these sources of bias operate consistently over the full course of time under study here. The proportion of landless men in the living population rose, and the functioning of the court system itself grew more efficient as it formalized procedures.

Another defect, universal to probate records in the southern colonies, consists of the omission of land from the inventories. Wills usually describe pieces of land owned and may even give their acreages, but land prices are hard to find and vary with the quality of the land. Much of the discussion that follows will confine itself to personal wealth alone, for which the data are much more complete.

Awareness of all these sources of potential distortion must inevitably curb our confidence in the estimates of various parameters and in conclusions based on them. On the other hand, the records are rich in detail, survive in abundance, and are all we have in the way of a systematic recording of economic and social data from these early years. The student of our colonial past can only feel gratitude, and apply the same kind of critical scrutiny to probate records as that traditionally brought to bear on more familiar kinds of sources.

The records list and value assets encountered by the court-appointed appraisers, who were usually neighbors of the deceased

---

[2] Appendix A provides a full discussion of this point.

and solid citizens of the community.[3] These assets can be described in the following way:

Financial Assets

Debts receivable, including book debts, domestic bills, and bills of exchange

Money, including foreign coins and bullion but not paper money, which was not introduced until much later

Consumption Goods

Apparel, usually the clothing of the deceased owner, occasionally that of deceased members of his family, often omitted in in- dividual inventories

Jewelry, watches, clocks, silver plate

Books, musical instruments, pictures, flower pots, window cur- tains, hangings, table linens

Furniture, bedding

Cooking and eating utensils,including pewter and brass

Riding gear, arms, ammunition, militia gear

Capital

Bound labor, including servants and slaves

Livestock, primarily cattle, horses, swine, and sheep, but also poultry, bees, and goats

Plantation tools, including carts and harness

Craft tools

New goods, including stocks of textiles, hardware, and other goods usually but not always imported, and never used

Boats and ships

Crops, including stored provisions

Operationally, the contents of personal estates were assigned either to "capital," or to "financial assets," and those not so assigned

[3] Values of assets were expressed either in terms of tobacco or money in the English system of pounds, shillings, and pence. Maryland currency was roughly equivalent to English sterling for most of the years in this study, although the official exchange rate between the two currencies was set officially at 133.33 to 100.00 in 1709 by act of Parliament. See John J. McCusker, *Money and Exchange in Europe and America, 1600-1775: A Handbook* (Chapel Hill, 1978), pp. 189-204. Prices in the inventories, however, did not rise to this level. Indeed, those of domestic produce and livestock fell between 1709 and 1717. See Appendix B on inventory prices in colonial Maryland.

were, by default, "consumption goods." Assignments were often arbitrary, but the underlying rationale will become clearer by means of a few examples. For instance, cattle, horses, sheep, swine, poultry, and bees are all livestock, and, as such, "capital." Canoes, rowboats, flatboats, sloops, and shares in larger vessels are capital, as are axes, hoes, adzes, saws, wedges, awls, and a lengthy list of other woodworking tools. The grindstones necessary to keep edged tools sharp are also capital. Plows, carts, and the harness gear needed to attach them to horses or oxen are capital, but saddles, pillions, bridles, and bits are consumption goods. Items for personal use, such as clothing and razors, spectacles and watches, are clearly consumption goods, as are household furnishings, cooking utensils, sheets, and tablecloths. Wooden containers for carrying or storing liquids and solids are consumption goods, except hogsheads designed to ship tobacco. If, however, a man kept an ordinary or inn, the large numbers of dishes and casks in his inventory ought rightfully to be assigned to capital.

The tricky part of distinguishing between assignments to capital or consumption arises when the owner's occupation is unknown. Since many men in early Maryland, particularly among the more well-to-do, pursued a variety of income-producing activities, occupational distinctions cannot always be adduced, and consistency of application, rather than confidence in the individual accuracy of each assignment, determined the placement of the ambiguous goods encountered in the inventories. Uncut cloth, for instance, was invariably coded as capital, whereas needles and buttons that were not part of lists of "new" goods or in the "store" were treated as consumption articles. Spinning wheels were also considered to be consumption items, but looms were treated as capital. All cider, stored grains, and salt meats were coded as "crops" and, therefore, as capital, simply because one cannot always distinguish between those intended as provisions for the family and those intended for sale.

Total personal property, comprising all of these components, will bear the tag GPW in the tables that follow, which stands for gross personal wealth. For many purposes, a slightly less inclusive version of total personal property will be used, PPW, or physical personal wealth, defined as gross personal wealth minus debts receivable, DR. Liabilities are not known for a majority of cases. When total personal wealth minus liabilities is estimated, however, it will carry the title, Net Worth, the equivalent of GPW minus gross debts payable or GDP.

51

The records used in this study are derived from a sample of six counties geographically distributed around the shores of the bay: Charles County, on the lower western shore, Calvert to the north of Charles, Anne Arundel to the north of Calvert, Baltimore to the north and east of Anne Arundel, Kent opposite Anne Arundel on the eastern shore, and Somerset on the lower eastern shore, bordering Accomack County in Virginia. Inventories from these counties begin in 1656, but the numbers remained few in these early years.[4] There were not as many as a dozen per year until 1664, or more than two dozen until 1670.

WHEN we turn to the probate records to inquire about the course of probate wealth over time, we discover that PPW per estate rose fairly consistently over the entire course of the period under study, 1650-1720. As Figure II-1 shows, mean PPW fluctuated widely from year to year, due to the occasional very wealthy case, but over time the compound rate of growth was over one percent a year. This is an impressive performance for a preindustrial economy, but it is surprising to find such growth continuing after tobacco exports had themselves ceased to grow after 1702.

Averages often mislead us, and the puzzle raised by rising mean wealth is clarified when we distinguish between strata of planters. In order to sort estates into separate classes for tracing the fortunes of poor, middling, and rich, we will arbitrarily draw dividing lines between percentages of estates ranked by their PPW. Thus the bottom 30 percent of estates averaged £11 PPW (and £16 GPW and £6 Net Worth) in the earliest period of the study, and this remained relatively unchanged over time. Table II.1 gives the results, having divided the years into five periods conforming roughly to the phases of the tobacco price cycle—although not precisely because to have done so would have produced very uneven numbers of estates in each period, a quality undesirable for other purposes of this study.

Depending on which definition of wealth becomes our measuring rod—PPW, GPW, or Net Worth—one's interpretation of how each class of men fared over the span of the study will differ. The source of the inconsistency lies in the behavior of financial assets. The ratio of debts receivable, DR, fell sharply for all ranks during the 1690s, and gross debts payable, GDP, also declined for all ranks above the bottom. Somewhat as a consequence of these movements, and aided

---

[4] A few early inventories may be found in *The Archives of Maryland*.

Figure II · 1

PERSONAL WEALTH IN SIX COUNTIES
OF MARYLAND 1660–1719

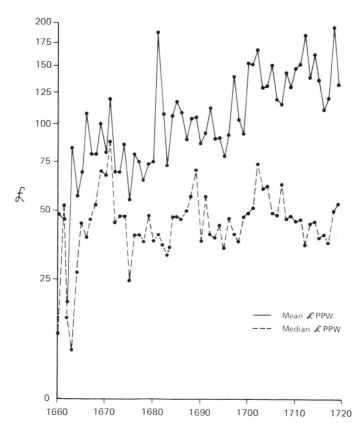

also by a rise in PPW, Net Worth actually rose during the depression years before 1697 for all but the poorest, and peaked during the boom of the interwar years for those in the middling ranks.

The richest 10 percent registered increases on all fronts the entire span of time. The bottom 90 percent of estates was perhaps a little better off, in terms of material goods, at the close of the period than they had been earlier, but the rich were far richer, no matter which measure we use. GPW and PPW for them more than doubled, and Net Worth rose over 300 percent.

Prior to the depression after 1702, economic growth had been

TABLE II.1

MEAN PERSONAL WEALTH OF RANKED STRATA OF MARYLAND PROBATED ESTATES
(£≈sterling)

Strata of Estates	1656-1683	1684-1696	1697-1704	1705-1712	1713-1719	% Change 1656-83/ 1713-19
Bottom 30%						
GPW	£16	£15	£14	£14	£13	− 19
PPW	11	12	13	13	12	+ 9
Net worth	6	0	5	0	0	− 100
Lower-middle 30%						
GPW	48	49	48	46	42	− 12
PPW	37	41	45	41	40	+ 8
Net worth	12	18	20	16	18	+ 50
Upper-middle 30%						
GPW	142	150	169	146	146	+ 3
PPW	108	122	164	138	139	+ 29
Net worth	59	76	99	87	91	+ 54
Richest 10%						
GPW	473	652	719	971	1009	+113
PPW	349	470	630	830	842	+141
Net worth	258	442	490	695	881	+241
Total no. estates	661	752	716	741	828	3699

SOURCE: Probate records of six counties, Maryland, in Hall of Records, Annapolis.
NOTE: GPW is gross personal estate, PPW is physical personal wealth, Net Worth equals GPW minus liabilities.

generally shared by the middling ranks of planters. Particularly was this true for their upper range, but they lost ground on all three measures—PPW, GPW, and Net Worth—in 1705-1712 and regained very little in the succeeding period. Table II.2 compares the wealth of the middle 60 percent of planters with the wealth of the richest 10 percent, revealing that the process of wealth accumulation was confined to the rich after 1700, further extending inequality in wealth holding. After 1704, the share size of the richest decile jumped to well over 60 percent; it had been 50 percent. The Gini coefficient, which measures the distance from absolute equality, rose from .65 in 1697-1704 to .72 for PPW and .73 for GPW, as Table II.3 shows.[5]

[5] A convenient summary of the characteristics of various measures of inequality may be found in chapter three of Martin B. Bronfenbrenner, *Income Distribution Theory* (Chicago, 1972). Alice Hanson Jones discusses the literature pertaining to the Gini coefficient and its limitations as a measure of inequality in *Wealth of a Nation to Be* (New York, 1980), pp. 424-25. A handy short-cut method for computing Gini

TABLE II.2

THE WEALTH OF THE MIDDLING PLANTERS COMPARED WITH THAT OF
THE RICHEST

Years	GPW		PPW		Net worth	
	M.60%	R.10%	M.60%	R.10%	M.60%	R.10%
1656-1683	£95	£473	£72.5	£349	£35.5	£258
1684-1696	99.5	652	81.5	470	47	442
1697-1704	108.5	719	104.5	630	59.5	490
1705-1712	96	971	89.5	830	57.5	695
1713-1719	94	1009	89.5	842	54.5	881
% Change 1656-1683/ 1713-1719	− 1%	+ 213%	+ 23%	+241%	+55%	+341%

SOURCE: Probate records of six counties, Maryland, in Hall of Records, Annapolis.

TABLE II.3

MEASURES OF WEALTH INEQUALITY IN EARLY MARYLAND
(probated decedents)

	1656-1683	1684-1696	1697-1704	1705-1712	1713-1719
GPW					
Share size, top 10%	43%	50%	50%	61%	64%
Mean/median	2.1	2.3	2.6	3.2	3.5
Gini coefficient	.59	.64	.65	.71	.73
PPW					
Share size, top 10%	43%	47%	49%	59%	61%
Mean/median	2.0	2.2	2.6	3.1	3.2
Gini coefficient	.58	.62	.645	.70	.72

SOURCE: Probate records of six counties, Maryland, in Hall of Records, Annapolis.

The rise in inequality is clearly due to the growth in the wealth of the richest planters whose estates appear in each successive time period, although the declining wealth of the poorer half during 1713-1719 also contributed to that effect. Two questions, then, must be addressed. The first seeks the origin of the remarkable stability of the mean, or average, of probated wealth for all the strata below the top, whereas the second probes the sources of the rising fortunes of the richest decile. Both may be consequences of

---

coefficients on hand calculators is in Charles M. Dollar and Richard J. Jensen, *Historian's Guide to Statistics: Quantitative Analysis and Historical Research* (New York, 1971), pp. 124-26.

the demographic transition in Maryland that took place between 1680 and 1720. A decline in the relative numbers of young, unmarried men in the population and the growth in the relative numbers of older men, with a probable increase in the accumulated savings or pool of assets in the colony, could account for both the stability in the level of wealth among the majority of decedents and the growth in wealth at the top.

Of necessity, then, we must analyze the age structure of the probated decedents and measure their wealth in terms of their relative age. Of the approximately 3,700 men with estates originating in the six counties before 1720, almost 2,000 left sufficient clues to be assigned into categories based on marital and family status: bachelors, those married and with young children, those who had at least one child of age and others under age, and those whose surviving offspring had all reached adulthood. We must substitute these categories for age classes because of the absence of birth and marriage records. The proportion of probated decedents in the older categories increased with time, from about 10 percent of estates in the early years to almost a quarter at the end of the century. Since mean physical personal wealth of the older men tended to be higher than the wealth of the younger men, and grew even higher with time, the rise in the mean for all estates that Figure II-1 disclosed may have been due entirely to the effects of Maryland's demographic transition. An exercise with weights and mean wealth figures for the age groups, fully described in Appendix A, demonstrates that almost all of the growth in mean personal wealth was indeed due to the changing age structure of probated decedents. Had that structure remained unchanged between 1656 and 1720, mean GPW would have fluctuated with tobacco prices.

Decedents	1656-1683	1684-1696	1697-1704	1705-1712	1713-1719
Fixed ages	£108	£ 95	£116	£112	£118
Changing ages	108	125	143	162	167

Changes in the age composition of probated decedents, therefore, accounted for much of the apparent economic growth recorded in the estate records, and contributed to rising inequality, as well—not because of the changing age mix, but because the more sizable accumulations of longer-lived men were perpetuated by means of gifts at marriage and bequests in wills.

The demographic effects on the level and distribution of wealth of probated decedents were analagous to those at work concurrently in the living population. The process is a difficult one to visualize, but one way to approach it is to see what happened to the distribution of wealth among a single age class, men with children all under age, called the "young fathers" for quick reference. Table II.4 displays their mean PPW as well as the median, and also provides Gini coefficients of inequality in each of the five time periods. One may note that the mean grew by half from the first period to the last, whereas the median increased by a fifth to its maximum size in 1705-1712, before declining sharply in the final period. The difference between the median and the mean widened, therefore, with the passage of time, just as the Gini coefficient registered increasing inequality. The effects of the demographic transition, therefore, not only raised the numbers of the older group of men in the population, it raised the wealth of their heirs, as well.

One might suppose that declining income from tobacco would have greatly eroded existing assets and that partitioning among children would have dissipated them, lowering the level of wealth and making its distribution less unequal. The effects, if any, of these countervailing tendencies are not apparent in the probate records before 1720. Savings, reinvestment, and the continuing scarcity of children surviving into adulthood acted to counteract the eroding forces that may have been at work. At least as important were the planters' own efforts to find alternative sources of income and to substitute domestic manufactures for imports. Analyzing the things people owned by means of the inventories of probated estates can provide vital clues to such activities.

First, let us spell out the options facing the planters and their families during periods of low tobacco prices: 1. they could move

TABLE II.4
SUMMARY MEASURES OF THE LEVEL AND DISTRIBUTION OF PPW
AMONG "YOUNG FATHERS" (£≈sterling)

PPW	1656-1683	1684-1696	1697-1704	1705-1712	1713-1719
Mean	£134	£151	£183	£205	£200
Median	44	47	50	53	40
Mean/median	3.0	3.2	3.7	3.9	5.0
Gini coefficient	.50	.54	.54	.59	.65

SOURCE: Probate records of six counties, Maryland, in Hall of Records, Annapolis.
NOTE: The "young fathers" consist of all married male decedents identified as having at least one child underage and none of age.

within the colony itself or leave it entirely to find their fortunes elsewhere; 2. they could stay where they were and work harder to grow more tobacco in order to earn the same amount of cash income; 3. they could continue to produce the same amount and mix of crops, livestock, and so forth, but buy less and make do with less; 4. they could cut back on their tobacco growing and devote the saved labor time to make at home what they formerly purchased; 5. they could sell these things or their services to others who continued to make and sell tobacco but imported less; or 6. they could seek new export markets, such as the provisions trade with the West Indies.

Individual response to poor prices—or, worse, no buyers at any price—depended on individual circumstances. Planters owning fertile, well-located lands and who dealt directly with London firms occupied the best situation for riding out the depression. These men constituted a small minority in Maryland, but such men could, and did, buy their neighbors' Oronoco at depressed prices and ship it with their own, undertaking the risk involved and bearing the charges for freight and customs. Those worst off were men without property or those whose debts could not be met out of the reduced proceeds from their crops of tobacco.

Probably as important as any other single factor determining the planters' decisions was the relative load of debt each carried. Some simply fled ahead of the sheriff. Within the colony, many moved to cheaper lands, where settlers perforce practiced a mixed style of farming either because their soil was too poor to produce the kind of tobacco in demand or they were too far away from deep water to attract buyers with heavy transportation charges.

The proportion of the colony's population living on marginal lands or in marginal areas grew, so that exports of tobacco per capita fell, but the best tidewater lands continued in full production, following the usual cycle of tobacco, then corn or other cereal, then pasture, and long fallow. Thus, the withdrawal of labor resources took place at the fringes rather than at the heart of the tobacco economy.

Tobacco remained the primary cash crop of three economic groups: the middling planters fortunate enough to own good land in accessible areas and in ample quantities; those poorer planters who, as tenants and debtors needed the crops of tobacco to pay off their debts and fulfill their contracts; and the richest planters with good land and lots of slaves. Different routes of diversification were followed by different classes and in different regions of Maryland.

Three may be distinguished: production of substitutes for imported goods (that is, home manufactures or commission work by artisans working full or part time); substitution of other crops for tobacco, such as wheat or flax; and extension of livestock raising and perhaps fattening animals for market.

For those not desperately in debt, it cost less in terms of income foregone to reduce their crop by withdrawing labor time and allocating it to other pursuits in periods of low tobacco prices than during periods of good prices. Thus, in bad times even the wealthiest planters became willing to assign some of their laborers' time to growing wheat, for instance, in order to enhance their own diet, or to manufacturing goods such as shoes and coarse woven materials for blankets and clothing, thereby reducing their cash outlays. Those forced to adopt the country-made cloth in place of even the cheapest English yardgoods suffered a diminution of their standard of living, since the home-produced textiles were seldom fulled, dyed, or otherwise finished, and were sleazy, inferior products. On the other hand, their supply was assured, and people may well have preferred such assurance to unexpected interruptions in trade goods from overseas.

The evidence for this comes from the composition of planters' assets in estate inventories.[6] We will sketch out the changing configuration of planters' holdings in each of the five time periods demarcated, separating the estates into fixed strata based on the value of their physical personal property, PPW.[7] The particular bounds of individual strata were set with two criteria in mind: that they hold nearly equal numbers of estates in each of the periods,

---

[6] Probate inventories list articles a man owned at his death but not how or when he acquired them. The composition of those assets, however, can help to date the introduction and spread of new tools, crops, and household and personal articles. Although one cannot retrace the actual steps of decision making, one can measure relationships after the fact between important independent variables such as relative wealth, county of residence, date of the inventory, and age (or stage in the life cycle) to composition of assets.

[7] The value of PPW was the single best predictor of how people lived and how they spent their time. County of origin proved of secondary significance once wealth itself had been taken into account, except that Calvert and Anne Arundel County planters owned significantly more slaves and greater amounts of new goods (stocks of unused or unopened goods, usually imported). Somerset County planters' estates listed significantly fewer debts receivable. This information was obtained by means of analysis of variance and difference of means tests carried out on the logarithmically transformed values of the various components of probate wealth using the ANOVA and ONEWAY programs in *The Statistical Package for the Social Sciences*, usually referred to as SPSS.

and that they reflect, insofar as such existed, actual gaps in the original distribution between groups of estates and between congeries of assets.[8] Obviously, some sort of compromise among competing criteria was necessary, but altering the specific boundaries would not greatly alter the substance of the findings.

Table II.5 shows the bounds finally selected, ranking the estates from poorest to richest in ten classes. Table II.6 summarizes the composition of wealth for each of the classes and provides ready comparisons among them. The various forms of capital composed the principal part of planter property at all levels of wealth, although the relative importance of capital increased from class to class. For the top estates, consumption goods represented only a fifth of their personal property, whereas for the poorest planters, such things were twice as important. Within the general category of capital, the bulk of the assets shifted progressively from livestock to bound labor as wealth rose, so that ultimately, for the richest 6

TABLE II.5
DISTRIBUTION OF MARYLAND PLANTER ESTATES BY PHYSICAL
PERSONAL WEALTH (PPW)

PPW	1656-1683	1684-1696	1697-1704	1705-1712	1713-1719	Average
£ 0-15	.22	.20	.19	.18	.20	.20
16-34	.21	.21	.19	.21	.22	.21
35-49	.14	.11	.13	.12	.13	.13
50-71	.10	.12	.08	.11	.09	.10
72-96	.07	.08	.08	.08	.08	.08
97-149	.10	.09	.09	.09	.08	.09
150-228	.07	.07	.08	.06	.07	.07
229-399	.06	.07	.08	.06	.07	.07
400-799	.02	.03	.06	.05	.03	.04
800-up	.01	.02	.02	.04	.04	.02
Total	1.00	1.00	1.00	1.01	1.01	1.01
Nos.	629	714	665	680	766	3454*

SOURCE: Probate records of six counties, Maryland, in Hall of Records, Annapolis.
* This excludes estates for which inventories were lacking.

[8] These latter criteria could only have been implemented in objective fashion if most of the various kinds of material objects actually mentioned in the inventories had been *each* individually coded and punched, a task that seemed far too expensive to justify the promised increases in clarity. Instead, intensive analyses of notes on the estates of "young fathers," men whose children were not yet of age, provided the approximate or probable boundaries. Key assets for this procedure were slaves, servants, beds, chairs, silver plate, and new goods.

Table II.6
Composition of Personal Wealth by Class (percent)

PPW	% in Class	Livestock	Bound Labor	Crops	New Goods	Other Capital*	Total in Capital	Cash	Consumption Goods	Total PPW
£ 0-15	20	40	0	15	2	3	60	0	39	99
16-34	21	47	2	11	2	3	65	1	34	100
35-49	13	51	5	8	2	2	68	0	32	100
50-71	10	48	8	9	2	3	70	0	31	101
72-96	8	45	11	9	2	2	69	2	29	100
97-149	9	41	15	9	3	2	70	1	28	99
150-228	7	35	22	10	4	2	73	1	27	101
229-399	7	29	27	8	7	3	74	1	26	100
400-799	4	25	33	9	7	4	78	1	21	100
800-up	2	19	34	9	12	4	78	2	20	100
Total	101									

SOURCE: Probate records of six counties, Maryland, in Hall of Records, Annapolis, 1656-1719.
* Includes tools of all kinds, boats, ships, and milling equipment.

percent of estates, bound labor took precedence over livestock as its share dominated the entire investment portfolio.

Of first and paramount importance in understanding the functioning of the tobacco economy is the fact that the planters were primarily farmers—they kept cattle, cleared land, dressed timber, built fences, and pursued the myriad activities that constituted the farm tasks of the day. Before going on to consider the processes by which Maryland planters adapted to the changing fortunes of the tobacco market, let us pause to examine more closely the composition of their agricultural capital, with special attention to the differences, and similarities, between the poor, the middling, and the rich.

The composition of farm livestock, for instance, varied little between classes of planters. Sheep form an important exception to this fact, since their numbers were confined primarily to the upper three-fifths of planter households. Cattle, on the other hand, occupied first place for everyone, ahead of horses and swine. Table II.7 divides the planters into four classes, from poorest to richest, and shows the average number of animals per household among those owning at least one of each kind. The poorest families, for instance, kept about 10 cattle, 2 horses, and 8 swine. Only a quarter kept sheep, and among these, the average number owned was 8. The middling planter owned twice as many cattle and three times as many hogs as did the poorer households, but fewer than half had sheep. The richest planters ran larger herds of everything: 76 cattle, 10 horses, 52 hogs, 33 sheep.

During the earliest years of settlement in the Chesapeake, farm animals of all sorts were both scarce and expensive, but after 1680 their relative costs declined as herds flourished and multiplied. Few

TABLE II.7

ESTIMATED AVERAGE NUMBER OF ANIMALS AMONG OWNERS BY CLASS
IN PROBATED ESTATES 1656-1719

Class PPW	Cattle	Horses	Swine	Sheep	% with Swine	% with Sheep
£ 0-49	9.8	2.2	8.6	8.2	75%	27%
50-149	21.2	3.3	19.2	13.2	90	45
150-399	34.2	4.9	24.0	20.6	92	58
400-up	76.3	9.9	51.7	32.2	100	81

SOURCE: Probated estates of men whose children were all under age, referred to as the "young fathers" sample from probate records of six counties, Maryland, in Hall of Records, Annapolis.

farmers, however, attempted to keep sheep before then because of wolves and the general lack of cleared fields for their pasturing, since thickets and shrubs tore away the wool from their coats. Most households probably raised chickens, but these do not appear in estate inventories before 1700. Growing numbers after that date reported bees, geese, and turkeys.

The central importance of cattle raising in the early South rested on the existence of an open range. Maryland planters generally made no attempt to restrain their animals, letting them run loose in the woods all year round. In the year 1681, for instance, three men and their horses spent several tiring days looking for two dozen cattle belonging to a Baltimore County man. General roundups were necessary every spring so that planters could mark the young animals by notching ears and branding hides. Most of the young male cattle were castrated then as well, since bulls were almost worthless as meat and troublesome to keep.[9]

Horses were the most difficult to catch during these roundups. One administrator charged a decedent's estate 100 pounds of tobacco for each of 14 colts he and his men had chased after. At 40 pounds of tobacco for daily wages to each man and his horse, it had taken some 35 man-days to accomplish the task.[10] Another administrator charged an estate 26 shillings for a similar chore, plus 2 bottles of rum to lighten the task.[11]

Planters exercised little care over this free-roaming stock except to provide occasional feed in winter. As early as 1669, however, one man's animals consumed some 15 barrels of corn in order "to preserve them," and the cost of the corn was equivalent to 10 percent of their appraised value.[12] In three other cases, wintering the stock, including the cost of feed, averaged about 60 to 70 pounds of tobacco per head for both cattle and horses, a cost that was almost 15 percent of their usual value.[13] Amos Cooke's estate was

---

[9] *Inv. & Accts.*, Liber 8, f. 7. See also Liber 31, f. 241, and Liber 29, f. 320. As early as 1677, Thomas Roper of Anne Arundel County kept some two dozen cattle and almost that many hogs in a "cow-pen." His five horses, however, remained somewhere out in the fields or woods. Ibid., Liber 4, f. 538. The average ratio of bulls to cows was about one to seven.

[10] This was Charles County. The inventory dated to the year 1678, but the account was not rendered until 1684. Ibid., Liber 8, f. 389.

[11] Ibid., Liber 37B, f. 109.

[12] *Testamentary Proceedings*, VI, f. 56. For similar cases in Kent County, the charges came to 13 percent and 16 percent of the inventory value of the animals so fed. *Inv. & Accts.*, Liber 31, f. 241 and Liber 29, f. 320.

[13] *Inv. & Accts.*, Liber 10, f. 470; Liber 16, f. 210, and Liber 35A, f. 237.

charged 200 pounds of tobacco in 1690 for keeping some six hogs in a pen for two months, which meant providing them with all their food. Almost 17 pounds of tobacco per head was charged per month, meaning that the cost was a little more than a shilling apiece monthly. In terms of corn, the hogs were eating about a barrel a month or a little less than a bushel each.[14]

Under the normal free-running regime, it is not surprising that quality suffered and that losses of livestock by starvation and disease were frequent. As Robert Beverly complained, the planters were guilty of "ill husbandry in not providing sufficiently for them all winter . . . they starve their young cattle or at least stunt their growth."[15] One account from Anne Arundel County reported that out of some 16 calves born in the year 1674, only 4 survived two years later. A Somerset County account reported far less dramatic losses, however. From an initial stock of some 49 cattle in 1685, 13 head had died three years later, including 2 in calving and 6 that had become mired and died from exposure and starvation. Out of 38 hogs, 14 had either died or strayed, and 2 out of the 10 horses were also deceased, one having hanged himself by chance.[16] A Charles County record mentioned losses of 3 out of 10 cattle and 7 out of 19 hogs.[17] Occasional reports such as these cannot give us very exact ideas about survival rates, but it seems clear that the youngest animals suffered the most from wintering out in the woods.

Inadequate food undermined the ability of the animals to survive occasionally severe winters, and the occurrence of epidemics inflicted unnecessarily heavy costs on the weakened animals. The latter part of the seventeenth century has been termed "the little ice age" by some historians, and livestock losses were unusually high. In the winter of 1694-1695, for instance, the colony was hit especially hard, and 25,000 cattle and 62,000 hogs died of disease and cold. Since the human population at that time numbered less than the roughly 35,000 noted in the 1704 census, this loss was at least the equivalent of a cow and two hogs for each resident.[18]

Despite high attrition rates, large numbers of cattle were reported as early as 1660 in the Chesapeake region, when even newly freed

[14] Ibid., Liber 10, f. 327.
[15] Beverly, *History*, p. 291.
[16] *Inv. & Accts.*, Liber 2, f. 224; Liber 10, f. 174.
[17] Ibid., Liber 26, f. 106 and Liber 29, f. 383. Frontier dangers inflicted other costs. Six sows belonging to a Baltimore County planter were killed by Seneca Indians in 1682 or 1683. These losses wiped out half the planter's stock.
[18] *Md.Arch.*, XX, 191-92, 270-71.

servants encountered little difficulty obtaining them. The average number of cattle in individual classes of planters did not vary much after these early years.[19]

Hogs were especially plentiful. They "swarm like vermin upon the earth," boasted Robert Beverly. "The hogs run where they list and find their own support in the woods."[20] They also proved a nuisance—one aggressive old sow finally got her comeuppance for killing lambs when she was caught in the act and dispatched without ceremony.[21]

Running loose led to haphazard breeding and small average size for all the farm livestock. Reliable evidence on actual sizes is difficult to come by, but scattered information suggests a norm for hogs of well under 100 pounds prior to 1700. After that, especially in the northern areas, farmers began deliberately to fatten their animals, and recorded weights there rose to nearly 200 pounds live, and about one-fourth less when dressed.[22] Higher prices for live hogs in these later years suggest heavier animals, but one cannot be sure. Although we lack firm evidence on the matter, a market may have developed elsewhere for Maryland pork, making it possible for growing numbers of planters profitably to exploit this opportunity.

[19] Numbers dipped during the period 1697-1704 as a result of an epidemic.

[20] Beverly, *History*, p. 318.

[21] *Inv. & Accts.*, Liber 11, f. 29½.

[22] Ibid., Liber 21, f. 294 reports a boar and sow of the "Essex Breed," about nine months of age and valued at £1. This is the only mention of any special breed encountered in the records. On hog weights, for Kent County: three weighed 204 pounds total, or an average of 68 each in 1698. Ibid., Liber 19, f. 117. Charles County: five weighed 80 pounds each, four 90 pounds, and eight others only slightly over 50 each, but these were all probably *dressed* weights, not live. Anne Arundel County: a 1707 account reported sixteen hogs dressed out at 119 each, on the average, and were valued at £1 each. Six others averaged 106. Ibid., Liber 27, f. 246. Baltimore County: a dozen hogs in 1717 yielded 1,900 pounds of pork valued at two pence per pound, each hog averaging 158 pounds of meat. *Inventories*, Liber 1, f. 41. These examples ranged from 50 to 158 pounds, dressed, and heavier hogs sold for £1 per head, live. Since the average price of "killable" hogs was from 12 to 16 shillings each, these hogs would have ranged in size between 72 and 96 pounds, dressed, about two-thirds the size of John Beale Bordley's preferred size for hogs, reached at approximately eighteen months of age. John Beale Bordley, *A Summary View of the Courses of Crops, in the Husbandry of England and Maryland* . . . (Philadelphia, 1784), pp. 180, 185, 187, quoted in James T. Lemon, *The Best Poor Man's Country: A Geographical Study of Early Southeastern Pennsylvania* (Baltimore, 1972), p. 166. Lemon estimated that the average hog at slaughter time weighed about 175 pounds live, so the difference between live and dressed weight was about a quarter of the live weight. If so, Bordley's hogs would have dressed out between 123 and 154 pounds.

In nontobacco growing areas of Somerset County, hog raising had long provided a significant source of income, and many debts were expressed in terms of pork rather than cash or tobacco.

Horses took longer to establish themselves in the Chesapeake than either hogs or cattle. Only half of the estate inventories, for instance, mention them in the years before the 1680s, when there were actually more servants and slaves than horses. The appraised values of horses, like those of other livestock, reflected this scarcity, averaging £ 4 each in the 1660s and 1670s but gradually falling to half that amount by the end of the seventeenth century.

Horses of better quality and training appeared in the eighteenth century, as appraisers began to append such descriptions to individual animals as "draught," "plow," "cart," "riding," and even "pacing" or "flying." Besides these more valuable animals, however, the usual undistinguished breed continued to flourish, many still being reported as "running in the woods." These nearly wild animals throve particularly well in the back country where mounted planters accompanied by dogs found both sport and profit in chasing them, for they were "shy as any savage creature." Horses provided the means to pursue other prey as well: Beverly gleefully reported full-speed chases on horseback through the woods after wolves, a dangerous but exhilirating sport for the bold.[23]

Horses also furnished occasional muscle power for plowing, carrying goods, and even for milling, but few men owned either carts or mills, and plows were little used before the eighteenth century. Hogsheads of tobacco were too heavy for a horse to carry and these generally had to be rolled, since it made little sense to construct cart roads from each tobacco shed down to the waterside. The extension of the population into the interior brought with it a greater need for roads, and as these were built, carts grew more common in the inventories.

Horses, then, were principally important as a means of communication and as a means of escape from the grinding routine of farm life on isolated plantations. In function they not only served as the principal mode of transportation for the planters and their wives, but they were prized for the freedom and independence they permitted. They offered, too, a highly visible means of asserting status, and the speedier mounts afforded exciting opportunities for sports, racing, and gambling.

Early Maryland probably contained as many farm animals per

[23] Beverly, *History*, p. 312. "Many people have taught their horses to . . . walk gently by the huntsman's side to cover him from the sight of a deer"; ibid., p. 308.

planter as did its neighbors to the south, and certainly more than
did the colonies to the north.[24] One must not underestimate, then,
their importance to the economy and to the well-being of their
owners, despite the central role of tobacco. A vivid demonstration
of this comes from a comparison of livestock holdings among the
poorer third of Maryland households with those of the landless
farm laborers in the west of England during the first half of the
seventeenth century.[25] Table II.8 shows that many more poor men

TABLE II.8

LIVESTOCK OWNERSHIP IN MARYLAND AND ENGLAND: MARYLAND
PLANTERS OF THE BOTTOM THIRD OF HOUSEHOLDS
AND ENGLISH FARM LABORERS

Group	% with Cattle	Average No. Cattle	% with Horses	Average No. Horses	% with Swine	% with Sheep
English laborers	90	0.8	30	0.4	30	45
Maryland £0-19	64	3.1	50	0.8	53	12
Maryland £20-39	93	8.5	83	1.9	71	27

SOURCES: Alan Everitt, "Farm Labourers," in Joan Thirsk, ed., *Agrarian History
of England and Wales*, IV (New York, 1967), 413-15; probated estates of men whose
children were all under age, referred to as the "young fathers" sample from probate
records of six counties, Maryland, in Hall of Records, Annapolis.
NOTE: The bottom third of heads of households was roughly equivalent to all
those with estates worth less than £50 PPW. The English farm laborers' estates date
from 1615 through 1640 and originated in the west of England.

[24] The median holding of cattle in Connecticut before the Revolution was ten,
from seven to ten in southeastern Pennsylvania after 1730, and twelve in Maryland.
Jackson Turner Main, *Connecticut Society in the Era of the American Revolution* (Hartford, Conn., 1977), pp. 28-29; Lemon, *Best Poor Man's Country*, pp. 163-65. The
average holding among landowners in late eighteenth-century tidewater Virginia
included a dozen cattle and two-dozen hogs, not far from the medians recorded in
early Maryland.

[25] A sample of "poor" married men, those with estates worth less than the median
of £ 50, was assembled for the specific purpose of analyzing their property holdings
in order to establish both the boundaries and the meaning of relative poverty among
free white settlers in the tobacco colony. The English evidence comes from Alan
Everitt, "Farm Labourers," in Thirsk, ed., *Agrarian History*, pp. 396-415. This article
reports an investigation of over 3,000 inventories from the sixteenth and seventeenth centuries taken from seventeen counties divided into six geographical regions
of England, of which the "west" formed one. The term "farm labourer" refers to
a socio-economic class distinguished particularly by nonownership of land, but the
designation was not clear-cut in the sources, and the author was forced to rely on
his own judgment in the majority of cases.

in Maryland owned livestock than did farm laborers in the west of England, and, of particular significance, it shows how many more of them they were able to keep, aided as they were by the vast tracts of empty land in which the animals could roam and forage for themselves. As a result, the poorest planters had far more meat available to them than did the majority of English countrymen whose access to commons and waste faced steady encroachment.

The craze for land commonly attributed to European immigrants to the New World may well have rested as much on the promise of a perpetual abundance of meat and dairy products as on its assurance of security.[26] The old European farm economy required a careful balancing of needs and land resources, since a significant part of the available land had to lie fallow in order to renew itself. The number of animals that could be kept, therefore, was sharply limited by the amount of winter feed that could be raised on that part of the land which was not resting or producing food for the farmers themselves.[27] Constraints imposed by the low level of farm technology, principally the failure to develop nitrogen-fixing fodder crops, governed the land-use budget and restricted the size of herds just as much as did the limited amount of land available. Inability to support greater numbers of animals led in a vicious circle to insufficient supplies of animal dung for manuring the exhausted soil, requiring scarce land to be withdrawn from use so that it might recover its fertility.

The stretches of unused land at everyone's back door inevitably shrank as population grew in the tidewater, which is why the opportunity to keep animals by running them in the woods likewise diminished. Post-Revolutionary Virginia tax lists, for instance, disclose that a quarter of the freemen had neither cattle for milk or meat nor horses for riding and recreation—a sad reversion to the poverty of the old world.[28]

Passage of time brought with it other consequences of a receding

[26] Everitt remarks that "until labourers began to grow potatoes, they were rarely in a position to rear and fatten swine"; ibid., p. 416.

[27] B. H. Slicher Van Bath, *The Agrarian History of Western Europe, A.D. 500-1850*, translated by Olive Ordish (London, 1963), chapter two.

[28] One should, however, beware of overstating the contrast between the two periods, since eastern Virginia had experienced a recent and quite sharp economic decline prior to the date of the tax list of 1787, from which these data come. Jackson Turner Main, "The Distribution of Property in Post-Revolutionary Virginia," *Mississippi Valley Historical Review*, XLI (1954), 243. The tax lists also overstate poverty among taxables because young men of good family may have had excellent prospects of attaining what their fathers then possessed, but prospects were not taxable.

frontier and a burgeoning population. After the best lands for tobacco were taken, the human overflow occupied areas less suited to the staple crop or further away from water transport. The prime tobacco lands of the lower western shore, for instance, were home to three-quarters of the poorest planter households in the years before the first prolonged depression of 1686-1696. The growing population then began spreading up into the northern reaches of the bay, up into lands at the head of creeks and rivers, and well down the eastern shore, particularly into Somerset County, where most settlers concentrated on cattle, hogs, and wheat.[29]

Planters living on poorer soils were the first to feel the effects of economic downswings, because no one would take poor quality tobacco in times of glut. Fewer ships came calling, and fixed freight charges made shippers especially choosy. Planters finding no buyers for their crop had no choice, then, but to diversify or leave. Their options were several: find a market for such alternative crops as wheat, barreled pork, and timber products, or make something someone else would pay for.

The provision trade with the royal navy and with the West Indies offered such markets, and ultimately came to play a very significant role in the region's economy.[30] Since imports of English goods always fell off sharply during downswings, country-made products not only filled their makers' needs but occasionally found buyers nearby. The longer the recession, the greater such demand would develop, so successively longer downturns in tobacco prices after 1680 gradually forced changes in the structure of farm and household tasks as purchases of new manufactured goods from abroad were postponed or abandoned.

During the early, expansive phase of Maryland's development, work activities not directly related to clearing land or cultivating tobacco and corn took up only a small portion of most planters' working lives. The reasons for this are obvious: while the price of tobacco was good, one's time was better rewarded raising it than

[29] Of married planters whose personal estates (PPW) came to less than £ 50, the distribution among counties altered most dramatically during the depression of 1686-1696, but the brief revival in tobacco prices at the end of the century only temporarily reversed the trend away from Anne Arundel and Calvert counties. Charles County, with its smaller average holdings and more equitable distribution of wealth, in particular experienced booms in population during "good" times and counteracted this long-term trend. Somerset county's population of small farmers, however, grew steadily after 1700 and dominated the six-county distribution of poorer estates after 1712.

[30] Clemens, *Atlantic Economy*, chapter six.

making the things that tobacco could buy. For those living along the extensive waterways, ships from England came to their very doors carrying hardware and uncut cloth: the cheaper kinds of English yard goods such as canvas, dowlas, and osnaburg for the poorer planters and the servants, and fine linens and woolens for those able to afford them. In addition, the cargoes included new hats and shoes, fine feather beds, and luxury food items such as sugar, spices, wines, and, after 1700, tea, coffee, and chocolate. Salt, hoes, axes, saws, carpentry tools, and nails rounded out the ships' stocks of goods for sale to the planters, because everyone who established a new farm had to have or borrow elementary carpentry tools. Heavy reliance on commercially forged metal nails resulted in savings in labor time that more than made up for their cost.[31]

Every household that could afford to do so sought to lay by what it needed for the rest of the year when, in the winter and early spring, the ships again came up the rivers trucking their wares for tobacco. For those who could not pay out in advance enough for a full year's necessities, enterprising neighbors offered these for sale, and thus there developed a network of small debts all over the colony that would be settled when the crop came in. Debt collection time often meant a hectic riding up and down the countryside, as creditors tried to beat each other to the crop. Many financial settlements were also made in a more leisurely and sociable fashion at the court house door during one of its regular sessions; those who had accumulated more debts than tobacco might, alas, find themselves inside the court room standing before a stern-countenanced judge.

Poor men were particularly in need of credit to carry themselves and their families over the year between crops. John Foukes of Kent County, for instance, died in 1680 owning some £17 worth of personal property. He ranked in the bottom fifth of all planters in terms of personal estate, which was administered after his death by his neighbor, Lewis Blangy, who was also his patron and chief creditor. Blangy's accounts charged Foukes' estate for the costs of maintaining the widow and children for four months at the rate of 250 pounds of tobacco per month, or about one pound sterling. Blangy also charged the estate for goods "delivered to the deceased in his lifetime," which included four yards of broadcloth, six and

---

[31] Chapter Four below, on housing in early Maryland, discusses at greater length the uses of nails.

a half ells of dowlas cloth, five yards of "trading" cloth, one pair of shoes, one pair of boots, two pairs of stockings, and one pair of bodices (a woman's undergarment). In addition, Blangy also charged for a weeding hoe, ten gallons of cider, five quarts of rum, and a bed cord—rope used to form the lacework suspended between the bed rails to support mattress and bedding. The total amount owed by Foukes to Blangy came to 1,281 pounds of tobacco or just over £5 in money, almost a third of the value of Foukes' entire estate, which consisted of three cattle, a mare and her colt, eight barrels of corn, four hogsheads of tobacco, and some household goods worth about £2 in money.[32]

Poor men such as John Foukes relied on well-to-do neighbors or landlords to supply them with clothing, tools, and drink in exchange for their annual crop, specializing in the latter to obtain the rest. Under these conditions, such a man needed relatively little capital of his own to set up as an independent planter and acquire a wife, although doing so placed him in a position of dependency on his supplier. By rigorously limiting his purchases and applying all his labor, and that of his wife, to extracting the maximum quantity of tobacco from the land, a planter could hope to build surplus credits and eventually acquire a servant to expand the crop still further. The cattle, horses, and hogs, meanwhile, were themselves providing supplementary earnings as well as passively increasing the planter's total capital worth. The vagaries of nature and the market did endow the enterprise with more risk than a poor man might care to undertake, but such has always been the lot of men who farm for a living.

As stated earlier, most planters above the poorest level attempted to acquire in advance a year's supplies of imported goods. This was particularly true in the early decades of generally good tobacco prices, when this was easier. Roughly a quarter of all estates before 1684 contained at least some items, usually cloth, that were being saved or stored. Declining income in the years that followed forced sharp cutbacks in such stocks, although in the brief period of prosperity between the wars, middling and rich planters again rushed to acquire English goods.

For many of the poor and middling classes, the decline in new goods available to them required a withdrawal from tobacco production, or at least a diminution of effort expended on that crop and simultaneous direction of energies into making substitutes for

[32] *Inv. & Accts.*, Liber 7A, ff. 257, 254.

them. For the rich, however, dealing in imported goods provided sources of income and thus afforded an important means of diversification.

Well into the depths of the long depression in tobacco prices that followed the reopening of the war in 1702, Governor Spotswood of Virginia succinctly explained to the British Council of Trade the effects of low prices on the staple economy. "The overproduction of tobacco," he wrote, "was felt in those parts of the Country where Tobacco is reputed mean, and the people being disappointed of the necessary supplies of Cloathing for their familys in return for their tobacco found themselves under necessity of attempting to Cloath themselves with their own Manufactures. And the Market for Tobacco still declining and few stores of goods brought in, other parts of the Country, through the like necessity, have been forced into the same."[33]

Home production of apparel in the tidewater South never approached in importance the levels reached later in the back country or in the households of northern farmers.[34] How early, and to what extent, tobacco planters of various classes engaged in wool and flax manufacture, however, has never been satisfactorily investigated. One historian of seventeenth-century Virginia has argued that the leading planters of the day adopted an energetic, indeed quite entrepreneurial stance in promoting economic diversification at home.[35] Another writer has stressed, on the other hand, the universal resistance of the planters to programs that their leaders attempted to impose on them.[36] Class, region, and timing played major roles in determining individual planter response. The distribution of certain indicator items, such as sheep, in probate inventories can serve as a rough index to the particular disposition of Maryland households to withhold resources from tobacco production, either to engage in home manufactures or to exploit alternative sources of income.

We have already noted the rarity of sheep in seventeenth-century Maryland. Only 7 percent of inventoried estates listed them prior to the 1680s. During the depression of 1686-1696, when tobacco prices hit their lowest levels of the entire colonial period, the proportion of households owning sheep rose abruptly to 28 percent.

[33] "Letters of Governor Spotswood," *Virginia Historical Collections*, new ser., I, 72.
[34] Rolla M. Tryon, *Household Manufactures in the United States, 1640-1860* (Chicago, 1917, repr. New York, 1966), chapter three; Gray, *Agriculture*, I, 232-33.
[35] Bruce, *Economic History*, II, 454-74.
[36] Rainbolt, *Prescription to Persuasion*.

In the short period of prosperity that followed, sheep keeping extended to a third of planter households, but the most impressive increase took place during the depression that followed, when Governor Spotswood pointed out the consequences. Almost two-thirds of the Maryland inventories of this period mentioned sheep. Rather predictably, however, the next upturn in tobacco prices brought with it a reduction in the proportion of estates with sheep.

Even in the eighteenth century, much of the increase in the relative numbers of sheepkeepers was confined to the counties of the eastern shore, reflecting the strongly regional nature of Maryland's adaptive response to stagnation in the tobacco economy. By moving onto lands that were farther away from shipping and markets or less productive, or incapable of yielding the varieties of tobacco in demand, the expanding population reallocated its energies into producing more things for domestic consumption. In counties on the lower western shore, where were located the best soils for raising marketable tobacco, only the better-off planters raised sheep, whereas on the eastern shore, residents on poorer soils in Kent and Somerset County were far more likely to keep sheep no matter which class they came from, particularly after 1700 (see Table II.9).

The expansion and regionalization of home manufacturing can also be detected by tracing the appearance of spinning wheels in estate inventories. Once again, the eastern shore counties of Kent and Somerset produced the highest proportions of estates with spinning wheels: roughly a fifth in the seventeenth century, three-quarters thereafter. As with sheep, affluence played a key role in distribution on the western shore north of Charles County, where more than twice as many planters owning more than £ 229 in personal wealth owned spinning wheels than did men in the classes below them. None of the inventories in the six-county sample mentioned looms before 1705, and only 8 percent did so thereafter (see Table II.10).[37]

The prolonged absence of sheep, spinning wheels, and looms from the households of Maryland planters strongly suggests that domestic manufacture of textiles played little part in the economy so long as tobacco prices did not go below the critical level of a

[37] Only one loom appeared in the inventories of the richest county, Anne Arundel, and it belonged to a poor weaver who died in 1718. Not a single estate among the richest 5 percent mentioned a loom. The only servant in the probate records of the six counties who was described as a weaver worked for a planter in Somerset County on the lower eastern shore. Shoemaking and repairing were more common.

73

TABLE II.9
PROPORTION OF ESTATES WITH SHEEP IN TWO PERIODS BY
COUNTY AND CLASS

PPW	Anne Arundel, Baltimore, Calvert	Charles	Kent and Somerset	Average*
	1656-1696			
£ 0-34	10%	0%	6%	7%
35-96	9	9	22	12
97-228	13	36	56	26
229-up	30	50	50	38
Average*	12	14	24	15
	1705-1719			
£ 0-34	0%	10%	57%	23%
35-96	38	29	89	25
97-228	70	42	92	76
229-up	71	60	93	77
Average*	33	28	77	48

SOURCE: Probated estates of men whose children were all underage, that is, the "young fathers'" sample from the probate records of six counties, Maryland, Hall of Records, Annapolis.
* Weighted by numbers of all estates in each county, class and period.

penny per pound, a price that could attract new resources in 1698-1702, but that later failed to do so as costs of labor, land, and local transportation gradually rose and population penetrated into lands further away from waterways. Even in the eighteenth century, however, the poorer half of planters living in regions containing prime tobacco lands did not make any of their own clothing.

The expansion of population on the eastern shore, on the other hand, extended that part of the Chesapeake economy which lay outside the tobacco market for much of the range of prices prevailing before the 1730s. These areas developed mixed farming supplemented by fishing and home manufactures. The crop that best distinguishes farming of this type is wheat, and the distribution of plows in Maryland inventories provides a very rough index of wheat growing. One did not need a plow to raise row crops such as tobacco, corn, beans, and squash, nor did one have to plow the land to raise wheat, although more extensive weeding is required by broadcast sowing of small grains, and this is what plows do better than hoes.

One cannot plow in a field full of obstructions, however, and tree stumps had to be removed from new fields if one chose to use

74

TABLE II.10
PROPORTION OF ESTATES WITH SPINNING WHEELS IN TWO PERIODS BY
COUNTY AND CLASS

PPW	Anne Arundel, Baltimore, Calvert	Charles	Kent and Somerset	Average*
		1656-1696		
£ 0-34	0%	0%	19%	4%
35-96	6	0	17	7
97-228	0	9	44	11
229-up	6	0	0	4
Average*	2	2	21	6
		1705-1719		
£ 0-34	18%	10%	60%	32%
35-96	20	14	60	39
97-228	20	25	92	47
229-up	45	20	93	57
Average*	23	15	75	40

SOURCE: Probated estates of men whose children were all under age, that is, the "young fathers'" sample from the probate records of six counties, Mayland, Hall of Records, Annapolis.
* Weighted by numbers of all estates in each county, class, and period.

a plow. Tobacco and corn so quickly exhausted the land that by the time the stumps of the original trees had rotted to the point that they could be easily removed, it was already time to allow the land to return to fallow. Thus, the ususal course of rotation in tobacco growing meant that a large portion of the total land area in the best regions for its growth would not be in actual production of tobacco but would remain in rough pasture, scrub, or woods.

Intervals of fallow played equally vital roles in mixed farming, to be sure, but grains such as wheat and barley could be grown for longer periods in the same soil than could tobacco and corn, and the fallow stage could be greatly shortened between cycles of use, so that fields sown only to grasses remained continuously clear of trees. Once the stumps were cleared, then, the plow proved a more efficient tool for planting and weeding in such fields than did the hoe, for corn as well as for wheat. Hoe culture is more labor-intensive than plow culture, once the land has been cleared and fenced, and the universally felt labor shortage prompted the gradual adoption of the plow, particularly where tobacco was only a marginal or intermittent crop.

The use of the plow did spread among the richer planters of the western shore (see Table II.11), but perhaps more as a result of their preference for wheat bread on the table than as their wish for a supplementary source of income. (The generally small amounts of wheat in estate inventories suggest this.) Consumption of wheat bread was a mark of superior social status and undoubtedly enhanced the sense of well-being among those who could afford to raise wheat for their own consumption.[38] Wheat contributed to nutritional welfare as well, for corn is seriously deficient in certain amino acids necessary to the human diet. Other grains raised by Maryland planters with the aid of the plow included barley and oats. The former was intended for brewing beer, the traditional drink of the Englishman, and oats improved the diet of their horses, or at least of those more valuable steeds appearing in the post-1700 inventories.[39] Plows, then, should perhaps more properly be viewed

TABLE II.11
PROPORTION OF ESTATES WITH PLOWS IN TWO PERIODS BY
COUNTY AND CLASS

PPW	Anne Arundel, Baltimore, Calvert	Charles	Kent and Somerset	Average
		1656-1696		
£ 0-34	0%	0%	0%	0%
35-96	1	0	9	3
97-228	11	0	44	16
229-up	24	0	0	15
Average*	5	0	10	5
		1705-1710		
£ 0-34	0%	0%	33%	12%
35-96	13	0	55	26
97-228	35	17	62	41
229-up	39	0	29	28
Average*	15	2	44	23

SOURCE: Probated estates of men whose children were all underage, that is, the "young fathers'" sample from the probate records of six counties, Maryland, Hall of Records, Annapolis.
* Weighted by numbers of all estates in each county, class, and period.

[38] Few New England families ate wheat bread, either, because wheat rust made it unprofitable to grow wheat successfully in most areas. Daily bread there and in Pennsylvania was made of cornmeal or cornmeal mixed with rye, popularly known as "rye 'n injun." Lemon, *Best Poor Man's Country*, p. 156.
[39] See Chapter Five for a discussion of beer and its manufacture in early Maryland.

as adjuncts to the production of luxury grains for home use or local sale in western-shore households that otherwise continued to raise tobacco as their major source of income. To the north and across the bay, however, the spreading use of the plow suggests a greater emphasis on raising cereals for the market.

Although planters at the very bottom of the scale on the western shore continued to hoe their tobacco and corn to the virtual exclusion of all other economic activity, some of their better-off neighbors could afford to follow more promising lines of investment in addition to their farming. A few of the middling planters in the counties of Anne Arundel, Calvert, and Charles, for instance, began making use of hides, leather, and shoemaking tools in the late 1680s, and by the eighteenth century, about 10 percent of those worth between £50 and £150 PPW had the means to make or mend shoes. Planters of the same rank living to the north in Baltimore County or across the bay in Kent and Somerset counties were even more prone to engage in such activity: a third were doing so before 1700, half by 1720.

Other occupational groups also began to appear in estate inventories after 1685 or so, although physicians and "chirurgeons" were present in the colony from very early times. Most of the craftsmen and artisans encountered in the records were those working with wood, principally carpenters and coopers, but also a few joiners, turners, and housewrights. Weavers, tailors, and shoemakers appear rather late in the records, as do smiths and millers. Table II.12 gives their numbers and the timing of their appearance, while

TABLE II.12
NONFARM OCCUPATIONAL GROUPS IN EARLY MARYLAND

Occupation	No.	% before 1700	% 1700-1719	Total %
Doctors, etc.*	40	48	57	100
Woodworkers	202	29	71	100
Weavers	51	2	98	100
Shoemakers	49	22	78	100
Smiths	30	17	83	100
Millers	13	31	69	100
Tailors	8	13	87	100
Total	393			
Probated Estates	3696			

SOURCE: Probate records of six counties, Maryland, in Hall of Records, Annapolis.
* Includes physicians and surgeons.

Adaptation under Fire

Table II.13 shows their geographical distribution. Anne Arundel, Calvert, and Charles counties produced three-fifths of the inventoried estates from the six-county sample, but 80 percent of the doctors practiced there, probably because the richest planters resided in these counties. Weavers and shoemakers, on the other hand, made their homes on the eastern shore and to the north of the bay, on the fringes of the tobacco-growing areas.

East and west, the richest planters continued to produce most of the tobacco actually exported during the deepest depressions, but they also diversified their economic activities, not just in order to cut back on their overseas purchases but also to exploit commercial and financial opportunities at home as a means of supplementing fluctuating incomes from their staple. In the first decades of the eighteenth century, for instance, William Byrd II of Virginia was busily staffing his old and new plantations with freshly imported Africans, but he also opened up an iron mine and began operations of a new saw mill.[40] Although Maryland of the same period could

TABLE II.13
REGIONAL DISTRIBUTION OF NONFARM OCCUPATIONS, 1656-1719
(percent)

Occupation	Anne Arundel	Calvert	Charles	Baltimore	Kent	Somerset	Total
Doctors, etc.*	32	32.5	12.5	10	7.5	2.5	100
Woodworkers	20	14	13	15	20	17	99
Weavers	6	6	2	12	8	67	101
Shoemakers	10	10	12	20	14	33	99
Smiths	20	13	17	3	17	30	100
Millers	8	0	23	8	15	46	100
Tailors	12.5	50	0	12.5	0	25	100
All estates	20	21	18	12	12	16	99
% of men enumerated in Table 13 (N = 393)	19	15	12	13	15	26	100

SOURCE: Probate records of six counties, Maryland, in Hall of Records, Annapolis.
* Includes physicians and surgeons.

[40] He also acted as physician and pharmacist to his family, slaves, and neighbors, engaged in moneylending and trade, and served in the provincial legislature and on the governor's council. He could do all of these things because of hired overseers and other trained help, but the slower pace of economic activity, geared as it was to the annual crop year, also permitted him the leisure to read and write extensively

78

not yet boast the likes of a William Byrd, this less glamorous of the "two sisters" had succeeded in making wealthy a small but enterprising class of men. Many had arrived in the colony in the years immediately following the Restoration in England—ambitious young men who brought with them capital or who had family connections with the Proprietor or his circle.[41] Other members of this wealthy group included sons and even grandsons of immigrants, most of whom had also begun their American careers with advantages beyond those available to the great mass of settlers, if only because of their initial status as freemen. Col. Henry Darnall, who owned over a hundred slaves in 1711, provides an outstanding example of the former, and Samuel Chew, Quaker and merchant-owner of the richest estate in our six counties prior to 1720, well illustrates the latter.[42]

An inquiry into the provenance and makeup of the estates of these men and of others like them can provide a crucial insight into the processes by which this class acquired its wealth and why it continued to amass more in spite of the difficulties encountered by the economy as a whole. By the close of the period of this study, not only did these men own most of the bound labor in the colony but their sons and grandsons came to hold most of the major and lesser political offices of the province, significant sources of income in themselves. Thus, their importance to their world, and to our study, far outweighs their small number.[43]

In a society still rude and only recently emerged from raw wilderness, many of Maryland's economic leaders had not yet acquired the wealth, the style, or the distinctive habiliments of a class apart. One would not expect to find among them men of aristocratic pretensions, nor would one expect to discover men with wealth so secure they could afford to sit back and await their accustomed revenues. There could be no coupon clippers in this society, for there were no coupons, and without banks in which to deposit savings or from which to borrow funds for starting up new enterprises, each man had to be his own money manager and his own financier.

---

and to engage in a great deal of visiting by horseback, everybody's favorite pastime. Byrd, *Secret Diary*.

[41] Jordan, "Political Stability," in Tate and Ammerman, eds., *Chesapeake*, p. 246.

[42] Darnall's inventory is in *Inv. & Accts.*, Liber 33B beginning on f. 221. Chew's is in *Inventories*, Liber 1, f. 464, and an account appears in *Accounts*, Liber 3, f. 193.

[43] Jordan, "Political Stability," in Tate and Ammerman, eds., *Chesapeake*, pp. 243-73, particularly p. 265.

In the old world, families of long standing and growing fortunes often served as financing institutions for business operations, but the geographic frontier in the seventeenth-century Chesapeake was a demographic frontier as well. Family connections had to be forged and wealth accumulated, sons launched and well married before kinship networks reached sufficient density to serve as reliable credit sources and firm bases of power in a new society—all of which took time, and which the lethal biosystem greatly hindered. By 1710, tidewater Maryland's incipient aristocracy had at last succeeded in erecting that lacy, tensile web of familial relationships around which wealth and power collect and coagulate.[44]

The richest 5 percent of probated decedents for the period as a whole were those with £450 or more in PPW. Most appeared after 1700 and came primarily from the better tobacco-growing areas in the six counties: Anne Arundel, Calvert, and Charles. These three contained on the average 59 percent of the total population of the sample counties and contributed roughly the same proportion of the probated decedents.[45]

Strong regional differences in economic organization mark these richest estates, just as they do all other levels. Table II.14 offers a summary view of the investment propensies of each county's economic elite. Those in Somerset showed a decided preference for maritime and mercantile pursuits, interests that were echoed in Anne Arundel across the bay, where planter-merchants engaged in moneylending and mortgage holding while continuing their acquisition of slaves to produce tobacco. Charles and Kent, by contrast, remained almost entirely agricultural. The merchant-planters who served their needs resided in adjacent counties: St. Mary's for Charles and Talbot for Kent.

Proportionate investments in slave labor rose higher with each successive set of probated estates: from 26 percent of personal wealth before 1697 to 38 percent after 1704. Table II.15 demonstrates that the increase in slaveholding furnishes the most striking example of the various changes that marked the regional economy during these years, although one should also note how sharply the

---

[44] Ibid., p. 267.

[45] Arthur E. Karinen, "Numerical and Distributional Aspects of Maryland Population 1631-1840," *MdHM*, LIV (1959), 365-407; LX (1965), 139-59. Of the 177 estates in this richest stratum, 131 (75 percent) came from these three counties. Anne Arundel's 57 were the most numerous and also the richest, averaging over £1,000 apiece, compared to £948 for Calvert's 51 estates in this stratum and £928 for Charles' 23. These are PPW, not GPW.

TABLE II.14

PRINCIPAL SOURCES OF INCOME FOR TOP FIVE PERCENT OF ESTATES BY
COUNTY, 1656-1719

County	Mercantile		Financial *DR/PPW*	Tobacco
	Mean £ (sterling) Boats and Ships	*% PPW in New Goods*		*% PPW in Bound Labor*
Somerset	£65.5	19%	.19	21%
Anne Arundel	27.8	12	.31	36
Calvert	14.3	11	.22	38
Baltimore	14.7	5	.44	36
Charles	7.1	8	.10	39
Kent	9.1	6	.18	29
Average	£21.9	11%	.24	35%

SOURCE: Probate records of six counties, Maryland, in Hall of Records, Annapolis.

TABLE II.15

FINANCIAL ASSETS, LIABILITIES, AND BOUND LABOR OF
TOP FIVE PERCENT OF ESTATES (£≈sterling)

Years	GPW	Liab.*	Net Worth	% Net Worth Bound Labor	% Net Worth in DR	Liabilities/ GPW
1656-1696	£1040	£260	£780	27%	39%	.25
1697-1704	834	267	567	44	19	.32
1705-1719	1399	280	1119	39	24	.20

SOURCE: Probate records of six counties, Maryland, in Hall of Records, Annapolis.
* Liabilities are known only for those estates leaving accounts of administration, roughly two-thirds of the members of this class. For these estates, percentages of GPW were calculated, averaged, then applied to the average GPW for the set.

volume of credit contracted during these boom years when tobacco prices were temporarily up and when cargoes of blacks direct from Africa were arriving in unprecedented numbers on the banks of the Potomac, the Patuxent, and the Severn, as well as the James, the York, and the Rappahannock.

In order to purchase the slaves as they became available, the richest planters probably drew on their credit balances while themselves curtailing new loans. As slaves increased both in numbers and as a proportion of total personal assets, outstanding liabilities among the rich apparently rose too, since estates before 1697 averaged a fifth of GPW in debts payable, but the proportion then climbed to a fourth in the succeeding period. After the boom years had passed, estates of this class registered more debts receivable, more slaves, and more of everything else but liabilities, which remained at the same level as previously. Charles County slaveowners, who had invested close to half of their personal wealth in bound labor, were forced to cut back during the years of low tobacco prices that followed, probably in order to pay off the liabilities contracted during the rush to acquire slaves.

The fall in the relative debt load of the richest estates as they expanded their property holdings suggests that some planters, at least, were proving nimble on their feet and versatile in their investment policies. Their continued cultivation of tobacco undoubtedly brought them losses in the years of very low prices, but tobacco must have proven remunerative enough in the long run to keep them in the game. Farming did offer security for their capital and provided a credit base for ventures into other fields.

A few examples will illustrate the variety of interests pursued by Maryland's economic elite.

Col. George Wells of Baltimore County, son of Richard Wells of Anne Arundel County, died in 1696, owning at least 3,670 acres of land, 4 servants, and 11 slaves. His total personal property came to £1748, of which £892 was in the form of debts receivable. (Since no account of administration for his estate survives, the amount he owed remains unknown.) Not only was the colonel the chief militia officer of his county, he was also a justice of the peace and a member of the Assembly. Judging from the composition of his assets as reported in the inventory of his estate, he acted as a doctor, merchant, and distiller as well as a planter.[46]

One of the colonel's sons, Mr. Bryant Wells, died just six years after his father, owning a dozen slaves but no servants. This third-generation Marylander appears to have adopted the life of a country squire, since his inventory reveals no occupational tools or apparatus other than those of the planter. His personal wealth totalled £495 plus debts receivable of £168. Again, liabilities are unknown.[47]

An early neighbor of Bryant's grandfather in Anne Arundel County was Nicholas Wyatt, who left a widow and two young children at the time of his death in 1674.[48] Planter Wyatt owned two plantations, which he operated with the help of two white servant men, two black slave men, one white woman servant, and probably occasional hired help as well. Interestingly, one white man and one

[46] *Inv. & Accts.*, Liber 15, f. 8. "Desperate" debts are excluded.
[47] Ibid., Liber 23, f. 318.
[48] Wyatt's inventory is in *Testamentary Proceedings*, VI, f. 212. Two accounts are in *Inv. & Accts.*, Liber 2, f. 246, 263.

black man, Negro Will, were paired off in charge of the Outward Plantation, where they maintained their own household and oversaw some nineteen cattle and twenty-two hogs. Neither, however, had the use of a horse, although nine were kept at the Lower Plantation.[49]

Wyatt's inventory included carpenters' and coopers' tools, frequent adjuncts to well-equipped farm households in early Maryland. Although no sheep appear in the inventory, husbandry tools included sheepshears as well as reap hooks, a pole ax, two other axes, and two hatchets, and a pair of cartwheels; several small craft were tied up at the landing. Cattle at the Lower Plantation comprised two cows with their calves, two other cows, fourteen yearlings, four "great" steers, and five other steers. In addition to the nine horses, there were some two dozen hogs but no poultry. Given the makeup of Wyatt's capital, there can be little doubt that his primary source of income was tobacco. At the quarter were the crops produced by three hands, totaling some 7,682 pounds of tobacco, an average of approximately 2,500 pounds each. In addition there were 2,000 pounds "more at the Quarter," plus "the crop at home" of 6,800 pounds, for a grand total of 16,482 pounds, which at a penny per pound would have been worth more than £68. Corn on hand included thirty barrels at the Outward Plantation, seven bushels in the cellar lofts at home, and one and one half barrels at the Lower Plantation, which, because it is listed along with the livestock there, may have been the remnants of winter fodder, since the inventory was taken in April.

Wyatt's cellar lofts also stored twelve bushels of wheat valued in pounds of tobacco at fifty pounds per bushel, or four shillings twopence in money. Thus, of the crops mentioned, tobacco was worth about £68, corn just under £14, and the wheat, £2½. The corn may have been intended as provision for both man and beast since there was more than enough to last the remaining four months until harvest for the master's household of four persons plus his five servants and slaves. Some of those nine cows, furthermore, provided the milk for which the churn, twenty earthen pans, and various tinware in the milkhouse were clearly intended. If all seven of those cows with calves were healthy and still "fresh," while being provided with winter fodder, the supply of milk should have been ample for both calves and humans.

---

[49] There were three beds at the "Outward Plantation," and the inventory also mentions three hands' crop at the "Quarter," so a third laborer, probably a hired man or a servant whose time was nearly out, also lived and worked with these two.

Planter Wyatt's farm organization is typical of others of his class for the times. He specialized in raising the staple crop with the aid of indentured servants and black slaves, but he also produced with their help ample provisions of meat, grain, and dairy products. The number of boats at his landing suggests that his men may have earned him some additional income transporting neighbors' crops, for which his coopers' tools probably helped provide barrels for the transoceanic voyage. Aside from these evidences of possible supplementary sources of income, little else in the estate records suggests much diversity of enterprise. Rather, the very comfortable furnishings in the main house reveal the life of a country squire who may have inherited his position, rather than that of an aggressive and ambitious parvenu.

Perhaps the most successful of the immigrant founders, in terms of the future fortunes of his family line, was Samuel Chew I, son of John Chew of Virginia, Gent., who originally kept a house and store at St. Mary's but then moved up to Anne Arundel County. His sons Samuel, Joseph, and Benjamin, and his grandson John, all appear in the top 5 percent of estates. Samuel II, indeed, left the largest of those recorded in the six-county region prior to 1720, over £5,000 in personal wealth (PPW).[50] All of the Chews were merchants, moneylenders, and slaveowners.

Benjamin died in 1700, worth £597 plus £53 in debts receivable, and left three servants, ten slaves, new goods in his storehouse worth £52, and a mill, of which the metal parts were valued at £12.[51] His brother Joseph died in 1705 with more than £2,000 in personal property, including four servants and twenty slaves. In land, he owned four plantations plus another 1,000 acres. He also owed more than a thousand pounds of tobacco. At the home plantation, the work force included a half-share in a miller for a term of two years. Joseph's plantations shipped 150 hogsheads of tobacco, two years' crop, which sold in England for £449, so that the annual income from tobacco alone in these years came to £224. In addition to the mill, Chew had bought a one-eighth share, valued at £230, of a ship of 160 tons burden, and one-sixteenth of another ship weighing 200 tons, this share worth £90. Corn, wheat, and meat on hand came to less than £20 in money, but this was on June

[50] *Inventories*, Liber 1, f. 464 and *Accounts*, Liber 3, f. 193.
Benjamin Chew's inventory is in *Inv. & Accts.*, Liber 19½B, f. 122. An account was rendered by his widow, who had remarried, and his son, Samuel, in 1728. *Accounts*, Liber 9, f. 293.

7, and the household provisions would have been depleted by this late date in the farm calendar.[52]

Joseph Chew well epitomizes the businessman-planter who made up more than half of his class in his home county of Anne Arundel. His Quaker connection prevented him from serving in public office, but gave him more time to devote to his business interests. To what extent the legal disability and his religious beliefs and associations channeled this energetic man's ample capital endowment along some lines rather than others is open to speculation, but none of the Chews seems to have nursed aspirations toward a life of reflection or ease.

The leading Catholic politician of the county and cousin of the third Lord Baltimore by marriage, Colonel Henry Darnall, also conducted a mercantile business as well as supervising his plantations.[53] This very rich and successful man died about 1712 worth at least £3,500 in personal property, possessing more than 18,000 acres of land and over a hundred slaves, with stocks of imported goods on hand worth better than £500. White overseers presided over three of his five quarters, but it was Darnall himself, apparently, who managed the Woodyard with the aid of his skilled slave carpenters. The store and the Woodyard clearly qualify Darnall to enter the ranks of the diversified planters, despite an investment in slaves amounting to almost two-thirds of his very sizable personal estate.

Darnall's slave force was exceptional in its size, yet the disposition of his assets was not. Systematic analysis of the composition of capital among the region's top planters reveals a strikingly limited number of patterns of business activity, of which Darnall's fell into a common mold. Although we cannot follow their decision-making process at firsthand, we can make limited but valid inferences about what the planters had been doing prior to their death. Since few of these men had retired, their end-of-life portfolios represent those of men still actively involved in business. The composition of capital in the richest estates thus furnishes us with patterns of past investments, and when studied in terms of the phases of the tobacco price cycle and of Maryland's major demographic and regional

---

[52] Joseph Chew's inventory is in *Inv. & Accts.*, Liber 25, f. 208, and an account is ibid., Liber 29, f. 131. A copy of the inventory may also be found in Box 16, f. 6, *Testamentary Papers*, Anne Arundel County.

[53] *Inv. & Accts.*, Liber 33B, f. 221. For more on Darnall, see Lois Green Carr and David William Jordan, *Maryland's Revolution of Government, 1689-1692* (Itahca, 1974), entries as indexed.

shifts, affords considerable insight into planter responses to changing market conditions. Factors associated with the relative proportions of key assets among individual estates of the economic elite
include relative wealth, date of death, county of origin, and, in
addition, imponderable influences such as religious affiliation, political officeholding, the nature and antiquity of family relationships, and, finally, the marital and economic status of children.[54]

[54] The interplay of tobacco prices, trends in the economy and in the makeup of
the population, and their effects on patterns of investment can be understood by
means of the analysis of the composition of personal wealth. The ANOVA program
of SPSS carries out analysis of variance using interval and categorical variables.
Application of various options in this program on logarithmically transformed values of the interval variables—debts receivable, capital, consumption goods, and debts
payable—disclosed that capital was the best predictor of the other three, and once
its effects were removed, the other three did not strongly correlate. When we then
introduce categorical variables, after removing the effect of capital, we find that all
three responded in different ways to such factors as the time period (phase of the
tobacco and demographic movements), county of residence, whether or not the
planter owned at least one book, whether he did, or did not, own £15 worth of new
goods (an arbitrarily set figure), and the stage in the life cycle determined by marital
status and relative ages of his children, if any. Had sufficient biographical information survived for more planters at all wealth levels, from all counties, all time
periods, and at all stages of the life cycle, we might then have been able to measure
some of the effects of family connections and religious affiliation on patterns of
investment and consumption goods.

Debts receivable were dominated by a downward trend that continued throughout
the period of the study except for a brief reversal during the depression years 1705-
1712. This trend was partially accounted for by the aging of the planter decedents,
the effects of which were not significant at the .99 level of confidence but were so
at .95. The regional redistribution of population, with the growth of Somerset
County, also accounted for part of the trend. However, when all three effects have
been removed, that is, those of rising wealth, changing age structure, and regional
diversification out of tobacco (distribution by county), the decline in debts receivable
persisted and must be viewed as an autonomous phenomenon related to the development of the economy and society itself.

Debts payable, too, showed a downward trend after the effects of other factors
had been removed, but that trend was not significant at the .99 or the .95 levels of
confidence. These debts proved highly correlated with debts receivable as well as
with capital, but were not significantly affected by the alterations in the age structure
of the population that had taken place. In the final years of the study, however,
new unmarried immigrants and slightly larger numbers of men old enough to have
grandchildren combined to lower significantly the level of debts payable in the
probated estates.

As with debts receivable, the county of origin proved significant in determining
the level of debts payable, but the differences between counties were not as great
or as readily subject to explanation in the terms of their differing economic structures as in the case of debts receivable.

Disaggregation of estates below the county level might well provide the clues to

To simplify things, one may identify four principal categories of assets:

1. farming with livestock, tools, and labor;[55]
2. mercantile investments composed of stocks of new goods, cargoes for export, boats and shipping;
3. home industry, such as milling, tanning, shoemaking and the leasing out of indentured and slave skilled craftsmen;
4. financial credits from loans, retail sales, practice of law.

Since crops represented income rather than capital, they will be excluded from the analysis that follows.[56]

We will view these various income-earning activities as having brought in a stream of new resources that flowed into "baskets" or categories of personal assets: livestock, labor, new goods, shares in ships, debts receivable (that is, past income not yet received and not yet converted into physical assets, and here treated as a form of accumulated savings), and consumption goods, which consist of assets not providing income. The contents of these five "baskets" made up the entire personal estate of each planter at his death, and by definition, exhausted the possibilities of what he could do with his income, aside from buying land, about which we know very little.[57]

Let us proceed to score individual planters on how much of the total money value of the contents of the four baskets rested in each: livestock, bound labor, mercantile assets, and debts receivable. First,

---

a more complete explanation of the behavior of the variables here considered. The only attempt at such disaggregation to receive public discussion is that by P.M.G. Harris, "Integrating Interpretations of Local and Regionwide Changes in the Study of Economic Development and Demographic Growth in the Colonial Chesapeake, 1630-1775," in *Working Papers from the Regional Economic History Research Center*, I (1978), 35-71.

[55] Other forms of capital include husbandry and craft tools, mill irons, and stocks of hides and leather.

[56] Not all tobacco shipped was of the planter's own produce but represented proceeds from debt settlements or outright purchase to fill a freight commitment. Inventories and accounts, however, do not provide sufficient information concerning the origin of the tobacco to allow us to distinguish between the crop of the decedent's own growth and that which he had acquired by other means.

[57] Again, note that plantation produce has been deliberately excluded from the analysis. A very practical consideration applies: the time of the year in which the inventory was taken determined if a particular crop would appear or not, and inventories were taken throughout the year. Variability in record keeping also contributed to the instability of debts receivable and debts payable, since most were listed in accounts rather than in the inventories themselves.

how important was agriculture to this class? If we assume for the sake of simplicity that all slaves were involved in farm tasks, we are not violating reality to any significant degree. To measure the importance of agriculture as an economic activity, we will inquire into the relative proportion of the total money value of the contents of the four baskets invested in livestock (LV) and bound labor (LB). One can divide the rich planters into three types on this basis:

I. Those who kept 85 percent or more of the total allowance in livestock and bound labor, LV + LB;
II. Those who put 50 to 84 percent of that total in LV + LB; and
III. Those who placed less than 50 percent of that total in LV + LB.

All estates fall into one of these investment types. We will sort them further by time and by relative amounts of resources available to them, as measured by the total value of all the assets resting in those four baskets: £200 to £599, £600 to £999, and £1000 plus. Finally, each estate is identified by county of origin. Of the 177 planters in the entire set, more than a quarter of them, 28 percent, invested 85 percent or more of their basket allowance in agriculture, LV + LB, identified in our scheme as Type I. Over half of them invested between 50 and 84 percent in agriculture, identifying them as Type II, and the remaining 35 estates fall into Type III. As Table II.16 shows, a clear economic basis underlay these divergent patterns of investment: the greater the resources, the larger the portion invested in nonagricultural pursuits.

TABLE II.16
PATTERNS OF INVESTMENT AMONG TOP FIVE PERCENT OF ESTATES
(numbers of estates)

Level of K*	Type I LV+LB More Than 84% K*	Type II LV+LB 50 to 85% K*	Type III LV+LB Less Than 50% K*
£ 200-599	31	45	5
600-999	13	23	10
1000-up	7	23	20
Totals	51	91	35

SOURCE: Probate records of six counties, Maryland, in Hall of Records, Annapolis.
NOTE: K* = capital plus debts receivable
LV = livestock
LB = bound labor

88

Certain regional variations in these investment patterns proved important, even after relative resource level had been taken into account. Somerset, the reader will recall, produced more men, proportionately, who engaged in shipping and merchandising than did other counties in the six-county sample, whereas Baltimore planters of this class kept greater amounts of their assets in the form of debts receivable, probably reflecting the newness of settlement there. Furthermore, neither county produced planters of the traditional stereotype, the squire who devoted his principal energies to farming and who invested heavily in slaves (Type I). This absence is not at all surprising in view of the fact that both counties lay outside the prime tobacco regions of the colony. Charles County, on the other hand, remained deeply committed to the staple crop, and the investment pattern among this county's wealthiest planters reflects that commitment. Even when we restrict our notice to those with investible funds of £600 and up (96 out of the 177), *none* in Charles County invested less than half in livestock and labor, and 5 out of the 12 with £1,000 or more in that county were of the squire type, those who placed 85 percent or more into LV + LB. Table II.17 summarizes the patterns by county, arranging them in order from entrepreneurial Somerset to squirelike Charles.

The majority of men from all counties in the top 5 percent of estates invested between half and 85 percent of the total value of assets in the four baskets identified above into agriculture, which

TABLE II.17
INVESTMENT PATTERNS OF MARYLAND'S CAPITAL-RICH PLANTERS,
1656-1719

County	No.	Type I LV + LB More Than 85% K*	Type II LV + LB 50 to 85% K*	Type III LV + LB Less Than 50% K*	Total
Somerset	5	0%	0%	100%	100%
Baltimore	6	0	50	50	100
Anne Arundel	35	11	54	34	100
Calvert	28	29	43	29	101
Kent	10	30	50	20	100
Charles	12	42	58	00	100
Total	96				
Average		21	48	31	100

SOURCE: Probate records of six counties, Maryland, in Hall of Records, Annapolis.
NOTE: Capital-rich planters are those owning capital and debts receivable together worth at least £600.

meant that a considerable portion of the rest was available for allocating into the other baskets. The range of allocation forms a spectrum from one end, estates that placed relatively more in debts receivable, to the other end, estates that allocated most of the non-agricultural capital into mercantile assets.

Financial assets were, on the whole, safer than mercantile capital. Ships did founder, cargoes got lost, spoiled, or failed to find a good market. Stocks of new goods at home might not find buyers when tobacco was depressed, and textiles quickly rotted in the humid summers. The relative isolation of customers contributed to problems that arose with communications and freight, and the principal suppliers of the imported merchandise also handled assignments of tobacco for the merchant-planters.

For most planters, a solid foundation in agriculture—investment in livestock and bound labor—took clear priority over alternative uses for their capital, but once this was established, the state of the economy (or their expectations concerning it) promoted or deflected interests in mercantile ventures. Risk taking was made worthwhile by the buoyancy of a rising market, on the one hand, and was less threatening to the total enterprise as the margin of income over costs in tobacco production expanded.

In the eighteenth century, a trend toward less risky or conservative investment behavior emerged despite substantial increases in the average value of disposable capital as compared with that available in the seventeenth century. The portion of those estates with £600 or more in total value of the assets contained in the four baskets rose from 43 percent of the richest estates of the period 1697-1704 to 54 percent of those in 1705-1712, yet this accompanied a drop in the relative numbers investing substantial portions in mercantile assets. Although such a shift may be explained as a consequence of the depression in the tobacco market and of demand for new goods, that conservative shift persisted into the years when tobacco prices reversed their course and British merchants turned bullish. Thus, despite another increase in the relative numbers of men with £600 or more in the four "capital" baskets (60 percent of estates in the top 5 percent after 1712), mercantile assets scarcely expanded at all.

To conclude this investigation into the investment patterns among Maryland's richest planters, one must again refer to the extraordinary level of slave purchases made during the brief prosperity between the wars, the financing of which was achieved primarily by reducing credits, if our reading of the probate records is correct. The contraction that followed served to liquidate the bulk of their liabilities—together with some of those liable—and redistributed the recently acquired slaves among the survivors. The closing years of this study then witnessed a brief renewal of expansion in the tobacco economy, but one that was accompanied by considerable hesitation toward commercial involvements. Higher fixed costs of slavery, as compared to those of indentured servitude, may explain this caution, but a satisfactory explanation must await investigation into subsequent years.

By 1720, then, the planters of tidewater Maryland no longer pursued a uniform, tightly integrated set of farming activities centered around tobacco growing. Some, indeed, no longer even raised tobacco. All continued to farm, however, and Maryland remained rural and agricultural. The long-term cumulative effects of saving and investment, especially among those relatively few families with successive generations of long-lived heads, gradually raised the level of wealth among the richest planters, and this widened the gap between them and the middling sort.

Before we conclude this already long chapter on the functioning of Maryland's economy, let us inquire into its effect on the social structure of the colony. The picture one gains from reading county court records of the middle decades of the seventeenth century reveals a social structure composed of a broad class of white servants and a smaller class above them of freed servants, out of which many men were working their way up toward householder status and eventually marrying and starting a family. With a population made up almost entirely of people of prime working age under conditions of an open frontier and a virtually guaranteed market for their crops, rates of capital formation were high.

At the top of this almost all-white society there presided a small class of planters consisting of two quite different sorts: successful men of the self-made variety, including even a few former servants, and a handful of true gentry who had emigrated with money, connections, or goods as stakes to the new world. During the expansive phase of the tobacco economy, of which the settlement of Maryland itself was a part, this small class was occasionally and erratically renewed by fresh infusions from below and more rarely from abroad. Its own internal growth, however, was glacially slow because the relatively high mortality rates cut down men in their

91

forties. Since most had married late, their orphaned children were still too young to take over where they had left off. Because of the preponderance of males among the immigrants, widows quickly remarried, and control of the heirs' estates passed into the hands of men unrelated to their fathers. Interposition of stepfathers thus effectively hindered the establishment of patrilineal dynasties. The class of men who could seek and use high political office, therefore, remained fluid and heterogeneous in membership until a significant number of transgenerational families could establish themselves and pass on power and wealth with the family name.[58]

Maryland's was a highly stratified society from its beginnings, although economic expansion made possible a high degree of economic and social mobility. Economic depressions, however, severely retarded opportunity and transferred assets from debtors to creditors, exacerbating the degree of inequality and consolidating the positions of the more fortunate. The increase in transgenerational families perpetuated and expanded such inequality.

The end of expansion in the tobacco market coincided with the beginnings of the demographic transition and the establishment of patrilineal families. Both brought exclusion from opportunity for gain and office, and denied growing segments of Maryland's white population the traditional avenues of upward mobility. Those who could not grow marketable tobacco also found themselves denied credit since they did not produce a crop that interested English merchants or their Maryland correspondents. Those who could do so exploited intercolonial opportunities for trade in goods that they could produce.

Land and slaves furnished the foundation for an elite class; these were longer-lived assets with secularly rising demand that yielded capital gains if one could keep them from the jaws of creditors.

Despite the disabilities experienced by all of Maryland's planters after 1702, they did succeed in protecting their assets and their standard of living. Indeed, that standard of living proved remarkably high when compared to that enjoyed by their counterparts in later years. Table II.18 shows the results of an estimating procedure using the probated estates from 1683 to 1719 weighted by age class to calculate wealth per living wealthholder and wealth per capita. Tables II.19 and II.20 go on to compare these estimates with those obtained for the thirteen colonies in 1774.

---

[58] Jordan, "Political Stability," in Tate and Ammerman, eds., *Chesapeake*, and "Maryland's Privy Council, 1637-1715," in Land, Carr, and Papenfuse, *Early Maryland*, pp. 65-87.

TABLE II.18
ESTIMATING WEALTH PER CAPITA IN MARYLAND CIRCA 1700
(£≈sterling)

1 Age Group	*2* Equivalent Stage of Life Cycle	*3* % Males 21-up	*4* Mean GPW c. 1700	*5* Col. 3 times Col. 4
21-25	Unmarried	31%	£62.6	£19.41
26-46	Married, with young children	56	160.5	89.88
47-57	Married, with older children[a]	12	188.8	22.66
58-up	Married, with grown children	1	247.3	2.47
Total GPW per wealthholder				£134.42
Real estate[b] per wealthholder				70.79
Total wealth per wealthholder				205.21

3,377 free adult males[c] times £205.21 divided among total population of 19,985 equals per capita 34.68

SOURCES: Probate records of six counties, Maryland, in Hall of Records, Annapolis; age structure from Darrett B. and Anita H. Rutman, " 'More True and Perfect Lists,' " *VMHQ*, LXXXVIII (1980), 60; Talbot County land figures and prices from Paul G. E. Clemens, *The Atlantic Economy and Colonial Maryland's Eastern Shore* (Ithaca, 1980), p. 231; Menard's corrections to the 1704 census in R. Menard, "Five Maryland Censuses," *WMQ*, XXX (1973), 619-21.

[a] "Older" means at least one child of age and one child still a minor.

[b] Real estate estimate based on land owners and their acreage in Talbot County, Maryland, and the average price of land in that county.

[c] 2,914 "masters of households" plus estimated 463 adult male nonheads of households equals 3,377 free adult males living in the six counties according to the 1704 census, as corrected by Menard.

The Maryland census of 1704 provides the earliest counts of men, women, and children, black and white, free and unfree, for the tobacco colony.[59] Good as the census is, it does not provide age information, which must be estimated in some way for the living adult males. We borrow for this purpose an age distribution constructed for a Virginia county's white population of the same general period.[60] We also lack age information on the probated de-

[59] The censuses are reported in *Md.Arch.*, XV, 50-54; XXV, 225; XXIII, 92. The totals for the six counties in 1704 have been recalculated following the corrections made by Russell R. Menard, "Five Maryland Censuses, 1700 to 1712: A Note on the Quality of the Quantities," *WMQ*, XXXVII (1980), 619-21.

[60] Darrett B. and Anita H. Rutman, " 'More True and Perfect Lists,' " p. 60.

TABLE II.19
ESTIMATES OF WEALTH PER WEALTHHOLDER, EARLY MARYLAND
AND THE THIRTEEN COLONIES, 1774 (£≈sterling)

Region, Time	Total Wealth	Less Bound Labor	Less Land	Less DR
Six counties, Md.				
c. 1700	£205	£179	£100	£78
South, 1774	423	290	107	81
Middle Colonies, 1774	252	245	129	64
New England, 1774	190	189	74	46

SOURCES: Alice Hanson Jones, *Wealth of a Nation to Be*, (New York, 1980), pp. 58, 98, 149-151; probate records of six counties, Maryland, in Hall of Records, Annapolis; and Table II.15.

TABLE II.20
ESTIMATES OF WEALTH PER CAPITA, EARLY MARYLAND
AND THE THIRTEEN COLONIES, 1774 (£≈sterling)

Region, Time	Total Wealth	Less Bound Labor	Less Land	Less DR
Six Counties, Md.				
c. 1700	£34.68	£31.18	£19.22	£16.24
South, 1774	58.60	40.20	14.60	12.36
Middle Colonies, 1774	56.60	54.90	27.30	14.64
New England, 1774	43.10	42.90	16.65	10.70

SOURCES: Alice Hanson Jones, *Wealth of a Nation to Be*, (New York, 1980), p. 96; probate records of six counties, Maryland, in Hall of Records, Annapolis, and Table II-15.

cedents, but we can measure the wealth of men at various stages of the life cycle and substitute stage for age in the estimation process.[61] Thus, we take each class's mean GPW and multiply it by the estimated proportion of free white men belonging to that class, which yields £134 per wealthholder. That figure times the 2,914 masters of households and an estimated 463 free adult nonheads of households among these enumerated as "free men and servants," gives the total amount of personal wealth of the six counties, £453,935. When divided up among the entire population of 19,985, that sum yields an estimated £22.7 per capita.

We can go a step further and estimate real wealth as well. A recent study found that an average of 380 acres was owned by

[61] Appendix A gives full details on definitions and measurements.

landowners in one tobacco-growing region on Maryland's eastern shore during the early part of the eighteenth century.[62] Since some men did not own land, the average for all, landowner and landless alike, will be lower. If we assume for present purposes that the numbers in the youngest age group of the freemen correspond to the number who were landless, that is, 31 percent, the average for all freemen would be 262 acres. The eastern shore data included an average price per acre, as well, which we will use to affix a value to the 262 acres: £0.27 times them yields £70.79, the estimated value of real estate owned, on the average, by wealthholders in early Maryland. That plus personal wealth equals £205.21 total wealth, and this figure times 3,377 freemen and divided by the total population results in an estimate of almost £35 per capita.

Given the fact that most of the people who had emigrated to Maryland in the seventeenth century arrived as propertyless servants, £35 per capita must be regarded as a major accomplishment. This appears especially impressive when we compare it with similarly derived estimates for the thirteen colonies on the eve of the American Revolution.[63] Although total wealth per wealthholder was only half that enjoyed by property owners of the pre-Revolutionary South, the difference is entirely attributable to unfree labor and land. Personal wealth *net* of these was almost as high in Maryland around 1700 as it was three-quarters of a century later for the South, and higher than that for the middle colonies or New England. On a per capita basis, moreover, Maryland's standard of living looks even more impressive, substantially ahead of that obtained by the pre-Revolutionary generation.

In terms of material goods, the tobacco economy of the seventeenth century had done well by its white participants. Of those who managed to hang on during the long depression that succeeded, even the poorer sort commanded assets of comparable worth to those accumulated by their kind in earlier, more prosperous times.

More important to Maryland's social structure than the fluctuations in the market for its staple crop was the decline in immigration of prime male servants from England, which paralleled the decline in income from tobacco. Coinciding with the diminution in man servants were politically inspired changes in the organization of the African slave trade and a pause in the expansion of the sugar

---

[62] Clemens, *Atlantic Economy*, p. 231.
[63] Jones, *Wealth of a Nation*, pp. 58, 96, 98, 149-51.

economy in the West Indies. This unhappy coincidence ushered in a new era for the Chesapeake, one that witnessed the creation of a caste system based on race and lent an exalted status to the minority of planters who came to acquire this new kind of capital. The story of the transition from servitude to slavery comes next, in Chapter Three.

SERVANTS AND SLAVES, SLAVES
AND SERVANTS

DEMAND AND SUPPLY OF BOUND LABOR IN
EARLY MARYLAND

England in the first half of the seventeenth century suffered from inflation, underemployment, wars, plagues, and a succession of harvest failures.[1] Large numbers of homeless poor wandered the countryside in search of food, shelter, and jobs, depressing further the wages of those fortunate enough to find employment. Men and women on the move sought opportunity in the market towns and port cities, and it was there that they encountered recruiters for the colonies.[2]

Most of the thousands of young English men and women who arrived each year in the early Chesapeake had freely consented to come, leaving their homeland and their kin in the hopes of one day marrying and acquiring a farm of their own. Because most had neither job nor money before leaving England, their fare and the cost of their keep for several months had to be paid for by someone else. These charges constituted a debt to be paid off by their labor, and their agreement to serve a fixed term of years guaranteed both the shipper and the planter that their expenditures would not go unrepaid.

Each indenture was a unique contract, a bargain struck in England between the prospective emigrant and the recruiter, who was

[1] For example, see Carl Bridenbaugh, *Vexed and Troubled Englishmen, 1590-1642* (New York, 1968), pp. 355-56.

[2] Mildred Campbell, "Social Origins of Some Early Americans," in *Seventeenth-Century America: Essays in Colonial History*, edited by James Morton Smith (Chapel Hill, 1959), pp. 63-89; David W. Galenson, " 'Middling People' or 'Common Sort'? The Social Origins of Some Early Americans Re-examined," with a "Rebuttal" by Mildred Campbell, *WMQ*, XXXV (1978), 499-540. A rejoinder by Galenson and a reply by Campbell appear ibid., XXXVI (1979), 264-286. See also Galenson, "British Servants and the Colonial Indenture System in the Eighteenth Century," *Journal of Social History*, XLIV (1978), 41-66; David Souden, " 'Rogues, Whores, and Vagabonds,' Indentured Servant Emigrants to North America, and the Case of Mid-Seventeenth Century Bristol," *Social History*, III (1978), 23-41.

usually a merchant or his agent.[3] The latter faced certain expenses in undertaking each bargain: cost of ship fare, food, and clothing for each servant sent. These costs placed a floor under the minimum acceptable asking price for the contract in the colonies. Since a shipment of servants tied up considerable sums of capital, no recruiter would undertake such a venture unless the expected returns from sales covered these costs and offered significantly greater returns than would the same sum invested for the same duration closer to home.

Given these fixed costs per head, the recruiter found it advantageous to seek out the fittest subjects for each venture and to send them to the colony that promised the highest bids for his human cargo. The prospective emigrant, on the other hand, had to be induced to go in the first place, and he or she would endeavor to select the most desirable colony under the easiest of terms. Indeed, since the recruiter wanted to place only healthy specimens aboard ship, a healthy emigrant might have extracted a bounty of some kind, such as extra bedding or clothing, or even cash. Choice of destination and the precise terms of the indenture itself, then, entered as separate and distinct elements into the total package. The more desirable the potential servant, in terms of age, physical condition, and skills, the more bargaining power that individual could exercise over the final agreement.[4]

The range of options open to servants not only included a veto over the colony of destination, but the length of the term of service, any special conditions of that service, such as restrictions on the kinds of tasks the master could impose, and the composition or value of the bonus paid at the close of service to the freed servant by his master, the so-called freedom dues. Because of the heavy mortality imposed by "seasoning" in the colonies and the relatively

[3] Examples of indentures may be found in *Md.Arch.*, XLI, 19, 385, XLIX, 103, 106, 189; LIII, 401, 462-63, 579-80; IV, 327, 464; X, 121, 305-306, 496. See also Warren M. Billings, ed., *The Old Dominion in the Seventeenth Century: A Documentary History of Virginia, 1606-1689* (Chapel Hill, 1975), p. 135. London innholder Richard Garford promised in June of 1654 to pay £10 sterling to Thomas Workman if he did not cause to be delivered to the latter a "sound and able man servant between Eighteene and 25 yeares of age that shall have fower years to serve at the least"; ibid., pp. 134-35.

[4] Galenson, "Immigration." However, some portion of the servants who arrived, and probably a proportion that grew with each passing decade, came without these contracts, and their terms of service were then set by laws prevailing in the Chesapeake colonies, which also specified freedom dues and governed the obligations of both servants and masters. See below.

high death rates prevailing even among survivors of seasoning, four years' service was probably the minimum term most planters would consider when bidding on new arrivals in their colony, so the length of service contracted for probably had a high floor to begin with, greatly narrowing the bargaining leeway for this particular component of the indenture contracts. Understandably enough, most indentures included references to the responsibilities of the master to provide sufficient clothing, diet, and lodging in return for service.

Servants with written indentures did not compose the entire body of white bound laborers, it should be noted.[5] Many, and probably a majority after 1680, came without prior contracts and served under the terms imposed by the "custom of the country," which was codified into law in all the colonies by the middle of the seventeenth century.[6] Those aged twenty-one or over served five years, according to Maryland law, if they had no contract stating a shorter period. Younger persons served longer, in proportion to their age. Judges in the county courts set these terms officially after viewing the new arrivals and estimating their ages. Any master expecting more than the customary five years' labor from a newly arrived servant had to seek the court's judgment on the matter within six months of the latter's arrival in the colony. Individual terms of servants without indentures, serving more than five years, then became a matter of record and could not be lengthened against the servant's will even if he were sold to another.

The willingness of merchants to recruit and finance potential servants, and the willingness of planters to purchase them, was tempered by the risk of losing them to illness, death, or running away. In the first half of the seventeenth century, servants had nowhere to run, but on the other hand, they suffered excessively from seasoning, the often lethal combination of illnesses visited on weakened newcomers who arrived after six weeks or six months of shipboard conditions. Mortality among arrivals during their first year of residence in the Chesapeake seems to have declined sometime after mid-century, with a consequent reduction in the risk to the investment borne by the planters who purchased them.[7] The settlement of North Carolina in the 1670s and of Pennsylvania in the 1680s opened up potential havens for escaped servants, but

[5] Walsh, "Servitude and Opportunity," in Charles County, Maryland, 1658-1705," in Land, Carr, and Papenfuse, eds., *Early Maryland*, 112.

[6] *Md.Arch.*, I, 353, 409, 428, 443-44, 453-54; II, 147-48, 335-36, 351-53, 527.

[7] Morgan, *American Slavery*, p. 181; Rutman, "Of Agues and Fevers," p. 42.

distances between settlements and the absence of roads continued to hinder their chances for succeeding overland. The risk to planters of losing their servants this way may have risen somewhat over the course of the century, but never seriously impaired the economy's functioning.

On the whole, it seems fair to argue that until the 1680s the indenture system worked well for both buyer and servant. Bound labor from abroad served a necessary purpose in the tobacco economy during its long phase of expansion because there existed no domestic source for planters to tap. Indian men refused such employment. They were unaccustomed to field work on a daily basis and preferred to withdraw to the interior during the critical summer months, when tobacco required constant attention. As for free labor, there was none. Freed servants started out on their own as quickly as they could, and heavy mortality and the scarcity of women hindered the propagation of sons to aid their fathers or to hire out to neighbors. Any planter who wished to expand output was forced to import his labor, and to place that labor under legal restraint to ensure the return on his investment.

Because servants stayed with their masters for fixed but relatively short terms, planters who merely wished to maintain current levels of production had to return to the market repeatedly to replenish their laborers. Freed servants, meanwhile, were busily accumulating enough to become buyers of labor, adding to the ranks of planters demanding new servants. The supply could not keep up. As Table I.1 revealed, the average rate of new arrivals from England in the Chesapeake declined from over 2,200 per year in the 1670s to fewer than 1,500 in the 1680s. Population grew from 41,000 in 1670 to 60,000 in 1680 and to over 75,000 by 1690. Judging from this, potential demand for servants was rising by some 3 percent per year, while the supply was falling at roughly the same rate. Worse, from the point of view of the planters, was the changing makeup of those who did come. No longer strong young men of good background, but boys, women, Irishmen and felons composed the newly arriving contingents.[8] Among white servants identified in the probate inventories of the six counties,

[8] Russell R. Menard, "Economy and Society in Early Colonial Maryland," Ph.D. dissertation, University of Iowa, 1974, pp. 414-17. Walsh, however, argues that the average age of servants may not have declined over the course of the century, and any such decrease would not have been sufficient evidence of any declining quality of the servants themselves. Walsh, "Servitude and Opportunity," in Land, Carr, and Papenfuse, eds., *Early Maryland*, p. 131.

the proportion who were adult males declined from two-thirds, in the years before 1684, to half or less thereafter. In 1684, the ratio of men to boys among them stood at 6.3 : 3.5, and then dropped to 2.15 : 1.0 in the depression years after 1702.

With fewer servants arriving, and fewer prime field hands among them, what were the planters to do? Those who could afford to, bought slaves. In attempting to explain the origins of slavery in the Chesapeake, some historians have stressed the potential for conflict between planters and landless freedmen. Bacon's Rebellion, according to this version, so frightened the planters that they turned to slavery rather than continue to add freed servants to the swelling ranks of the propertyless. Other historians have argued that English laborers were inefficient and unruly, whereas Africans were docile, more resistant to the diseases that killed off whites, accustomed to unremitting labor in a hot, humid climate, and capable of flourishing on a diet that neither pleased nor sustained Englishmen.[9] Once acquired, they were therefore cheaper to keep, and they lasted longer, found it more difficult to run away, and could be made to work more steadily, if not harder, than English servants. As a bonus, they also reproduced themselves.

When the disadvantages of indentured servitude are laid alongside the advantages of slavery, the combined effect appears to be a decisive argument in favor of the greater profitability and desirability (to the landowner) of slavery. Persuasive as the logic may seem, however, one cannot put any firm numbers into the implied equation. Moreover, one scholar has recently argued the reverse: it seems unreasonable to him that kidnapped aliens from another culture should be as productive at the complex tasks involved in raising and curing high-quality tobacco as men who understood the language and ways of the planters themselves.[10] In attending to the timing of the switchover to slaves, he finds that the average price of adult male servants rose prior to that event. Thus, planters turned to slaves only after the reduced supply, and hence the higher price, of these servants made slaves more attractive. Table III.1 provides the data on prices and relative numbers of slaves and

[9] Gray, *Agriculture*, I, 349-50, 361-71; Thomas Jefferson Wertenbaker, *Planters of Colonial Virginia* (Princeton, 1922), pp. 126-29. More recently, Edmund Morgan has stressed the deficiencies of servants and the threat from freedmen in "Slavery and Freedom: The American Paradox," *Journal of American History*, LIX (1972), 25-27 and in *American Slavery*, pp. 295-315.

[10] Menard, "Servants to Slaves," pp. 355-90.

TABLE III.1

RELATIVE PRICES OF SERVANTS AND SLAVES AND THEIR
PRESENCE IN PROBATE INVENTORIES (£≈sterling)

Years	Prices of Prime Adult Males in Md. Inventories			Ratio of Slaves to Servants in Inventories	
	Slaves	*Servants*	*£ Slaves/ £ Servants*	*Six Co., Md.*	*York Co., Va.*
1674-1676	£23.0	£8.0	2.88	0.28	
1675-1679					0.52
1677-1679	23.5	9.0	2.61	0.18	
1680-1682	25.5	11.0	2.32	0.51	
1680-1684					0.53
1683-1685	23.0	10.5	2.19	0.31	
1686-1688	23.0	11.5	2.00	0.66	
1685-1689					3.70
1689-1691	22.0	12.0	1.83	0.98	
1690-1694					14.29
1692-1694	24.5	10.0	2.45	1.86	
1695-1697	25.5	10.5	2.43	2.94	
1695-1699					50.00
1698-1700	26.5	11.5	2.30	0.97	

SOURCES: Russell R. Menard, "From Servants to Slaves: The Transformation of the Chesapeake Labor System," *Southern Studies*, XVI (1977), 361 and 372; probate records of six counties, Maryland, in Hall of Records, Annapolis.

servants in the inventories of Maryland and in York County, Virginia.

Judging from the probate evidence in the table, Virginians raising sweet-scented varieties jumped into the market for slaves more aggressively than did Marylanders raising Oronoco and lesser types. Such men tended to be richer than the average Chesapeake planter, and conducted much of their own marketing through agents in England for the English market, rather than for reexport to the Continent, where most of Maryland's tobacco was destined. The trend toward slaves in Maryland was much less dramatic but still clear enough. The route of the transition, as well as its timing, explains the reasons for the shift: first, the Virginia evidence suggests that only planters of means and with reliable outlets for their crops could afford to buy slaves. Many, of course, were excluded on grounds of cost alone, whereas others were excluded from both forms of bound labor by the disruptions of their overseas markets during the war years 1688-1697 and, again, 1703-1713. Men with estates worth £150 or more, particularly those living in the prime

TABLE III.2
MARYLAND ESTATES WITH NEITHER SERVANTS NOR SLAVES (percent)

PPW	1656-1683	1684-1696	1697-1704	1705-1712	1713-1719	Average
£ 0-34	90	96	94	98	98	95
35-49	59	78	74	87	92	78
50-71	28	47	58	72	90	59
72-149	17	29	24	54	44	34
150-up	1	5	6	9	4	5
Average	53	59	55	68	68	61

SOURCE: Probate records of six counties, Maryland, in Hall of Records, Annapolis.

tobacco-producing regions, simply switched over from servants to slaves. Fewer than half of such men owned even a single slave prior to 1684, but virtually all were slave owners after 1712. Inventories of men who had lived in Anne Arundel, Calvert, and Charles counties enumerated 78 percent of all servants listed in the probate records of the six counties in the seventeenth century, and 76 percent of all slaves in the eighteenth century. Yet these same counties contained less than half of the white population of the six counties in 1710, as compared to more than two-thirds in 1680.[11]

The secular decline in the supply of servants, therefore, mainly affected planters below the top quintile of estates (those worth less than £150) who continued to specialize in raising tobacco for the market: mainly those living in Anne Arundel, Calvert, and Charles in the six-county sample. Men with estates under £72 in physical personal wealth (67 percent of estates at the beginning of our study, 63 percent by the end) had almost entirely ceased to acquire servants in the course of the transition, and simply could not afford slaves. Those owning estates in between these two boundary figures, £72 to £149, made up less than a fifth of all estates in any time period studied. Such men averaged 2.8 bound laborers apiece in the earliest years and only 1.0 by 1713-1719. The ratio of servants to slaves in their inventories fell from 12 to 1 in the early period to 1 to 1 by 1713-1719.

The transition to slavery, then, came as a result of a diminished supply of high-quality white laborers, but was confined to the richest quintile of planters. The more general transition away from servants was further abetted, however, by the decline in demand

---

[11] Menard, "Five Maryland Censuses, 1700 to 1712," p. 624; and "Growth of Population," pp. 5, 9. See also Karinen, "Numerical and Distributional Aspects of Maryland Population," pp. 139-59.

for them arising from reduced production of tobacco in rapidly growing regions of the colony. A still further reduction in demand resulted from the demographic transition within the population as the increasing proportion of native-born among them provided a growing source of a third type of unfree labor: children. Table III.3 discloses that in one tobacco-producing region on the eastern shore, the number of sons mentioned in wills did not surpass the numbers of men writing them until the 1690s. Among testators in the six counties, men identifying at least one adult among their children constituted only 20 percent of all fathers before 1684. This group grew to 37 percent in the twenty years following, and had climbed to almost half by the end of the period.

As a result of the decline in servitude and the rise of slavery, a new class of large-scale owners emerged after 1700, and the social structure of whites in Maryland came to be characterized by a large class of white planters who owned neither servants nor slaves, a narrowing middle stratum of men who owned a few bound laborers of either type, and at the top a small but growing class of men who almost monopolized the available pool. In 1656-1683, for instance, only 6 percent of estates entering probate included six or more laborers, but by 1713-1719, that percentage had doubled. Only 1 percent had owned as many as twenty before 1700, over 3 percent did so afterwards. Calculations of Gini coeffecents of inequality effectively summarize the change in the distribution of bound laborers in planter estates. These rose from .65 prior to 1684, to .73

TABLE III.3
MALE REPLACEMENT RATES IN
TALBOT, KENT, AND QUEEN ANNE'S COUNTIES

Years	No. Wills	No. Sons	Rate
1669-1673	15	4	0.3
1674-1678	54	36	0.7
1679-1683	30	26	0.9
1684-1688	63	62	1.0
1689-1693	17	8	0.5
1694-1698	60	82	1.4
1699-1703	97	136	1.4
1704-1708	95	142	1.5
1709-1713	121	185	1.5

SOURCE: Paul G. E. Clemens, *The Atlantic Economy and Colonial Maryland's Eastern Shore: From Tobacco to Grain* (Ithaca, 1980), p. 65.

by the turn of the century, and to .83 in the years thereafter. Inequality in the possession of such labor rose as the switchover to slavery proceeded through depression, prosperity, and depression again.

One can see now that the decline of indentured servitude and the rise of slavery were interrelated events. The former was not a consequence of the latter but actually preceded it. A kind of ratcheting effect had been at work in Maryland. In times of poor tobacco prices, servants whose terms expired were not replaced, but slaves necessarily stayed on. This being so, fewer laborers were needed by their owners the next time they chose to expand production. When they bought additional laborers, they chose not to mix newly arrived servants with resident slaves. This reluctance can be observed in the ratios of slaves to servants among those owned by planters having at least six laborers: in the years before 1684, these groups averaged one slave to 3.6 servants, or almost one out of four. That ratio declined to one slave for fewer than two servants in the following period, 1684-1696, and then shifted over entirely thereafter as laborers became predominantly black rather than predominantly white.

The growing presence of slaves in the tidewater areas of the Chesapeake may well have acted as a deterrent to servant enlistment, as it seems to have been for West Indian sugar planters anxiously bidding for servants in order to strengthen internal security forces against the threat of slave uprisings.[12] Certainly from the point of view of an arriving servant, the presence of numerous slaves already on the plantation must have been seriously disturbing. Working alongside slaves at the same task undermined the status of whites, unless the latter exercised some authority, even if only minimal. Since close to half of all servants belonged to planters with six or more laborers in the years between 1684 and 1704, many owners sought to avert trouble by working them in groups separate from slaves. Most eventually chose to sidestep the problem entirely by switching over to slaves. Even owners of smaller numbers of bound laborers ceased acquiring servants after acquiring slaves, as suggested by Table III.4.

The proportion of servants working singly and living with the master's own family actually rose slightly from period to period, while those living and working with only one or two others, and

[12] Richard S. Dunn, *Sugar and Slaves: The Rise of the English Planter Class in the English West Indies, 1624-1713* (Chapel Hill, 1972), pp. 87, 205, 230.

TABLE III.4
STATUS OF GROUPS OF BOUND LABOR: PERCENT SLAVE

Years	Number of Laborers in Group	
	2-5	6+
1656-1683	9% slave	40% slave
1684-1696	18	57
1697-1704	32	70
1705-1712	66	89½
1713-1719	68	94

SOURCE: Probate records of six counties, Maryland, in Hall of Records, Annapolis.

probably still within the bosom of the master's family, even came to predominate among the relatively few servants living in Maryland during the closing years of this study. This was a result of the bifurcation of the servants into a skilled or managerial elite on the one hand and common field workers on the other. The first worked for slaveowners, the second for masters without slaves.

From the slaves' perspective, newcomers to Maryland encountered very different conditions in the years before the 1680s from those that prevailed after 1700. Fewer than two out of every ten worked in all-black groups in the early period, more than half did so later. Contact with white servants performing similar tasks to their own, then, had virtually ceased as the bound labor force shifted its color, its status, and its distribution.

To summarize, the two types of bondsmen had been more or less interchangeable for much of the seventeenth century, playing equally crucial roles in the formation of Chesapeake society. Time, however, drove them apart. Far from merging into a unified class, they came to live in different areas, work for different people, live different lives. The next two sections will examine their living conditions, work arrangements, and for the servants, assess their chances to make it in freedom's wake.

CONDITIONS OF WHITE SERVITUDE IN EARLY MARYLAND

As we have seen, the majority of servants in the early period lived and worked as common farm hands in an all-white environment. The advent of large-scale slavery wrought a major change, dividing servants into two distinct groups: an elite made up of those with special skills or talents who worked for rich slaveowners, and the rest, who worked for planters owning only a few bound laborers of either race.

106

David Boughan of Calvert County offers a case in point. In 1670, his estate inventory listed no slaves but three servants: a man, a woman, and a seventeen-year-old boy.[13] Boughan's servants illustrate a further truth about the makeup of the white labor force after the 1660s: it had come to include members of both sexes and drew from a relatively broad age range. One-fourth were women, whereas the proportion of younger servants, chiefly boys, continued to rise as the total number of servants fell.[14] The supply of men servants responded with particular sensitivity to the price of tobacco, and their relative proportion in the overall supply of servants did not reverse its decline until the very end of the period of this study.

That resurgence marked a change in the function of the adult male servant in Maryland's society during these years, as we have said. Those who had specialized in certain crafts at home could then supply the slaveholder with shoes and clothing for his slaves at a cost to the planter substantially lower than that of imports. Some craftsmen, such as coopers, carpenters, and joiners, were imported chiefly to teach the master's own slaves how to ply their trades, whereas others were hired on terms very favorable to themselves because of special skills.[15] William Byrd I, for instance, asked

---

[13] *Testamentary Proceedings*, V, f. 21.

[14] Paul Clemens counted 56 men, 28 women, and 27 children in Talbot County inventories of the 1680s, a male/female ratio of two to one in this centrally located county on Maryland's eastern shore. In headright claims made in this county, up to the early 1680s, the names of males outnumbered females by two and a half to one. Clemens, "Economy and Society," p. 161. Lorena Walsh estimated that prior to 1706 about three times as many men as women came as servants to Charles County on the lower western shore, and that women were older, on the average, than men. Walsh, "Servitude and Opportunity," p. 111.

[15] Bruce, *Economic History*, II, 475-77; *Md.Arch.*, IV, 283; *Inv. & Accts.*, Liber 2, ff. 320, 343; Liber 7B, f. 98; Liber 19, f. 18; Liber 33B, f. 166; *Inventories* Liber 1, f. 279. Robert "King" Carter paid the wife of his servant, a "painter," £5 for a year of the man's service, according to the contract between them. The servant's wife and child were still in England, and he planned to send for them the following year. Carter praised the man: "He's really an honest, careful, sober fellow and may be able to get a comfortable livelihood when he comes to be his own man"; Carter, *Letters*, p. 23. Bruce found five Negro artisans in late seventeenth-century Virginia inventories: two carpenters, two coopers, and "Tom," a tanner; *Economic History*, II, 405-406. The earliest black artisan to appear in the inventories of the six counties in Maryland is "Cooper Jack," owned by Col. Edward Pye of Charles County in 1697. Pye's neighbor, Col. Diggs, had a mulatto carpenter and a Negro cooper. Cole, a Negro carpenter belonging to Mr. Thomas Todd of Baltimore County, commanded one of the highest prices encountered in the records, £38 (current money) as compared to £25, £28, and £32 for others among his colleagues. *Inv. & Accts.*, Liber 15, ff. 132, 318; Liber 37C, f. 53. Richard Markham of Prince George's

his London correspondent in 1686 to "procure me a tailor for mine is allmost free." Sewing the year's clothing for the "family," which included both servants and slaves, he pointed out, was surely worth more to Byrd in Virginia than what a tailor could hope to command in the marketplace at home. Thus his offer, Byrd felt confident, would surely attract takers at once.[16]

Maryland planters owned servant men who were tailors, carpenters, joiners, millers, shoemakers, and even a doctor in one case, but such skilled individuals made up fewer than 4 percent of all male servants who were described in the inventories and whose terms were mentioned. The fate of most servants in colonial Chesapeake, and of most white men for that matter, was to work at the hoe and the ax. It is not so clear, on the other hand, what constituted the tasks of the women, who, together with a very small number of young girls, made up one-quarter or more of all the indentured servants encountered in the probate records. In the period before 1684, roughly a quarter of the women servants were owned by planters of the poorer classes, those worth less than £100 in physical personal wealth. These women were often the only servant in the household (29 percent) or worked with just one other servant, usually a man (another 29 percent).[17] Women in these circumstances probably spent a good deal of their time working on the tobacco crop. Robert Parnafee's "servant wench" was credited with a share of the tobacco crop of 1,140 pounds, and her corn crop was valued at 402 pounds of tobacco, comparable to what the other two hands had each produced, 1,572 pounds' worth. This woman must have worked full time in the fields, alongside the men.[18]

Traditionally, the English disapproved of field work for women except at harvest, and scorned continental countries where female peasants reportedly worked side by side with their men. Given such an attitude, English women may well have felt demeaned by such labor, and rumors that the tobacco planters might require them to work at the hoe did not aid recruitment efforts. Alice Rogers of York County, Virginia complained in 1669 that her master made her "work in the ground," a task that she expected the court to

County owned thirty-five adult male slaves, of whom two were carpenters. The younger of these two men held the highest appraisal value among the entire group of thirty-five. *Inv. & Accts.*, Liber 30B, ff. 223-26.

[16] "The Letters of William Byrd I," *VMHB*, XXV (1917), 130.

[17] Only two women in this group lived in the same household.

[18] *Inv. & Accts.*, Liber 7B, f. 205.

exclude from her regular duties.[19] Thomas Cocke of Henrico County, Virginia, stated in his will, dated about 1690, that his mulatto girl, Sue, was not to be forced to "beat at the mortar or to work in the ground."[20]

Apologists for the planters attempted to reassure English women that female servants were "not (as is reported) put into the ground to worke, but occupie such domestique employments and house-wifery as in England, that is dressing victuals, righting up the house, milking, employed about dayries, washing, sowing, etc. . . . yet some wenches that are nasty, beastly and not fit to be so employed are put into the ground" in order to pay for their keep and their transportation over.[21]

Since the poorer sort of planters who acquired these female servants did not run dairies or own much in the way of household equipment, women in such households probably spent little time pursuing "domestique employments." However, the proportion of women servants in the possession of poorer planters declined after 1683, and this may have led to more desirable working conditions. Only about one-third worked alone or with just one other servant, usually a man or a boy as before, compared to the 58 percent who had done so previously. Another third lived in groups of three to five servants, where, again, they were generally the only bound women present and very probably did "dress victuals" and tend "dayries." Only 5 percent of all women servants belonged to the big planters, who seemed to prefer slave women for household duties.[22]

Given the general scarcity of marriageable women, most found husbands soon enough after gaining their freedom. Ironically, their working conditions may actually have deteriorated after their wedding, since most of them married poor freedmen with little to offer in the way of material goods.[23] Only a quarter of all free women

[19] Bruce, *Economic History*, II, 15. Robert Beverly stated that "a white Woman is rarely or never put to work in the Ground, if she be good for any thing else: And to Discourage All Planters from using any Women so, their Law imposed the heaviest Taxes upon Female-Servants working in the Ground, while it suffers all other white Women to be absolutely exempted: Whereas on the other hand, it is a common thing to work a Woman Slave out of Doors; nor does the Law make any Distinction in her Taxes, whether her Work be Abroad, or at Home"; *History*, pp. 271-72.

[20] Bruce, *Economic History*, II, 103. Sue was given to Cocke's daughter along with the "weaver's loom" to be used by Sue.

[21] Hammond, *Leah and Rachel*, in Force, *Tracts*, III, No. 14.

[22] For more on houses and housekeeping, see Chapters Four and Five below.

[23] Most freed women found ready suitors. George Parker's administrator paid

in Maryland after 1683 lived in households staffed by even a single servant or slave.

One final point about women servants needs to be made before we turn to the others: they were primarily valued as workers, not as sexual partners, by their masters. This is not to deny that men living in a predominantly male society far from the purview of the customary guardians of morals and consciences consistently resisted temptation and seduction.[24] It is important, however, to emphasize that fear of impregnating their sexual partners played a strongly inhibitory role for men in this society. Masters lost valuable services when their maid servants got pregnant and could demand recompence, whereas county or parish officials moved quickly to exact from the offending father all charges in the raising of bastards. Two servants in 1671, for instance, asked their master's permission to marry. He gave them that liberty, but they had to promise to serve extra time for every child they had while in his service, not only to compensate him for the loss of the woman's time, but for the trouble and charge of bringing up the children.[25]

In an indenture signed in 1666, John Cooper agreed to serve Randall Revell two years in return for two years of the term of Revell's servant woman, Susanna Brayfield, and to serve four years if she died in childbirth. Cooper also promised to pay Revell for the loss of her time from pregnancy and childbirth and for care of the infant. The contract further states, "Cooper is to take away the child & to provide a nurse for itt att his owne Cost & Charge soon after her delivery." Revell, in turn, promised to deliver up his servant to Cooper at the close of the two years "to dispose of her as he shall think fitt with Corne & Clothes according to the tenur of her Indenture."[26] What Susanna Brayfield thought of all this remains hidden.

William Caughey for "his wife's" freedom corn and clothes sometime before 1690. *Inv. & Accts.*, Liber 10, f. 356. That wives worked in the fields is argued by Carr and Walsh, "The Planter's Wife," pp. 561-63. Clemens infers this to have been the general case among farm tenants in Talbot County from the substantial difference in crop sizes between married and unmarried men. "Economy and Society," p. 156.

[24] Indeed, they did not! One poor woman was not only raped by her master, but caught a venereal disease from him as a result. *Md.Arch.*, XLIV, 69. Women must also have regretted their enforced celibacy and occasionally given way to temptation.

[25] Ibid., pp. 44, 518.

[26] Nothing was said about Cooper's marrying the woman, but it is a reasonable inference. Still, the terms settled between the two men utterly ignored her interests as a third party to the negotiations; ibid., p. 622. John Cooper died about twenty years later, a widower, with approximately a hundred acres of land and personal property worth £105, plus debts owing to him of £85. Cooper did not make a will, and the account of administration makes no mention of children.

The cold language of these contracts treats human relationships as mere business propositions, caricaturing their real meaning to the people involved, but servants were a species of property, and should a pregnant woman die if overworked or in childbirth, her master's investment aborted as well.[27] He would not take kindly, therefore, to anybody's attempt to win the sexual favors of his female servants, nor would he lightly choose to do so himself.

In summary, most female servants, as well as male, stayed single, and presumably celibate, during service.[28] Their legal and economic circumstances simply forbade marrying, and punishment for extracurricular activities included more than bodily chastisement: extension of their terms of servitude, as well.

Although young immigrants from abroad furnished the overwhelming majority of servants, many poor orphan children were also put out to service in early Maryland.[29] Free people of limited means, when writing their wills, implored friends and benefactors to watch over their children and to endeavor to protect them from such servitude. The language of the Orphans' Court, set up to protect the property inherited by minors who had lost their fathers, makes the same point. Wards of the court who had sufficient estates were not to be "turned to Common Labor" by their guardians, and were to be "exempted from the How and the Mortar" or from the ax and the hoe in order that they might learn skills that would offer them better advantages in adult life.[30]

In practice, however, many orphans were put to work in the field. Children whose property provided insufficient income to pay their keep were to be bound out as servants, according to a law of 1663.[31] One orphan boy complained to the court that his master was not teaching him to be a boatwright and carpenter as he was supposed to, but was using him for common work at the ax and

[27] In the malaria-ridden areas of the tidewater Chesapeake, it is probable that men outlived women. Darrett and Anita Rutman argue that malaria was the probable cause of the exceptionally high death rate among pregnant women which they observed in Middlesex County, Virginia. Rutman and Rutman, " 'Now-Wives and Sons-in-Law,' " in Tate and Ammerman, eds., *Chesapeake*, pp. 160, 172, 178-82.

[28] Examples of married servants are rare, but see *Inv. & Accts.*, Liber 22, f. 32; Liber 27C, f. 98; Liber 35, f. 248; *Md.Arch.*, XLIV, 375, 28.

[29] Boys were assigned many of the same duties as men, but in addition, they seem to have borne the task of "beating Corn" in the mortar. For more on this particular chore, see Chapter Five.

[30] Walsh, "Charles County," p. 117; Lois Green Carr, "The Development of the Maryland Orphans' Court, 1654-1715," in Land, Carr, and Papenfuse, *Early Maryland*, p. 42.

[31] Ibid., p. 43.

hoe. His master defended his usage by arguing that the boy was "so younge and small that as yett he was not fitt to work at his trade." The court agreed, and sent the boy back to the fields.[32] William Watts' sons complained that the executor of their father's estate had put them to hard labor in the ground "equall to any servt or Slave."[33] Nor were girls immune; Margaret O'Daniell protested that her stepfather made her work for him at the hoe "as hard as any servant."[34]

John Clarke's mother accused her son's master of reneging on promises made before she had "put" John to him. He "Doth not use him as a son but a servant or rather a white Negro [,] clothing him in such things as Negroes are usually clothed and putting him under an Overseer to make Tobacco and Corne instead of gooing to Schoole."[35] This list of complaints makes three specific charges of ill usage: putting the child to common labor, putting him under an overseer, and dressing him in clothes such as only Negroes wore. Perhaps one can detect here a scale of priorities held by the people of the times. Men might have sought to avoid, for their wives and children if not for themselves, clothing that was demeaning, working under an overseer, and field labor.

Yet toiling in the fields was not only the lot of servants and slaves, and of unfortunate widows and children, but of most freemen as well. "Some of the masters and their wives [,] who pass their lives here in wretchedness, do the same [as the servants and slaves, that is, make tobacco]."[36] Robert Beverly put it rather more cheerfully: "The work of their servants and slaves is no other than what every common freeman does."[37] Tatham, writing many years later, made much the same observation, stating that many masters and their sons worked alongside their bondsmen.[38] Oldmixon did not think it wrong, and assumed his readers would agree, that the children of free white Carolinians were set to work at eight years of age.[39]

[32] Walsh, "Charles County," p. 123.

[33] Carr, "Orphans' Court," in Land, Carr, and Papenfuse, eds., *Early Maryland*, p. 41.

[34] Walsh, "Charles County," p. 117.

[35] Ibid., p. 139.

[36] *Journal of a Voyage to New York and a Tour in Several of the American Colonies in 1679-80 by Jaspar Dankers and Peter Sluyter of Wieward in Friesland*, translated by Henry C. Murphy (Brooklyn, 1867), p. 216.

[37] Beverly, *History*, p. 271.

[38] Tatham, *Historical Essay*, in Herndon, *William Tatham*, p. 19.

[39] John Oldmixon, *The British Empire in America*, 2 vols., (London, 1741; orig. ed. 1708).

Despite their relative helplessness, servants and children were not bereft of all rights.[40] "Sufficient" food, clothing, and lodging were the legal responsibilities of masters, as stated and restated in a series of laws passed by Maryland's legislatures.[41] Servants' material condition was actually no worse than that of many planters, when we compare the value of their bedding, clothing, and other accomodation.[42] Servants and slaves were separated from ordinary whites more by status than by the nature of their tasks or accommodations. It is their treatment as disposable property, rather than their material circumstances, that makes their position appear so degrading.[43]

Maryland laws also prohibited ill treatment. Masters were not to burden their people unreasonably beyond their strength or keep them from necessary rest, and whippings were not to exceed ten lashes for any one offense.[44] The modern reader recoils in horror from the harshness of punishments meted out to servants then, but he should remember that English law and custom of the times could comprehend only two alternatives for the punishment of transgressors: fines or physical chastisement. Those without legal command over property, such as servants, married women, and children, could not be fined since they could not pay. The court could force poor persons into temporary servitude or extend the

[40] Carr, "Orphans' Court," in Land, Carr, and Papenfuse, eds., *Early Maryland*, pp. 43-44.

[41] *Md.Arch.*, I, 500.

[42] See Chapter Six below.

[43] The Dutch mariner, David De Vries, commented disparagingly on the prevalence of gambling among the Virginia planters in 1633. He particularly criticized their practice of using servants as pawns in a wager. Parr, *Voyages of David De Vries*, p. 242. These were boom times and reflected that atmosphere.

[44] On the legal status and rights of servants, see Richard B. Morris, *Government and Labor in Early America* (New York, 1946), pp. 390-512; Lois Green Carr, "County Government in Maryland, 1684-1709," (Ph.D. dissertation, Harvard University, 1968), pp. 315-19, 583-84. The laws cited may be found in *Md.Arch.*, IV, 35-39. Any magistrate, on proper complaint of the master, might order a servant to receive more than ten but not more than thirty-nine lashes. Whippings of servants that involved laying on more than ten lashes appear regularly in the county court records. See Raphael Semmes, *Crime and Punishment in Early Maryland* (Baltimore, 1938), chapter five, "Servant Discipline and Punishment," pp. 80-118. In one case, two servants were punished for forging a pass, each to receive twenty lashes. A third had his punishment remitted "upon future good behavior" and on the condition that he be the one to apply the whip to his fellows. *Md.Arch.*, X, 516-17. For Virginia, Bruce cites Hening's *Statutes at Large*, III, that no master was permitted to whip a white servant on the naked back without special authority from the court; *Economic History*, II, 12.

113

terms of servants, but whipping made its point at once, a considerable psychological advantage in the eyes of both judges and parents.

Courts of law in Maryland and Virginia were legally bound to protect the rights of servants who petitioned for redress of grievances against their masters or others. The terms of their indentures, furthermore, had the full legal force of any contract and were as binding on the masters as on the servants, just as Hammond argued. Although "servants complaints are freely harkened to, and (if not carelessly made) there [*sic*] Masters are compelled either speedily to amend, or they are removed upon second complaint to another service."[45]

There can, however, be no assurance that servants were treated gently. The county court records contain many cases of abuse.[46] Many servants ran away, a few even committed suicide.[47] One poor fellow was ordered by the court to serve ten days additional for each day he was away without leave, because he had given no real cause for running away, expressing to the court only the fear of what his master might have done to him because he had "over soaked his corn to beat."[48]

Contemporaries were divided in their assessment of servants' status in Chesapeake society. The visiting Labadists, Dankers and Sluyter, viewed the entire tobacco system as destructive and de-

[45] Hammond, *Leah and Rachel*, in Force, *Tracts*, III, No. 14, p. 295. Here is one example: Simon Bird, servant to Mr. Thomas Truman was hired out to another man, one Robert Taylor, in 1654 and was forced to petition the court because the new master had failed to supply him with necessary clothing, "which Complaint appeareth to this Court to have Sufficient ground" and thereupon the judges ordered Taylor to supply Bird with what he needed; *Md.Arch.*, X, 401.

[46] Semmes, *Crime and Punishment*, chapter five, particularly the outrageous behavior of Captain and Mrs. Thomas Bradnox, he a justice of the peace in Kent County during the 1650s (pp. 96-99 and 105-109 for other cases of brutality). Captain Bradnox had, at various times, been guilty of rebellion, sedition, rapine, theft, robbery, and drunken brawling. County commissioner, sheriff, and captain of militia are some of the offices of public trust occupied by this ignorant and vicious man. His fellow judges refused to convict him of any felony, not because they condoned his behavior, but because they could not find any one else of his "quality" and property to put in his place. The Bradnox maid, Sarah, ran away repeatedly to escape harsh treatment, once turning up at a neighbor's "newly come out of the woods & almost starved with eatinge Trash"; *Md.Arch.*, LIV, 179. See the profile of Bradnox in Edward C. Papenfuse, Alan F. Day, David W. Jordan, and Gregory A. Stiverson, *A Biographical Dictionary of the Maryland Legislature, 1635-1789*, Vol. I: A-H (1979), 159.

[47] *Md.Arch.*, LIV, 362-63; also pp. 179, 184; X, 416, 511, 515-16.

[48] Ibid., LIV, 297.

humanizing. Of servants, they said in 1680, "they are by the hundreds of thousands compelled to spend their lives here and in Virginia, and elsewhere in planting that vile tobacco . . . this insatiable avarice must be fed and sustained by the bloody sweat of these poor slaves."[49] Monsieur Durand, a Huguenot visitor to Virginia around the same time, approved the system, but he, too, labeled the servants "Christian slaves."[50] The heroic explorer, John Lawson, condemned indentured servitude as tyrannical; "in my opinion, it's better for Christians of a mean Fortune to marry with the Civiliz'd *Indians*, than to suffer the Hardships of four or five years Servitude, in which they meet with Sicknesse and Seasonings amidst a Crowd of other Afflictions, while the Tyranny of a bad Master lays upon such poor Souls, all which acquainted with our Tobacco Plantations are not Strangers to."[51]

Robert Beverly, on the other hand, stressed that "neither is any Servant requir'd to do more in a Day, than his Overseer . . . generally their Slaves are not worked near so hard, nor so many Hours in a Day, as the Husbandmen, and Day-Labourers in *England*."[52]

Thus, contemporary attitudes toward servants and their condition varied rather widely. Those who approved of the system saw it as beneficial to those who practiced the desirable virtues of a working class: industry, abstemiousness, and honesty. An open system, such as existed in the early Chesapeake, probably justified the more optimistic viewpoint. The England of that day was not hospitable, after all, to the propertyless. Two modern scholars have thoughtfully concluded that those who worked for the lesser planters were probably no worse off than members of the family. Because such planters could not afford to maintain separate servants' quarters, they argue, the servants and free laborers "must have been fully integrated into family life, sharing meals, sleeping under the same roof. . . . Shared social experience as well as common social origins must have diminished differences in status between freedmen and their employers."[53]

[49] Dankers and Sluyter, *Journal*, p. 192. This was in the year 1680.

[50] Durand, *Frenchman in Virginia*, p. 113. Monsieur Durand referred to the white servants as "Christian slaves" to distinguish them from the others.

[51] Lawson, *New Voyage*, p. 238.

[52] Beverly, *History*, p. 271. He goes on, "The Male-Servants, and Slaves of both Sexes, are employed together in Tilling and Manuring the Ground, in Sowing and Planting Tobacco, Corn, &c. Some Distinction indeed is made between them in their Cloathes, and Food."

[53] Lois Green Carr and Russell R. Menard, "Immigration and Opportunity," in Tate and Ammerman, eds., *Chesapeake*, pp. 228-29.

The courts were particularly careful to protect the rights of servants who had fulfilled their side of the bargain. The records contain scores of cases in which servants successfully sued their masters for compliance with the terms of their indenture, particularly for payment of freedom dues.[54] Servant James Loyler, for instance, had been included in one estate inventory and appraised at £6, but the terms of his indenture explicitly provided for his automatic freeing in the event of his master's death. The administrator, therefore, dutifully freed James and debited the estate for £6 as a consequence.[55] Imagine the pleasurable surprise of another servant, Thomas Abbott, who by the "custom of the Country" was legally free some months prior to the visit of appraisers to the plantation where he worked, when he was informed by them that he had already served beyond his time. The estate's administrator was thus compelled to make good the overtime, some 68 days, for which he paid Abbott 680 pounds of tobacco at the then customary rate of 10 pounds per day.[56]

Two servant boys were set free by the court in yet another case, leading the administrator to lament their loss, "being half their best time." Freedom granted a girl and boy in 1711 cost another estate £2 and £3, respectively.[57]

Indentures occasionally provided for the payment of wages to servants at the expiration of their term, in addition to their freedom corn and clothes. William Stradder promised to serve Walter Cooper, Gent., for two years nine months, in return for his passage, meat, drink, apparel, and lodging, "with other necessarys," and at the expiration of his term, £20 sterling or the value thereof "at prices Current."[58] In 1657, William Wardiff engaged to serve Mr. John Wade one whole year upon these conditions: that Wade cure him of his disease and besides the cure, pay him at the end of the year 1,000 pounds of tobacco, give him a kersey or broadcloth suit, two shirts, two pairs of stockings, three pairs of shoes, and one barrel of corn or 100 pounds of tobacco, during which year Wade was

[54] *Md.Arch.*, IV, 361, 447, 456, 470, 471, 539; X, 48, 52, 218, 238, 247, 254, 261, 382, 406, 436, 505, 506; XLI, 67, 417, 418; LIV, 416, 442, 448, 468, 498, 575.
[55] *Inv. & Accts.*, Liber 10, f. 442.
[56] Ibid., Liber 7A, f. 31.
[57] Ibid., Liber 13A, f. 187; Liber 33A, f. 243; *Will Book* 3, f. 551.
[58] *Md.Arch.*, X, 121. This latter sum was disputed later when Cooper sold Stradder and the purchaser had understood the payment at expiration of the term to have been only £10.

also to "find" him diet and lodging, all of which surely totaled more than 2,000 pounds' worth of tobacco.[59]

For servants without indentures, the law required masters to give, as freedom dues, "one good Cloth Suite of Kersey or Broadcloth a Shift of white linen one new pair of Stockins and Shoes two hoes one axe 3 barrels of Corne and fifty acres of land five whereof at least to be plantable."[60] The right to land became in practice only a "warrant" to the land that enabled the would-be owner to obtain a deed to his fifty acres only after he had first located vacant, undeeded land and then had it professionally surveyed and officially recorded by the county clerk, all of which cost time, effort, and money. The Proprietary government discontinued this practice after 1683.[61]

The value of freedom dues thus varied, depending on the terms of the indenture, or in its absence what was afforded by custom or stipulated in law and the changing value of tobacco itself. A judicial inquiry in 1648 estimated the "customary" freedom dues at only 429 pounds of tobacco, but the staple was then worth two or three times as much as what it came to be a half-century later.[62] Lewis Evans' administrator kept careful account of the freedom dues paid Evans' servant: three barrels of corn, a gown, shoes, stockings, hoe and ax, worth 600 pounds of tobacco or roughly £2.5 in 1704.[63]

Some twenty specific references to the value of freedom dues in the probate records prior to 1697 averaged 685 pounds of tobacco, or less than £3 in money at a penny per pound. Thirty-two observations from the years 1698 through 1715, the date of the last one uncovered in our period, averaged a bit higher than those earlier, 822 pounds, or just under £3.5.[64]

Some fortunate men were occasionally able to put together a

---

[59] Ibid., p. 496. A jury trial had to be called in Kent County in 1670 in order to force one man to pay his servant the £10 he had promised him, besides whatever else the indenture may have stipulated. In 1684, one "John," was also promised £10 for his service at the end of three years, whereas a few years before, Elizabeth Cole received 1,000 pounds of tobacco for a year's wages plus her freedom clothes. Ibid., LIV, 293; *Inv. & Accts.*, Liber 7A, f. 119.

[60] *Md.Arch.*, I, 80, 97; XXII, 22, 445; XXX, 286.

[61] Earle, "Environment, Disease, and Mortality," in Tate and Ammerman, eds., *Chesapeake*, p. 43.

[62] *Md.Arch.*, IV, 470-71; see also p. 271.

[63] The inventory was dated 1691 and did not mention any women servants. The account was rendered April 1704.

[64] The intercept was 631 pounds, slope only +.074.

117

little capital before the expiration of their terms, gaining a small headstart on the minimum stake necessary to set up on one's own. One pamphleteer assured his English audience that servants who were "industrious" could gain a "competent" estate before freedom, since "most" masters allowed their people a "parcel of clear ground . . . [which] he may husband at those many idle times . . . allowed him." Keeping pigs or a calf would be profitable as well, he added, "but this must be gained (as I said) by Industry and affability, not by sloth or churlish behavior."[65]

The extent to which servants might work for themselves is unknown, but occasional records suggest that opportunities to do so were not entirely absent. One instance is offered by servant Robert Kemp, who, in 1687, owned a heifer, a steer, a chest, a carbine, a drawing knife, and a wedge, besides a debt owed him by his master of £7.5. William Earl affords another example of the "industrious" servant and/or the benevolent master. Earl paid his master 385 pounds of tobacco in consideration for setting him free before the expiration of his full term of service. At his death a few years later, Earl possessed a chest, clothing, tools, two horses and a saddle, all worth £8.[66] Buying out of an indenture could not have been possible in most cases, although workers with special skills were in the best circumstances to succeed. Thomas Todd, "glover," agreed to deliver his master 50 dressed skins each year for his remaining term and guaranteed to dress the 46 skins "now in the lime pitt" and to make up from them a dozen pair of breeches and a dozen pair of gloves "in the best manner."[67]

As we have seen, servants did receive a small stake as a reward for completing their terms, but their newly acquired status did not carry with it any guarantee of material betterment. Although freedom's true value cannot be measured in monetary terms, it is surely empty of meaning without economic opportunity. Let us, then, inquire into the fate of freedmen in early Maryland.

The earliest servants appear to have enjoyed generally good fortune in their later careers. Of some 158 former servants who had

[65] Hammond, *Leah and Rachel*, in Force, *Tracts*, III, No. 14, p. 292. Other sources of income included occasional tips. William Byrd II, for instance, recorded in his diary that he had given out some £3 in tips to a half-dozen servants on the occasion of the governor's birthday celebration. *Secret Diary*, p. 118.

[66] *Inv. & Accts.*, Liber 25, f. 255.

[67] *Md.Arch.*, IV, 283. On the other hand, another man, who had been sold at York River in Virginia to a planter in Kent County, Maryland, made a bargain with his new master to serve him an additional year if he would teach him the trade of cooper; ibid., p. 191.

arrived in Maryland before 1642 and survived to earn their freedom, better than half definitely succeeded in acquiring land. Others who emigrated may well have done so, too. Half also served in local political offices of various kinds, including jury duty, whereas some compiled "remarkable" records of public service in the course of their later lives. Opportunity to acquire land and to win local office declined after 1660 or so, as population grew and the cost of land rose commensurately.[68]

Beyond humble aspirations to a place of one's own and the respect of one's neighbors, however, only a handful of those freed after 1674 in Charles County, for instance, eventually succeeded in acquiring the wherewithal to rise above small planter status.[69] Time was against them: the streams of freed servants had to travel further and further away as the years passed. The experience of one man dramatizes the growing difficulties facing the freedman in a decelerating economy. About the year 1695, John Young received his freedom corn (worth 300 pounds of tobacco) and freedom clothes, hoes, and axes (worth 600). He died unmarried ten years later. He had been living in another's household, and his meager estate included six horses worth only £9, clothing valued at £3.5, some cash, and a few small debts. The sum came to roughly £20, which made his estate equivalent in rank to the twenty-fifth place from the poorest for every hundred men entering probate in the period in which he died. Young's landlord was also his chief creditor and the executor of his estate, and in his accounts he charged for two years' accomodations at 800 pounds of tobacco per annum, or a little less than £7 total. Other debts owed by Young, plus the usual probate fees, brought the total bill against the estate to some £16, leaving a net worth of only £4, which seems rather a small sum to show for ten years' effort.[70]

In order to accumulate the wherewithal to set up independent housekeeping, the newly freed servant usually began working for wages or for shares or as a tenant on a leasehold. Wages during good times could be quite high, but in the latter part of the century fell slightly.[71] Some eighteen observations on yearly wages appear

[68] Menard, "From Servant to Freeholder," pp. 37-64. See also Carr and Menard, "Immigration and Opportunity," in Tate and Ammerman, eds., *Chesapeake*, pp. 206-42.

[69] Walsh, "Servitude and Opportunity," in Land, Carr, and Papenfuse, eds., *Early Maryland*, p. 123.

[70] *Inv. & Accts.*, Liber 13A, f. 367 and Liber 25, f. 129.

[71] Manfred Jonas, "Wages in Early Colonial Maryland," *MdHM*, LI (1956), 27-

in the probate records of the six-county group. These range from a low of 960 pounds of tobacco in Somerset County in 1684 to a high of 2,100 pounds in Anne Arundel County in 1703. Undoubtedly the wage bargains varied with the state of economy and the tasks performed.[72]

It is difficult to evaluate these data on wages from the point of view of freed servants and their chances for economic success. A Virginia county court record, however, provides a valuable clue to the amount that a man could save in a year. In 1661, a year following one of good tobacco prices, former servant John Deane was judged an "idiot" by the court and placed with Robert House for the year. House promised to give Deane meat, drink, washing, and lodging "above the degree of a common servant," to pay Deane's levies, keep him "well and justly cloathed," and to take care of his cattle and their increase. At the expiration of the year, Dean would be freed, and in the meanwhile, at the completion of the crop, 350 pounds of tobacco were to be paid over by House to a trustee who would employ this pay for Deane's particular use and benefit. That 350 pounds represents, then, savings over and above all costs for the year and should be viewed as a minimum, given the potential problems arising to House for employing one not fully competent, mentally or psychologically (one cannot be sure of the particular disorder designated by the term "idiot").[73]

In 1661 that 350 pounds would have yielded approximately £2 in money, though in other years, when tobacco prices more closely approached the long-term level of a penny per pound, that value shrank to £1.5. If this case provides a reasonable guide to the level of savings over the long run in the tobacco economy, a servant could look forward to accumulating 4,613 pounds in ten years, given an interest rate of 6 percent, or just over £19 at a penny per pound. With luck, his livestock would have been increasing in the meanwhile, so his total stock would have been even more. This sum may not look impressive, especially when one compares it with the fees some professional men of the times earned, but for an

---

28. Daily wages for unskilled workers ranged from 15 to 20 pounds of tobacco per day in accounts of administration, but these were rates set by the court. Yearly contracts paid lower wages figured on a per diem basis, but these also included room and board. Examples of such contracts may be found in *Md.Arch.*, I, 166, 173-74, 201, 286, and 468.

[72] Another man in Anne Arundel County was owed over £13 for a year's service in 1718, but by that time currency inflation had set in. *Inventories*, Liber 2, f. 112.

[73] Billings, ed., *Old Dominion*, pp. 92-93.

unlearned man starting out with nothing more than a few head of livestock, a year's supply of corn, and the clothes on his back, that fund of cumulative savings would have been enough at the end of a decade to purchase a place of his own.

Tenancy, however, offered more immediate advantages, and many freed servants chose this route. The rents were usually quite small in the seventeenth century, only 100 to 300 pounds of tobacco per year for fifty or a hundred acres of virgin land. The landlord benefited by having his land "seated," which confirmed his title; the improvements were made at no expense to himself, and the tenant meanwhile had a place to farm independently without having to lay out purchase money or entry fee. As more land came under tillage, however, the incentives for the landlord shifted from capital improvements to rental income. Late in the period, lease terms showed a strong tendency to rise, perhaps doubling as the price of the land itself had done.[74]

Renting a plantation also offered a means of starting out, and working for shares of the crop furnished still another. The distinctions between sharecropping, renting, and leasing were never clear-cut, so that considerable room for negotiation always existed between the interested parties. Tatham, a careful observer, explained succinctly the principal forms taken by such options a century later: "If A . . . furnishes the land, and finds everything necessary to its cultivation, and B undertakes the labour of the culture, A will share two parts, and B will share one. If, on the contrary, A finds the land only, and B furnishes the labour and necessaries of cultivation, A will share one-third part, and B will take two."[75]

Actual arrangements in the seventeenth century varied over a wider range. William Fenix, for instance, lived and worked on leased land, but also supplemented his income by working for a share of the crop on his neighbor's land.[76] Robert Maine lived in his landlord's household and worked rented ground, while also doing wage work for his landlord, who had initially advanced him the tools and clothing to get started.[77] The landlord, acting as

[74] Leases of lands owned by one affluent eastern shore family showed a median rent of 600 pounds after 1720. Prior to that time, tenants had been paying 100 to 400 pounds of tobacco a year for rent. A new guardian for the heirs instigated a general increase in rents when he took charge, so that the median rose from 200 to 600 pounds. Clemens, "Economy and Society," pp. 155-56.

[75] Tatham, *Historical Essay*, in Herndon, *William Tatham*, p. 101.

[76] *Inv. & Accts.*, Liber 31, ff. 153, 321.

[77] Ibid., Liber 13B, f. 69.

administrator of Maine's estate, debited the account as follows: "to his corn ground ready fenced, 1 40-foot house and tobacco ground, 600; pr. yarn hose 35; weeding hoes 25 [and] hilling hoes 18," for a total charge of 1,519 pounds. Credits included 600 on the crop, a gun, "unfixt," for ten shillings, and a debt of six shillings from his landlord for wages earned for thrashing and cleaning twenty bushels of wheat.

Getting started obviously required capital, and the records offer a few valuable glimpses into some of the routes taken by people of the times. Patrick Westin, for instance, obtained house, ground, and diet for some 400 pounds in 1683, plus four barrels of corn for 300. He paid his levy for that year, 130 pounds, and owed 510. He already possessed two horses worth 1,600, and a number of people owed him debts totaling altogether 450. Westin's corn crop eventually came to be worth 800 after harvest, and his crop of tobacco, 2,400 weight. His clothing and tools probably amounted to less than 400 pounds in value, although these are not known. He died suddenly, and his landlord had to charge his estate 700 for finishing the crops; "gathering, husking, and stripping" cost 200, "taking up two horses," 400, and for six hogsheads to package his crops, 150. At his death, then, Patrick Westin owned 2,050 pounds in assets, plus his clothing and tools, and a crop of corn and tobacco that together totaled 3,200 pounds in value. His debts and debits came to 1,340 plus the cost of the hogsheads and getting in his horses, and, in addition, the labor charges for finishing his crop, 1,050, for a total of 2,790 against 5,250 in credits. Funeral charges were a modest 350 and probate fees an immodest 776.[78] He had, therefore, acquired before he died an estate of £10 to £12, net of debts and charges, a substantial and worthy stake for a beginner.

One more example of the process of getting started in early Maryland, this one from 1710, will suffice. John Rains of Charles County made an arrangement with Henry Tanner, who advanced him the following: a cow and yearling (700), two yards "checks" (44), two knives (16), broad ax and hoe (36), a bottle of rum plus a pound of sugar (25), a bottle of molasses (30), a peck of salt (12), three barrels of corn (360), and two hogsheads for his crop of tobacco, a total of 1,272 pounds of tobacco owed by Rains to Tanner. In addition to this series of debts, Rains also owed 20 pounds of tobacco at "Mr. Williams Store," 60 pounds to a tailor, and to

[78] Ibid., Liber 8, f. 80.

122

Henry Tanner (again) for "washing and mending," 90. Rains' levy for the year came to 102 pounds, so his total debts were 1,544. His crop was only six bushels of corn and 1,400 pounds of tobacco, worth 1,520 pounds altogether, so poor Rains actually slipped behind for the year.[79]

It was Rains' misfortune to have arrived late on the scene. Economic opportunity passed with the frontier as population growth pushed up land prices and depressed those for the staple crop. Men with both capital and connections gradually built a more familiar kind of society in the meanwhile, one more stable and more stratified, and one into which freed servants could fit only as landless, voteless, voiceless tenants or else leave in search of yet another frontier.

CONDITIONS OF BLACK SERVITUDE

White servants had rights and, after freedom, options. Blacks enjoyed neither.[80] Even more than the servant, the slave was at the mercy of his master, because he lacked the critically important right of petition to the courts to secure compliance with the laws that were supposed to protect him. Englishmen of the day were not necessarily harsher toward their servants and slaves than toward their own children or those of their friends, but the absence of legal recourse placed the slave in a particularly vulnerable position.

The surviving records tell us where the slaves lived, how many of them there were, and something about their ages and sex, but very little about their lives. We can, at the very least, examine their numerical and chronological distribution. Two-thirds of all slaves in the six counties between the years 1656 and 1720 worked for just 6 percent of the planters, that is, those with £400 or more in physical personal wealth. Four-fifths of the black chattels appear in estates dated after 1696, and, of these, more than four-fifths worked for masters who owned six or more laborers.[81]

Given these facts, it seems correct to say that the typical slave

[79] Ibid., Liber 31, f. 111.

[80] For examples of free Negroes, see Billings, *Old Dominion*, pp. 155-58; Bruce, *Economic History*, II, 123-24; *Md.Arch.*, LIV, 675, 757, 760. Mungoe, Jupiter, and Peter were also exceptions. *Inv. & Accts.*, Liber 34, f. 32; Liber 22, f. 106; and Liber 10, f. 78. See the general works on the subject by James M. Wright, *The Free Negro in Maryland 1634-1860* (New York, 1921), and John H. Russell, *The Free Negro in Virginia* (1913).

[81] After 1696, close to two-thirds of the slaves lived in just two of the six counties, Anne Arundel and Calvert.

worked in a less intimate environment than the typical servant, especially after 1700. Indeed, for the two decades at the start of the eighteenth century, better than a third of the slaves lived among holdings of twenty or more, and in just the three principal tobacco counties: Anne Arundel, Calvert, and Charles. These larger plantations used relatively few servants, as we have seen: ratios of slaves to servants among them ranged from six to one in Charles, twelve to one in Calvert, and a whopping twenty-six to one in Anne Arundel.

The existence of these large labor holdings in colonial Maryland did not mean that slaves worked in "gangs" on tightly coordinated tasks, nor did they necessarily live in extensive "quarters." Quite the contrary, workers dispersed in relatively small groups all over the landscape.

In the earliest years, blacks were racially isolated. Only about one-tenth of the slaves actually worked with other blacks. They were scattered rather thinly among the white servants and freemen, and little segregation on the basis of race or status took place. In this period there were only a few planters who owned more than a dozen workers, and only four estate inventories enumerated all-black groups of six or more.

For slaves in these early years, the situation of James Hume's Negro man, valued at just under £12, was typical. His all-white coworkers included two men, a woman, and a boy.[82] Another representative example is that of the old Negro woman who worked for Henry Lewis, a tanner and justice of the peace in Anne Arundel County. She lived with his four servants, two men and two women, all of whom may have helped at the "pitts," to run the bark mill, and to make shoes. Elsewhere, Moll Bryant, "a Malotta" aged about twenty years, worked with four white servants, one of whom was a woman.[83]

Until the arrival late in the century of the first cargoes direct from Africa, most slaves had come to the Chesapeake by way of the West Indies, or were the offspring of those who had done so. Their exact origins and times of arrival cannot be traced, and probably were haphazard in any case, and the less than optimal physical condition of most of these involuntary immigrants suggests that they were castoffs and rejects of the sugar growers there.

These West Indian blacks spoke at least some English and under-

[82] *Inv. & Accts.*, Liber 4, f. 69.
[83] Ibid., Liber 7, f. 156; Liber 5B, f. 8; Liber 4, f. 116; Liber 6, f. 683.

stood what was expected of them. They had already accustomed themselves to a modified European-style diet and had survived the rigorous "seasoning" of the Caribbean. Already masters of survival by the time they appear in Maryland records, their spirit and grit made them desirable and marketable in the labor-short Chesapeake, despite physical disabilities such as missing limbs or advanced age.

In a society chronically short of women and their skills, the household help rendered by even quite elderly slaves released others' more valuable time, making the cost of their upkeep worthwhile. For this reason, the numerous old Negro women who appear in early inventories had a value to the estate, even when they were appraised at only a pound or two. Henry Lewis' slave mentioned above was typical of these.[84]

There did exist, however, a few black men of prime age and health among the slaves living in early Maryland. These may have been sons of immigrants or immigrants themselves. In 1663, for example, Captain William Battin owned a five hundred-acre plantation in Charles County that was stocked with one man servant, two woman servants, one of them lame, an old Negro woman, and a Negro man with his wife and daughter. Captain Battin also had land in Virginia and kept a Negro couple there. Edward Keen's Negro boy, seventeen-year-old Mingo, was appraised at 5,000 pounds of tobacco, just about top price in 1676. Alexander Magruder's man, Sambo, went for that price the following year, as did William Parker's Negro man in 1680. Peter Archer's Negro man, James, sold for £25 sterling in 1683.[85] Slave prices such as these were peak values, and declined after the early 1680s, not to rise again until the late 1690s. The values of other slaves, however, tended to be lower, occasionally much lower, than those for prime males, strongly suggesting that the majority of slaves present in Maryland for most of the seventeenth century could not have been in the full vigor of youth and health.

The ages and general health of the black population could not have been conducive to strong natural growth. As Table III.5 dis-

---

[84] See previous note.

[85] *Testamentary Proceedings*, Liber 1D, f. 84, pp. 163-67. At a penny per pound, 5,000 pounds equals about £21. *Inv. & Accts.*, Liber 2, f. 149; Liber 4, f. 606; Liber 7A, f. 128. The highest prices in these early years were in Anne Arundel County, at 6,000 and 6,500 apiece, but in the latter case, an account of administration dated some two years later reduced the valuation to 5,000. *Testamentary Proceedings*, Liber 2, f. 85; *Inv. & Accts.*, Liber 8, f. 109.

TABLE III.5
SEX RATIO, ADULTS/CHILDREN AMONG NEGRO SLAVES INVENTORIES OF ANNE ARUNDEL AND CALVERT COUNTIES

Years	No. Men	No. Women	Ratio M/W	No. Boys	No. Girls	No. Children	Total Children	Ratio Adult/Children	Ratio Boys/Girls	Corrected Ratio*	Ratio M/F
1656-1696	88	58	1.52	41	9	16	66	2.21	4.56	2.82	1.83
1697-1700	79	45	1.76	15	10	25	50	2.48	1.50	1.22	1.58
1701-1707	122	67	1.82	28	22	22	72	2.63	1.27	1.18	1.61
1708-1714	181	110	1.65	76	47	36	159	1.83	1.62	1.45	1.57
1715-1719	154	84	1.83	74	42	37	153	1.56	1.76	1.53	1.71

SOURCE: Probate records of two counties, Maryland, in Hall of Records, Annapolis.
* Corrected by assuming ratio of boys to girls among children not identified by sex is 1:1.

closes, women in prime childbearing years were relatively scarce, and this, together with the general dispersal and isolation of blacks in these early years, strongly inhibited family formation, just as it must have deterred the development of any sense of black community or of social or kinship networks among blacks.[86] For a man and a woman to establish close, supportive ties under such circumstances must have been difficult.

Before natural growth could take place, some kind of "critical mass" was necessary, one that furnished propinquity of numbers plus a balance between men and women in relative youth. North of the Potomac, that "mass" did not come into being until well into the eighteenth century.[87] Numerous cargoes direct from Africa at the end of the previous century actually worsened the already lopsided ratio between the sexes and reduced the proportion of children among inventoried slaves, but during the "dormant" period of 1708-1714, when tobacco prices were depressed and no more slaves were delivered, the relative numbers of children increased and the sex imbalance among adults eased a bit. Rising tobacco prices after 1715 then reversed this process, as more men were again imported. However, the proportion of children enumerated continued to rise, evidence that family formation had taken place at an unprecedented rate in the previous years, pushing the birthrate well above the death level.

Mulattoes appeared early in Maryland history, testimony to other consequences of racial propinquity. Like all the other British colonies in the New World, Maryland reversed the usual English practice in which the condition of the children normally followed that of the father. Many white men, therefore, came to treat their own children as property, denying them all claims on themselves as parent. Illegitimate white children could press no claims under English law, either, but they were born free. The zealous protection of property rights so characteristic of English society, with its rigorous insistence on the sanctity of contracts and patrilineal priority, here seems to have gone awry. Racism and greed combined to override English justice.

For much of the seventeenth century, then, most blacks in Maryland were immigrants, the products of an unorganized and uncertain slave trade with Virginia and the West Indies, or of white

[86] Allan Kulikoff, "The Beginnings of the Afro-American Family in Maryland," in Land, Carr, and Papenfuse, *Early Maryland*, pp. 171-96.

[87] Table III.5 contains data from the inventories of Anne Arundel and Calvert counties. See also Menard, "Maryland Slave Population," pp. 29-54.

emigrants carrying their human chattels with them. Marginal in number and marginal in status, most of these blacks lived and worked among whites. Whether their loneliness and homesickness were assuaged or exacerbated by protracted intimacy with members of a dominant and alien race, we can only ponder.

ONE of the more remarkable facts to come to light about the workaday world of Maryland slaves and servants is their dispersal into small groups, and the relative isolation of these bands. The purpose for such decentralization of operations in the tobacco economy was twofold: first, to allow the cattle and hogs to live off the land, and second, to place the laborers close to the best lands for raising tobacco. Thus, farming activity repeatedly shifted location in order to make use of scarce labor resources more efficiently.[88] Table III.6 provides an overview of the distribution of bound laborers among work sites in the early eighteenth century. The groups of laborers generally consisted of a core of four or five field hands supplemented by one or two women who cooked, washed, and supervised the children, who also formed an integral part of these little communities. Workers tended cattle and hogs as well as corn and tobacco, but few had horses. The numbers of cattle per hand ranged around seven or eight, and of hogs about five or six.

Living conditions at these outlying quarters can only be described as spare in the extreme. For those whose primary duties centered on the tobacco crop, there was no reason to stay on at these quarters once the crop was in. They may have returned to the home plantation for the winter months and perhaps a round of socializing, since the biggest planters often had Negro quarters at the home plantation as well as camp facilities at the outlying work sites.

Let us turn to specific examples of the disposition of servants and slaves among work sites in order to examine more closely the conditions of slavery in Maryland, not only to reconstruct the material content of their daily lives but to probe their spatial relationships with whites, particularly with servants. In that way, perhaps, we can detect unspoken attitudes toward their race and status among both blacks and whites.

In the early period, as outlined above, blacks and whites generally worked together and lived together in relatively small households. Bedding, clothing, and diet were much the same for everybody

[88] Surpluses of farm animals were not necessarily sold or killed off, but loaned to lessors or tenants on shares as an encouragement to take up and improve underused lands owned by the larger planters.

TABLE III.6

DISTRIBUTION OF BOUND LABORERS AMONG WORK SITES IN ESTATES WITH FIVE OR MORE SERVANTS AND SLAVES, 1700-1719

Average No. Slaves and Servants	Average No. Work Sites	Average No. Slaves and Servants per Site[a]	Average No. "Hands" per Site[b]	Average No. Cattle per "Hand"[c]	Average No. Hogs per "Hand"[d]
5-9	1.85	3.7	2.2	—	—
10-19	2.5	5.7	3.4	7.35	6.3
20-34	3.6	7.5	4.2	8.4	7.0
35-49	4.8	8.8	5.0	6.75	6.0

SOURCE: Probate records of six counties, Maryland, in Hall of Records, Annapolis.

[a] Correlation coefficient R^2 + .347 between no. sites and no. servants and slaves, "S & S."

[b] Correlation coefficient R^2 + .407 between no. sites and no. "hands," here defined as white men, and black men and women in good health and under age 45, where age is known.

[c] Among those with 11 or more bound laborers, 28 observations were possible, which yielded these correlation coefficients: no. cattle with no. "hands," + .731; no. cattle with no. S & S, + .782; no. cattle with no. work sites, + .537.

[d] Among those with eleven or more bound laborers, 27 possible for calculating a correlation coefficient between no. hogs with no. "hands," + .795.

except the richest planters and their families. That primitive intimacy and propinquity between the races eroded as the numbers of slaves rose and as their white companions vanished, never to be replaced. We must beware, however, of sentimentalizing the relationships between slave, servant, and master in the halcyon days of an expanding frontier. Masters demanded obedience and respectful behavior from their bondsmen, and whites regarded blacks as a race apart.

The rather remarkable case of Colonel Benjamin Rozer provides a concrete example of a wealthy planter who owned large numbers of bound laborers and used them at a variety of tasks on scattered work sites. Rozer's work force in 1681 consisted of sixty-nine men, women, and children—black, white, even red among them. This racial diversity was not unusual in the period 1680-1700, when the immigration from England had slackened and the more affluent planters were turning to slaves to supplement the insufficient numbers of prime white man servants. What was unusual about Rozer's work force was its abnormal size, the largest encountered in the probate records of the six counties before the eighteenth century. All other assemblages of forty or more appeared after 1696 and were overwhelmingly black.[89]

Colonel Rozer was a wealthy Protestant who had married Charles Calvert's daughter, making him triply valuable to the proprietary party in Maryland, the members of which were at some pains to appoint Protestants loyal to their cause to important provincial offices.[90] Rozer served as receiver-general and provincial secretary, among other profitable offices, and owned more than 4,000 acres at his death in 1681. His principal plantation, in Charles County at St. Patrick's above the head of Port Tobacco Creek, lay across the wide Potomac from Virginia. On Augustin Herrman's beautifully detailed map of 1670, six plantations appear along this creek, effectively boxing in Rozer's capability to expand from home base.[91] He solved some of his space and management problems by entering into a partnership with another planter at "Bracewick," where seven of his servants, including one Indian, worked. Rozer's work force was further scattered among other sites: one contained five white man servants plus a servant couple, a man and his wife who were to serve three years and four months from the date the inventory

[89] Rozer's inventory begins on f. 198 of *Inv. & Accts.*, Liber 27C.

[90] Carr and Jordan, *Maryland's Revolution of Government*, pp. 32-43.

[91] Augustin Herrman, *Virginia and Maryland . . . Surveyed and Exactly Drawn* (London, 1673), in the Library of Congress, Division of Geography and Maps.

was taken. To another site, "Jack's," he sent two men servants, and at the dwelling plantation on Port Tobacco Creek there were twelve more servants, four of them women. Two slaves also lived there, a Negro man and an Indian man who was described by the appraisers as a servant for life.

Elsewhere the work force was entirely colored: at "Indian Field," there were three Negro men and an Indian lad, plus three Negro women and seven Negro children. At "Tomboy's," seven Negro men (one of them old), two Negro women, and four Negro children lived. Finally, the twelve stationed at "War Captain's Neck" included six men, two women (one of them old), and four children.

As this distribution of Rozer's people demonstrates, whites and blacks owned by the same man did not necessarily live and work side by side. They more often lived in small clusters that tended to be all white or all colored. Captain John Bayne's workers provide another illustration of a racially diverse assemblage. When he died in 1703, his inventory listed twenty-four Negro and mulatto slaves and fifteen white servants, the largest number of servants owned by any one man in the probate records of the six counties after 1696.[92] At Bayne's home plantation, eleven black slaves worked under two man servants. A servant tailor also resided there. Besides the home plantation, Bayne operated five other work sites, two of which were run on shares by free tenants. Nine servants, meanwhile, worked at Pascataway Quarter, and four Negroes operated Aberdeen Quarter. Only at Forest Quarter did a truly mixed crew reside. A Negro man, woman, and four-year-old girl lived there, probably as a family, with three man servants.

Regardless of the racial makeup of large holdings, where and how the members were used varied from planter to planter. Some masters concentrated their workers at just one or two sites and hired overseers on annual contracts to supervise them from first sowing to the housing of the crop, or even to the final stripping and packing, a task that required considerable skill and experience. Other planters, by contrast, spread their work force thinly and left them without close supervision.

The nature of the site determined the primary tasks of the workers assigned there, and this in turn regulated the numbers necessary. Let us take a closer look at these patterns of labor usage among large slaveowners. Henry Darnall's estate in 1712 provides an ex-

---

[92] This is my reconstruction based on three inventories, one of which included his wife's "reserve," taken in 1702 and 1703. *Inv. & Accts.*, Liber 22, f. 32, and Liber 24, f. 134.

ample of relatively concentrated distributions of slaves presided over by hired white overseers.[93] He operated his home plantation with eighteen Negroes, staffed five other quarters with some forty-five more under three overseers, and placed the "Woodyard" under the direction of two slave carpenters who presided over a black community of some thirty-eight individuals. Not all of these slaves were of prime quality and age—nor were those in our previous examples. This point requires emphasis, since the dispersion and tasks assigned many were also shaped by the needs of dependent slaves such as children, nursing and pregnant mothers, and the elderly. Planters using servants only did not have to tailor each individual assignment so closely. Only half, or even fewer, of the Negroes in any large work force were healthy young adults, prime field hands, as contrasted with the preponderance of such workers among white immigrants. On Darnall's home plantation, for instance, out of the eighteen slaves only nine were fit adults. Overseer William Fisher's sixteen slaves included four little girls and a baby, whereas overseer James Willard's twenty-three included a dozen children plus an old woman "past labor."

If we count "hands," rather than heads, we find that nine of Darnall's hands worked at home, twenty-four at the Woodyard, which was not a farming site but a lumbering facility, and an average of five or six at each of the other five locations. No separate sleeping arrangements for the Negroes at home were identified as such by Darnall's appraisers, but they were probably housed together, since a frying pan, four iron pots, a kettle, a bell-metal skillet, and two spits were grouped together at the close of the listing of goods at the "Dwelling House." William Fisher's two quarters were equipped with five iron pots and a frying pan, and presumably Fisher slept in the only bed mentioned, a flock tick with rug worth £2. James Walland's two quarters were similarly stocked, but two fowling pieces there promised welcome variety in the edibles. The third overseer, Darby Conners, had only an old flock bed to sleep in, worth just six shillings. His all-black crew cooked with four iron pots and two frying pans, but, again, we know nothing about their sleeping arrangements. It would be reasonable to suppose that no slave had a bed worth as much as the overseer's, even if the overseer were a mere Irishman, as Conners apparently was.

In sharp contrast to the highly concentrated siting of work operations in Darnall's case, Captain Richard Smith, Esquire, carried

[93] Ibid., Liber 33B, f. 221.

132

on operations at ten different locations, while also acting as a share-owner in a mill on St. Leonard's Creek, where one of his Negro men worked.[94] Smith kept cattle on an island, but he did not place any of his people there. Some twenty-three Negroes were "at home and at Okee's," of whom only eleven were "hands." Elsewhere, still fewer, on the average, worked at each site. Fifteen hands ran seven quarters stocked with an average of six cattle and seven hogs per hand. The individual circumstances varied a good deal. Only one Negro man was stationed at Spelman's Quarter, where he watched over ten cattle, seven hogs, four sheep, and a "plow mare." Two men and one woman worked at Hector's Quarter, taking care of thirteen cattle and thirty-five sheep. Their cooking equipment consisted of just one iron pot and a small frying pan. The two men at Cox Town Quarter not only had two iron pots, but a hand mill as well, which was a luxury. They had the care of three horses, fifty-five hogs and pigs, and twenty-three cattle. Nine Negroes at Old Jack's Quarter used one frying pan and nothing else, if the appraisers listed everything. There were no cooking utensils at all at Spelman's, Jenkins', Benedict Town, or Locust Thicket.

Only one bed, three pots, and two frying pans constituted virtually the entire housekeeping equipment at all these sites, so that we must assume that the workers walked out to them every day or that they merely camped there for a season, carrying their bedrolls and cooking things back and forth as needed. The absence of these things from the individual site inventories makes it difficult to assess the conditions of daily life, but it is doubtful that the number and variety of things packed in and out would have been any greater than the contents of poor planters' homes, which we will be considering in Chapter Five.

The inventory of George Plater's estate does include lists of the "necessaries" of daily life on quarters away from the home plantation, although the lists may not be complete.[95] Plater used white servants, not freemen, as local foremen in residence where the Negroes worked.[96] Associated with servant Edward Malone, for instance, were three blacks: a man, woman, and child, probably a

---

[94] Ibid., Liber 36C, f. 1.

[95] Ibid., Liber 28, f. 26.

[96] One particularly notable foreman in the present case was Daniel Dulany I, who managed the home plantation with its fourteen slaves, of whom only three men and three "lads" qualified as full-time, full-strength laborers. For an account of Dulany and his son, see Aubrey C. Land, *The Dulanys of Maryland: Daniel Dulany the Elder (1685-1753) and Daniel Dulany the Younger (1722-1797)* (Baltimore, 1955).

family, although the appraisers did not describe them as such. This little group tended twenty-eight cattle, fourteen hogs, fifty sheep, a cart horse, two geldings, and two mares with their colts. The household furnishings consisted of two flock beds, one worth £1, the other only five shillings, one old bed "for the Negroes" at six shillings, an iron pot, a little iron kettle with "one bale broke off," an iron pestle, an old gun, and some tools.

At another site, servant boy John Browne's Negro companions included two men, George and Tom, and three women: old Bess, Diddy, and Jenny Cukenson, plus a lad, thirteen-year-old Gregory, and two smaller boys, Andrew and Tom, for a total of eight.[97] This assemblage watched over seventeen cattle, twenty-three hogs, and a mare and her colt, a far smaller number of animals per person than Edward Malone's people took care of. Indoors, Browne's groups used three iron pots for cooking and two pestles for grinding corn. There were neither kettles nor frying pans. The only bed listed, presumably Browne's, was appraised at £1.5, whereas "old bedding" for the Negroes was valued at just ten shillings, or fifteen pence apiece.

On two of Plater's plantations in adjacent Charles County, the same kind of pattern reappears. Servant William Verling presided over a small company of Negroes at Popes Creek, which included an old man, Jack, a woman, Hester, and two boys, Ned and Tobie. They cared for twenty cattle, twenty-five hogs and pigs, and three horses. In this case, no bedding at all was listed for the blacks, but a flock bed was valued at £2.75. Equipment for food preparation consisted of two small iron pots and a pestle, but they also had two pails—for water and milk, perhaps—and a common bowl for eating.

At Nanjemy, servant John Bell worked with Negro men Peter, Scipio, Andrew, and Tom, and with women Judy, Agathy, and Betty. Four little girls, Moll, Jenny, Nan, and Caty had each other for company, and Ned and little Frank completed the ensemble. Again only one bed is listed, which at £4 was the single most valuable one encountered outside a "big house" on any plantation anywhere in the inventories of the six counties. One suspects that Plater himself used it when he arrived for an inspection.

The relationship between individual white male servants and slaves of both sexes and all ages on George Plater's plantations resembles that between a supervisor and his crew. A similar pattern

---

[97] Note the inclusion of a last name for Jenny Cuckenson. The appraisers were uncomfortable about it. They carefully wrote out, "a Negor woman called Jenny Cukenson," estimating her value at less than Diddy's but more than Old Bess's.

prevailed among many other large planters' dispositions of their work forces. Colonel William Dent, for instance, owned thirty-three Negro, mulatto, and Indian slaves, plus two mulattoes who were to serve only until age thirty-one, and five white servants.[98] At the home house and quarter at Nanjemy, perhaps near Plater's place there, a white man servant lived along with seven hands: the two young mulatto servants, the Indian woman and boy, two Negro men and two Negro women, one old, and a Negro boy and girl. No servant, however, is listed with the twelve mulatto and Negro slaves at the quarter at Portobacco, where possibly a hired overseer had charge. A white man and woman worked with three Negro men at the lower quarter at Mattawoman, and a white man and boy worked at the upper quarter there, with ten Negroes and mulattoes. Four iron pots and a hand mill supplied the limited kitchen equipment at Portobacco, where they also had a fowling gun, but it was "much out of kilter."

The marsh ducks were just as safe from Dent's work crew at Mattawoman Creek, since the two old gun barrels there were quite useless. The lower quarter had two old iron pots, but nothing more. The upper quarter had two frying pans, three pots, and even some pewter, rare materials for mere servitors' quarters. No beds or bedding were identified as specifically for the use of the Negroes. The only one at the upper quarter was worth £3, and the one at Portobacco was valued together with the two iron pots at only eight shillings, so it was not much of a bed.

Working in widely scattered areas in small groups, under the eye and direction of servants or overseers, most slaves in early eighteenth-century Maryland lived in bare, camp-style settings, as the foregoing illustrations have suggested. Native Americans and West Africans did not use tables, chairs, bedsteads, and so forth, nor did they use much metalware, so it is inappropriate to condemn the furnishings supplied to the slaves as "inadequate." More troubling, however, is the absence of sufficient bedding. Coastal Maryland's climate is decidedly raw and cold for five or six months out of the year, yet the housing provided for the work crews, including servants and freemen, offered scanty shelter, and "parcels of old bedding" were insufficient as well as unsanitary. Indians and Africans would have supplied themselves with wall hangings to cut off drafts.

It is fair to say that the condition of both slaves and servants varied more from owner to owner and site to site than it did between

[98] *Will Book 3. Inv. & Accts.*, Liber 25, f. 390.

slave and servant. Those in supervisory positions, whether white or black, were more likely to have real beds of significant monetary value listed in the inventories of their masters, and this leads one to the conclusion that everyone else made do on inferior pallets, most likely piles of tree boughs or marsh reeds on which were spread blankets and clothing. For added warmth, perhaps the dogs were called inside, Indian-fashion. Fleas were surely preferable to chillblains, and one can eventually build some tolerance against their bites.

The slaves' food was the same as the Indians' and poorer planters', although they probably received less meat than did servants, and both probably got less than their master and his family if he were among the more affluent.[99] Despite the difficulties presented by the sources, we can also conclude that slaves, servants, and poor planters did not dress very differently from each other.[100] None possessed very good or adequate clothing by modern standards.

Mortality may not have favored one race against another in the tidewater, although we know rather little about the relative immunities each enjoyed or lacked. Concentration on tobacco, however, required the workers' presence during the months of heavy mortality associated with polluted estuaries and mosquito-borne diseases.[101] Native Amerindians of the area traditionally withdrew

[99] Food and cooking styles are discussed more fully in Chapter Five below.

[100] Analysis of clothing for all classes is found in Chapter Six below.

[101] Malaria, dysentery, and smallpox were among the primary causes of ill health and early death, and probably influenza should be added. Actual mortality conditions varied locally. In Charles Parish, Virginia, the average age at death among adult males, native-born and white, was only 39.9. On the lower western shore of Maryland it averaged 46.0, and in Middlesex County, Virginia it reached 48.8. In New England, it was well over 60 in the seventeenth century. Daniel Blake Smith, "Mortality and Family," pp. 403-27, cites all the relevant studies. Carville V. Earle argues provocatively that the fresh water-saltwater transition zones of the river estuaries of the Chesapeake were the most dangerous, particularly in summer, due to pollution of the ground water by human wastes. "Environment, Disease, and Mortality," in Tate and Ammerman, eds., *Chesapeake*, pp. 96-125. There is some dispute about the relative health and immunity of Amerindians. Lawson argued that those who lived in the hilly back-country were the healthiest, citing their "Gigantick Stature, and Gray-heads," Lawson, *New Voyage*, p. 82. By implication, the lowland Indians must have been less healthy or long-lived. William Hranicky examined 316 skeletons of early Virginia Indians, all currently housed at the Smithsonian, of which some 164 were adults, and only eleven were estimated to have been older than age 55. The median may have been under age 40. The Rev. John Clayton asserted that the English and the Indians were alike, if they lived "past 33 they generally live to a good age, but many die between 30 & 33." William Jack Hranicky, "A Plaeodemographic Study of Prehistoric Virginia Skeletons," *Quarterly*

136

to the healthier and cooler piedmont regions of the interior when warm weather arrived, but the planters and their "families" stayed behind and suffered the consequences.

Living conditions for slaves were harsh, but they were little better for servants, freedmen, or poor planters, and may have improved for all with the passage of time. Social changes did meliorate slaves' lives as the growth of their numbers improved opportunity to marry, form families, establish kinship relations, and develop real communities.[102]

In the early period, most slaves did not have the comfort of family life. Theirs, like that of the whites, was a heavily male society, and the sheer hopelessness of it all must have greatly added to their burden. Fortunately, their work did not consist solely of hoeing corn and tobacco. Chopping firewood, hewing timber, clearing brush, mowing marshgrass, drawing water, lightering goods, rounding up cattle, pressing cider in the fall—these and many other tasks relieved the monotony of fieldwork. Winters were "slow" times to be spent indoors, providing frequent opportunities for relaxed socializing, whereas holidays such as Christmas and the king's birthday brought celebratory drink, festive foods and other treats, along with dancing, singing, and other party delights. The rest of the year, servants and slaves had time off on Saturday afternoons and Sundays, by general custom, and slave funerals occasioned large gatherings, which not only gave relief from work and master, but provided the means to build community identity through shared ritual.[103]

Bulletin of the Archeological Society of Virginia, XXX (1975), 1-17; *The Reverend John Clayton, A Parson with a Scientific Mind; His Scientific Writings and Other Related Papers*, edited by Edmund and Dorothy Smith Berkeley (Charlottesville, 1965), 38. Finally, Kenneth F. and Virginia H. Kiple discuss the differences between whites and blacks in their immunities to yellow fever, which was not a factor in Chesapeake mortality of the period under discussion, and of malaria as well: "Black Yellow Fever Immunities, Innate and Acquired, as Revealed in the American South," *Social Science History*, I (1977), 419-36. Despite different resistance and immunity patterns that characterized the three races, it is doubtful that the area proved any more mortal for whites living outside that fresh water-salt water transition zone along rivers than for captive slaves who had no choice, or for Indians foolish enough to disregard their own inherited folk wisdom.

[102] Slave families, specifically labeled as such by appraisers, appear as early as 1663, for instance, and gradually became more common as time went on. *Testamentary Proceedings*, Liber 1D, f. 163; *Inv. & Accts.*, Liber 2, f. 127; Liber 10B, f. 3; Liber 13A, f. 120; Liber 34, f. 170; Liber 37C, f. 7.

[103] "R. G." asserted that servants got Saturday afternoon off by the custom of the country. "Virginia's Cure, or an Advisive Narrative Concerning Virginia: Discov-

Opportunities for socializing probably occurred more often among members of larger holdings than for servants and slaves living in their master's own household. One such occasion emerges vividly from court depositions in a case heard in 1681 by William Byrd I and a fellow justice in Henrico County, Virginia. On a hot afternoon in August, a group of freemen and servants, including one woman, all in their twenties and thirties, had gathered together to drink the planter's cider with half a dozen Negro and mulatto slaves after spending the day cutting down weeds in the orchard. The supply of the mildly alcoholic beverage proved more than ample, as one woman, a guest among them and the wife of a Quaker who lived in the neighborhood, began to exhibit that cheerful relaxing of decorum often associated with light intoxication. Her openly amorous attentions were focused on the young slave boys, and on one handsome mulatto lad in particular. Since she later accused him of raping her while she was returning home that day, the judges were concerned to discover whether she might not have actually seduced him and then sought to avoid her husband's wrath by accusing her lover of forcible rape. Witnesses of her behavior earlier clearly believed that she had brought it on herself, but we do not know the outcome of the case and what punishment, if any, the young slave ultimately received. No one, be it noticed, had rushed out to string him up, and the long-suffering husband merely warned him off when the terrified slave attempted to apologize to him for his act.[104]

The picture that at first emerges from the depositions of the white witnesses suggests a congenial mingling of free persons, white servants, and black slaves, but closer reading of the evidence reveals that racial boundaries were carefully observed. The tipsy coquette was actually engaged in a cruel teasing, and the young male slaves sought earnestly to avoid offending both her and the white men present. Their studied decorum succeeded in fending off criticism

---

ering the true Ground of that Churches Unhappiness, and the only true Remedy. As it was presented to the Right Reverend Father in God Guilbert Lord Bishop of London, September 2, 1661," in Force, *Tracts*, III, 10. Two masters punished on complaint of their servants for making them work on the Sabbath may be found in *Md.Arch.*, X, 474, 485. One complaint dealt with beating corn and baking it, the other for hunting with a gun! An Act "for Preventing Insurrections among Slaves" stated that "whereas the frequent meeting of considerable numbers of negroe slaves under pretence of feasts and burialls is judged of dangerous consequence . . ." and was passed as early as 1680. Hening, *Statutes at Large*, II, 481-82 quoted in Billings, ed., *Old Dominion*, p. 173.

[104] Ibid., 161-63.

and possibly worse. This becomes clear in the remarks of the white men in court, most of whom were not only contemptuous of the woman involved but also utterly indifferent to the helplessness of the slaves. Since slave testimony was not admissible as evidence, the records do not let us hear their side of the story.

Servants and slaves worked together, drank together, often lived together, in the early years of plantation society, sharing the same rough life, the same hardships, the same abuse. They had much in common and seemed to have associated more equally than we might have supposed, but they were not equal, just as servants were not equal to freemen, nor ordinary planters to their "betters." Differences in status counted, in life chances and in sense of self. White servants often acted as overseers to blacks; the reverse rarely occurred.[105] Servants rather than slaves supplied most of the skilled craftsmen. Sexual opportunities for white male servants may have been more frequent than for black men in the seventeenth century, but neither had enough by modern standards. Whites, however, had elected their lot and could look forward to eventual freedom and a chance, somewhere, to get a place of their own. The most burdensome legacy of enslavement, surely, was its hopelessness.[106]

[105] There is mention of a Negro overseer in the complaint made by a woman servant who resented it, quoted in Bruce, *Economic History*, II, 18. This took place in 1669.

[106] Some Virginians began to regret their headlong purchases of Africans. In 1710, the Virginia House of Burgesses supported an increase in duties on imported slaves after referring to an abortive slave insurrection that had recently taken place. Of that insurrection, the *Journal* noted, "freedom wears a Cap which Can Without a Tongue, Call Together all Those who long to Shake of the fetters of Slavery." Quoted in Rainbolt, "Alteration," p. 429.

139

Chapter Four

HOUSING IN EARLY MARYLAND

Perhaps the most striking thing about seventeenth-century Maryland is how long it remained in a frontier condition. If it were possible for us to step back in time and ride a boat going up one of its rivers, we would see vast unbroken stands of gigantic trees along the spines of higher ground, interspersed by abandoned fields and overgrown thickets with occasional sagging houses and dilapidated barns. The long intervals of green shoreline are only occasionally interrupted by villagelike clusters of small buildings that mark the home plantations of the larger planters, but nowhere would we see great mansions rising from grassy knolls or long sweeps of lawn leading down to the waterside. The landings to which we tie up our boat lead us instead to small wooden houses, unpainted and unadorned. No formal space stands before or behind the principal structure, if one can so be defined, nor is there an orderly disposition of the farm buildings. Only the beaten pathways between link them together into a working whole.

If the untidy, unplanned, and unsymmetrical layout of the typical plantation is dismaying, the interiors of the homes prove even bleaker. There we find few comforts and no conveniences. Most colonial furniture consists of homemade pieces from local soft woods, roughly dressed and nailed together. Dirt or plank floors bear no coverings, nor do curtains hang at the glassless windows.

The beautiful old homes and furniture displayed in the picture books are misleading. That was not the way most tidewater planters and their families lived, not even in the eighteenth century. The houses they lived in and the things they used have disappeared with the years. What survives is unusual because it has survived. Houses are particularly deceiving because we see them as they are, not as they were. Few authentic structures from the seventeenth century still stand, and the early dating of many supposed specimens is open to serious question.[1]

[1] Cary Carson, Norman F. Barka, William M. Kelso, Garry Wheeler Stone, and Dell Upton, "Impermanent Architecture in the Southern American Colonies," *Winterthur Portfolio*, XVI (1981), 135-96. Careful searches by archeologists and historians have turned up fewer than seven surviving seventeenth-century buildings in Mary-

Existing buildings in their present guise are in no way typical of the past. The differing survival values of wood and brick overwhelmingly favor the latter. As the passage of time shrinks the sample, structures of brick—chimneys, walls, or foundations—come to dominate. Since people tend to save and repair only objects of unusual value, including homes of superior quality, this too biases the sample. Repairs, additions, and improvements in the meanwhile can so alter the original as to make it difficult to identify the authentically old within later layers of encasement. Seldom does one get the opportunity to dissect an old house, but only so radical a course can really restore it to its condition when it was lived in by the people who built it.

Most of the great colonial houses of Maryland standing today—and of Virginia as well—are the products of the eighteenth century, and of another world. For the first century of settlement, the planters lived in straggling wooden boxes dribbled over the landscape without apparent design.[2] These structures were of wood because the forests offered an abundant supply of building material, with which most English immigrants were familiar. Clearing fresh ground was a never-ending process in an agricultural system that relied on very long fallow periods to restore the fertility of the soil. An experienced hand could dress a log quickly with his ax, cleave clapboards, rive shingles, and hammer in a nail cleanly. Such skills were sufficient for finishing the box-frame structures that dominated wooden building construction in old England.[3]

Architectural styles of farmhouses in the mother country were diverse, nevertheless. England in the sixteenth and seventeenth centuries did not form an integrated culture, but consisted of separate regions, each with its own folkways, dialects, and material culture, and all were still isolated from each other as well as from the world at large.[4] In the south, for instance, the hall still kept its traditional central importance and rooms were added at the "parlour" end, one of which might be a service room, variously called

---

land and Virginia. This fine article summarizes the technical findings and offers an explanation that differs little from that offered here.

[2] "Dribbled" is Henry Glassie's inspired adjective. See his provocative but ahistorical study of folk architecture in Virginia, *Folk Housing in Middle Virginia* (Philadelphia, 1975).

[3] R. W. Brunskill, *Illustrated Handbook of Vernacular Architecture* (London, 1970), pp. 50-51. James Deetz, *In Small Things Forgotten* (Boston, 1972), p. 102, reports on evidence of a cruck structure in Flowerdew Hundred in Virginia.

[4] The discussion that follows is based on M. W. Barley, "Rural Housing in England," in Thirsk, ed., *Agrarian History*, pp. 696-766.

kitchen, milkhouse, or buttery. Preparation of meals, however, continued in the hall itself. An upper story, a "loft" if reached by ladder and a "chamber" if by stairs, was over the parlor and open to the hall. This upper story was used primarily for storage and only secondarily as sleeping quarters, depending on the size of the farm household. Even in wealthy Kent, yeoman farmers did not attempt to house servants or hired hands under their own roofs before 1660 or thereabouts.[5]

Farmhouses in the northern counties, which were poorer than those in the south, were built along simpler lines. These consisted of the hall or "hall house," possibly with a kitchen or milkhouse, and maybe one or two chambers, all on the ground floor. In the west, "kitchens" were sometimes detached from the farmhouse itself, but the name was also used for a brewhouse or bakehouse, that is, for any room with a special hearth and equipment.[6] This being so, such rooms, even when attached, may not have been regarded as part of the house where the family lived, ate, and worked together, much as today's attached garage is viewed as being outside the house. The western farmer's concept of a house, apparently, differed from those of farmers living elsewhere in England, because rooms with differing functions were often built as separate structures loosely disposed around a central courtyard. In southeastern England, by contrast, the improving farmer built upward, formally integrating rooms of various functions into a single, imposing pile.

The houses of farmers, who formed a distinct and propertied class in England, must be distinguished from the usual abode of the great majority of rural inhabitants, the farm "labourers." Such was always termed a "cottage." "Cottage" and "labourer" were class terms, the former determined by its association with the latter, arising strictly from the fact that a man had to offer himself for hire. Thus, "cottage" referred to a structure usually, but not necessarily, distinguished by small size and mean materials, housing a family that was dependent to some extent, or even totally, on employment by others. The general insubstantiability of construction

---

[5] The extended farm household became more common in the eighteenth century, as both the scale and organization of farming altered.

[6] Gervaise Markham, *Country Contentments . . . The English Housewife: Containing the inward and outward vertues which ought to be in a compleate Woman: as her Phisicke, Cookery, Banqueting-stuffe, Distillation, Perfumes, Wooll, Hemp, Flaxe, Dairies, Brewing, Baking, and all other things belonging to an Household* (London, 1615; repr. New York, 1973), p. 127.

is attested by the fact that no authentic English cottage dating before 1700 has survived, despite the earnest endeavors of hundreds of field searchers to locate one.

Small size and insubstantiability, therefore, characterized the dwellings of a numerous class in the rural areas of England, one noteworthy for its dependence on the propertied class. Since most Maryland planters and their families occupied structures that were likewise small and insubstantial, upper-class visitors to the colonial Chesapeake tended to regard such dwellings as evidence of low status for their occupants. Misled by their own preconceptions, they failed to appreciate the true rank of such people, and often found themselves disconcerted by the boldness of their carriage.

English immigrants to the New World carried with them, then, not a single, homogeneous building tradition but a bundle of possible housing styles from which to choose. The prevalence of timber and the humidity of the summers in the Chesapeake guided their selection toward low and airy structures rather than toward the compact, upright houses designed to conserve heat that flourished in New England. Old England provided the models and technology in both cases, nevertheless. Colonists in both areas rejected Indian models, and did not erect log cabins.[7] Their first houses used saplings stuck into the ground at close intervals, not unlike the Indian wigwam, but this was also a technique familiar to forest inhabitants of contemporary England. These "punches" were overlaid with riven boards, however, and not with wattle and daub as in England or with the skins of animals or woven mats, as among the Indians.[8] When resources and time permitted, planters built box frame struc-

[7] Harold Shurtleff so effectively demolished the "log cabin myth" that it is with temerity that one offers a few scattered examples of log structures serving as habitations in Maryland. Three "loged hows" occur in the Charles County court records for the years 1658, 1662, and 1663; *Md.Arch.*, XLIII, 232, 381-82, 356-57. Baltimore County Court Proceedings and Land Records, at the Hall of Records, Annapolis, mention log houses with lofts in 1693 and 1694. Another was described in 1703 as "old" and "ready to fall down" (pp. 143-44). Some log houses also appear in Kent County in the early eighteenth century. *Inv. & Accts.*, Liber 28, f. 186 and Liber 32, f. 40. C. A. Weslager, *The Log Cabin in America: From Pioneer Days to the Present* (New Brunswick, N.J., 1969), chapter 6, "The Maryland Planters," pp. 135-47. Charles County and Baltimore County references appear on pp. 142-44. The former cannot be explained by Scandinavian influence, since this county is on the lower western shore and was settled from Virginia. For Shurtleff's coverage of Virginia and Maryland, see *The Log Cabin Myth: A Study of the Early Dwellings of the English Colonies in North America* (Cambridge, Mass., 1939).

[8] Records of the Virginia Company, IV, 259, quoted in Morgan, *American Slavery*, p. 112.

tures sided with clapboard and roofed with shingles.[9] Such continued to be the dominant type of housing throughout the colonial
period, greatly to the chagrin of Thomas Jefferson, who complained that "the private buildings are very rarely constructed of
stone or brick, much the greatest portion being of scantling and
boards, plastered with lime. It is impossible to devise things more
ugly, uncomfortable, and happily more perishable."[10]

[9] See "A contract for a Frame House, Henrico County Deed Book, 1677-1692,"
in Billings, *Old Dominion*, p. 306. This was forty feet long and twenty feet wide, with
a partition through the middle, two outside chimneys, weather boarded, to cost
1,200 pounds tobacco and cask. Another such contract, quoted in full, may be found
in *WMQ*, XV (1907), reprinted in Henry C. Forman, *Early Manor and Plantation
Houses of Maryland* (Easton, Md., 1934), p. 246. One Paul Simpson paid over a bill
of exchange for 20,000 pounds of tobacco in 1653 to Thomas Wilford of North-
umberland County, Virginia, in return for "Sufficient wholesome meate drink Ap-
parell both Linen and woolen lodging washing and all other Necessaryes well be-
seeming and fitting a Gentleman, and when Nayels and Carpenter can be had to
build him a fifteen foot house Square with a welsh Chimney, the house to be floored
and lofted with Deale boards, and lined with Riven Boards on the inside
. . ."; *Md.Arch.*, X, 301-302. See also Thomas Cornwallis' description of the house
he was building in 1638, in *Calvert Papers*, I (Baltimore, 1889), 138. Leonard Calvert's
own house is mentioned in *Md.Arch.*, IV, 189, 320-21. Edmund Plowden described
Virginia in 1648, which he disliked, as "most of it being seated scatteringly in wooden
clove board houses, where many by fire are undone"; Force, *Tracts*, II, no. 7, p. 4.
John Hammond, on the other hand, defended them as "Pleasant in their building,
which although for most part they are but one story beside the loft, and built of
wood . . . usually the rooms are large, daubed and whitelimed, glazed and flowered,
and if not glazed windows, shutters which are made very pretty and convenient."
Leah and Rachel, in Force, *Tracts*, III, no. 14, p. 29. Dankers and Sluyter expressed
nothing but contempt for the English clapboard houses they encountered in New
Jersey and Maryland, "the dwellings are so wretchedly constructed, that if you are
not so close to the fire as almost to burn yourself, you cannot keep warm, for the
wind blows through them everywhere." *Journal*, p. 173. Two articles by historical
archeologists report on three seventeenth-century Maryland houses, all of the box
frame type, in Gary Wheeler Stone, "St. John's: Archeological Questions and Answers," *MdHM.*, LXIX (1974), 146; and Cary Carson, "The 'Virginia House' in
Maryland," ibid., p. 186. As late as 1765, the twenty-eight dwellings of tenants living
on a Calvert family manor in Charles County were mostly one or two rooms, and
only a few had chimneys made of brick; Gregory A. Stiverson, "Landless Husbandmen: Proprietary Tenants in Maryland in the Late Colonial Period," in Land,
Carr, and Papenfuse, *Early Maryland*, p. 202. See also Richard Pillsbury and Andrew
Kardos, *A Field Guide to the Folk Architecture of the Northeastern United States* (Hanover,
N.H., n.d.), pp. 77-78. The best general work on late colonial Maryland architecture
is Henry Chandlee Forman, *Maryland Architecture: A Short History from 1634 through
the Civil War* (Cambridge, Md., 1968).

[10] Thomas Jefferson, *Notes on the State of Virginia, 1781*, edited by William Peden
(Chapel Hill, 1955). Monsieur Durand, however, reported that he saw "a number
of houses" in Virginia during his visit of 1686 which were built "entirely" of brick.
Durand, *Frenchman in Virginia*, p. 112.

Most colonial houses were structures framed with heavy posts hewn from nearby trees and assembled on the site. When the frame was raised into place, wooden pins inserted into the mortise-and-tenon joints held the parts together. Boards, more often split than sawn, of five or six feet in length, were nailed onto the outside of this frame, with ends overlapping. Since the wood had not been aged, gaps between the boards developed and widened as the wood warped while drying. These openings had to be filled in from the inside of the dwelling, which must have given the interior walls a curiously mottled effect. "The best people plaster them with clay," explained Messers. Dankers and Sluyter in 1680.[11] An early Pennsylvania pamphlet offered very precise instructions on how to build such a house, with a lower floor of dirt and an upper one of plank, reckoning the time to erect and finish it at only five or six weeks if a skilled carpenter were in charge.[12]

As the preferred roofing material, shingles replaced thatch despite their voracious appetite for nails. A well-made thatch roof will long outlast one of shingles, if a fire does not intervene, but repairing a shingle roof is a simple matter.[13] Thatch roofs were a far worse fire hazard, but it was for other reasons as well that they disappeared from southern homes. First, thatching took skill and experience, and special skills were always rare in the Chesapeake. Second, the materials were not abundant since straw-producing crops and suitable grasses were scarce. Finally, shingle making was an indoor, wintertime chore, whereas thatch must be gathered, cured, and applied in summertime, thus competing with corn and tobacco for a man's attention.

Brickmaking appeared early in the tidewater, but the construc-

[11] Dankers and Sluyter, *Journal*, p. 173.

[12] William Penn, *Information and Direction to Such Persons as are inclined to America, more Especially Those related to the Province of Pennsylvania* (London, 1684), cited in Shurtleff, *Log Cabin Myth*, pp. 124-26. The real author of this promotional pamphlet was probably not Penn himself.

[13] Thatch roofs are also very heavy, but the oak frames of the time could have supported them with ease. The process of riving shingles with a froe is beautifully described by a "life-long" resident of Metcalf County, Kentucky, in William Lynwood Montell and Michael Lynn Morse, *Kentucky Folk Architecture* (Lexington, Ky., 1976), p. 43. Riving and other woodworking chores are carefully illustrated by Eric Sloane in *A Museum of Early American Tools* (New York, 1964), upon which I have relied for its visual rendering of both the tools encountered in the inventories and how they were used. In nineteenth-century Kentucky, shingles were laid down only when the moon was full or "when it is growing." Folk belief had it that to put them on while the moon was dark or "shrinking" would cause them to curl up at the end, no matter how tightly they were pegged down. Montell and Morse, *Kentucky Folk Architecture*, p. 46.

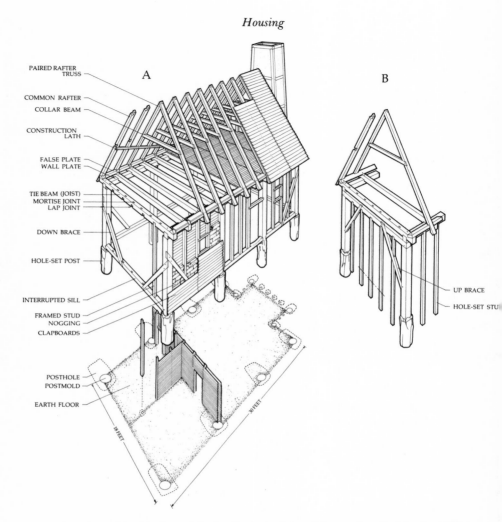

Reconstruction drawing of the "ordinary beginners" house described in the 1684 pamphlet *Information and Direction to Such Persons as are inclined to America.* Interpreted as a conventional Chesapeake hole-set frame house, with the addition of a timber chimney based on archaeological evidence . . . from River Creek (see Appendix 2:23). (B) Variation without sills showing hole-set studs, up braces, tilted false plates, and a possible interpretation of the two 18-foot spanning plates called for in the specifications that are otherwise difficult to explain. (Drawing, Cary Carson and Chinh Hoang.) Reprinted from *Winterthur Portfolio*, XIV, Nos. 2/3 (Summer/Autumn 1981) by permission of the University of Chicago Press. From Carson, Barka, Kelso, Stone, and Upton, "Impermanent Architecture in the Southern American Colonies," p. 143.

tion of brick chimneys was a demanding art.[14] Most planters in the seventeenth century settled for a "welsh" chimney, a wattle-and-daub affair variously described as of "catted" or "cribbed" poles laid crosswise one above the other, the interstices filled with clay daubing.[15] These chimneys were generally built on the outside of a gable end to reduce the danger from flying sparks.[16] Although brick chimneys gradually replaced wattle-and-daub stacks in houses of the more well-to-do planters, the pace of the transition was slow. As late as 1737, a Virginia statute continued the century-long struggle to banish these fire hazards from the province.[17]

After forty years' settlement, St. Mary's, the capital "city" of Maryland, consisted of "not above 30 houses spread five miles along the river's length and the buildings (as in all other parts of the Province), very mean and little, and generally after the manner of the meanest farmhouses in England."[18] Even by the end of the century, the brick construction at the new capital of Annapolis of the state house and the school was an accomplishment enthusiastically acclaimed because they "made a great shew among a parscell of wooden houses."[19] Nevertheless, a decade later, the provincial capital was lampooned as still a poor place, "where scarce a House will keep out Rain."[20]

In Virginia of the same period, most dwellings continued to be of wood. Although Robert Beverly did report that "severall gentlemen built themselves large brick houses of many rooms on a floor and several stories high," it is clear from his account that these were exceptional.[21]

For the vast majority of the residents in the tidewater region, then, the only changes that took place in house construction for at least a century were these three: the replacement of thatch by

[14] Bruce, *Economic History*, II, 143 cites a court case in 1674 in which one man sued another for the "negligent manner" in which he had built brick chimneys.

[15] Montell and Morse, *Kentucky Folk Architecture*, p. 2, illustrates this type of chimney with a photograph. Morgan, *Slavery*, p. 173 reports a Virginia contract of 1645, which included specifications for this kind of chimney.

[16] An outside chimney is in the diorama pictured in Richard Walsh and William Lloyd Fox, eds., *Maryland: A History, 1632-1974* (Baltimore, 1974), p. 14.

[17] W. W. Hening, ed., *The Statutes at Large, Being a Collection of All the Laws of Virginia* (1619-1792), V, 430.

[18] *Md.Arch.*, V, 363-64.

[19] Michael G. Kammen, ed., "Maryland in 1699: a Letter from the Reverend Hugh Jones," *JSH*, XXIX (1963), 372.

[20] Cook, *Sot-Weed Factor*, p. 24.

[21] Beverly, *History*, p. 152.

shingles, the gradually spreading use of brick in chimneys, and to an extent still unknown, the substitution of glass for oiled paper or empty space in windows protected by wooden shutters. The richer planters lived in expanded versions of the same houses, but their chimneys were of brick and they used stairs instead of ladders. The principal differences between rich and poor lay not in size and quality of housing but in the number of structures. "According to his means, each planter provides as many of such houses as he needs. They build also a separate kitchen, a house for the Christian slaves, another for negro slaves, and several tobacco barns, so that in arriving at the plantation of a person of importance you think you are entering a considerable village."[22] About this same time, William Fitzhugh was trying to sell his estate in Virginia's Northern Neck and described his plantation layout with undisguised satisfaction, "all houses for use furnished with brick chimneys, four good cellars, a dairy, dove cot, stable, barn, hen-house, kitchen, and all other convenienceys."[23]

A generation later, Robert Beverly reported similar building styles: "All their drudgeries of cookery, washing, dairies, etc., are performed in offices detached from the dwelling houses which by this means are kept more cool and sweet."[24]

Repeated efforts by governments to upgrade the planters' housing and improve their aesthetic sense failed, just as did their attempts to force the planters to adopt the "balanced" farming and settlement patterns of the more advanced parts of contemporary England. As early as 1642, the Privy Council ordered Virginia's Governor Berkeley to require everyone owning 500 acres or more to build a brick house of 24 feet long and 16 feet wide with a cellar, "and also not suffer men to build slight cottages as heretofore . . . And to remove from place to place, only to plant Tobacco."[25] The five hundred acres must have seemed very grand to people living in England at the time, and so misled them into thinking that those who could acquire that much land also had the wherewithal to build houses of brick, if only they would.

[22] Durand, *Frenchman in Virginia*, p. 113.

[23] William Fitzhugh, *Letters and Other Documents, 1676-1701*, edited by Richard B. Davis, (Charlottesville, 1963), pp. 175-76.

[24] Beverly, *History*, p. 152.

[25] *VMHB*, II (1894-1895), 284, 287. "An Act for Building a Towne," passed by the Virginia House of Burgesses in 1662, was expected to accomplish the same goals. Each county was required to build a house in Jamestown of brick, forty feet long and twenty feet wide, with roofs of slate or tile; Reps, *Tidewater Towns*, p. 52. The houses were never built.

Why didn't they build with brick? There were kilns and brick-makers available and some planters did use brick in chimneys and cellars, and occasionally even more extensively.[26] The missing ingredient must have been the skills of the bricklayer. Of the hundreds of men identified in the Maryland records by craft affiliation or who were paid for exercising special skills, only one owned tools specifically identified as those of a bricklayer.[27] Carpenters, coopers, joiners, and boatwrights, shoemakers, tailors, physicians, surgeons, clergymen, and schoolteachers—all were more common than brick-makers or bricklayers. In 1681 William Fitzhugh begged his London correspondent to procure him both a bricklayer and a carpenter, because they would "save me a great deal of money in my present building, & I would be willing to advance something extraordinary for the procuration of them or either of them . . . be sure to send in their tools with them."[28]

The bricks themselves were cheap to make, but they had to be made close by the construction site or else near the water where they could be floated downstream to sites convenient to shipping.[29] One account of administration, dated 1701, listed bricks as nine for a penny sterling, which compares favorably with inch plank at a penny per running foot in the same account.[30] How many were needed to build a house? Would a brick house have cost more than a wooden one, assuming that a skilled craftsman were available to supervise the work? House sizes varied greatly, from 12 to 40 feet in length and 12 to 20 feet wide.[31] A one-story house measuring

[26] See some of the references to brick foundations and chimneys in note 9 above. Governor Berkeley's houses at Green Spring and Jamestown were of brick, according to Bruce, *Economic History*, II, 139. Barley states that until after 1775, "a brick house in an East Midlands village was a rarity." M. W. Barley, *The English Farmhouse and Cottage* (London, 1961), p. 27.

[27] *Inv. & Accts.*, Liber 31, f. 125 (1710). A remarkable indenture signed in 1643 appears in *Md.Arch.*, X, 213. A brickmaker agreed to three years' service in return for meat, drink, apparel, and lodging, and at freedom, a 200-acre freehold with a house twenty-five feet long and sixteen feet wide, plus two cows, two sows with pig, two goats with kid, five barrells of corn, a bed stuffed with feathers or wool flocks, a pillow, one rug, two dishes, one pot, and six spoons. The brickmaker reneged!

[28] Fitzhugh, *Letters*, p. 92.

[29] Byrd, *Secret Diary*, p. 14.

[30] *Inv. & Accts.*, Liber 20, f. 213.

[31] Bruce lists the following sizes for Virginia houses recorded in county court records: 40 × 20, 20 × 16, 20 × 15, 20 × 20, and one brick house 60 feet long in Surry County! Bruce, *Economic History*, II, 140-44. In the *Md.Arch.* there appear the following sizes: 15 feet long, 20 feet long, and three 30 feet long. One of the latter was planned to be 18 feet wide and to have two chimneys; Vols. X, 476, 363-

20 × 16 feet with walls 9 feet high, to take a hypothetical but reasonable case, would require approximately 4,656 bricks, minus the openings for doors and windows, plus the bricks in the chimney, if we assume that the bricks with their mortar measured 8 × 2½ inches.[32] At nine to the penny, the bricks necessary to build the walls of the hypothetical house would have cost slightly over £2 in money, or 518 pounds of tobacco at a penny per pound.

The frame alone of an ordinary wooden house cost £6 in one instance.[33] The number of clapboards necessary to sheathe the walls of our imaginary dwelling would have come to just under 400, if these are assumed to have been 5 feet long and 6 inches wide, and overlapped 2 inches, as reported in the partial description of such a house in the 1680 journal of Jaspar Dankers, "they split the boards of clapwood, so that they are like cooper's pipe staves, except they are not bent. . . . They are about five or six feet long, and are nailed on the outside of the frame, with the ends lapped over each other."[34] An estimate of their cost comes from an Annapolis estate account which, in 1712, charged £2 for 500 new clapboards, or about two per penny.[35] Although this may have been stated in slightly inflated currency, let us use it in order to compare the costs of clapboarding a frame structure with those of brick construction.[36] The 392 clapboards at two per penny would then cost £1.12.9. A house built before or during 1669 used 4,450 nails, worth 308 pounds of tobacco. The price of the latter that year was 1.15 pence per pound, so the nails would have cost £1.9.7 in money.[37] We have no idea

---

64, 405; IV, 175; and XLIV, 79-80. Robert Right of Charles County owned a house 25 × 25, valued at less than £5; *Inv. & Accts.*, Liber 10, f. 77. Robert Maine rented a 14-foot house in 1695; ibid., Liber 13B, f. 69. In 1712, there is mention of a 25-foot house, a 10-foot hen house, and part of the ground on which these stood valued at £20 in all; ibid., Liber 33, f. 146. A log house in Maryland dated by Henry Forman as c. 1683 was measured by him at 26 × 24½. Forman, *Early Manor Houses*, p. 204. Captain Neale's contract specified a 40 × 20 foot framed house of two stories with five rooms on the ground floor and with two chimneys, material unspecified; ibid., p. 246.

[32] These measurements come from the brick fireplace of a modern home. The estimate is devised solely to gain some idea of the relative costs of building in wood and in brick.

[33] *Inv. & Accts.*, Liber 36, f. 176.

[34] Dankers and Sluyter, *Journal*, p. 173.

[35] *Inv. & Accts.*, Liber 33A, f. 241.

[36] Costs of labor not included.

[37] Ibid., Liber 1, f. 61; tobacco prices that year estimated by Menard, "Farm Prices," p. 85. The construction of two tobacco houses in 1694 required 6,000 nails. *Inv. & Accts.*, Liber 12, f. 139.

how many nails would have been needed to build the walls of our 20 × 16 foot structure, but if they numbered half (the other half going to shingle the roof) and cost the same, as in this example, then the combined price of clapboards and nails, £2.7.6, was *higher* by 10 percent than the £2.3.2 for the bricks. A long string of "ifs" adds up to the conclusion that the colonists did not forego brick houses because they objected to the cost of the bricks. The true difficulty lay in obtaining, and paying, the masons and bricklayers to do the job.[38]

Monsieur Durand, who reported on the "village" effect of the numerous buildings serving the plantation owner and his labor force, did not know why the planters, "whatever their estates," chose to build as they did.[39] Beverly argued that "they don't covet to make them lofty, having extent enough of ground to build upon, and now and then they are visited by high winds which incommode a towering fabric."[40] Thus he presents two practical reasons why the people did not build their houses in stories but added separate structures as needed. They had plenty of space, and low-lying buildings were safer from wind damage than taller structures.

Neither reason is compelling, in view of the fact that many men in the years ahead did decide to build such houses. But in the seventeenth century, people built the simplest houses in the simplest way they knew, using their time and resources for purposes other than architectural expression. "Adequacy" rather than aesthetic need seems to have been their guide. Let us explore the dimensions of that adequacy by counting rooms and noting their functions among houses owned by the different economic classes of Maryland planters. The route we shall follow lies through that small subset of probate inventories that the appraisers organized room by room.[41] Although such lists tended to originate more often

---

[38] As late as 1722, two-thirds of the houses in Boston continued to be of wood, where they surely posed a far greater fire hazard than they did scattered about the countryside, as in Maryland. [Capt. John Bonner's Map of] the Town of Boston in New England, cited in David H. Flaherty, *Privacy in Colonial New England* (Charlottesville, 1972), p. 42.

[39] Durand, *Frenchman in Virginia*, p. 112.

[40] Beverly, *History*, p. 152.

[41] For the six-county sample of Maryland records, 1656-1719, 111 room-by-room inventories were found. For an early appreciation of the possibilities of this kind of source material for American architectural history, see the review by Wendell D. Garrett of Abbott Lowell Cummings, ed., *Rural Household Inventories: Establishing the Names, Uses and Furnishings of Rooms in the Colonial New England Home, 1675-1775* (Boston, 1964) in *WMQ*, XXII (1965), 360-62.

among the wealthier estates, one can readily counter the effect of this bias toward the wealthy by matching each such inventory to its relative position in the overall distribution of wealth among the planters, and then treat each room-by-room inventory as illustrative of its respective stratum within that distribution. Thus we can guard against the tendency to treat "frequent" as "typical."

One must, however, acknowledge that in Maryland's case, almost no room-by-room inventories originated in the bottom half of the wealth distribution as a whole, nor in the bottom third of married householders. It makes sense to infer that the poorer families lived in fewer rooms than did their more affluent neighbors, simply because personal wealth and the number of rooms and "places" in the inventories are highly correlated. A strong presumption arises therefore that families in the bottom third lived in only one room; appraisers had no reason to note which room they were in if there was only one room. Literary evidence supports this assumption.

Table IV.1 summarizes the results of the survey among the probate records of six counties in early Maryland, reporting the number of rooms inside the dwelling houses of each stratum and, in addition, the numbers of subsidiary structures, either nearby or at other sites belonging to the owners. For households under £50 in

TABLE IV.1

ROOMS, BUILDINGS, "PLACES" BY WEALTH CLASS,
MARYLAND HOUSEHOLDS, 1660-1719

PPW Class	Percentile Rank Households[b]	Main House Average No. Rooms	Other "Places"[a] Average No.	Total Rooms Plus "Places"
£ 0-15	0-6	1?	0.0	1.0?
16-34	7-21	less than 2	0.0	less than 2
35-49	22-34	2.0	0.5?	2.5?
50-71	35-46	2.8	0.6	3.4
72-96	47-56	3.1	1.0	4.1
97-149	57-69	3.1	1.0	4.1
150-228	70-79	5.0	1.5	6.5
229-399	80-89	5.3	3.1	8.4
400-799	90-95.5	6.0	3.1	9.1
800-up	95.6-99.9	6.3	5.1	11.4

SOURCE: 111 room-by-room inventories in the probate records of six counties, Maryland, in Hall of Records, Annapolis.

[a] Includes all habitable outbuildings and quarters of home plantation and elsewhere. Excludes tobacco houses, closets, cellars, garrets, etc.

[b] Households of all married men in probate records of six counties, N = 1,863.

physical personal wealth, roughly coinciding with the poorest third of planters' families, members lived in one or two rooms, whereas the middling third had three rooms, usually two rooms on the ground floor with a loft above. This stratum also had an auxiliary structure, sometimes a separate kitchen or quarters for the servants or slaves. Above £150, families lived in five or six rooms, and added more buildings rather than more rooms when they needed additional space.

Thus we find that the middling planter and his family lived in a very modest structure indeed, and only those in the upper third of society lived in a house with more than three rooms. Between the three-quarters mark in the distribution and the top 5 percent or so, houses stretched out, seldom up, to an average of five rooms, with two outbuildings providing additional space. Among the very rich, some built larger structures with ten or twelve rooms, but these were extraordinary. Of the 46 room-by-room inventories drawing from this top group, 27 were from houses of six rooms or less, and 10 were from houses of only four rooms or less.

The houses of the Maryland planters, then, tended to be small, inconspicuous, and inconsequential. Built entirely of green wood, they required frequent repairs, and became virtually uninhabitable after a decade unless they were substantially reconstructed. Since they were inexpensive to build in the first place, it may often have been preferable to build anew rather than repair the old, with the additional advantage that one could relocate closer to fields under current cultivation. A process such as this eventually left a scattering of abandoned houses in various stages of decay for shocked visitors to moralize about. Throwaway houses became a new American tradition.

Although the smallness of the houses and inconsequential nature of the construction methods and materials may strike some readers as evidence of the impoverishing effects of market-oriented agriculture, recent studies suggest that the farmhouses of seventeenth-century England and New England were probably neither larger nor better built. Table IV.2 provides figures for the Midlands village of Wigston Magna and for two counties in rural Massachusetts, all based on room-by-room inventories in probate records. An average of 45 percent of the Wigston Magna lists describe houses with three rooms or less, compared to 55 percent in Essex County, Massachusetts, between 1638 and 1664, 33 percent in Suffolk County between 1675 and 1699, and 30 percent for the six-county sample from Maryland prior to 1700.

153

TABLE IV.2
NUMBERS OF ROOMS IN HOUSES, ROOM-BY-ROOM INVENTORIES

Region	Percent with					Average No. Rooms
	2 Rooms	3 Rooms	4 Rooms	5+ Rooms	Total	
Wigston Magna, England						
1621-1641	15%	22%	15%	49%	101%	4.9
1675-1725	29	24	16	31	100	4.1
Average	22	23	15½	40	100½	4.5
Essex Co., Mass.						
1638-1664	35	20	23	22	100	3.3
Suffolk Co., Mass.						
1675-1699	5	28	20½	46	99½	4.6
1700-1724	0	13	20	67	100	5.7
Six counties, Maryland						
1660-1699	13	17	20	50	100	5.1
1700-1719	8	8	19	65	100	5.6

SOURCES: W. G. Hoskins, *The Midland Peasant* (London, 1965), 297-302. *The Probate Records of Essex County*, 3 vols., 1635-1681 (1916-1920); Abbott Lowell Cummings, *Rural Household Inventories: Establishing the Names, Uses and Furnishings of Rooms in the Colonial New England Home, 1675-1775* (Boston, 1964); probate records of six counties, Maryland, in Hall of Records, Annapolis.

By relating individual inventories to percentile ranks of heads of households, we earlier arrived at an estimate of two-thirds for those living in three rooms or less in Maryland. For Wigston Magna, such a distribution is not available, but hearth tax assessments for the year 1670 provide a convenient means of making such an attempt in this case as well. Of the 161 households listed, three-quarters (120) paid for just one hearth, whereas 25 paid for two, 9 for three, 2 for four, and 5 households paid for five fireplaces each. One can reasonably assume that a single fireplace heated no more than three rooms, so the conclusion follows that three-quarters of the village families probably lived in three rooms or less that year, more than in Maryland for roughly the same period.

It is not possible at present to locate Massachusetts inventories within a wealth distribution for heads of households, but still another English study proves useful here in attempting to evaluate Maryland's housing standards.[42] The sizes of farm cottages from

[42] One must first distribute the estate inventories of married heads of households by physical personal wealth (PPW) to locate the room-by-room inventories by stratum within that distribution, that is, richest decile, poorest quintile, and so on. I propose to carry out such a procedure on probate records from the three counties

regions all over England in successive periods dating from the late sixteenth and early seventeenth centuries have been estimated, based on the house sizes of farmers or farm laborers whose personal estates came to £10 or £15 sterling, depending on the time period under study.[43] These money values cannot be readily translated, but we can feel reasonably confident that these estates draw from a sizable class near, but not at, the bottom of English society before the Civil War. According to the room-by-room inventories from 1630 to 1640, numbering eighty out of the total of three hundred gathered for those years, at least 62 percent lived in three rooms or less. This must be viewed as a minimum estimate of the proportion doing so, because the author of the study did not attempt to determine the relationship between relative wealth and house size. The extent to which these are positively related tends to underestimate the proportion of households living in three rooms or less, but in any event the results are more generous than what one would expect from the Wigston Magna hearth tax of 1670, cited above. Maryland houses were no smaller, in either case.

Despite ambiguities arising from problems inherent in the sources, data from the several studies offer a firm basis for several conclusions. First, the immigrant exservants of early Maryland who survived and married lived in houses in which the number of rooms compares quite favorably with those built by their New England contemporaries. Second, colonists of both regions were living in houses little different in construction methods or size from those of the least affluent farmers of England. Finally, colonial houses in the eighteenth century may have become larger and more substantial than they had been previously, representing a real improvement in the material standard of living in the older settlements along the seaboard, but this is a point that requires further investigation.

Regional differences in house styles did evolve as a result of differences in climate, available materials, and wage structures. In the north, most houses were built over a cellar, huddled around a central chimney stack, and with a lower-story extension at the rear that extended the roof line down to the ground: the "cat-slide." In the south, houses were built on posts set into the ground, usually without cellars; extensions tended to run laterally, extending the

---

of Massachusetts spanning the colony from the Connecticut River to Boston for the period up to 1750.

[43] With some qualifications and adjustments; Everitt, "Farm Labourers," pp. 396-465.

155

roof line horizontally; and chimneys stood at the gable end(s) of the house.

Initially, both regions drew on diverse building traditions from various areas of Britain, and we are only now becoming aware of the true complexity of their origins and paths of evolution in the New World.[44] Yet the similarities between the regions should not be forgotten: both built wooden box frames, sheathed them in wooden clapboards, and roofed them with wooden shingles. Both used large quantities of metal nails in the process.

By Thomas Jefferson's time, as we all know, the great planters of the tidewater had erected substantial dwellings, usually placed on knolls overlooking their river landings. Wealthy merchants of the great northern ports likewise built themselves homes that embodied aspirations beyond mere considerations of size and comfort. The emergence of a self-conscious and formal style of architecture among well-to-do colonials produced houses of greater permanence as well as of imposing proportions, which required trained staffs of servants to maintain them. Concurrently, there came to be a division of living and working quarters between the two classes of people inhabiting the same building as well as between those inside and those only temporarily in, and therefore, not of, the household. The Georgian house used a formal, symmetrically organized layout, indoors as well as in its façade, with two rooms, back to back, opening off each side of a central hall whose sole purpose was to keep visitors isolated from the house's occupants by a phalanx of closed doors. In such homes, only a few hanging portraits and mirrors broke up the expanse of walls and doors that greeted the new arrival.

The Georgian style not only made an aesthetic statement, it successfully kept servants and strangers at arm's length, even within the confines of the house. This was an extraordinary departure for tidewater homes, since the usual pattern was a front door leading directly into the hearth room of the planter's house, the room in which everyone gathered, and where, therefore, everyone was di-

---

[44] James Deetz has argued for an evolution in colonial New England from initial diversity to broad-based uniformity in house styles, and then later to an overriding concern for visual symmetry about the middle of the eighteenth century. The first phase, he suggests, was strongly influenced by the demands and resources of the physical environment itself. The later stage, however, was a product of something else, perhaps of growing wealth, new cultural aspirations, and/or a shift in the "mindset" of the people. In this last suggestion, he is echoing Henry Glassie's argument as stated in *Folk Housing of Middle Virginia*. Deetz, *In Small Things Forgotten*, pp. 104-107.

rectly accessible if he were at home at all. As noted earlier, the big brick houses we associate with the planters of Virginia and Maryland did not supersede the small wooden "vernacular" homes of even the richest class until well after 1700, and the biggest of these did not adopt Georgian styling until 1740 or later. The accumulation of sufficient wealth necessary to support both house and staff over the entire course of the economic cycle may have taken a full century to accomplish, but more was required than mere wealth to bring about what appears to have been a fundamental shift in perception.

We can draw closer to an understanding of perception or life style among the planters of early Maryland by noting their preferences among classes of material objects, particularly among those inside the house. These embodied qualities or fulfilled functions deemed more or less desirable by those acquiring them. Any list of their potential utilities would have to include comfort (or the absence of discomfort), convenience, cleanliness, order, privacy, decorative effects, and an ineffable yet recognizable quality encompassing and transcending all of these—"civility." The relative presence or absence of each of these, as exhibited by actual living arrangements and furnishings among planters of various classes and in various time periods, throws considerable light on the deeper attitudes of transplanted Englishmen and their children toward the environment and toward those with whom they shared it. Changes in living arrangements go to the heart of all social relationships, even though the precise psychological processes at work cannot be laid bare by the mere contemplation of objects in space.

First, let us establish a rough index to that space in terms of the numbers of rooms occupied by Maryland households of various size. Chesapeake families often included cousins and stepchildren, servants and orphans, so that households frequently teemed with as many people as those of New England, where colonial families grew to legendary size.[45] Radically different family structures may have produced disparate patterns of intrahousehold dynamics, but the question we shall here attend to is how much space the Maryland household had and needed. Just how crowded were the families?

We argued earlier, despite the lack of direct evidence, that the poorer third of households lived in smaller houses than their richer

---

[45] Darrett B. and Anita H. Rutman, " 'Now-Wives and Sons-in-Law,' " in Tate and Ammerman, eds., *Chesapeake*, pp. 153-82. Average household size is not the same as completed family size, however, and most of the New England studies have focused on the latter.

neighbors because personal wealth and house size proved highly correlated in the visible part of the wealth distribution, that is, the upper two-thirds whose inventories were occasionally organized on a room-by-room basis.[46] The number of rooms occupied by the poorest third, therefore, would have been no more than two. The possibility exists that they needed no more. If these families were younger and smaller than those in the middle and upper ranges, the planter may have added on as his family and his means expanded. To discover whether this might be true, we will combine the house size information in the room-by-room inventories with data on family size in young fathers' estates, and in doing so, control for differences in wealth and age simultaneously. Table IV.3 does this, adding servants and slaves to the pool of information as well, so that we answer two questions with one table: how many family members were there per room, and how many people per "place," counting the other structures and quarters as additional places of habitation?

The information in Table IV.3 indicates that average family size among this age group did not vary with wealth above the very poorest strata, so we can state with some assurance that the poorer families did not choose to live in fewer rooms: the choice was not theirs to make. Stating it another way, planters who could afford to do so added rooms and additional buildings as their means permitted, rather than in response to the pressure of numbers alone. Indeed, scanning the relationship between size of family and number of rooms in the table, one can see that the planters formed at least three distinct classes based on life style, each class consisting of just about a third of all the households. At the top, a thin layer of very rich had formed—the cream, as it were—consisting of those planters who operated more than one or two plantations and staffed these various work sites with a numerous labor force.

The poorest third of families, few of whom owned any bound labor, were still the most crowded, simply due to the lack of available space, averaging about two-and-a-half persons per room or "place."

[46] House size, measured in terms of the number of rooms, did not vary with wealth among estates worth more than £450 PPW in the room-by-room inventories, roughly equivalent to the richest 5 percent of all estates, nor were there any trends in house size over the period of the study despite the increasing proportion of wealthier estates in the room-by-room sample and in the records as a whole. What did vary directly with wealth was the number of auxilliary structures and secondary living sites. The dividing line between those with more than one secondary site and those with one or none was about £850 PPW.

Table IV.3
Household Size and Habitable Space in Maryland, 1660-1719

Households[a] Percentile Rank	Main House Average No. Rooms	Family Size[b]	Family Members per Room	Other "Places"[c]	Average No. Servants[d]	Average No. Slaves[d]	Total No. People	Average No. People per "Place"
0-6	1?	3.72	3.72?	0.0	0.01	0.00	3.73	3.73?
7-21	less than 2	4.49	less than 2.25	0.0	0.11	0.01	4.61	more than 2.31
22-34	"2"	5.39	"2.70"	0.5?	0.23	0.04	5.66	"2.26"
35-46	2.8	4.91	1.75	0.6	0.53	0.07	5.51	1.62
47-56	3.1	4.72	1.52	1.0	0.88	0.22	5.82	1.42
57-69	3.1	5.17	1.67	1.0	1.17	0.46	6.80	1.66
70-79	5.0	4.84	0.97	1.5	1.52	1.51	7.87	1.21
80-89	5.3	5.08	0.96	3.1	2.07	3.13	10.28	1.22
90-95.5	6.0	5.51	0.92	3.1	2.47	7.71	15.69	1.72
95.6-99.9	6.3	5.33	0.85	5.05	3.28	21.79	30.40	2.68

SOURCE: Probate records of six counties, Maryland including 111 room-by-room inventories, in Hall of Records, Annapolis.

[a] Households of all married men in probate records of six counties, excluding those not positively identified as married or widowed; N=1,863.

[b] Includes stepchildren and orphans, where known, who were not servants. Does not include boarders, lodgers, or free servants residing with the family, because of uneven evidence. Data taken from estates of "young fathers."

[c] Includes all outbuildings and quarters on the home plantation and elsewhere except for tobacco houses, cellars, closets, garrets, etc.

[d] Data from all estates in wealth classes of original distribution of probated estates of six counties.

The middling planter's family, however, was considerably more comfortable. Averaging about five members per household, they lived in three rooms and also used another structure nearby. Non-members, however, gradually ceased to share the "home" space. Four-fifths of these households had owned bound labor before 1683, but only half that proportion did so after 1700. Of those with servants or slaves, fewer than half had built separate sleeping quarters for them, although the higher the number present, the greater the probability they would sleep apart. When analyzed overtime, the room-by-room inventories originating in this class did not reveal any significant trends in housing of bound labor. Insofar as sleeping arrangements suggest status differences, distinctions between family and servant among those households with only one or two did not widen, nor did the growth of slavery in the society at large alter the relationship at home between master and servant or master and slave.

As we have seen, greater wealth increased the size of the resident work force, not the size of the family. Those laborers owned by planters worth less than £150 most often lived with the family itself, sleeping in the "outer" rooms or halls, in kitchens or kitchen lofts. Separate quarters for servants and slaves more particularly characterized estates above £229 in personal wealth, the upper quintile of households. In racially mixed labor groups, more common in the period before 1700 than after, no clear pattern of segregation in their living quarters emerged in the room-by-room inventories.

That poorer families suffered more crowding than did richer ones is not surprising, but merely counting people and rooms need not exhaust our inquiry into the quality of life among the planters of all classes, since the room-by-room inventories not only tell us how many rooms there were but how they were designated, and list their contents, as well. Maryland room designations drew on a bank of English terms. In the houses of men whose estates fell below the 70th percentile (£150), the number of rooms seldom rose above 4, but 17 different terms were used to distinguish them. Among a total of 44 individual rooms given names, 7 were called kitchen, 5 each were called outward room, chamber, and milkhouse. "Hall" and "inner room" each generated 4 references. Hall, room, kitchen, and milkhouse applied to ground-floor rooms, chamber generally applied to those in an upper story.

The houses and auxillary structures of richer planters added more names to the list of potential room and building designations. Table IV.4 ranks the sixteen most common usages by wealth class

TABLE IV.4
PERCENT OF ROOM-BY-ROOM INVENTORIES WITH AT LEAST ONE
OF THE DESIGNATED ROOMS (percent)

Rooms	Wealth Classes					Average	Weighted Average*
	Under £150	£150-270	£271-450	£451-861	£862-3223		
Kitchen	50.0	64.7	80.7	73.7	85.2	71.2	57.5
Hall	45.0	76.5	73.1	68.4	77.8	67.6	54.0
Milkhouse	25.0	35.3	34.6	31.6	37.0	32.4	28.0
Quarters	15.0	35.3	30.8	47.4	29.6	30.6	21.3
Porch	5.0	23.5	15.4	31.6	55.6	27.0	11.7
Parlor	10.0	23.5	34.6	31.6	25.9	25.2	15.9
Closet	5.0	0.0	23.1	31.6	48.2	23.4	9.6
Cellar	0.0	17.7	7.7	26.3	51.9	21.6	6.4
Inner room	25.0	29.4	15.4	10.5	22.2	19.8	23.5
Outer room	40.0	23.5	11.5	10.5	11.1	18.0	32.4
Loft	10.0	23.5	15.4	10.5	25.9	17.1	12.7
Shed	10.0	11.8	23.1	0.0	11.1	11.1	11.0
Buttery	10.0	11.8	7.7	0.0	3.7	6.3	9.1
Store	0.0	5.9	26.9	31.6	80.0	33.9	8.4
Garret	0.0	0.0	7.7	5.3	7.4	4.5	1.4
Study	0.0	5.9	7.7	0.0	3.7	3.6	1.6
Nursery	0.0	0.0	0.0	5.3	7.4	2.7	0.6
Number of room-by-room inventories	20	17	26	18	27	111	
Weights*	.69	.11	.10	.06	.04	1.00	

SOURCE: 111 room-by-room inventories in the probate records of six counties, Maryland, in Hall of Records, Annapolis.
* Derived from actual distribution of estates of Heads of Households.

of the estate, showing what percentage of the room-by-room inventories in that class specified each label. The kitchen was the most common room for all but one class of estates, and the hall came second. Relative wealth played a key role in ranking and rate of appearance for most of the other names, but other factors were also at work. "Buttery," for instance, dropped out of common usage before 1700. "Parlor" appeared in fewer than a third of the estates, even among the richer planters, and may have been more narrowly regional in origin than other terms. Similarly, "milkhouse" appears almost as often in the group of estates worth £150 to £270, which averaged 6.5 rooms and structures, as in estates worth £850 or more, which averaged 10.7 rooms and structures.

"Loft," on the other hand, which occurred equally often in the

room-by-room inventories of these same two wealth classes, proved
quite uncommon in those of poorer men. This can perhaps be
explained as part of the physical process of house expansion. When
the planter added new space for storage, for sleeping, or for carrying out a specialized task, he first added on by building out, then
he built up, then he built a new structure entirely.

Core pairs of rooms, around which the rest of the house was
built as additions were made, consisted of "inner and outer" rooms,
or "hall and chamber" or "hall and kitchen" combinations. In the
first two pairs, cooking took place in the hearth room, the outer
or hall room, which occasionally took the name "house" or "lodging" room. Whenever one of the rooms was designated "kitchen,"
however, the cooking invariably took place there, as evidenced by
the presence of the cooking pots.[47] Terms for rooms in addition
to the core pair usually express their location with reference to
them, as for example, inner, middle, upper, lower, or adjoining.
Rooms situated upstairs were usually, but not always, called chambers and identified by the rooms lying under them, as porch chamber, hall chamber, and so forth.[48] Most chambers and rooms had
beds in them, as did the halls of smaller houses.

The route of expansion also can explain the otherwise anomalous
disappearance of separate quarters for the bound laborers in the
richest class of estates. At that level, most of the laborers lived away
from the home site, living at other quarters on the same plantation
or at other plantations. The remainder at home slept in the kitchen,
in the kitchen loft or room attached to the kitchen, or in other
auxilliary structures. Some even slept in the main house itself, on
the floors or under the beds of their owners. Since no beds or
bedding of any kind appeared in the garrets of the few houses that
had them, one may infer that these were intended as storage areas
only.[49]

The glossary of room names in Appendix D should prove useful
in understanding what each room was used for, and provides comparisons with seventeenth-century English usage as determined by

[47] "Old" kitchens, usually separate structures, were occasionally turned to other
uses.

[48] Porches were probably not enclosed and stood in the front of the door leading
into the hearth room. Rooms built over such porches were used for storage rather
than for sleeping.

[49] "Garrets" imply a third story, but were probably only loft spaces above the
chambers on the second floor.

one authority (Appendix E).[50] The latter attends to regional variation but does not attempt to quantify usage. The Maryland glossary
attempts some assessment of this and whether the passage of time
produced any changes in usage or in function.

Many of the terms found in English farm inventories made no
appearance at all in Maryland: cockloft, dish house, firehouse, or
fire room, for instance. The cheese house and dairy were structures
that were probably more highly specialized than the milkhouse, a
standard term in Maryland. Other terms not mentioned in the
English glossary relate to outbuildings and are self-evident: shop,
cider house, corn house, corn loft, mill house, salt house.

Books could be found almost anywhere in the main house, but
most often in the hall, closet, study, and inner room. "Studies"
found no place in English farmhouses. Only six parlors and three
kitchens held reading matter, generally Bibles or prayer books, in
Maryland inventories. Planters who owned works dealing with law
or history stored them in rooms especially designed for them, although a few men used their bedchambers as all-purpose rooms,
even using them for the dispatch of business.

Planters with closets or studies containing books came primarily
from the very richest strata of Maryland society, a fact that comes
as no surprise, since few people had the leisure or education to
appreciate books for themselves. Everyone, however, had to find
space for certain unavoidable functions of daily life, and it is interesting to track these activities through the room-by-room inventories. Grinding corn, for instance, had to be done at home and
almost daily, because few mills then existed.[51] Most of this grinding
was accomplished by means of an iron pestle thumped up and
down in a deep-sided wooden mortar. Hand mills, using a small
pair of matched quernstones (imported), set in a wooden frame,
gradually replaced pestles for beating corn, although never entirely
and not everywhere. Pestles and hand mills most often were found
in kitchens and quarters, locations convenient to the lodgings of
both servants and slaves, the principal persons elected to this task
among households enjoying their services.[52]

[50] M. W. Barley, "Glossary of Names for Rooms in Houses of the Sixteenth and
Seventeenth Centuries," in I. D. Foster and J. Alcock, eds., *Culture and Environment*
(London, 1963), pp. 483-95.
[51] Chapter Two mentions the scarcity of mills. Corn also stored better if left
unhulled and unshucked, so that frequent grinding in small quantities made more
sense than hauling large amounts over any distance at longer intervals.
[52] The grinding took place in either the kitchen or the quarters. On plantations

Other chores that required daily attention for much of the year included clearing and breaking ground, planting, and weeding, all tasks using the ax and hoe. Felled trees required splitting, riving, and sawing for making fence rails and pales, shingles, staves, and firewood, important byproducts of farming in early America. These chores required froes, drawing knives, saws, axes, mauls, and wedges, which appear in the inventories of virtually all planters who owned their own land or of those who leased new land. Well over half of the places around the farmhouse where such tools were stored were kitchens, lofts, quarters, and other outhouses of various descriptions, and in "stores," where new equipment of all sorts were kept. It is symbolic of the life style of the planters, however, that these tools of husbandry could be found in places that seem unlikely to our more orderly sense. Seven percent of occurrences were in halls and outer rooms, 6 percent in closets (before 1700, none afterwards), 13 percent in other rooms and chambers, 5 percent in milkhouses, 3 percent in cellars, and the rest scattered in sheds, garrets, and once each in a study and a parlor.

More specialized woodworking tools belonging to the trades of carpenter, cooper, and joiner were also scattered about the plantation. Just under half were stored in such places as kitchens, quarters, lofts, outhouses of various kinds, and in stores. The rest were in bedchambers (16 percent), sheds, closets, milkhouses, and "outer" rooms (5 percent each), and once each in a parlor, a cellar, and a study. These tools became more important in the eighteenth century, as the larger planters attempted to become more self-sufficient during the economic downswings, and as the poorer planters turned to them to supplement their incomes.

As Chapter Two showed, depressions in the tobacco market not only prompted people to try new sources of income, but also to make clothing they had hitherto been accustomed to buy from overseas. Only 18 percent of the room-by-room inventories dated prior to 1700 mention any of the tools associated with woolen, linen, or cotton manufacture, such as cards, worsted combs, hackles, spinning wheels, or looms. After 1700, however, almost all listed one or more of these tools. These were dispersed all over the home plantation, and even occasionally appeared in quarters located else-

having both (twenty-five in the room-by-room inventories), grinding took place most often in the quarters (64 percent), less often in both places (20 percent), least often in the kitchen alone (4 percent). Several inventories failed to mention either pestle or mill. For households without kitchen or quarters, the grinding tools were in the hall or outer room.

164

where. At home, these tools could be found anywhere in the house itself or in outhouses.

Rooms in the main house, excluding the hall, kitchen, etc.	33%
Hall	13
Kitchen	13
Milkhouse	7
Closets	8
Parlor	2
Garret	3
Shed	2
Loft, cellar, store	0
Outhouses	15
Quarters	3
Total occurrences	99%

The fewer the rooms and auxilliary structures present, the less specialized became the remaining rooms. However, even on quite large plantations, as we have seen, the storage and use of tools might occur in any number of places. Similarly, eating, drinking, and sleeping were not spatially separated. Indeed, only in a very few plantation homes would we encounter a dining room or a room intended primarily as such. Less rare, but still far from common, was the hall or outer room without a bed. In the smallest houses, of course, these rooms served all the functions of the household, including grinding the daily corn. Table IV.5 provides a rough

TABLE IV.5
ROOMS AND OUTBUILDINGS ON MARYLAND PLANTATIONS AND THE
AVERAGE NUMBER OF FUNCTIONS PERFORMED IN THEM

Room	Average No. Functions	Major Function	Secondary Function
Kitchen	1.9	cooking	other household chores
Quarters	1.8	sleeping	cooking, household chores
Outer room	1.7	sleeping	eating
Hall	1.3	eating	sleeping
Inner room	1.25	sleeping	eating
Parlor	1.2	sleeping	eating
Milkhouse	1.1	dairying	cooking

SOURCE: Room-by-room inventories in probate records of six counties, Maryland, in Hall of Records, Annapolis.

165

guide to the functions to which various rooms were put in early Maryland. Eating and sleeping took place in all but the milkhouse.

The principal impression one carries away from close study of the room-by-room inventories is the helter-skelter quality of objects and functions. If there were any passion for order or symmetry in this culture, its symptoms have not survived in the lists compiled by appraisers. Furthermore, few planters, even among the rich and powerful, cared to introduce any decorative note to the interior furnishings of their homes. Perhaps the most appropriate adjectives to apply to the Maryland life style are "simple and unaffected." One is tempted, however, to add "crude, untidy, even dirty." The smaller houses must have been very crowded, particularly when the weather drove everyone indoors. Certainly they were drafty and cold in the winter, insect-ridden in the summer.

We will return to a consideration of the qualitative aspects of life in early Maryland after taking a more detailed tour through planter households and their furnishings. We must go beyond the numerically inadequate and biased sample provided by the room-by-room inventories in order to generalize about who owned what and when. Once these have been laid out, perhaps we can then speak with greater confidence about the needs, perceptions, and priorities of the people themselves.

Chapter Five

THE POORER PLANTERS AND
THEIR FAMILIES

As we have seen, the poorest planters lived in the smallest houses. The interiors of the one or one-and-a-half story box-frame structure probably consisted of a single room into which the visitor entered directly as he crossed the threshold. The fireplace stood to one side from the doorway, at a gable end. If any partition existed, it ran perpendicular to the door, setting off an inner room to one side, away from the fireplace.

By just opening the door, one could view the room and see the fire on the hearth, as George Delty's statement makes clear: "One night he came to the house where Edward Hudson and Robert Holt's wife did live together and he did see them both lyeing in bed together before the fire."[1] Seldom where there any chairs visible, but benches standing at the table and one or two chests against the wall served for seating as well as for storage.[2] The only bed was the one near the fireplace, where it too served as a place to sit. The windows were shuttered against the cold in winter, making the interior quite dark except for the light from the fire. In summertime, however, light and fresh air entered past the opened shutters, since neither glass nor screening intervened.

Unless the chinks between the clapboards had been carefully filled or the walls sheathed from inside, the open fire on the hearth in winter sucked in great drafts of cold air from outside, making everyone indoors hug the fire. Some of the "dwellings are so wretchedly constructed," complained Dankers and Sluyter in 1680, "that if you are not so close to the fire as almost to burn yourself, you cannot keep warm, for the wind blows through [the walls] everywhere."[3]

Part of the little house would perhaps have been ceiled over with

[1] *Md.Arch.*, X, 110.

[2] Roughly a quarter of planters with estates in the bottom third of the distribution of wealth in early Maryland possessed chairs. Households with books were twice as likely to have chairs as those without books.

[3] Dankers and Sluyter, *Journal*, p. 173.

movable planks to make a storage and sleeping loft. Unshucked ears of corn, flitches of bacon, strings of onions and apples hanging from the rafters, a few tools not currently in use—these might be stored out of the way overhead. The hearth fire warmed the entire chimney stack, which radiated some of that heat to anyone sleeping nearby. Although comfortably snug in winter, lofts such as these would be unbearably close and hot in summertime.

The hearth room served as kitchen, dining room, living room, and workshop, its contents ranging from the large cast-iron cooking pot hanging over the fire to the beds, chests, dishes, and work tools that constituted virtually all the family's personal possessions. The floor was of beaten earth, and the rough plank walls bore neither paint nor pictures. A few shelves held the dishes and other utensils, most of them made of wood, the rest of pewter. A few pieces of spare clothing hung from pegs or were stored in the chests along with extra shoes, scraps of cloth, and other little things not in current use.

The assortment of such furnishings varied widely from household to household, but it is possible to establish certain minimum essentials that the planters and their wives deemed necessary for keeping house. It is possible, moreover, to discern levels of priority among potential additions to the list of basic necessities by comparing the inventories of planter estates at successive levels of personal wealth. Table V.1 organizes a selected group of household goods by their presumed function and shows the proportion held among households in each of three wealth classes drawn from the bottom third of planter families entering probate in six counties of Maryland prior to 1720.[4] Table V.2 rearranges these selected items by the rank order of their proportionate appearance. At the top of the list, one finds beds, which appeared in the most inventories of each stratum of wealth. The rest are ranked in declining order of their average proportion among the three strata.[5]

---

[4] This is the set of married men's estates gathered from the bottom third of the wealth distribution of married heads of households, those with PPW of less than £50, N = 240. Marital status was positively established for each individual in the sample by specific references in the documents pertaining to the estate.

[5] The basis of selection of individual goods or of setting up categories of goods rested primarily on convenience to the researcher, but the resulting list of eighteen separate consumption goods provides good coverage of the range actually available to these households, with one major exception: woodenware. Objects of wood appear in every inventory in a multitude of forms for a multitude of purposes, contibuting a significant portion of the total value of consumption goods among poorer estates. The sheer abundance of forms rendered their separate analysis too tedious, and it is unlikely that there would emerge significant differentiation between strata.

TABLE V.1

PERCENT OF POORER FAMILIES IN MARYLAND OWNING SELECTED
HOUSEHOLD GOODS, 1656-1719

Function	Goods	£1-15	£16-34	£35-49	Weighted Average[a]
Sleeping	Beds	88.0%	93.2%	94.3%	92.7%
Cooking	Pots or kettle	72.8	93.3	96.2	90.8
	Fry pans, skillets	37.9	60.6	62.8	57.4
	Hand mills	11.5	16.2	54.3	29.9
Eating	Spoons	11.5	10.9	15.3	12.7
	Pewterware	52.0	66.1	82.6	69.9
	Earthenware	27.5	34.8	41.3	36.0
Clothing	Men's apparel	53.85	54.4	54.9	54.5
	Spinning wheels[b]				
	before 1700	0.0	13.3	5.6	8.0
	after 1700	7.0	15.1	21.2	16.0
Cleanliness	Soap	0.0	0.0	4.3	1.6
	Washtub	0.0	1.7	1.4	1.3
	Smoothing iron	16.1	19.4	32.7	23.9
Convenience	Chairs	22.0	27.2	21.7	24.2
	Warming pan	2.8	3.0	3.8	3.3
	Candles or holders	12.9	13.5	24.8	17.7
Civility	Tablecloth, napkins	10.5	10.5	18.4	13.5
	Chamber pot	4.0	4.2	10.6	6.6
Education or religion	Books	26.0	26.7	32.9	28.9
Personal appearance	Looking glass	13.5	23.9	16.7	19.3

SOURCE: Married heads of households in probate records of six counties, Maryland, in Hall of Records, Annapolis. Based on records of married heads of households with PPW less than £50, corresponding to the poorest third of decedents in the probate records.

[a] Weights are derived from the distribution of married heads of households: for estates worth £1-15 PPW, .177; £16-34, .441; £35-49, .382. N=240 in sample.

[b] Excludes Somerset County estates.

As one might expect, sleeping, cooking, and eating were activities that required certain articles that came very close to being indispensable, whereas other goods associated with these activities or with their qualitative aspects, such as cleanliness, convenience, and civility, ranked lower in the scale of material needs. Hand mills, for instance, were not necessary for grinding corn, since a heavy pestle used as a pounding weight achieved satisfactory results, though at greater expense of time and labor.[6] Hand mills, furthermore, were expensive, costing about a pound in money, more than a "killable" hog but not as much as a cow. Few estates below £35

[6] Smaller grains than corn, such as wheat, cannot satisfactorily be ground by mortar and pestle alone.

TABLE V.2
HOUSEHOLD ITEMS RANKED BY PERCENT OF POORER
MARYLAND FAMILIES USING THEM

Rank	Weighted Average* % Estates	Goods	Monetary Value
1	93	Beds	10s to £7
2	91	Pots, kettles	3d a pound, 10s for a forty-pound pot
3	70	Pewterware	6 to 12d a pound, 1s for plate, 3 to 4s a flagon
4	57	Fry pans, skillets	3d a pound for iron, 12d to 15d for brass
5	36	Earthenware	1 to 5d per piece
6	30	Hand mills	15 to 25s
7	29	Books	6d to 6s
8	24	Chairs	wooden, rush, or leather 1 to 6s
9	19	Looking glass	3 to 8d, hand-held
10	18	Candles, holders	3 to 8d
11	14	Tablecloth, napkins	6s to £2
12	8-16	Spinning wheels	6 to 15s
13	7	Chamber pot	pence if earthen, shillings if pewter
14	3	Warming pan	brass: 6 to 8s
15	2	Soap, washtub	pence

SOURCE: Married heads of households in probate records of six counties, Maryland, in Hall of Records, Annapolis.

* Weights derive from the distribution of married heads of households; for estates worth £1-15, .177; £16-34, .441; £35-49, .382.

could afford them, yet more than half of those in the level above did choose to acquire them.

Initial cost played a key role in the patterns of acquisition of consumer durables such as hand mills. Once some invisible but real income/wealth barrier had been surmounted, families then felt they could afford certain items, and proceeded to buy them. Not so readily explained is the puzzle raised by comparing the rankings of pewterware and earthenware. The latter was cheap and useful but not very durable. Pewter, on the other hand, was not only durable, but when worn out, could be melted down for reuse, so it continued to retain significant value even when temporarily laid aside. Its enduring quality and persistent value greatly enhanced the chances that some pieces of that metal alloy would turn up in the inventories of even quite poor men, despite its high cost in

170

relation to alternative materials.[7] Cheap earthenware, domestic as
well as imported, was in widespread use in the early Chesapeake,
but in any single inventory, the number of pieces would be few,
and none worth more than a few pence.[8] This pattern of usage
implies that poor quality limited the usefulness of clay products:
they may not have been cheap enough, given their fragility.[9]

Since virtually every inventory mentioned items of quite small
monetary value, we must beware of dismissing certain persistent
patterns of omission from the inventories as resulting from oversight on the part of hasty appraisers. Why, for instance, did so few
families own spoons?[10] Among those mentioned were both wooden
and metal ones, and none cost very much in relation to their obvious
utility. The most persuasive explanation for their widespread absence from inventories lies in the availability of found objects, such
as oyster shells, as substitutes.[11] Thus the absence of spoons from
some four-fifths of these poorer estates need not imply that four-
fifths of the people ate with their fingers only.

Such items, and probably many others simple enough for any
one to fashion, carried no market value for precisely that reason,
and it would serve no purpose for appraisers to include them among
assets having resale value. Certain other kinds of property having
positive market value also did not appear in inventories of estates.
Perishables and current food supplies were generally omitted, for
reasons that are not difficult to find. Pets never appear, even though
some, such as dogs, must often have been highly regarded as hunting aids, watch and guard animals, or merely as companions.[12]

---

[7] Large drinking vessels, in particular, require a malleable, durable, lightweight
material, and useful substitutes for pewter seem to have been lacking. Objects made
of tin cannot support a large volume, and glass of the period was too fragile for
mealtime use. Earthenware and stoneware were heavy, awkward to use, and also
fragile. Homemade objects, such as cattle horns and gourds, do not appear in the
inventories, although tanned leather "jacks" occasionally turn up.

[8] Earthenware was used primarily for small dishes and bowls, and for shallow
milkpans in which milk was set out to allow the cream to rise and curds to form.

[9] Cheap imported earthenware of more sophisticated manufacture and greater
durability became available to colonial families of moderate means in the course of
the eighteenth century, but this ware replaced pewter rather than domestic pottery.

[10] Knives and fingers were undoubtedly the primary utensils in use for eating.
Forks did not come into general use until the second half of the eighteenth century.

[11] These served the Indians as eating implements, according to at least one traveler's account. Captain Norwood, "A Voyage to Virginia" (1649), in Force, *Tracts*,
III, 37.

[12] The one case in which a dog did appear in an inventory carried a later notation
that the inclusion of the animal had been a mistake. *Md.Arch.*, IV, 74.

171

Negative evidence is the hardest kind to evaluate, and the absence
of particular items raises questions that can never be definitively
settled. If the inventory mentions no beds, for example, does this
mean there were indeed none at all, or did the appraisers deliberately exclude the only one present for the benefit of the poor
widow? Clothing and other personal items belonging to wives, children, and servants were technically the property of the master, but
creditors did not expect them to be sold in satisfaction of their
debts. In cases of insolvency, moreover, when creditors might be
inclined to push for the last farthing, the court intervened to set
aside things for the widow "to keep house with." In one such instance, the widow of Daniel Smith was allowed her bed, some corn,
and a frying pan, for which she would not have to make account
to the court.[13] Legally, the widow was not permitted to hold back
anything that belonged to her husband's estate. She could claim
her lawful "thirds," which were hers by "dower right," but only
after payment of funeral and medical expenses, legal fees, and
creditors had all taken their due. Even the land might be sold, with
the court's permission, to satisfy outstanding debts, before any heir,
including the widow, could claim a share.

Yet there are clear cases in the records in which certain items
normally included have been deliberately withheld from the inventory. "Madame's" room, for instance, might include all the things
one usually encounters except the bed. The omission in such a case
is striking, although the precise reason for it is unknown. Perhaps
"Madame" was the owner, possibly as stated in a prenuptial agreement for which we now have no record. In other cases, the deceased
made certain last-minute bequests that were honored prior to the
taking of the inventory. These were usually included in the inven-

[13] The inventory of the estate of one Daniel Smith of Charles County was drawn
up by several appraisers on February 7, 1701. Six months later, when it was examined by a clerk, it bore the following request: "[Smith's] widow & relict . . . is a
very poor widow having four children, therefore it is considered for sippor and
relief of the said widow and children that there be deducted and allowed out of
the said estate her bed and furn., 3 barrels of corn, one fatt, and frying pan at such
time the widow pass her account." (*Inv. & Accts.*, Liber 20, f. 217.) The total value
of Smith's personal estate came to approximately £14; the bedding was worth £1.5,
his apparel £1.65, and the household furnishings, which included besides the bed
and bedding, three boxes, a dozen bottles, three razors, a jug, three wooden chairs,
two chests, a sifter, assorted wooden ware worth 2 shillings; two iron pots and a
frying pan worth 8 shillings; some pewter, tin, and earthenware, and three brass
skillets worth only 3 shillings all told.

172

tory, however, with a notation to that effect, and then debited to the estate in a later account of administration.

Since procedures in probate cases gradually became more closely regulated over time under the direction of the Provincial Court and with the aid of successive acts of the Assembly dealing with testamentary matters, it is probably true to say, in the most general kind of way, that widows came to rely on the court to protect their means of livelihood from the press of creditors as both the latter and the judge came to demand fuller accounting from appraisers and administrators. Earlier, however, the records were probably less complete under the less rigorous supervision of the court, and sympathetic appraisers may well have conspired with the widow to hide from the creditors essential household goods.[14]

Recognizing the possibility of such omissions does not permit one to argue the reverse, however. If a family appears to have had no bed, it may in fact not have had one. In cases where the wife died before the husband, for instance, no point was served by omitting any articles of housekeeping from the official inventory, yet we find in a number of such cases bedding but no bed.[15]

If there are no beds or chairs or chamber pots in an inventory, does this mean that there was literally nothing in that house to sleep on, or to sit on, or to relieve oneself into? Obviously the answer must vary with the circumstances, but the inference seems sound that many people did sleep on the floor, or on tables, and one could sit on any number of things besides chairs. A chamber pot, however, did not lend itself to alternate roles, nor could other items serve its function. The absence of a chamber pot thus meant no chamber pot, and the inference follows that people went outside when nature called.[16]

To summarize the reasons why certain classes of objects did not get inventoried: first, some were homemade or free. Others were perishable if not used within a short time, perhaps less than a

[14] The willingness of appraisers to act as accomplices in this illegal act perhaps rested on their perception of her probable future. If she appeared highly marriageable, she might need less help and protection from them.
[15] These are in the sample of fathers of under-age children where family membership is known.
[16] Lawrence Stone notes that members of Charles the Second's court made use of fireplaces, room corners, and so forth. While this might be a measure of aristocratic arrogance, one also suspects such behavior was not confined to a single class. Stone argues that Englishmen of the period cheerfully tolerated very low standards of cleanliness and personal hygiene. *Family, Sex and Marriage in England, 1500-1800*, New York, 1977, pp. 77, 80, 159, 257.

month. Third, some species of property were not customarily subject to the auction block: clothing worn by children, wives, and
servants, for instance. Servants' bedding may also have fallen under
this dispensation. Fourth, property might belong to the widow prior
to the decease of her husband, who had waived his rights to it in
a formal agreement.[17] And finally, there was the poor widow's
reserve in cases of insolvency, which had originally been recognized
in custom and gradually became formalized in regular court procedure.

This long excursion into questions dealing with missing items
has been necessary in order to clarify our interpretation of household contents as reported by probate inventories, and we can now
return to a reexamination of Table V.1. Despite the ambiguities,
one can compare among successive wealth classes the proportions
of estates that listed various consumer goods, and distinguish between high- and low-priority items. Beds and cooking pots were
clearly essential, as chamber pots and warming pans were not. Hand
mills proved highly desirable, though expensive, but chairs and
looking glasses did not fill a need so generally felt.[18] When resources
permitted, artificial light took precedence over tablecloths and napkins, but the high cost of the latter probably acted as a critical
deterrent. Smoothing irons appear before soap or washtubs, so
people did wash their clothes, but not in the way we might imagine.
They may have gone down to the waterside to do the job, or used
the cooking pot to boil them.

The individual items that might be found in planters' houses of
the late seventeenth or early eighteenth century number in the
hundreds, and our discussion so far has focused on a limited class
of objects in order to simplify matters and provide some sense of
the relative importance of things. Because the range of possibilities
for equipping households of even the poorest families was quite
broad, a complete quantitative analysis would be too costly an undertaking. The data contained in Tables V.1 and V.2, however,
guided the following attempt to develop budgets for housekeeping

[17] Such agreements were uncommon for first marriages, but if a woman were a
second wife and the husband wished to exclude her from the usual "widow's thirds"
in favor of his children, a prenuptial agreement to that effect must bear her sig-
nature.

[18] The first looking glass to appear in Wigston Magna inventories was found by
Hoskins in the estate of Francis Smith, Gent., in 1677. Not until 1706, in the
inventory of another "Gent." did he encounter a second. Hoskins, *The Midlands
Peasant*, p. 307.

that range from a minimum list of basics to one incorporating the goods generally found in households living at a level we might tentatively lable as comfortable but not luxurious. Not only have we attempted to contrast budgets, however, but we have also sorted the additions into priorities based on impressionistic readings of approximately a thousand sets of detailed notes on household furnishings in early Maryland. Intuition is a fallible guide, and the results of this exercise, contained in Table V.3, should not be taken as definitive.

A clear functional bias underlies the table: eating, sleeping, and things to hold things. Additions to the bare material necessities take one of three forms: more of the same, elaborations of the same, or departures from the composition of previous acquisitions. More beds or better beds, chairs and stools to replace makeshift seats, a cloth for the table, curtains for the bed, razor and looking glass, gun and saddle, books and candles—these are some examples, but the order or logic in the sequences displayed in Table V.3 are as much imposed by the researcher as inherent in the inventories on which they are based. This is a fundamental problem raised by our use of the sources, because we cannot track the decision-making process at firsthand. All we know is what a man owned when he died, not how or when or in what order he obtained his goods.

The absence of some goods often tells us more than does the presence of others. For instance, the wives of the planters did not bake in big brick ovens, nor did they dip candles, spin flax, or weave homespun for the family's clothing. Indeed, the planter's wife probably spent a lot of her time doing men's tasks as well as "dressing the victuals," "righting up the house," and rearing children.[19]

The actual division of labor between the sexes in early Maryland deviated from the English ideal for the yeoman class, because a man who owned land in England could more readily call upon the labor of others than could one in the New World. Gervaise Markham, the prolific writer of how-to-do-it books in early seventeenth-century England, explicitly distinguished between the roles of man and wife. "The Perfect Husband-Man," he averred, "is the father and master of the family . . . whose offices and imploiments are ever for the most part abroad or remoued from the house as in the field or yarde . . . our english Hous-wife . . . is the mother and mistris of the family, and hath most generall imployments within

---

[19] See Chapter Three for discussion of the tasks performed by servant women.

175

Table V.3
Minimum Housekeeping Equipment for Maryland Families circa 1700

Basic List		First Priority		Second Priority		Third Priority		Fourth Priority	
flock bed	20s	feather bed	45s	bedstead Bible	2s	extra sheets	10s	curtains for best bed	20s
straw bed	10s								
2 iron pots and hooks	10s	frying pan	1s6d	brass skillet	5s	brass kettle	5s	iron pot, hooks tongs, flesh fork	6s
pewter tankard	1s	tin pan	6d	tin dishes	2s			gridiron	1s
pewter basin	2s	pewter dishes	8s	pewter dishes	8s			andirons	1s
wooden bowls	1s	wooden trays	1s	earthenware	2s			candlesticks	12s
cutting knife	1s	sifter	1s	milk trays	1s	stone jugs	1s		1s
spoons	6d			glass bottles	2s				
iron pestle	4s			hand mill	20s	another table	3s	three chairs	6s
table, form	3s	trunk	5s	chair or stool	1s	tablecloth, napkins	10s		
chest	3s6d			another chest	3s				
box	1s					another chest	3s		
2 pails	2s			wooden tubs	2s	tubs, cask	10s	saddle, bridle	10s
				razor, hone	3s	gun	12s		
				smoothing iron	1s				
Total	59s	Total	62s	Total	55s	Total	54s	Total	57s
Cumulative total	£2.95	Cumulative total	£6.05	Cumulative total	£8.80	Cumulative total	£11.50	Cumulative total	£14.35

Source: Inventories of probated estates of six counties, Maryland, based on heads of households with PPW worth £16 through £49, equivalent to the poorer third of all such heads of households in the probate records of these counties before 1720.

the house." He works outside and away from the house, she confines herself indoors—Markham continues, somewhat sanctimoniously, "[she] courting less to direct then to bee directed." Let her be "comely, cleanly, and strong, . . . of chaste thought, stout courage, patient, untyred, watchfull, diligent, witty, pleasant, constant in friendship, full of good neighbour-hood, wise in discourse but not frequent therein," and so on, at a length that violates one of his own maxims.[20] The housewife's only outdoor tasks included tending an herb and "sallat" garden, gathering other greens in the wild, managing the dairy, and tending the poultry.

These tasks continued to be associated with the woman's realm in the colonies and for generations to come. More than a century after Markham wrote, there appeared in a Philadelphia newspaper an advertisement seeking a housekeeper for a motherless household. It set out employments similar to those outlined by Markham as appropriate "Female Concerns of Country Business." These included "raising small stock, dairying, marketing, combing, carding, spinning, knitting, sewing, pickling, preserving, etc., and occasionally to instruct two Young Ladies in those Branches of Oeconomy."[21] In seventeenth-century Maryland, nonperformance of housekeeping duties by the wife were grounds for legal separation.[22]

Since there existed certain assumptions about which of the entire array of farm activities were suitable for females, there must also have existed notions about which were inappropriate, and it is precisely in this realm that questions arise. John Lawson explained, writing in the early years of the eighteenth century, that the white women in North Carolina helped in the fields only "when the season of the Weather requires Expedition."[23] John Oldmixon asserted that the Carolina women "take care of . . . cattle, make butter and cheese, spin cotton and flax, help to sow and reap corn, wind silk from the worms, gather fruit and look after the house."[24] Accurately or not, these Englishmen did not include daily work in the fields as among the normal or usual activities of white women.

[20] Markham, *Country Contentments* (London, 1615; reprinted New York 1973), pp. 1, 4.

[21] Quoted in Carl Holliday, *Woman's Life in Colonial Days* (Boston, 1922), p. 110.

[22] Walsh, "Charles County," p. 102. William Byrd II reported proudly of his daughters, "They are every Day up to their Elbows in Housewifery, which will qualify them effectually for useful Wives and . . . for Notable Women"; letter to Lord Boyle in *VMHB*, XXXII (1924), 39.

[23] Lawson, *A New Voyage*, p. 84.

[24] Oldmixon, *British Empire*, p. 518.

John Hammond, who was attempting to overcome contemporary English prejudices about servants' life in the Chesapeake, asserted in 1659, "the Women are not (as is reported) put into the ground to work, but occupie such domestique imployments and housewifery as in England, that is dressing victuals, righting up the house, milking, employed about dayries, washing, sowing, &c." Yet, he said, "some wenches that are nasty, beastly and not fit to be so imployed are put into the ground."[25] To work at the hoe, therefore, meant not only that one was servile, but "nasty, beastly, and not fit" for housewifery or the worthy estate of wife and mother. Orphan Margaret O'Daniell protested to the local county court about her stepfather, Thomas Denton, because he made her work for him at the hoe, "as hard as any servant."[26] Robert Parnaffee's servant wench likewise worked as hard as any man: the size of her crop was the same as that produced by either of the two men also employed by Parnaffee.[27]

A maid-servant in Cook's famous satire complained that she had been kidnapped in England and sold as a servant in Maryland where

> . . . things are changed now,
> at the Hoe I daily work,
> and Bare-foot go,
> In weeding Corn or feeding Swine,
> I spend my melancholy Time.[28]

Not only servant women were condemned to lives at the hoe, said some observers, but "some of the masters and their wives who pass their lives here in wretchedness, do the same."[29] Perhaps the key word here is "some." Not all women, servant or free, worked in the fields, simply because the ordinary tasks of running the household expanded with its size and status. Women carried out those chores for which men had no time, training, or inclination. On John Weaver's plantation in Kent County, for instance, there worked five men servants and one woman. Only five shares of

[25] Hammond, *Leah and Rachel*, in Force, *Tracts*, III, 12.

[26] Walsh, "Charles County," p. 117.

[27] She made a crop of 1,140 pounds of tobacco in 1681, and her share of the corn crop was valued at 400 pounds of tobacco, for a total value of 1,540 pounds. Two male hands, also working for Parnaffee that year, produced crops of tobacco and corn valued at 3,144 pounds of tobacco, or an average of 1,572 each. *Inv. & Accts.*, Liber 7B, f. 205.

[28] Cook, *The Sot-Weed Factor*, pp. 6-7.

[29] Dankers and Sluyter, *Journal*, p. 216.

tobacco were reported in the inventory of Weaver's estate in 1706, indirect evidence that the woman did not participate in the fields.[30] Her work presumably released the others from domestic duties, allowing them to concentrate on earning a cash income.

That some division of labor within the farm household was more efficient than efforts of an undifferentiated work force is strongly suggested by certain partnership agreements surviving from the early years of Maryland's settlement, when the male/female ratio was perhaps as high as six to one. Under such circumstances, free men could not expect to marry as soon as they were economically able. They therefore often joined together with other men in similar circumstances, whom they then referred to as mates. With these they agreed to hold their property in common and to work for equal shares of the crop.[31] Here is one example dating from 1655: John Erickson and Edward Tarret divided 100 acres between them. The former promised to share equally in clearing and fencing enough ground to contain 3,000 corn hills and clearing ground for 6,000 tobacco hills, unfenced, and to bear equal charges in building a "walplate" tobacco house 40 feet long and 20 feet wide. This latter chore was to be performed by Edward by "next March if nailes are then to bee gott."[32] Another pair, Thomas Osborne and Luther Ayers, agreed to dissolve their partnership in the event of disagreement or if either married.[33]

Still other partnerships were formed between married men and single men. Walter Peake and John Slingsbury agreed in 1649 to plant for equal shares for five years, "Only the sd. Peake his Wife is to have her wearing clothes, & her childs, & one bed furnished, & to give each of the children a Cow-calf, the first that doth fall to Us."[34] Similarly, Robert Martin and Henry Ashley consented to an equal partnership in cattle, hogs, and land, crops of tobacco and corn, "only the sd Robert Martin resseruinge to himyselfe three

[30] Kent Co. *Inventories*, Box 2, f. 4. Neither did Weaver, need it be added. He lived part of the time in Bristol, England, and owned a library of books that included some concerning medicine, divinity, and law. Since the inventory also included two wigs, hair powder, and eighty-one quire of paper, he may have practiced law in Maryland.

[31] More examples of such agreements or references to them may be found in *Md.Arch.*, XLIV, 20, 27, 37, 44, 54, 79-80, 91, 162, 218, 244-45, 313, 394; IV, 479; and X, 297, 479.

[32] Ibid., XLIV, 54.

[33] Ibid., p. 218.

[34] Ibid., IV, 479. Peake made another, similar agreement in 1653 with Paul Simpson, ibid., X, 297.

Cowes for my three Children." This contract was scheduled to end
in three years, at which point they intended to make equal division.[35] The terms of another partnership stated that it would remain in force until one or the other quit the country, the bachelor
married, or they dissolved the pact by mutual consent.[36]

The agreements between two men, one of whom was married,
not only provided mutual help in planting chores and in the exchange of materials and skills for the betterment of both, but the
married man provided his wife's housekeeping services as part of
the bargain. Hubert Pattee agreed to grant William Turner, with
whom he promised to live the "present yeare," two and a half shares
"provided the Said Turner Should get a new hand and the Said
Patee was to lay in 4 barrells of Corne and a Cowes Milk and more
if he had it and to find Soap and William Turner his washing."[37]
The half share must surely have been offered in return for laundry
and in recognition of the wife's contribution in the form of domestic
tasks. Consider the following arrangement between John Salter and
John Raby: Salter was to give Raby sufficient ground to plant corn
and tobacco for the ensuing year and housing for his crop, the two
planting together for equal shares. Salter was to "find" Raby meat,
drink, and lodging for twelve months, and Raby in turn promised
to help make fence. In addition—and this throws a flood of light
on the division of labor in farm households—Raby promised to
beat corn for bread for himself, Salter, and Salter's wife and child
during the year "and to assist in anything needful to be done about
the tobacco" and further, to pay 600 pounds in tobacco in consideration of Salter's, and Salter's wife's, taking care of household
matters and providing the land.[38] In yet another agreement, the
married man's wife was to do "all their household employment"
and to wash and mend the partners' linen.[39]

In none of the contracts did the terms specify that the wife would
work in the field. Furthermore, in the depositions of female witnesses taken in court proceedings during this period, the work
activities that these women described pertained only to housewifery—most commonly cooking, serving, and cleaning. The absence
of any references to fieldwork can be explained by the bias natural
to such records. Only those in a social setting could be on the scene

[35] Ibid., XLIV, 91.
[36] Ibid., X, 297.
[37] Ibid., p. 479.
[38] Ibid., XLIV, 151.
[39] Ibid., p. 394.

when something germane to a court case took place and could therefore be called upon to give testimony. Anyone who had been out in the field or woods at the time would have nothing of value to contribute to such investigations and would not be included on the roster of witnesses. Despite the weight of the argument for viewing the activities of witnesses in court cases as not necessarily representative of women's usual activities, it still seems impressive that the activities mentioned failed to include hoeing, suckering, worming, and so forth, or for that matter, making fence, staves, or shingles.

One finding that does emerge from the survey is that white women did not expect to work at the hoe or to beat corn as part of their regular work routine. Poverty or the avarice of a cruel master might force them to it, but neither task was considered suitable or appropriate for them. These tasks must therefore have been experienced as both unpleasant and degrading. Recall Hammond's statement that only those women who were "nasty, beastly" and unfit for housewifery were put to work in the ground.[40]

Although travelers' accounts, pamphlet writers, and court proceedings do not provide us with a direct description of women's typical and usual tasks, the inventories do afford limited but valid evidence of what they did not do—to return to our original point. Brewing beer, for instance, was women's work in rural England, according to Markham.[41] Relatively few Maryland inventories, however, mention malt, barley, hops, brewing vats, or beer barrels. Beer certainly was made, as attested by occasional funeral expense accounts, but only a few households seem to have engaged in brewing. Indeed, John Hammond had castigated as lazy the housewives of Virginia and Maryland for neglecting so nourishing a drink and so virtuous an activity.[42]

Ponder the rather limited range of possible activities posed by the goods listed in one man's inventory, by no means atypical of his class, taken in the year 1697 (Table V.4). The variety of indoor actions suggested by the household goods belonging to this man's estate appear to have been limited to cooking, eating, shaving, ironing, reading, and carpentry. Outdoors, the possibilities included splitting logs, tending the crops and the animals, and hunting, if the gun still worked and if our man could get ammunition for it.

[40] Hammond, *Leah and Rachel*, in Force, *Tracts*, III, 12.
[41] Markham, *Country Contentments*, p. 122.
[42] Hammond, *Leah and Rachel*, in Force, *Tracts*, III, 12.

TABLE V.4
GOODS IN ONE INVENTORY, 1697

Livestock	Tools	Cooking Utensils	Other
2 horses	4 gimlets	tin kettle	5 spoons
4 cattle	crosscut saw	flesh fork	smoothing iron
6 hogs	wedges	pair pothooks	3 small books
	carpentry tools	2 iron pots	2 razors, hone
		iron skillet	2 chests
		brass kettle	pewterware
		iron pestle	an old gun
			woodenware
			2 glass bottles

SOURCE: *Inv. & Accts.*, Liber 15, f. 242. The account of administration added a cow.

The conclusion follows: if members of this class, male or female, did not spin, make soap, brew beer, or dip candles, neither did they sit idly by sipping tea. They were outside hoeing tobacco and corn, splitting rails, perhaps hunting, maybe visiting the neighbors. What are the implications of these findings? First, their relative poverty would have acted to spur them on to produce *more* tobacco, not less, when its price foundered, even though the ultimate result of such effort was to worsen the glut, at which point one might not be able to sell the crop at all.

If no one would take their crops, the planters' families could not obtain the things they depended on the market to provide: clothing, shoes, tools, nails, powder and shot, or salt—to name only the most important. Their reliance on imports made them critically vulnerable to shipping interruptions of any kind as well as to cyclical downturns in the market. So long as anyone would take their tobacco, they were lured into staying. If no one took it, they were not only destitute but helpless. That vulnerability underlay many of the fitful attempts at provincial legislation to promote domestic manufactures in the seventeenth century.

Making wearable cloth and leather shoes required skill and time. The scattering of the population and the success of staple agriculture had inhibited the development of local markets for these home manufactures, so skilled craftsmen found neither profit nor security in abstaining from the culture of tobacco in order to supply local demand when imports ceased. The failure to develop and rely on things of one's own making, or of one's neighbor's, resulted from a thoroughgoing concentration on raising tobacco that could only be broken by prolonged and severe depression. Yet one shudders at the devastation visited by market fluctuations on families so wedded to a single crop as were the majority of those in the poorer third of Maryland's white population.

As Chapter Two showed, the spread of tools associated with home manufacture of cloth was confined to upper-class households and to the planters living on the lower eastern shore.[43] Flax growing and preparation was time-consuming and interfered with processing tobacco, since flax had to be cut down before it went to seed if its fibers were to be any good for linen cloth, but it ripened at about the same time that tobacco did.[44] Cotton was imported from the West Indies but could be purchased only if one had the means of exchange.[45] Wool, the one local source of textile fiber was not

[43] Tracing the course of spinning wheels in inventories yielded a simple guide to the timing and location of such activities (see Chapter Two). Few households among the poorer planters owned spinning wheels, but more did so after 1700 than before. Somerset County on the lower eastern shore of Maryland proved the most frequent site.

[44] William Byrd explained to his English readers why hemp and flax were not more generally grown in the colonies despite ideal climate and soil conditions: "Labor is not more than two-pence a day in the East Country where they produce hemp, and here we can't compute it at less than ten-pence, . . . our freight is three times as dear as theirs, the price that will make them rich will ruin us." Since half an acre provided ample material with which to clothe a family, the supply of land did not pose a critical obstacle to flax and hemp production, even in areas of relatively poor soils. Tryon, *Household Manufactures*, p. 207.

[45] Spotswood, *Letters*, II, 105, reports cotton imported from the West Indies into Virginia and some planting of both cotton and flax in response to low prices for tobacco. The Board of Trade had earlier expressed concern over the potential competition of cotton with tobacco in Virginia. *Calendar of State Papers, Colonial Series*, XIV, 518-19. Thirty years earlier, Governor Berkeley claimed to have lost more than £1,000 sterling in his efforts to raise flax in Virginia; ibid., 1661-1668, VII, 316. Late in the eighteenth century, Timothy Pickering estimated that good rich land would produce 2,000 pounds of seed cotton per acre, which would reduce to 500 pounds after ginning. Quoted in Gray, *Agriculture*, II, 674. If one can gin a pound a day, 500 pounds will take 500 days. If the cost of labor per day is 10 pounds of tobacco (the low end of the range for our period), then the cost to gin the crop from a single acre is 5,000 pounds of tobacco. If one pound of ginned cotton yields five yards of spun fiber per pound (two days' spinning, more or less), this yields two to four yards of cloth, depending on the closeness of the weave. At one day's wages per yard of cloth woven, the price of cotton cloth per yard is 3½ pounds of tobacco plus 10 for spinning plus 10 for weaving plus the cost of clearing, weeding, harvesting, and seed for the cotton. Therefore two shillings does not cover fixed costs, only the labor costs associated with the manufacture. The only reason to undertake its production, under these circumstances, is to use more intensively a labor force you are already supporting, and thus avoid or reduce your balance on account with an outside supplier. Only planters owning numerous slaves would

of very high quality. The fibers produced by Maryland sheep were not strong enough to bear close, tight weaving, and fulling of the resulting cloth was limited by the capacity of the human arm. The results were not praiseworthy.

So time-consuming was the production of "countrymade" cloth that even in times of low tobacco prices it cost as much per yard in the inventories of estates as did the imported kerseys with which it chiefly competed.[46] One author estimated that it took "a good day's work" to spin two double skeins of linen thread or to weave six yards of linen cloth.[47] The Virginia indentured servant, John Harrower, counted thirty-one work days for two people to spin a total of six pounds of wool and eight and a half pounds of cotton, to "run nigh five yards pr. lb." If he was correct, those thirty-one work days produced only 72½ yards of mixed thread, or 2⅓ yards of yarn per day.[48]

Yet for all the investment in time and effort that it required, homemade cloth was likely to be ugly, coarse, and scratchy. Given its price, there should be little wonder that the inhabitants preferred the professionally finished materials imported from abroad, which in most years their tobacco could purchase.

Imported or domestic, shirts and shifts, breeches and petticoats were necessary items to seventeenth-century Englishmen and women, not just for warmth, but for decency's sake, as well. A Christian covered his body, in summer as well as in winter, because he regarded the naked body as shameful. Such views were common to all Western Europeans, it should be observed, and were not limited to Puritans, English or otherwise. The comments on the habits of the American Indians by foreign travelers make this point clear, for they all as a matter of course linked nakedness with heathenism, sexual promiscuity, and moral laxity.

A lack of clothing, then, was a serious matter, even in warm weather, since it compromised one's moral stance. Yet poor women, who were supposed to be indoors and spinning, among other tasks, were out in the fields, alongside their menfolk and children, all

---

be likely to find themselves with underused labor, and thus only slaveowners would be likely to raise or import sizable quantities of cotton for home production of cloth.

[46] Eighteen to thirty pence per yard.

[47] Alice Morse Earle, *Colonial Dames and Good Wives* (Boston and New York, 1896), p. 312. This seems high for loom output.

[48] This was in 1776. Riley, ed., *The Journal of John Harrower*, edited by Edward Miles Riley (Colonial Williamsburg, 1963), p. 138. Harrower contracted with a young black woman to spin cotton for him at the rate of three shillings the pound.

dressed in whatever their tobacco could buy, or what remained after the year's accounts were cleared. During very bad years, they made do with old clothes and even rags. Judging from the scarcity of soap in the poorer estate inventories, one might also question how thoroughly the planter's wife washed the clothes. When they wore wool, which could not be washed without disastrous results, they were condemned to lice and other vermin. Even daily washing of hands, feet, and face could not provide relief from itching in an infested household, and no one in those days bathed his entire body all at once. Those who could afford a regular change of linen and frequent brushing and airing of their woolen garments might escape infestation, but such were the prerogatives of the affluent. Combing and "picking" were among the accustomed maternal duties of the seventeenth-century housewife.[49]

Although colonial and English hygiene left much to be desired, it was not entirely lacking. Despite the general absence of soap and laundry equipment in the inventories of the poorer planters, a fifth actually did own smoothing irons, the reader will recall, so linens did get washed occasionally. The laundry was probably done at the waterside instead of at home, perhaps using soap purchased especially for the day's needs. Or, perhaps, some local, homemade substitute was pressed into service. Maryland housewives did not, however, make the soft, scummy jelly obtainable from wood ashes and house grease. Such soap-making required boiling in a very large pot over a great, hot fire, a chore best done out of doors and away from the highly combustible materials of their little wooden houses.[50] It was nasty, hot work. Imported hard soap must have seemed far more desirable to those who could afford it, and one suspects that most Marylanders did so or went without.

The frequency of razors in the inventories suggests that most men shaved. Since keeping hair clean and free of lice was a continuing problem, many rich men such as William Byrd solved it by having their heads shaved as well, substituting powdered wigs or

[49] The guardian of a pair of twins described his chores as "washing, lodging, combing, pickeing, nurseing and fostering them"; Walsh, "Charles County," p. 108. Stone found picking lice to have been one of the tasks assigned servant maids in upper-class homes in seventeenth-century England. Stone, *Family, Sex, and Marriage*, p. 558.

[50] Earle, *Colonial Dames*, pp. 302-303. Few poor planters could afford such a pot in the first place. *Md.Arch.*, XLIV, 71 contains an entertaining account of going to "Mr. Hatton's next to Uties store" to get soap and finding none there so stealing some from Utie, instead. This was in 1656.

colorful turbans for their troublesome hair.[51] Ordinary men could not afford these niceties, and they also eschewed the Indian method of insect control: bear grease liberally applied. Directed primarily at mosquitoes rather than at lice, the grease stiffened with drying, so it was not quite so messy as it might seem, but the smell proved pervasive and memorable.

It is possible to make some generalizations about the kinds of clothing worn by the planters and their families. Not very surprisingly, those of the poorer sort owned very little, ranging in value from a few shillings' worth to as much as two pounds in those inventories that included the apparel of the deceased. This sum does not include the clothing worn by the rest of the family. It is interesting, though, that the men's clothing averaged about 6 percent of the total value of their personal estate, very close to the 7 percent calculated for English farm laborers in the first half of the seventeenth century. These wore coarse canvas or leather pants and linsey-woolsey shirts for work, but might own holiday wear consisting of a suit of woolen or mixed linen and woolen cloth, containing about six yards of material, which could last several years with care.[52] Maryland's poorer planters owned clothes of the same sort, although they may have needed less covering for much of the year: "Shirts and Drawers of Scotch-cloth Blue / With neither Stockings, Hat or Shoe," sneered Cook in *The Sot-Weed Factor*.[53]

Servants and slaves wore clothes that were little different in value or cut from those worn by poor white folks. A kersey suit for one servant cost 300 pounds of tobacco in 1681, another was valued at twelve shillings in 1688, and new clothing for three servants, including one Negro man, averaged £2.87 each in 1692, or 690 pounds of tobacco at a penny per pound.[54] A new shirt for a servant in 1701 cost two shillings six pence, and a suit for another servant five years later cost £1.16 or the equivalent of 279 pounds of tobacco.[55]

Let us outfit a hypothetical servant at these prices, giving him a pair of shoes worth 50, a pair of stockings at 30, a suit of light or small clothes at 70, a shirt for 30, a kersey suit at 280, and a hat

[51] Byrd, *Secret Diary*, p. 14.
[52] Alan Everitt, "Farm Labourers," in Thirsk, ed., *Agrarian History*, p. 450: "At the end of each year of service, their master might provide them with a new smock or shirt, and a pair of shoes and stockings, and at harvest time with a pair of gloves."
[53] Cook, *The Sot-Weed Factor*, p. 2.
[54] *Inv. & Accts.*, Liber 2, f. 149; Liber 7B, f. 11.
[55] Ibid., Liber 11, f. 29½; Liber 13B, f. 92; and Liber 28, f. 350.

186

or cap at 50, all of which come to 480 pounds of tobacco, representing a minimum outlay for a complete outfit of new clothes. Probably no one, servant or free, got all new clothes at once, but a reasonable guess would include at least one new shirt, one set of underclothes, one pair of stockings, one pair of shoes, and a pair of britches or a new jacket every year, resources permitting. This would come to about 275, perhaps a little more some years and a little less in others.[56]

By comparison, planters of the class worth £16 to £34 PPW owned clothing worth around 240 or £1. Nicholas Carr, for example, owned a hat, waistcoat, breeches, two pair of shoes and an old coat, all of which were sold or given away after his death but valued prior to their disposal at 180 pounds of tobacco.[57] Robert Vernon, whose inventory was dated 1717, owned two pairs of stockings, a hat, and a pair of "tick" britches worth twenty shillings, all told; but he also had twenty-four yards of colored linen and three yards of kersey worth fifteen shillings, part of which could have been intended for a shirt and jacket using the mohair thread and some buttons also mentioned in the inventory.[58]

Clothing for slaves is more difficult to estimate. Daniel Parke of York County, Virginia, left a will directing that a certain Negro be freed after his death, and that he be given annually, as long as he lived, a kersey coat, a pair of breeches, a hat, two pairs of shoes, two pairs of yarn stockings, two shirts, and a pair of drawers.[59] This was surely as fine an endowment as a freed black man could hope for, and may be viewed as a kind of maximum or upper limit to the annual cost of clothing a slave. A minimum money estimate, on the other hand, is represented by a particular account of administration that charged a debtor's estate for clothing the mulatto slave who had been surrendered to a creditor, £1.18, or roughly 275 pounds.[60] Since this was what the poor fellow required immediately in the way of clothes, it may be understood as the min-

[56] *Md.Arch.*, IV, 274 (1644); and Bruce, *Economic History*, II, 8-9 (1660, 1694) provide examples of menservants' clothing, and *Md.Arch.*, LIII, 168, of a woman servant's freedom clothes. Administration accounts provide vivid detail on clothing provided for George Beckwith's orphans and servants in 1676; *Inv. & Accts.*, Liber 2, f. 329-46 and 179-86. A Charles County account accepted by the court in April 1721 charged an estate the equivalent of 240 pounds of tobacco for a servant and for a child, per year, for their clothing; *Accounts*, Liber 4, f. 88.

[57] *Inv. & Accts.*, Liber 5, f. 106. The year was 1677.

[58] Ibid., Liber 39C, f. 80.

[59] This was about the year 1690. Bruce, *Economic History*, II, 278-79.

[60] *Inv. & Accts.*, Liber 35, f. 332.

imum necessary to clothe a slave in a year's time or less. A maximum money estimate is offered by another account that charged £6.30 for the "well appareling" of a Negro woman during the years 1710 to 1714, or 378 pounds per year if four years, 302 if five.[61] Finally, an estate in 1730 was charged the equivalent of 300 pounds apiece for clothes and tools for "the Negroes," adjusting for price changes.[62] Judging from this rather poor assemblage of evidence, adult slaves received clothing worth between 275 and 375 pounds a year. The latter is a very generous maximum, and the majority of slaves could probably have expected clothes worth about the lower estimate of 275, almost the same for servants and poor planters.

Fashions for men shifted during the course of the seventeenth century away from the broad shoulders and deep chest associated with military bearing, as the doublet and hose gave way to breeches and coat. Two inventories from the same year, 1638, contrast the old and the new in early Maryland. John Bryant owned two "suits" and a doublet with three and a half (!) shirts, two pairs of linen drawers, one pair of stockings, one coat, two neckcloths, a cap, two hats and a pair of boots with spurs. Richard Loe's apparel consisted of two pairs of breeches, a coat, a canvas jacket, a waistcoat, two pairs of stockings, a pair of shoes, and a cap.[63]

Although knee breeches became stylish, they were confining, and many farmers probably wore instead short, floppy trousers extending to a little below the knee.[64] Breeches made of crudely tanned leather do appear in Maryland inventories, but must have been hot for ordinary fieldwork and were probably intended for the messy tasks of tanning, butchering, and the like. For special occasions, if he could afford them, the planter wore a linen shirt bleached as white as his purse allowed, cloth breeches a little baggier than those fashionable in the eighteenth century, cloth or knitted stockings, leather shoes with wooden heels—and at the very end of our period these last were sewn and buckled rather than closed

[61] Ibid., Liber 35, f. 259.

[62] *Accounts*, Liber 10, f. 280. See also *Accounts*, Liber 2, f. 263, in which £10.55 is charged for "clothing and other necessaries" for fourteen slaves, three of them children. Runaways' clothing are reported in Bruce, *Economic History*, II, 106.

[63] *Md.Arch.*, IV, 30, 74.

[64] Peter Copeland, *Working Dress in Colonial and Revolutionary America* (Westport, Conn., 1977), p. 41. This book is organized by occupational group and is copiously illustrated, mostly with the author's own drawings and sketches. The original sources from which many of the illustrations were taken are foreign, however. An attached glossary, although very brief, is useful.

by ties.[65] With the breeches, the planter wore a cloth waistcoat over the shirt and under the coat, for a complete outfit. Only the most affluent men wore a greatcoat in wintertime; the others just kept moving.

If people wanted greater warmth, they added more clothes, or perhaps a blanket. Long winter underwear did not become popular until the nineteenth century. Indeed, in the colonial period a man's shirt served as his underwear, reaching to his knees and loosefitting for comfort. His trousers usually had a drawstring top, and front and back were indistinguishable. Breeches had a front flap held up by buttons sewed on the waistband. The seat of the breeches was cut very full to allow the wearer to sit down.[66] The waistcoat was worn over the shirt and breeches, under the coat, and tended to be long rather than short in the seventeenth century. The precise meaning of "jacket" as opposed to waistcoat and coat is not clear, but perhaps it combined both functions in a single garment and was for work rather than for dress.

Work clothes for women were also designed for comfort. A simple linen shift, with or without sleeves, tucked into a full skirt that ended above the ankles composed the basic outfit. Over the shift, what we would now call a long blouse, a woman wore a pair of "bodies" if she could afford them. This garment could be short or long, and might even have sleeves. For warmth, she added more petticoats, as skirts were called, and to keep them clean, an apron over all.[67] Freedom clothes for one woman servant in early Maryland included three pairs of shoes, two pairs of worsted stockings, a pair of "bodies," and a petticoat of broadcloth.[68]

Probably no woman of the poorer classes wore stays, the boned foundation garment often placed on children and young girls, which continued to be used by women of the middle and upper classes.

[65] Handsome buckles of pewter or silver became an article of adornment in the eighteenth century.

[66] Marjorie Hicks, compiler, *Clothing for Ladies and Gentlemen of Higher and Lower Standing: a Working Pamphlet to Aid the Imitation of New England Citizens of the Eighteenth Century* (Washington, D.C., 1976), pp. 14-21. This little book is unique in that it relates clothing styles to bodily carriage and general posture: the *image* that the wearer hoped to project. Although the author's primary purpose is to provide patterns for sewing period costumes, she also describes how they were to be worn, and how it should feel to wear them.

[67] Women wore neither brassieres nor underpants, both of which are inventions of the nineteenth century. C. Willett Cunnington and Phillis Cunnington, *The History of Underclothes* (London, 1951), p. 22.

[68] *Md.Arch.*, LIII, 168.

Fieldwork, particularly at the hoe, is not conducive to that upright posture so greatly in favor among the better sort at the time, so the dumpy figure and stooped carriage of the poor woman served to declare her status, even before her weathered face and horny hands could give it away.

The cooking and eating utensils found in the probate inventories provide additional clues to a life style that appears to have valued a strong back, a good bed, and a full stomach more than cleanliness or "niceness." The usual diet of the seventeenth-century English-man consisted of one-dish meals eaten with a spoon. When roasted meat made its uncommon appearance on the common man's table, the meat was carved and served by the housewife into plates or trenchers shared by two people sitting side by side. Young children found it easier to stand at the table, since seating was always a problem for them. The meat was taken up in the hands to be eaten. Forks did not come into common usage until much later.[69] Such ready use of the hands at table meant that people had to wipe them on something, and households of the middling and better sort were usually well supplied with napkins. Among the poorer planters, however, these carried a far lower priority, as we have seen. Of the poorer estates worth less than £35, for instance, only 10 percent owned table linen, but in the next step up, those worth £35 to £49, almost twice as many had acquired them.

Wherever they may have wiped their hands after dipping them into the dish they shared with their neighbor at table, do so they must if they were to get a sure grasp on the large drinking pot as it was handed around. When full, the pewter vessel must have been far too heavy for children to handle, and a nearby adult probably helped the little ones to drink.[70]

[69] James Deetz says they were not in general use in New England until the third quarter of the eighteenth century. *In Small Things Forgotten*, p. 123. The first reference to forks in Maryland records seems to be the four, two "new" and two "old," listed in Stephen Yeo's inventory taken in 1667, in *Testamentary Proceedings*, 2, f. 206. Whether these were actually table forks is not clear, but there seems no reason for a family to have owned more than one flesh fork, and few planters had even a single dung fork. Planter Yeo and his wife and her two children also owned six ivory combs and five horn combs, which suggests they were a family of no ordinary background.

[70] One writer reported an experience from his nineteenth-century childhood in Connecticut on the occasion of visiting a country family: "The only drinking vessel on the table was one of the quart Staffordshire mugs . . . which was filled with water, milk, or cider . . . and passed around the table at the demand of any thirsty one. The family consisted of a man and his wife, an ancient grandmother, and

All the cooking, serving, and eating took place in the hearth room for middling planters' families as well as for the poorer sort, and for both the fireplace served as the real center and focus of family life. On the hearth itself, the principal utensils for cooking were always in ready position. The single most important piece of that equipment was the cast-iron pot or kettle. About nine-tenths of the poorer planters' inventories mentioned them, whereas only half owned frying pans or skillets. The big iron pot was suspended over the hearth by a long hook hanging from a bar fixed into the chimney, usually a stout pole of green wood laid crosswise into notches in the chimney walls. Eventually the pole would burn through, and if not replaced before the inevitable rupture, a sudden break could throw both pot and contents in a scalding stream over the unwary. Since the floor in front of the fire was a favorite sleeping and resting place in winter, a tumbling pot posed a recurrent hazard; stories of small children scalding to death are not uncommon in the literature.[71]

Readers will recall that most seventeenth-century chimneys in Maryland were not made of brick, so there could be no oven in the structure itself. Even on wealthier plantations, the oven was usually a structure separate from the kitchen fireplace, in order to disperse the heat. For most families, baking took place in an iron kettle placed among the coals on the hearth, with more coals heaped on the kettle's top.

A single pot or kettle filled any number of functions in the planter's household, but the one-pot cooking style of the period epitomizes an entire way of life. No one had to watch it when it and its contents were placed well back, and up, from a banked fire, providing a perpetual promise of a warm dish of porridge or soup to the hungry traveler or to the sore-armed and weary workers in from the fields.

The people cooked everything the same way, or at least began almost every dish by first boiling the ingredients. Meat, corn, beans, greens—all were cooked in a pot with plenty of water to cover. Soft, motley messes were the rule, taken with a spoon, mopped up with cornbread. Everyday diet consisted of "hog meat and hoe

---

several children with not too clean faces. I couldn't refuse the mug when urged upon me and selecting a place on the brim at the right of the handle, I drank, when one of the children exclaimed, 'See, mar! He's got granny's place.' " George Dow, *Every Day Life in the Massachusetts Bay Colony* (New York, 1935; reprinted 1967), p. 30.

[71] Ibid., p. 40, recounts one such tragedy.

cake."[72] This, indeed, formed the diet for all the English colonists of North America in the seventeenth century, in New England as well as the Chesapeake. Indian corn "is the cheifest Diett they have," announced one visitor in 1706. "They beat itt in a Mortar and gett the husks from itt and then Boyle itt with a Peice of Beefe or salted Porke with some Kidney Beanes [,] which is much like to Pork and Pease att sea [,] butt they Call it hommony."[73]

Although wheat was grown by many of the more affluent families to supply flour for leavened bread and pastry for pies, Indian corn remained the "support of many of the meaner sort of People as well as of Servants and Slaves."[74] The Frenchman, Durand, explained in 1686 that "the peasants make only a few bushels of wheat on each plantation, intending it for pastry because of the great abundance of venison and apples." He went on to describe the cornbread, "as white as paper, and good to the taste, but rather heavy on the stomach to those unaccustomed to it."[75] Beverly attributed the planters' general failure to grow wheat to the laziness of the "poorer sort [who] don't mind to sow the ground because they won't be at the trouble of making a fence particularly for it. And therefore their constant bread is pone." Durand, however, was told that the return from corn was so much better than from wheat that the latter did not seem worth the effort.[76] Corn still in the husk could be stored longer and with less trouble than wheat, and did not have to be harvested at the moment of ripeness, as did wheat. Indeed, corn could stand in the field well into winter, and could wait until after the tobacco crop was finished and shipped.[77] Wheat, moreover, required a more elaborate milling process than corn.[78]

Although the Indians prepared the hard kernels of corn by roasting or parching them, the great effort required to grind the kernels with the teeth fails to extract the corn's full potential for nourish-

[72] This is the title of a recent study of the food production of the antebellum South: Sam Hilliard, *Hogmeat and Hoecakes: Food Supply in the Old South, 1840-1860* (Carbondale, Ill., 1972).

[73] "Narrative of a Voyage to Maryland, 1705-1706," *AHR*, XII (1907), 335, 336.

[74] Governor Drysdale of Virginia in 1724, quoted in Harold B. Gill, Jr., "Cereal Grains in Colonial Virginia," report prepared for Colonial Williamsburg Foundation, Inc., October 1974, p. 15.

[75] Durand, *Frenchman in Virginia*, p. 106. Corn flour cannot be rolled into pie pastry.

[76] Beverly, *History*, p. 153; Durand, *Frenchman in Virginia*, p. 106.

[77] Gill, "Cereal Grains in Colonial Virginia," p. 19.

[78] Gray, *Agriculture*, I, 161.

ment. Only corn just in the "milk" yields readily to human mastication without prior preparation of the kernels.[79] Hard corn can be cooked whole as a vegetable if it has first been soaked in an alkali compound to soften the kernels, but more often it was ground to coarse meal after the preliminary soaking, and then sifted.[80] The finer grains were reserved for making bread, and the rest boiled into porridge, served with milk or cider if these were available. As two visiting Dutchmen explained, "the corn . . . has to be first soaked, before it is ground or pounded, because the grains being large and very hard, cannot be broken under the small stones of their light hand-mills, and then it is left so coarse it must be sifted. They take the finest for bread and the other for different kinds of groats. The meal intended for bread is kneaded moist without leaven or yeast, salt, or grease, and generally comes out of the oven so that it will hardly hold together, and so blue and moist that it is as heavy as dough; yet the best of it when cut and roasted, tastes almost like warm white bread."[81]

The handmills referred to arrived late on the scene, and, as we have seen, few of the poorer planters could afford them.[82] Unlike New Englanders, few tidewater residents could resort to grist or saw mills.[83] The most common method for preparing corn remained beating up and down with a heavy iron pestle in a deep, bucket-shaped wooden mortar. Inside the mortar was a smooth concave surface that allowed the whole, and therefore heavier, grains to remain at the bottom during the pounding.

Beating corn was hard work. A sixteenth-century Spanish writer, Girolama Benzoni, wrote, "there is much work involved in making this bread. . . . Traveling in uninhabited districts, and with necessity

[79] Sweet corn, as the modern American knows it, was not developed until late in the eighteenth century.

[80] *Md.Arch.*, XLIV, 297, for the case of the runaway servant whose only excuse was fear of punishment for oversoaking his master's corn prior to "beating" it.

[81] Dankers and Sluyter, *Journal*, p. 217.

[82] See Table V.1 above.

[83] A traveller in 1649 reported only five watermills and four windmills in Virginia but there were, he said, a "great number" of horse and hand mills. "A New Description of Virginia," in Force, *Tracts*, II. An act of the Maryland Assembly cited the lack of watermills as the reason why cultivation of small grains was "but coldly prosecuted" there; *Md.Arch.*, XIII, 534. See ibid., II, 211-14 on the same subject. Since probate inventories enumerate only personal property, that is, "movables," one cannot count mills directly, but references to millstones, gear-works, mill houses, and so on, are just as rare as are references in wills. Only a dozen positive statements mentioning mills or horse mills appeared in the entire sample of young fathers' estates.

for my guide, I learned to grind it in order not to eat it raw or roasted. On account of its great hardness the grinding is very severe work." He recalled how sore his arms became from the daily chore.[84]

A dramatic story of shipwreck and rescue by friendly Indians also provides an illustration of the laboriousness of corn grinding. Exhausted and nearly starved, an English exile during the Civil War, one Captain Norwood, was guided by his Indian rescuers toward their village somewhere on Maryland's lower eastern shore, which they finally reached after a long journey. The morning after his arrival, he walked through the wigwam. "In passing the spaces betwixt fire and fire, one space amongst the rest was blinded with a traverse of mat; and [led] by the noise I heard from thence, like the beating of hemp . . . by standing on tiptoe for a full discovery, I saw a sight that gave me no small trouble. The same specifical queen (whose courtesy for our kind usage the other day can never be enough applauded) was now employed in the hard servile labor of beating corn for the king's dinner. . . . I wish'd myself in her place for her ease [but she waved him off]."[85]

As this story so strikingly attests, grinding corn was squaws' work among the Indians. Among whites, it was servants' work. Teenaged boys in particular were assigned the task. So tedious and exhausting was it, servants often sought to exclude it from their regular labors, and parents drawing up their wills attempted to protect their orphans from such service. One boy was made so distraught by the assignment that he drowned himself.[86] The use of hand mills spread about the time that the available supply of "mortar boys" was declining, yet ownership of the mills was positively correlated with wealth. Indeed, the biggest planters often owned several of them, one for each quarter. "While the Indian corn was soft [in the fall of the year] the block and pestle did very well for making meal for johneycake and mush but were rather slow when the corn became hard."[87] The hand mill offered clear advantages, but the stones

[84] Quoted in Weatherwax, *Indian Corn*, p. 99.

[85] Norwood, "Voyage to Virginia," in Force, *Tracts*, III, 37.

[86] *Md.Arch.*, IV, 166; XLIV, 391; XLIII, 406, 415-18. The will of Thomas Allen stated that he did not want his sons sold for "slaves or mortar boys"; ibid., IV, 404.

[87] Joseph Doddridge, *Notes on the Settlements and Indian Wars of the Western Parts of Virginia and Pennsylvania from 1763 to 1783, Inclusive, Together with a Review of the State of Society and Manners of the First Settlers of the Western Country* (Pittsburgh, 1912, reprinted from the 1824 edition), p. 141. Hugh Jones, in 1724, speaks of "the Indian invention of pounding hommony in mortars burnt in the stump of a tree, with a log for a pestle hanging at the end of a pole." *The Present State of Virginia*, edited by Richard L. Morton (Chapel Hill, 1956), pp. 86-87. Doddridge describes

had to be imported from abroad and periodically dressed by an expert. "It was made of two circular stones, the lowest of which was called the bed stone, the upper one the runner. These were placed in a hoop, with a spout for discharging the meal. A staff was led into a hole, in the upper surface of the runner, near the outer edge, and its upper end through a hole in a board fastened to a joist above, so that two persons could be employed in turning the mill at the same time. The grain was put into the opening in the runner by hand."[88]

In families without servants or hand mills, husband and wife may have shared the duties at the mortar until the children were big enough to take over the task. Since many Englishmen despised Indian males for treating their women as pack animals and servile laborers, perhaps their sense of appropriateness led them to take over the grinding chores, just as they did the heaviest fieldwork.[89]

Corn, cooked into "sampe," hominy, or into the various kinds of quick breads called johnny cake, hoe cake, or "pone," formed the foundation of colonial cuisine. Served with butter, milk, meat, or beans, or malted into beer, corn furnished at least half of the calories of almost everyone's diet, rich or poor, slave, servant, or free.[90] Besides corn, and "there is plenty of that . . . they have good Beefe and Bacon[,] sometimes Mutton[,] and abundance of Greenes as Cabbages, Parsnips, Turnips, Carrots, Potatoes . . . squashes and

---

that particular device very well: "This was a pole of some springy elastic wood, thirty feet long or more, the but end was placed under the side of an house, or a large stump, this pole was supported by two forks, placed about one third of its length from the but end so as to elevate the small end bout fifteen feet from the ground, to this was attached a large mortise, a piece of a sapling, about five or six inches in diameter and eight or ten feet long. The lower end of this was shaped so as to answer for a pestle. A pin of wood was put through it at a proper height, so that two persons could work at the sweep at once"; Doddridge, *Notes*, pp. 141-42. No evidence has yet appeared to suggest that the sweep was in use in the Chesapeake before 1720.

[88] Doddridge, *Notes*, p. 142. An illustration of a hand mill may be found in Henry Chandlee Forman, *Old Buildings, Gardens, and Furniture in Tidewater Maryland* (Cambridge, Md., 1967), p. 47. Mill picks, made of metal, were necessary for sharpening the grooves in the stones. The Smithsonian Institution includes several in its agricultural collection: John T. Schlebecker, *Agricultural Implements and Machines in the Collection of the National Museum of History and Technology* (Washington, D.C., 1972).

[89] That great gentleman and slave owner, William Byrd II, remarked of the Indians, "[They] make the poor women do all the drudgery . . . the weakest must always go to the wall and superiority has from the beginning ungenerously imposed slavery on those who are not able to resist it"; Byrd, *Secret Diary*, p. 397.

[90] Only a few ate any differently from this: those who, like Byrd, had acquired the education and habits of the English gentleman.

water mellons and also abundance of other things."[91] This list of foods was drawn up in the early part of the eighteenth century, and represents a considerable improvement over the ordinary diet of fifty years before. The cultivation of root crops had been almost unknown in England itself, with the consequence that vegetables traditionally played a minor role and cereals remained the principal food.[92] In the list above, the writer includes the Indian contribution to the planters' fare: squash and potatoes, the latter almost surely being the sweet potato rather than the Irish.

Thus, Marylanders ate an American diet cooked in old English style, not very dissimilar from what the colonists of New England ate. Corn, pork, peas, and beans also formed the foundation of Yankee cuisine, although northerners mixed their Indian with rye, and the better off in both regions substituted wheat when they could.[93]

White and black, servant and master—all liked their meat and vegetables cooked together in the large pot over the fire, and the cornbread baked on the hearth. "Pot likker," into which stale pone could be crumbled, provided nourishing victuals as well.[94] Robert Beverly, that fond son of the Virginian Eden, also emphasized the rich variety of fruits available, both cultivated and wild. Strawberries, cherries, grapes, berries of many kinds, and peaches grew in such quantities that they supplied the tables of all who would stoop or stretch to gather them.[95]

[91] "Narrative of a Voyage," p. 336.

[92] Jack Cecil Drummond and Anne Wilbraham, *The Englishman's Food: A History of Five Centuries of English Diet* (London, 1939), pp. 116-18, 123-24, 133-34.

[93] John Josselyn is the best source on late seventeenth-century New England's dietary regime, "Account of Two Voyages to New England," in *Massachusettes Historical Collections*, III (Massachusetts Historical Society, Boston, 1798), 311-54. Even before King Phillip's War, wheat rust had so "blasted" their grain that New England coastal towns were forced to import their wheat from other colonies. Farm families of the interior, except for the Connecticut River Valley, had to give up wheat bread entirely. These statements are based on my research in the probate records of Suffolk and Hampshire counties, Massachusetts.

[94] Hilliard, *Hogmeat and Hoecakes*, p. 51; Mary Randolph, *Virginia Housewife* (Philadelphia, 1855), pp. 103-104.

[95] Beverly, *History*, pp. 129-31, 133, 314-15; Lawson, *New Voyage*, pp. 76-77. John Harrower, a Scots indentured servant living in Virginia on the eve of the American Revolution, took deep pleasure in his garden and reveled in the abundance of fresh fruit, particularly in the big watermelons he grew himself. *Journal of John Harrower*, pp. 95, 112, 117, 142, and 151. Apple, peach, pear, and cherry trees were reported to be abundant in Virginia even before the middle of the seventeenth century; Edmund Plowden, "New Albion," in Force, *Tracts*, II, No. 7, p. 31. Francis Brooke of Kent County on Maryland's eastern shore, when accused of beating his pregnant

The single most important fruit in the early Chesapeake, however, was the apple. An eighteenth-century writer in England counted sixteen different varieties suitable for cooking and eating raw, nineteen for desserts, and six that were especially good for cider. At least one of these varieties made its way to Jamestown only a few years after settlement.[96] Habitual transiency and short lives delayed the spread of orchard planting, and the absence of bees to pollinate the blossoms stinted their yield. But by 1700, both bees and apple orchards had become common in the Chesapeake colonies and contributed to the diet of every family. Although apples furnished fruit for pies and mast for pigs, their principal use was in the form of cider.[97] One recent scholar has pointed out that cider drinking provided vital nutritional elements previously missing from the Virginian diet, while also offering a highly palatable substitute for water drawn from shallow and easily contaminated wells.[98]

Sweet cider readily ferments, and probably most of the cider consumed by the planters and their families was mildly alcoholic. The Englishmen of the period preferred anything alcoholic to plain water, although they drank that when they had to.[99] Besides water and cider, perry (from pears) and quince drink, some planters or their wives brewed beer, using corn, persimmons, sweet potatoes, pumpkins, or even Jerusalem artichokes.[100] Among the choicer

wife to death in the year 1656, claimed she had fallen out of a peach tree. *Md.Arch.*, X, 465.

[96] Phillip Miller, *The Gardener's Dictionary*, cited in Phipps, *Colonial Kitchens*, p. 123; Gray, *Agriculture*, I, 25. Father White particularly advised prospective settlers to bring with them the seeds of the pippin; "Father White's Relation," in *Narratives of Early Maryland, 1633-84*, edited by Clayton Coleman Hall (New York, 1910, reprinted New York, 1946).

[97] Cider casks began to be common in Maryland inventories after the 1680s. On apples and their uses, see Dankers and Sluyter, *Journal*, p. 218; Durand, *Frenchman in Virginia*, p. 117; Beverly, *History*, p. 154.

[98] Morgan, *Slavery*, pp. 182-83. This point plays a critical role in Morgan's argument about the shift from servants to slaves in the tobacco economy, since he links the high risk of the laborers' dying to planters' early reluctance to invest in higher-priced slaves.

[99] Dankers and Sluyter pitied the poor servants they saw in northeastern Maryland because they had to work so hard on a diet that the travelers thought consisted only of corn and water. Since they also commented on the excellent flavor of the abundant cider, they were implicitly denying that servants had access to it, but since these two were heavily prejudiced against the tobacco-based economy and its social consequences, they may have overstated the "misery" of servants and masters alike; *Journal*, p. 218. Beverly included water among the Virginians' "small drink" in 1705; *History*, p. 154.

[100] Beverly, *History*, p. 154; Lawson, *New Voyage*, p. 109; Durand, *Frenchman in Virginia*, p. 34.

drinks the newcomer might sample in the Chesapeake was a beer brewed from corn stalks and pumpkins with wild hops. On the other hand, "in the hot summers, rock-cold water, with an eighth of Peach Vineagar is the best Beaverage," one writer declared.[101]

Although some of the more adventurous planters experimented with exotic beers and tried to make wine from grapes and other fruits, hard cider probably provided most of the available alcohol.[102] Sweet cider works itself into hard cider naturally, but if not drawn off periodically, the working eventually produces vinegar, so the planter had to maintain constant vigilance to keep his family in drinkable supply.[103] As were the home-brewed beers, fermented cider was only mildly alcoholic, but when allowed to stand open and freeze during cold weather, fermented cider will yield small amounts of pure alcohol that can be tapped off, furnishing a very potent dram indeed. Hard cider can also be distilled into brandy, just as can the juices of any pressed fruit, and there were a few stills recorded in Maryland inventories that could have been used for this purpose.[104] Most, however, were quite small affairs used primarily for the preparation of medicinal spirits.

Distilled grain spirits, then called drams, were imported from England during the first half-century of settlement in the Chesapeake, but the expansion of sugar production in the West Indies produced quantities of cheap molasses as a byproduct from which rum could easily be distilled. Rum from the West Indies and New

[101] Plowden, "New Albion," in Force, *Tracts*, II, No. 7, p. 31.

[102] Jones, "Maryland in 1699; A Letter from the Reverend Hugh Jones," p. 370. Lawson favored quinces, which he reported "very pleasant" when eaten raw. The wine made from them, he stated, "I approve of beyond any Drink which that Country affords"; *New Voyage*, p. 109. The wines of the period stood somewhere in between beer and cider on the one hand, and brandy and rum, on the other, in the degree of their alcoholic content. Although Beverly and Byrd, and divers others, experimented with wine making, wines were generally imported from the Azores, Portugal, and Spain, and were a favorite drink of those who could afford them. Sack in the earliest years, madeira and canary later were the most common of these imported wines, which planters drank straight or mixed with water or fruit juice; Byrd, *Secret Diary*, pp. 25, 72; Beverly, *History*, p. 154.

[103] On cider and its properties, see John Hull Brown, *Early American Beverages* (Rutland, Vt., 1966), p. 47. William Byrd picked up a valuable hint on how to slow down the inevitable process, which he carefully noted in 1732: "keep a lighted match of brimstone under the cask for some time. This is useful in so warm a country as this," he explained, "where cider is apt to work itself off both of its strength and sweetness"; *The Prose Works of William Byrd of Westover*, edited by Louis B. Wright (Cambridge, Mass., 1966), p. 349.

[104] The amount of alcohol varies with sugar, acid, tannin, and nitrogen in the apples from which the juice is expressed. *Encyclopedia Brittanica*, V, 765.

England ultimately replaced all other strongly alcoholic beverages in the poor man's diet, just as cider gradually crowded out beer.[105]

Rum was most often taken neat, straight out of the bottle or tossed off from a dram cup that was then refilled and passed to the next person in turn. Rum and cider, mulled with sugar and spices, made a popular drink for large gatherings such as funerals. Rum served more than just convivial purposes, and offered readily available anesthesia for surgery, tooth extraction, and childbearing. Furthermore, it fended off the rigors of winter and kept the work crews going in harvest time. In 1678, for instance, the winter may have pressed especially hard: two neighbors called in to appraise a man's estate consumed in the course of four days two quarts of rum, six gallons of hard cider, and a quart of brandy.[106] These amounts work out to eight ounces of rum, three quarts of cider, and four ounces of brandy per person per day. This sounds like a good bit, even in winter, and it is interesting to try to estimate how much alcohol might have been consumed. If the cider were 7 percent alcohol, and the rum and brandy 40 percent, each man was taking in an average of eleven and a half ounces of alcohol during each of four successive days. The cider alone contributed well over half the potent ingredient, if these calculations are reasonable.

Rum, although cheap, cost far more than cider, and required an outlay that poorer planters tried to avoid if they could. Milk and milk products also played a far smaller role in their diet than cider. Both milk and cider were seasonal in nature, and the periods of their availability did not overlap. The supply of cider commenced with the first apple harvest, usually in August, and the final racking-off took place in March. Thereafter the drinkable supply dwindled rapidly. Indeed, one suspects that the last of the cider and of the stored apples and vegetables, as well, were probably consumed even earlier by most families, leaving a long stretch of time every spring in which everyone ate monotonous fare of salt meat and corn cakes.[107]

The cows freshened with calving in the early spring, and after a period during which the calves sucked freely and gained strength,

---

[105] *Md.Arch.*, X, 331, 391, 485; XLIV, 222, and numerous mentions in the inventories and accounts. Ebenezer Cook's first meal in Maryland, he said, was 'pone and milk served in wooden dishes, and followed as a matter of course with rum and a pipe; *The Sot-Weed Factor*, p. 5.

[106] *Inv. & Accts.*, Liber 5, f. 268. See also Liber 23, f. 81.

[107] See Jared Van Wagenen, Jr., *The Golden Age of Homespun* (Ithaca, N.Y., 1953), p. 98, although this is based on the nineteenth century.

the family then claimed its share. "To secure what milk they require they keep the calves shut up in a cow pen until they have milked the cows and only then permit the calves to suck."[108] Not all families bothered to make butter or cheese, although most of them kept at least one cow. Due to the exceptionally rich bacterial environment afforded by milk, dairying utensils required plenty of hot water, soap, and elbow power after every use. Otherwise they smell sour and impart that odor to the next batch. Poorer families chose to merely collect and drink the milk as it came without attempting to store it or make butter, thus simplifying their lives and probably avoiding the effects of ingesting unfriendly bacteria.[109]

The cattle of that time were of no special breed, but consisted of a mongrel assortment of descendents from the survivors of Atlantic crossings. These animals were used for draft, meat, and hides as well as for the supply of dairy products, and so served competing needs. In any case, the colonists were more interested in numbers than quality. Judging from contractual arrangements found in deeds and leases, the female cattle were used primarily to build the herd and only secondarily to provide milk, whereas the males, after gelding, were intended for meat. They were rarely used for draft purposes in the seventeenth century, when one finds few references to oxen, carts, or plows.[110] Bulls were never valued as highly as steers or cows, were a nuisance to keep, and their numbers restricted to the necessary minimum for breeding, which seems to have been about one bull for six or seven cows.

A common practice of the times illustrates the capital gains expected to accrue from possession of female cattle. This was the gift from godparents to their godchildren of young heifers. Not only did the child benefit from the gradually increasing value of the animal itself, but he also enjoyed the products of its reproductive system.[111] The income from the animal came in the form of milk,

[108] Durand, *Frenchman in Virginia*, p. 117.

[109] Rickets were not unknown, but apparently not common, since travelers are silent on the subject. In fact, Lawson, speaking of the native-born North Carolinians in the early part of the eighteenth century, praised their health and physical beauty; *New Voyage*, p. 123.

[110] In the level and often sandy soil of the tidewater, there was less need for slow, steady pulling, the kind of task at which oxen excel. The stone-free surface, moreover, provided such ideal working conditions for horses that these tender-footed animals did not even require shoeing. This advantage can best be appreciated when it is recalled that horses are particularly vulnerable to leg injuries, most of which result from loss of footing; Beverly, *History*, p. 125.

[111] When the keeper of the gift animal was not the child's own parent, any male offspring went to the keeper in exchange for his trouble and care.

but the real purpose of the initial investment fulfilled itself in the birth of calves.

Beef and pork furnished the staple meat diet for Maryland families and were thus their principal sources of protein. Pork was almost always made into bacon and ham. This was the preferred meat because beef did not smoke or pickle as well. In season, however, venison, wild fowl, fish, and oysters lent the menu a delicious variety.[112] Indian hunters hired themselves out in the fall to supply the planters' tables or sold freshly killed deer from door to door.[113]

Although the Chesapeake region and the country to the south became famous for large herds of cattle roaming at will in the woods year round, those herds took some time to build. One writer estimated in 1649 that the number of cattle in Virginia was about 20,000, a figure just slightly outnumbering the 15,000 English and 300 Blacks he guessed to be living there.[114] In the latter part of the century, the number of cattle in Maryland averaged between three and four head per person.[115] The relatively small size of the herds in the first half-century of settlement necessarily curtailed the supply of meat and dairy products, and the shortage may not have been rectified by protein from fish and game, particularly during the summer months when daily fieldwork made its heaviest demands. Six servants went on strike at one plantation in 1663, announcing that "if they had not flesh they would not worke." The judges of the county court inquired of the master what the problem was and he replied, "I had not flesh then to give them . . . until that time they have not wanted for the most part since the Crop of Tob. was in, to have meate three times in the weeke & att least twice." Since he had no meat to give his servants, he had provided instead sugar, fish, oil, and vinegar. "Moreover I did offer them to give them a note from under my hand for three or foure of them to take my Boate & to spend a weekes time or more, to see if they could buy any provision or flesh or any thing else, & I would pay for it, though never so deare bought." The striking servants insisted to the contrary, that "hee will allow us nothing but Beans

[112] Beverly, *History*, p. 153; Durand, *Frenchman in Virginia*, p. 120; "Voyage to Maryland," p. 336. Peter Kain or Caine owned a barrel of salt shad fish worth £1.25 in 1708; *Inv. & Accts.*, Liber 29, f. 333.

[113] "Voyage to Maryland," p. 337.

[114] "A Perfect Description of Virginia," in Force, *Tracts*, II, No. 8, p. 3.

[115] For tidewater Virginia in 1787, some one hundred years later, tax lists enumerated eight cattle for every adult male, which represents a point well below saturation for the tidewater because planters had already begun the conversion from tobacco to wheat, which required more for pasturing livestock; Main, "Distribution," p. 244.

& Bread." The judges listened to the master, not very surprisingly, and ordered thirty lashes for each, but pardoning two who were then to inflict the ascribed whippings to the others. However, the entire penalty was remitted upon their asking forgiveness and promising obedience.[116]

Whatever the rights or wrongs of servant grievances, the foregoing case suggests that people of all stations expected to eat meat on a regular basis, and viewed it as a necessary part of their diet. When a master did not give it to his servants, he apologetically explained that he had none left; the servants disputed his story but did not have to defend their "right" to meat in the first place. Corn bread and beans were not enough either in the eyes of the judges or in the opinion of the servants.

Corn is not a perfect food, as we now know, because it lacks certain vital nutrients. When corn makes up 75 percent or more of the human diet, pellagra will develop, and this very unpleasant skin disease was probably responsible for many of the cases of so-called scurvy that are reported in the records.[117] A diet consisting only of salt meat and cornmeal bread would bring on symptoms of nutritional deficiency within a few weeks, and some Englishmen, at least, were aware of this.[118] Complaints about insufficient diet, however, focused on a lack of meat as the cause, not the lack of variety, which was accepted as inevitable.

Contracts itemizing yearly food allowances, according to one careful student, always specified rations of three barrels of corn per hand and sixty to two hundred pounds of beef or pork.[119] In a certain marital dispute that came before a court, the judges ordered the husband to allow his wife, "for and Towards her maintenance," three barrels of corn, three hundred pounds of meat, and a thousand pounds of tobacco yearly. The tobacco was intended to serve as money with which to purchase clothing and other necessaries.[120] In 1662, an administrator of an estate told the court he had expended twelve barrels of corn and eighteen "middle" pieces of bacon, plus sugar, salt, spices, and biscuit for a household containing five children and four servants.[121] A side of bacon from a full-

[116] *Md.Arch.*, XXXIX, 8-9.

[117] *Encyclopedia Brittanica* (1966), Vol. 4.

[118] "Newes of Sir Walter Rauleigh," in Force, *Tracts*, III, No. 4.

[119] These contracts in the Charles County Court Records were used by Lorena S. Walsh, "Charles County," p. 267.

[120] *Md.Arch.*, IV, 320.

[121] No beef appeared in this account. The children ranged in age from 3 to 13. Walsh, "Charles County," p. 112.

grown hog weighed about twenty to twenty-five pounds, but the definition of a "middle" piece is unclear.[122] If this were just another term for flitch or side, and if each averaged 22½ pounds, then 18 × 22.5 = 405 pounds, divided among nine people is only 45 pounds of meat per person, or if we treat two children as equivalent to one adult in annual consumption, 62.3 pounds per person, certainly on the low side of the range specified in the hiring contracts mentioned above.[123]

One Maryland planter's "family" included, besides the planter, his wife, two sons and a daughter, twenty-four Negroes and eighteen white servants. After the planter's death in 1702, an account of the administration of his estate for the intervening year noted that the following had been killed to feed "the family": four steers, three cows, and a bull, plus sixteen hogs weighing a total of 1,112 pounds.[124] Although we do not know how much meat the slaughtered cattle yielded, we can estimate the quantity of beef, for instance, by comparing prices. Beef was generally worth only two-thirds to three-quarters as much as pork. In the case at hand, pork was worth twopence a pound. If the price of beef then stood at 1.5 pence, eight cattle worth the equivalent of 3,348 pence probably dressed out to 2,232 pounds of beef total, or 279 each. Thus, the combined weight of the beef and pork probably came to something like 3,344 pounds of meat to feed 47 people for one year, or roughly 73 pounds per person, man, woman, and child.

In another case, we find "An Account of What hath been expended and made use of, for, and towards the maintaining of the . . . Adm[ex] and her 5 children in meate & clothing, during the time of her widdowhood, as followeth." For 1685: nine hogs and three steers. Killed in 1686, nine hogs and two steers. In 1687, ten hogs, two sows, two young bulls, and one steer were required, and by August of the following year, another bull and one ram were added.[125] The inventory had listed only one servant, but the account mentioned servants' wages of 1,450 pounds of tobacco for the three-year period and also recorded the loss of a servant. Let us assume,

---

[122] *Md.Arch.*, XLIV, 231.

[123] Walsh, "Charles County," p. 267.

[124] *Inv. & Accts.*, Liber 24, f. 134; and Liber 22, f. 32.

[125] Ibid., Liber 10, f. 175. Clothing the family for the entire period required cloth worth 2,986 pounds of tobacco; for the making of the clothes, 400 pounds, and for 75 pairs of shoes, 2,600. Leather for unspecified use cost 2,000 pounds of tobacco. Old clothes given to the servants were valued at 1,000 pounds. Excluding the old clothing given the servants, the cost of clothing the family came to 8,000 pounds or 1,333 per person for six persons. Dividing this into three years yields an annual average expenditure of 222 per person, just under £1 sterling at a penny per pound.

then, that the household included the widow, five children, and one servant, and calculate the average number of pounds of meat consumed per person, using the weights from our previous example to supply the missing data. For the years 1685, 1686, and 1687, six steers, two young bulls, twenty-eight hogs, and two sows supplied meat for the family. The young bulls were valued at two-thirds the value of the steers, and we will estimate their yield accordingly. We will also assume that the sows provided the same average amount of meat as did the hogs. For six steers at 279 pounds, two young bulls at 195 pounds, and twelve hogs at 69.5 pounds, the total estimate for three years comes to 2,898 pounds of meat, 966 per year, which when divided among the household of five children, one servant, and the widow, averaged 138 pounds of meat per person per year. Similar calculations for another family consisting of a widow and four small children provided an estimate of 129 pounds of meat per person.[126]

These four examples, all taken from accounts of administration in Maryland probate records, have yielded estimates of the annual meat consumption per person ranging from 45 to 138 pounds per year. Undoubtedly there exists wide room for error in these calculations: children require less than adults, servants and slaves may have been given less than freemen. No account, furthermore, has been taken of meat and fish from other sources such as hunting and fishing. Be that as it may, compare this range with the "budget" developed by James Lemon for farm families in southeastern Pennsylvania for the eighteenth century: 153 pounds of pork and beef for each person of an "average" family. Lemon's hypothetical family ate close to half a pound of meat per day per person—a cholesterol-rich diet, indeed. Closer in allowance to Maryland's, although further away in time, is the estimate by Fogel and Engerman for slaves in the American South on the eve of the Civil War: 133 pounds of meat per capita per year.[127]

Not only did Lemon's Pennsylvania farm family gorge on meat, it consumed thirty bushels of wheat, rye, corn, and buckwheat—almost half of this in wheat.[128] This comes close to twice the allotment given the seventeenth-century field hand in Maryland, which was fifteen bushels. Fogel and Engerman's slaves ate sweet potatoes

---

[126] Ibid., Liber 8, f. 460.

[127] Lemon, *Best Poor Man's Country*, p. 155. Robert William Fogel and Stanley L. Engerman, *Time on the Cross: The Economics of American Negro Slavery* (Boston, 1974), II, 97.

[128] Lemon, *Best Poor Man's Country*, p. 155.

and peas, as well as their corn, so their average allotment was half that in early Maryland.[129] As *The Sot-Weed Factor* remarked of the planters' diet about 1700,

> Pon and Milk, with Mush well stoar'd,
> In Wooden Dishes grac'd the Board,
> With Homine and Syder-pap,
> (Which scarce a hungry dog wou'd lap)
> Well stuff'd with Fat from Bacon fry'd,
> Or with Mollossus dulcify'd.[130]

Sufficiency has its appeal, nevertheless, and for the poorer planters of the Chesapeake, a full belly and a good smoke could be mighty satisfying.

[129] Fogel and Engerman, *Time on the Cross*, II, 97.
[130] Cook, *The Sot-Weed Factor*, p. 5.

Chapter Six

THE MIDDLING AND AFFLUENT
PLANTERS AND
THEIR FAMILIES

Until now we have been concerned primarily with the poorest third of planter households, but much of what has been said about them applies equally well to their more affluent neighbors. The differences in their life styles were more a matter of degree than of substance, and most particularly was this true of their clothing and food. The apparel of planters in the middling third averaged about twice the value of those below. Similarly, the clothing of the richest came to twice that of the middling—expenditures that accorded with the differences between them in overall wealth. The poorest, having the fewest options, devoted 15 percent of their consumption assets to their apparel, whereas the middling allocated 10 percent, and the richest, 8 percent. Although the range between individuals could be very great, from about £3 for the more frugal to £30 or £40 for the extravagant, there did not appear among the vast majority of Maryland planters of this period any general tendency to acquire extensive or costly wardrobes.

The chief distinction in clothing of those in the upper third of the population lay in their ability to keep for special occasions a well-cut suit of good quality, with perhaps a wig, a cane, a silver watch, and handsome buckles on their shoes. William Hemsley's "best suit of clothes," for instance, was worth almost £7. Robert Carter ordered a new winter suit from his London correspondent in 1720, to be of broadcloth and to cost "between 8 and 10 pounds."[1] "King" Carter could afford anything London had to offer, but an appropriate color and well-made cloth satisfied the sober tastes of this prudent businessman. Carter abhorred ostentation in dress, but enjoyed riding to church in his coach.

Maryland women spent more on their clothing than did their menfolk. There are several possible reasons for this, the most ob-

---

[1] Carter, *Letters*, p. 48. Hemsley's estate inventory may be found in *Inv. & Accts.*, Liber 21, f. 20.

vious being that they required more yards of cloth for their gowns and petticoats. However, good clothing, like household linens, also offered a form of savings readily convertible to cash should the need arise. More subjectively speaking, pretty clothes, though perhaps seldom worn, brought secret comforts to lonely women living in an exhausting world not of their own making. In a society that counted capital goods—servants, cattle, and acres—as rungs on the ladder of importance, women hoarded a bit of finery or a costly gown as much for the satisfaction of looking at it as for the far rarer pleasures that came from wearing it or from the knowledge that one could bestow it on a favored relative when the time came.[2] Mary Goldsmith Boston, for instance, had packed away a black silk gown and petticoat with gold and silver lace on them, plus a gown of silver color to wear with a red silk petticoat, also decorated with silver laces. With these was a similar set, in sky blue and trimmed in laces of precious metals. These treasured garments of Mary Boston's were, all together, worth more than a healthy man servant with four years to serve, but their psychic income surely exceeded even what the labor of such a man could bring.[3]

Although only a few women were fortunate enough to enjoy such treasures, there were also some who indulged themselves extravagantly. One wealthy widow, Mary Truman, left six gold and two diamond rings, along with eight gowns, seventeen petticoats, four pairs of stays, six waistcoats, one embroidered stomacher, two muffs, six pairs of gloves, a pair of red satin sleeves, seven girdles, fourteen hoods, eleven pairs of laced shoes, two pairs of slippers, thirty-two shifts, twenty-eight pocket handkerchiefs, two fans, and a "parcel" of linen aprons, quoifs, headbands, sleeves, and other personal linens. The value of these garments and accessories, plus a few oddments not here mentioned, came to £66; close to two-thirds of all the estates inventoried in the six counties prior to 1720 were worth less than £66.[4]

More typical of wives of the middling planters was "Misteris" Francis Cox, who died shortly after her husband in 1648, a few years after their arrival in the colony. Their deaths orphaned a daughter, Elizabeth, and a young son, Will, who had not even been christened when his mother died. Mrs. Cox's inventory included a pair of "bodies," an old holland apron, a handkerchief, an old black

[2] Alice Earle reports that she was able to trace the same gown and "manto" through four successive owners by their wills; *Two Centuries of Costume* (Boston, 1903), I, 10.
[3] *Inv. & Accts.*, Liber 1, f. 389 (1675).
[4] Ibid., Liber 9, f. 205.

bag, a pair of gloves, a "stuff" gown, a petticoat, a cloth "joomp," a small piece of taffeta, a smoothing iron, a looking glass, an old suit of Mr. Cox's and a hat, besides the household goods, livestock, and two boats.[5]

Among the wooden containers in Mistress Cox's house was a brewing tub for making beer. The diet of the middling and affluent planters was based, as was that of the poorer sort, on corn and salt meat, but households with sufficient land and hands were more inclined to plant orchards, fence in wheat, build dove cots, and make beer, cheese and butter. The upper third added molasses, sugar, spices, and, late in the period, coffee, tea, and chocolate to their stores. The middling planter purchased from them rum, sugar, and molasses in occasional small quantities, but otherwise his diet paralleled that of his lesser neighbors. Over the course of the century, the supply of meat greatly improved as cattle and hogs thrived on the land, roaming the woods for their sustenance or grazing on the extensive stretches of marsh grass along the bay's edge. Meat, cider, and wheat, plus roots and cabbages, provided vitamins and amino acids not present in the earlier diet, which had relied heavily on dried beans and corn.

In contrast to these modest but important additions to the planters' diet, William Byrd's diary offers a guide to the bill of fare available to the planter-gourmet with a well-stocked larder: beef and pork, of course, but also fowl with bacon, fish, and mutton. Among the more interesting but less common entrees were squirrel, blue-winged teal, pigeon, partridge, turkey, goose, and duck. Oysters and geese came to the table entirely too often during one particular trip to the eastern shore. Too much of a good thing was worse than none at all for the well-tuned palate of a Byrd.

Venison, lamb, and veal also made their appearance on his table, as did beans and bacon, the commoners' fare, but they are remarkable for their rarity. In spring, his menus included asparagus everyday, and strawberries and cherries when they were in season, as well. Shad, new green peas, turnips, and raspberries followed with the calendar. Byrd was a temperate man, though particular, and preferred simple, digestible foods in moderate quantities. For breakfast, he usually had only milk, boiled or in a custard, but when entertaining or being entertained, he drank chocolate and ate bread and butter. The only times he ate eggs were during convalescence

[5] *Md.Arch.*, LIV, 97 (1648).

after illnesses or when he was traveling and had to put up at the home of an ordinary planter.

For dinner at home, which Byrd usually ate in the early or middle part of the afternoon, he generally restricted himself to one kind of meat, but when visiting others of his own rank, he was expected to sample a variety. After such visits, Byrd occasionally noted, "I did not keep to my rule of eating but one dish."[6] Along with many other mundane matters of ordinary routine, he generally reported what he ate everyday, so it is possible to distinguish which were the most important meats in his diet and which only occasional. Over the course of two years, between 1709 and 1711, beef dominated the daily menu. Whether roasted, boiled, or otherwise prepared, beef contributed more than a third of all the meats identified. Mutton placed a surprising second (14 percent), whereas fish, pork, and chicken were each served about 10 percent of the time. These were followed in importance by goose, blue-winged teal, venison, turkey, oysters, pigeon, and duck. Squirrel, partridge, beans and bacon, lamb, veal, and eggs appeared only two or three times each.

One of Byrd's favorite dishes was mutton hash, and one such serving he pronounced "as good as ever I ate in my life."[7] Another favorite was blue-wing, one occasional source of which was a neighbor whom he supplied with ammunition in return for the meat, while the hunter kept the feathers. Chicken, or fowl, especially when roasted with bacon around it, proved another popular dish.

Beef dominated Byrd's diet, however, even in winter. Between December 1, 1709, and March 1, 1710 (old style), beef occurred in twenty-four out of forty-three references to meat, pork only five times, mutton three, fish, goose, turkey, and chicken twice each, and venison, pigeon, and duck once each. The beef was either boiled or roasted, both about equally often during this short period, but when one scans the full stretch of years the diary covers, boiled beef appears more often, as logically it should, since this was corned meat that kept reasonably well. Byrd's immediate family was too small to consume an entire steer before it spoiled. Perhaps someone else also got fresh meat when Col. Byrd dined on roast beef. One wonders if the slaves, whom he regularly referred to as "my people," ever got a taste.

Fresh fruit in season brought both Byrds the greatest delight. His temperamental wife was a rather desultory diner who seldom

---

[6] Byrd, *Secret Diary*, p. 15.
[7] Ibid., p. 86.

took pleasure in the ordinary meals served at her table, but the fruit they picked in season from their own trees and bushes they shared together in companionable indulgence. The variety and goodness of fresh fruits in Virginia and Maryland occasioned many rapturous comments from visitors and residents alike, but many of these were available only to those who could keep gardeners. Allocation of labor time for those on a pinched budget probably inhibited the planting and tending of fruits, as it did vegetables, but it seems likely that apples and peaches had become so abundant by the early eighteenth century that no one was stinted when these fruits ripened.

The daily diet of the ordinary planter was monotonous in the extreme, as we have already observed, but custom required feasting on those important occasions when the birth of a child or the departure from this life of relatives or neighbors demanded public notice and ceremonial acknowledgment. Accounts of administration in the probate records often itemized funeral expenses, which held legal priority over all debts contracted during the decedent's lifetime, except for the doctors' and nurses' fees during the final illness.[8] Since creditors were understandably anxious about the possible expenses of this social ritual, administrators often felt compelled to itemize the costs involved in burying the deceased, and thus provided historians with invaluable clues to the eating and drinking of early Americans.

The abundance of good food and good cheer expended at a funeral banquet in colonial times was intended to testify to the virtue and quality of the departed, thereby honoring his or her memory. In theory, the only proper limits to such expenses were the extent of resources available, although heirs and creditors interposed demands considered equally legitimate. In the absence of large debts or close kin, therefore, the sky was the limit. This sentiment appears most clearly in a judgment expressed by one jury called to decide a suit brought to disallow as excessive the sums spent on the funeral of a widow and her only two children. The jury approved the costly entertainment as legitimate and right, "so long as an Estate sufficient was left. If it had bin more it would have only redounded to the credit and the memory of the Persons deceased."[9]

The greater the dignitary, the more impressive the quantity and

---

[8] *Md.Arch.*, I, 190.
[9] Walsh, "Charles County," p. 150.

quality of the viands offered. Food at the funeral of William Burgess, a wealthy merchant of Londontown in Anne Arundel County, included wheat and butter for cakes, besides sugar, spices, and fifteen gallons of rum.[10] William Drewry's funeral was even grander: fifty-five gallons of cider mulled with brandy, sugar, and spices, and served with a dinner "dressed" by two maids. The exact menu, alas, does not appear.[11] An account from Virginia mentions two turkeys, two geese, "dunghill" fowl (chickens), and a hog, plus two bushels of wheat flour and twenty pounds of butter. Beverages included the usual cider and rum, six gallons of each.[12]

Cakes and cider laced with rum, or a rum punch, became the standard offerings at well-conducted funerals by the third quarter of the seventeenth century, and everyone, even the poor man, was so honored. John Young, for example, had been a servant, and had received his freedom dues in 1695. He died in 1704, naming his landlord as executor of his modest estate. The account for his funeral expenses included ten gallons of cider, two gallons of rum, and a bushel of wheat "for cakes."[13]

Planters drank to the memory of even the poorest man, especially when his estate could foot the bill. Loling Moloney, for instance, owned nothing but the clothes on his back and one "sorry" horse. When he departed this life with neither creditors nor kin to mourn him, it was no accident that the charges for his funeral, plus the court fees, just balanced the full value of his scanty assets: a winding sheet and shirt in which to bury him, the coffin, and a gallon of rum to commemorate his passing.[14]

Funerals were not the only occasion at which planters drank.[15] A French traveler in Virginia described the punch served at a wedding he attended. It consisted of three portions of beer to three portions of brandy, mixed with three pounds of sugar, plus nutmeg and cinnamon: "Stir them well together and as soon as the sugar is melted they drink it. While one punch is being consumed another

[10] *Inv. & Accts.*, Liber 19½B, f. 153. For more on Burgess, see below.
[11] *Inv. & Accts.*, Liber 5, f. 268.
[12] Bruce, *Economic History*, II, 237.
[13] *Inv. &Accts.*, Liber 25, f. 129.
[14] Ibid., Liber 30, f. 173, and Liber 31, f. 108.
[15] Not everyone subscribed to the belief that alcoholic toasts were the most appropriate modes of honoring the departed. One man in York County, Virginia, stated in his will, "Having observed in the daies of my pilgrimage the debauches used at burials tending much to the dishonor of God and his true Religion, my will is that noe strong drinke bee p'vided or spirits at my burial"; Bruce, *Economic History*, II, 217.

is brewing. As for me," he added, "I did not drink anything but beer."[16]

One can seldom discover how many guests partook of the quantities recorded, but the amounts of sugar used in these holiday libations seem high. In one case, twenty-five pounds of sugar sweetened an equivalent number of gallons of cider, to which had also been added ten gallons of wine and six gallons of rum, or one pound of sugar to each 1.6 gallons of drink.[17] In another case, six pounds of sugar were added to twelve gallons of cider and two gallons of wine.[18] In yet another instance, fifty pounds of sugar were added to the same number of gallons of cider, into which six gallons of rum and ten gallons of wine had been mixed.[19]

Large quantities of liquor did not necessarily entail drunken orgies. Sugar and alcohol are more readily metabolized by hardworking farmers, with relatively less damage to their livers and kidneys than similar quantities produce in more sedentary folk. Consumption of alcohol was an important means of sociability and recreation for both sexes in early Maryland; the general absence of alternative sources of amusement, such as playing cards or musical instruments, leads us to this conclusion, although one should not forget the possibility of nonmaterial means of group recreation, such as games, songs, dances, and tale-telling. The pleasant buzz induced by taking intoxicating beverages, however, made neighborly visiting back and forth all the more attractive in the scattered settlement system of the tobacco colonies of the early Chesapeake.

The following incident, for example, took place in January of 1656 on the "Lord's day." The person recounting the story was a neighbor woman, aged thirty-five, named Ann. She was at the home of Edward Copedge on that day, along with Mary Baxter, who told "the woman of the house" that she would give her a dram. Copedge's wife insisted to the contrary that *she* would be the one to provide it, and brought out a pint pot then and there. The man of the house thereupon fetched some in turn. Overwhelmed by this bounty, Mary Baxter left to bring back yet another contribution to the party. "After this was drunk[,] came in Misteris Hinson and Misteris Morgan and then Mary would goe & fetch more but they pursuaded her not but that she should carry it home to her husband

---

[16] The poor man was plagued with an uneasy stomach his entire time in Virginia; Durand, *Frenchman in Virginia*, p. 34.

[17] *Inv. & Accts.*, Liber 29, f. 254.

[18] Ibid., Liber 39C, f. 101.

[19] Ibid., Liber 15, f. 173.

and children." After these two well-meaning women had left, however, Mary Baxter "rayelled upon her naybours& did sweare very desperatly many oaths."[20] Swearing on a Sunday afternoon was the charge on which the court was convened.

The records of the county court, in which accounts like these appear, often focus on the more tragic aspects of life, and the stories they convey may distort our sense of "how things must have been." They do contain the telling details, though, without which we are left to contemplate terse and formal language as though the words had never been said by real human beings. In another court case, this from the year 1663, a planter named Daniel Clocker wanted to cross the river after visiting another planter, Henry Ellery. Finding his host's canoe "something small," Clocker spent the night with him before setting out in the morning to inquire of a neighbor of Ellery whether he would give him a "cast" over the river. The neighbor, John Furnifield, readily acceded to Clocker's request and brought along a pint of drams, "which they drank out there amongst them." Clocker then walked back to his host's house to fetch his things while the neighbor brought around the canoe. At this point, Ellery's wife brought out an earthen pot of drams containing about a quart, which they shared around as a kind of "bon voyage" toast. They drank up most of the pot's contents before the two men got into the canoe, with the neighbor at the stern. Alas, somewhere "between the Indian Poynt at West St. Maries & the Church Poynt over against it, the said Furnifield fell out of the canoue & . . . drowned."[21]

Such celebrations and misfortunes united all ranks of Marylanders, but those with a little extra cash enjoyed or suffered them more often, just as they ate a little better and dressed more comfortably. The same distinction, again more of degree than of kind, extends to their houses and furnishings. As readers will recall, men whose estates fell below £50, roughly the poorest third of householders, probably lived in small houses of just one or two rooms each. Those in the middle range, £50 to £149, built slightly larger houses, averaging three rooms each. Their plantations also boasted an outbuilding of some kind, which meant less crowded conditions under the home roof. As Table VI.1 shows, most of the estates in this range owned at least one servant but very few owned slaves. The average size of the household, including any laborers present, con-

---

[20] *Md.Arch.*, LIV, 87-8.
[21] Ibid., XLIX, 29.

TABLE VI.1

HOUSES, OTHER BUILDINGS, AND SIZE OF HOUSEHOLD, YOUNG FATHERS' SAMPLE, 1656-1719 (£ decimals≈sterling)

PPW Class	Average No. Rooms Main House	Average No. Other "Places"[e]	Average Size Family	Average No. Servants	Average No. Slaves	Average No. Family Beds	Average £ per Family Bed	Family Bedding £ per Person
£ 0-49[a]	1-2	0	5	0	0	2	£1.3	£0.6
50-149[b]	3	1	5	1	0	3	2.5	1.6
150-799[c]	5-6	3	5	3	4	6	3.4	4.0
800-up[d]	6+	5	5	8	21	11	4.2	8.6

SOURCE: Young fathers' estates, probate records of six counties, Maryland, in Hall of Records, Annapolis, Maryland.
[a] Equivalent to poorest third of all planter households.
[b] Equivalent to middle third of all planter households.
[c] Equivalent to upper third of all planter households, excluding the richest 3 percent.
[d] Equivalent to richest 3 percent of all planter households.
[e] "Places" includes only those likely to house human beings, and excludes tobacco houses.

sisted of about six people, judging from the young fathers' sample. The richest third of planters lived in houses that, at six rooms, were twice the average size in early Maryland, and there were, in addition, two or three other structures on the home plantation. The wealthiest of this class owned several working plantations, dividing up their work force of some two dozen or so laborers into smaller work groups.

At all levels of wealth, beds and bedding constituted the single most valuable group of furnishings in the household. They generally cost more than horses, for instance, and the most elegant were worth as much as the average annual tobacco crop of four hands, which at a penny per pound, would come to £25, the price of a prime field slave.

The best bed of most planters, however, was considerably cheaper, about £4 or £5. This consisted of a mattress stuffed with feathers resting on a rope latticework strung between the sides of an oak or walnut bedstead, and further equipped with a pair of fat bolsters, which are long, very plump cushions used to support the sleeper in a semi-upright position. In addition to the bolsters, there would also be a pair of feather pillows, covered with a strong twilled fabric, as was the mattress tick itself. Over the sheets lay a pair of blankets topped by a rug—a heavy, densely woven coverlet—and occasionally over that, a decorative coverlet or quilt. The tall posts of the bestead supported a suite of curtains to keep out the noxious vapors of the night air as well as the strong, cold drafts created by the fire burning on the broad open hearth. The curtains offered privacy as well, since there was usually more than one bed to a room.

The parents, by right, claimed the best bed, and the rest of the family slept on simpler and cheaper furniture. The inventory of Stephen White of Anne Arundel County, taken in 1677, listed a bed with curtains valued at a little more than £4 and two others, one stuffed with cattails, the other with wool flocks, together valued at slightly more than £1.[22] The structure of bed values within households changed as one proceeded up the economic ladder. In the poorest families, of course, there was little bedding, and that was of the cheapest quality, but as soon as farm income allowed, the planter and his wife bought a feather bed. Servants slept on hammocks or on the floor in a bed roll or on ticks stuffed with cattails or rushes, covered with a pair of blankets and a rug.

[22] Planter White was worth £28 in personal wealth and ranked in the twentieth percentile among heads of households; *Inv. & Accts.*, Liber 4, f. 13.

The most common type of complete bed was the flock bed, a mattress stuffed with handfuls of wool pulled or sheared from the sheep. In beds like these, the covers were worth more than the mattress. A pair of good blankets and a rug, the usual complement, might be double or triple the value of the flock mattress. Feather mattresses, on the other hand, were very expensive items, and were generally reserved for the master and his wife in families fortunate enough to own one. It took forty to eighty pounds of feathers to stuff a tick properly, which at a shilling per pound for the feathers cost anywhere from £2 to £4—and the sacrifice of a lot of poor chickens in the process.

For servants' bedding actually appearing in their masters' inventoried estates, a rare occurrence, the average appraisal value was 124 pounds of tobacco per bed or per servant in the period through 1683. At a penny per pound, these beds were worth about ten shillings. Over the next two decades beds or bedding for servants declined in value to seven and a half shillings, but then jumped in value later, when the numbers of servants plummeted.[23] "Negro" bedding cannot be distinguished from servants' in the early years, leading one to conclude that the two were at first treated indifferently. Conditions changed as the numbers of slaves increased. The earliest inventory to distinguish explicitly between bedding for a servant and for "the Negro" was dated 1692. The servant slept in a "flock bed" worth fifteen shillings while "the Negro" slept on bedding worth six shillings.

By the end of the century, the bedding for the two kinds of bound laborers were consistently separated in the probate inventories, but the appraisal values did not significantly differ until after 1704, when that for slaves halved in price while servants' bedding doubled. The principal reason for this widening distinction is that those few men servants remaining in the colony after the onset of that long depression were serving in superior capacities and were

[23] References to servants' beds or bedding are rare. Out of 283 inventories during the years 1656 through 1683 that listed servants, only 34 mentioned their bedding and its value. Why servants' bedding is so commonly omitted is not clear. The usual view may have been that such bedding belonged, in right if not in law, to the servants and not their masters. It is also possible that such bedding simply had no monetary value whatsoever. Insofar as the servants were sleeping on straw, one would not expect to see this explicitly stated, but covering of any real utility would have had some monetary value, no matter how little. More likely, the bedding used by the servant on board ship when he made the crossing was regarded as his own and was carried by him wherever he went, in the modern student's manner of backpack and sleeping bag.

216

more often given real beds to sleep on rather than the miscellaneous piles of covers that most had used previously. "Negro" bedding more often than not consisted only of such miscellany, generally "old," and getting older as planters put off new textile purchases during the depression in tobacco prices.

Those fortunate slaves who slept in the main house or in the kitchen were supplied with real beds and were not unduly crowded. Those sleeping in quarters or elsewhere must have slept in groups on the floor, perhaps on heaps of straw under covers that generally escaped the appraisers' notice but, when inventoried, were valued at pathetically low prices.

When comparing beds and bedding by wealth classes of planters, one can observe a gradual convergence in the values of the beds in individual estates. Whereas the poorer families with more than one bed strove to acquire a good one, better-off families improved the quality of their secondary beds. At the very top of the planter hierarchy, however, one finds a reversal of this trend. Here one finds estates with a half-dozen beds of good-to-excellent quality but, in addition, another half-dozen beds of quite indifferent value. These are not servants' beds, for which we have already accounted, but must have been assigned to free hired men or itinerant laborers. These lower-quality beds are found in a wide variety of places on the home plantation and away, whereas the best feather beds are always in the main house, usually one to a room. For solitary beds such as these, curtains served less to provide privacy than warmth or show.

The average number of beds per household, excluding those for servants and slaves, ranged from fewer than two for the poorest families to almost nine for the richest decile of estates, and eleven for the top 3 percent. As in house sizes, this distribution resembles the pattern one finds in the room-by-room inventories of rural Massachusetts in the same period. (see Table VI-2). The chief difference between the two regions lay in the relative poverty of Maryland's lower range of households and in the greater affluence of its upper range. Since the Massachusetts probate data probably pertained to older men far more often than did Maryland's, most of the differences between the living standards exhibited by these two sets are probably attributable to age differences.

When one knows the number of people living under the same roof, as we generally do with the young fathers' sample, we can gain some sense of how crowded most families must have been at the time. Dividing the number of family beds by the size of the

217

TABLE VI.2

COMPARING ROOMS, BEDS, AND BEDDING IN TWO COLONIES

	Rural Suffolk, 1650-1699			Maryland, 1656-1719		
	No. Rooms	No. Beds	£ Best Bed*	No. Rooms	No. Beds	£ Best Bed
Bottom Third	2	3	£6	1-2	2	
Middle Third	3-4	3	6	3	3	£6
Upper Third	5	3	6	5-6	6	
Richest	6	7	9	6+	11	

SOURCES: Young fathers' estates, probate records of six counties, Maryland, in Hall of Records, Annapolis; A. L. Cummings, *Rural Household Inventories.*

* Deflated to sterling.

family also provides a useful index of crowding. In Maryland, an average of more than two persons per bed characterized young families at the bottom of the economic ladder, whereas at the top there were twice as many beds as people. Table VI.3 provides the summary. Since hired help, relatives, and lodgers may also have been living under the same roof and could not be counted with any certainty, these measures of crowding offer only *minimum* estimates of the average numbers of people living and sleeping together.

The value of the family bedding made up a very sizable portion of the total value of goods in the house, as we remarked earlier: approximately a third for most, but only 18 percent for the richest families, despite the large number of beds owned by this class. Next in importance to beds came the kitchen equipment. Planters of the middling sort usually built a kitchen separate from the hall, where the principal chores of cooking and food preparation were carried out and where the larger quantity of utensils could be stored. Even in houses where the cooking continued in the main hearth room, there would be a milk room or buttery to store articles for which there was no longer room in the hall. At this more affluent level,

TABLE VI.3

COMFORT VERSUS CROWDING: BEDS AND FAMILY SIZE
(YOUNG FATHERS' ESTATES), 1656-1719

	PPW Class	Average No. Family	Average No. Beds	Persons per Bed
Bottom 34.5%				
Heads of Household	£ 0-15	3.72	1.12	3.32
	16-34	4.49	1.66	2.70
	35-49	5.39	2.61	2.07
Middle 34.5%				
Heads of Household	50-71	4.91	2.69	1.83
	72-96	4.72	3.07	1.54
	97-149	5.17	3.90	1.33
Upper 27%				
Heads of Household	150-228	4.84	4.40	1.10
	229-399	5.08	5.81	0.87
	400-799	5.51	8.04	0.69
Top 3.9%				
Heads of Household	800-up	5.33	11.12	0.48

SOURCES: Young fathers' estates, probate records of six counties, Maryland, in Hall of Records, Annapolis.

the basic equipment for cooking and food preparation expanded in number and variety, including such things as andirons to support the fire on the hearth, tongs, fire shovel, and bellows for better control of the temperature. The andirons were often designed to carry spits for small roasts such as poultry, and several pots hung from the trammels or ratchet hooks that, by providing for exact positioning of the pot, permitted control over the cooking temperature without adjusting the fire itself. In addition to the pots, there would be a brass kettle, several skillets also of brass, and an iron frying pan. Some households added a chafing dish, a toasting iron, or a gridiron. Even more specialized ware such as patty pans, biscuit tins, fish boilers, and so forth, characterized the richest households.

Not only were cast-iron pots very heavy but they were also very brittle and susceptible to burning out, so they were not ideal cooking utensils. On the other hand, they were cheap and could be patched by a blacksmith. Pot iron in early Maryland cost about threepence a pound, and cooking pots weighed from 20 to 60 pounds or more, so that one cost from four to fifteen shillings. The more expensive brassware, at about fifteenpence per pound, was much lighter and could take the banging around of normal use without cracking. For this reason, brass was ideal for smaller utensils such as kettles and skillets. The latter, by the way, were what we would now call saucepans. They had steeply vertical sides and very long handles. The people of the period used the term "pot" for the larger vessels, with capacities usually measuring in the gallons, fitted with loop handles and hooks for suspension over the fire, not seating them in the fire. The smaller capacity of "kettles" was generally measured in quarts, and these had lids, whereas pots did not.[24]

Roasting took place in front of the fire, not in an oven, with a dripping pan placed beneath. By suspending the meat from the lug pole or the mantle piece, one need not turn it on a spit. In either case, the cook basted the roast with salt water and drippings from the pan. Well-to-do families may have served roasted meats frequently, but most dined just as did the poorer sort, on "messes," boiled in a pot and eaten with a spoon.[25] Maize porridge, cooked

[24] All generalizations such as these can be readily disproved with examples to the contrary, so distinctions drawn here should be understood as guides rather than as fixed rules.

[25] This preference for messes spiced with herbs may have disappeared in the eighteenth century among more sophisticated households. English cookbooks published in America made no mention of this style of cooking.

to a thick consistency in water and served with milk and butter when these were available, provided the fundamental "fill." Even in affluent households, the use of sugar and molasses as sweeteners for porridge was not common, nor was the cornmeal usually salted.

Boiled dishes incorporated salt meat, cut in small pieces, and dried beans, peas, and/or hominy, all cooked together for a long time and perhaps flavored with herbs and greens gathered from woods and fields nearby. Preserved meats salted the dish. By 1700, Marylanders could get honey from their own bees or trade for some with their neighbors, but only the rich regularly kept sugar and imported spices on hand. Few even of the rich stored large supplies of vegetables such as cabbages, onions, turnips, carrots, and sweet potatoes over the winter, as did New Englanders. Beans, peas, and corn, washed down with cider, provided the staple winter diet in the early eighteenth-century Chesapeake.

As the previous chapter noted, the poorest planters did not have the facilities for making large quantities of butter and cheese for long storage. With no means of cooling during the six months of warm weather, such households consumed their current production and then went without. The more affluent planters had substantial supplies of dairying equipment and made butter and cheese in the spring and fall. The latter, however, was probably not of very good quality, since there are far fewer references in the literature to cheese and cheesemaking equipment than to butter.[26]

The poorer planter families worked and slept in the same room in which they cooked and ate. There was only one woman to handle the cooking and laundry chores until a daughter grew big enough to help. There was neither room nor time for elaborate cooking under such circumstances. When the cooking moved out of the hall, however, the other heavy, hot chores left with it. A serving maid, hired or indentured, joined the family at this stage to help the overburdened housewife cope with the hearth-related tasks such as brewing, washing, and ironing.

With the hall cleared of cooking utensils, space became available for furnishings that made the place more convenient for sitting and visiting. The hall still served as a bedroom, but there were chairs to sit on, and usually a cupboard to hold the pewter and wooden dishes. For example, Captain Thomas Todd of Anne Arundel County, who died in 1677 leaving a widow, one son, and

---

[26] Proper cure of cheese requires temperatures below 60 degrees. Average daily temperature in the coastal counties of Maryland today rises above 55 degrees for six months or more in the year.

221

three daughters, lived with his family plus a woman servant and a "lad" in a three-room house. The inward room contained a bed, a trundle bed, two chests, a few tools, and a parcel of table linen. The outward room contained a "conoe" with a servant's bed in it, a table and form, and another table with an old chair. The room also contained two guns, with shot jug and horn, and a hand mill. In the milkhouse were the cooking utensils, pewterware, and carpentry tools. For eating, there were only six trenchers, but exactly eight spoons for two adults, four children, and two servants—not a luxurious style of living, but adequate.[27]

Members of John Day's family, like Captain Todd's, lived with their servants in a three-room house, but more comfortably.[28] In the "new" room, there were five leather chairs, a table, a trunk, and two chests with extra linens stored away, besides a curtained bed. In the outer room was another bed with curtains, a flock bed, a cradle with blankets and rug, and a couch with bolster that probably served as a bed as well. Besides the table and form, there were two wooden chairs, plus a chest and a gun. A chimney cloth covered the mantle over the fireplace, a sign of gentility. The two chamber pots and bedpan were stored in the kitchen, where the cooking utensils and pewterware were kept. The kitchen hearth boasted a pair of andirons with spit, bellows, two pairs of tongs, and a fire shovel. There were four drinking pots and a dozen trenchers, and a candlestick, a "falling" (folding) table, two Bibles, and a looking glass completed the room's equipment. Two iron pestles plus a small brass mortar and pestle served for all the grinding chores, which probably fell to the lot of the three men servants and one maid servant who shared the house with the family.

Neither the Todd nor the Day household had any utensils for making butter or cheese, not unusual for the times, but the family of Cornelius Howard did do some dairying, to judge from some of the articles in the "lower" room that served as a kitchen.[29] Planter Howard had a wife, two sons, three daughters, and two servants— a man and a boy. Their three rooms were quite crowded with furniture as well as with people. The "little" room contained not only three beds, but a quantity of spare linens in a chest with a decorative carpet over it, and a cupboard, lined with a cloth, that

[27] Capt. Todd, who arrived in Maryland in 1650, served as a justice of the peace; *Inv. & Accts.*, Liber 4, f. 149.

[28] *Testamentary Proceedings*, Liber 1B, f. 53 (1660).

[29] *Inv. & Accts.*, Liber 7A, f. 307 (1680). See the profile in Papenfuse et al., *Biographical Dictionary*, I, 465.

displayed several pieces of silver, a looking glass, and a Bible. The "upper" room also contained three beds, plus six old wooden chairs, a dozen turkey-work chairs, a chest with carpenters' and coopers' tools, and an inkhorn with three books. The "lower" room held the fireplace and cooking equipment, a couch and chair, three tables, and six joint stools. A dozen trenchers, two earthen dishes, and a basin supplied the eating ware. A churn, a parcel of earthen pots, and milk trays were used for making butter and farmers' cheese, but there was no cheese press or anything else to suggest that the family cured any cheese on the premises. A hand mill and iron pestle served for grinding the corn, smoothing and box irons for ironing clothes, four old candlesticks of wood and iron supplied holders for candlelight, but there was no looking glass by which to shave with the razor. Also stored in this room were cartwheels, old gears, a grindstone, wedges, saw, axes, frow, and other old ironware plus five guns, only three of which happened to be "fixt."

The Todd, Day, and Howard families all lived in three-room houses in the years before 1680 when households of their economic level (the middle third of the distribution of all households) normally kept servants. All, obviously, lived at close quarters with one another. Of the three, only the Howard menage showed any clear-cut signs of spatial separation between family and servants, at least in terms of sleeping arrangements. Everyone ate together, drank together, and worked together, even if they did not sleep in the same rooms.

The three men servants belonging to Nicholas Ruxton of Baltimore County, however, lived out in a quarter, where a saucepan, a spit, and a dripping pan provided limited cooking facilities.[30] Ruxton's family all slept together in the three beds crowded together in the inner room. The outer room had a fireplace and a few pieces of cooking equipment plus a copper drinking pot and a silver cup, several books, and three chairs, as well as the usual guns, powder, and shot. The buttery and shed held the pewter and principal cooking utensils and eleven milk trays for setting out the milk to let the cream rise. Out in the quarter, besides the scanty means for cooking, were a hand mill, two sifters, an iron pestle, a servant's bed (worth only four shillings), tools for carpentry and farming, plus some beans, wheat, and barley, as well as soap and salt.

Dommack Dennis, a planter from Somerset County, died in 1717,

---

[30] *Inv. & Accts.*, Liber 7A, f. 95 (1680).

almost forty years later than the planters whose homes and furniture we have been describing.[31] Dennis' personal property placed him on approximately the same economic level as the others, but he and his family lived in a four-room house with just one man servant. Since Dennis had at least one grandchild, he was probably a little older than the others. His will mentions two sons and two daughters besides his wife. Upstairs in the house, there were two chambers, one containing two feather beds with curtains, the other holding another, likewise with curtains, plus a spinning wheel and twenty-four pounds of wool. Downstairs in the parlor were three feather beds, two of them with curtains, two chests, and some uncut cloth. The beds ranged in value from £3 to £5—adequate but not luxurious. In the hall were two tables, a bench, a couch, and seven chairs. The larger table held a clock and two old looking glasses, one of which was cracked. Casks and other woodenware and tools of various kinds, including sheep shears and a flax hackle, lay all about the room, while in one corner sat a bed stuffed with chaff, worth less than five shillings. Cooking equipment at the hearth included pot racks, two frying pans, a chafing dish, a gridiron, a spit and dripping pan, two small brass kettles plus a larger one, and several iron cooking pots weighing altogether 150 pounds. The pewter pieces, which were not individually identified, weighed 66 pounds. In addition to the pewter and iron, there were three earthenware pots, three cups, three porringers, two plates, and two small basins of clay. The copper drinking pot was broken, so perhaps among the pewter there were some flagons or other containers for beverages.

Salt, vinegar, stored tallow, miscellaneous articles of clothing, and even a bag of thriftily preserved feathers were all in this same room, together with the candlesticks and table linen. In the Dennis house, the hall was clearly an all-purpose room, with laundry equipment, cooking utensils, husbandry tools, and even two sides of leather for making or repairing shoes in the evenings. The family slept downstairs as well as up, and the servant and hired help probably slept in the hall.

The families of middling planters, such as we have been considering, had little opportunity to develop any decorative sense in the placement and storage of their things. Clothing not in current use hung from pegs on the walls or lay packed away in chests, along with extra linens. A sizable minority did own cupboards for storing

[31] Ibid., Liber 39C, f. 160.

their eating ware, but few had chests of drawers. Besides the beds, then, there were rather few pieces of substantial furniture in the houses. Only a quarter of the poorer third of households owned chairs, the reader may recall, and only half of the middling third did so. Members of the household sat on a miscellany of things including beds, benches, chests, and stools.

When resources permitted, planters provided their families with more of the same utensils and furniture and generally of better quality, but they also added more variety: more tables, sets of chairs, candlesticks in every room, pewter, brass, and earthenware in greater profusion to fill a lengthening list of household needs and chores. The larger the household, the more things it acquired, and alas for the housewife, the more tasks greeted her each day. Life at this level was not much different from that of the poorer families except for the addition of a servant to help, perhaps, and the greater comfort afforded by the better beds, extra linen, separate cooking facilities, and the prevailing air of abundance and security.

When we compare the living conditions and material goods of the middling planters with those more affluent, the principal differences are two: clearer separation of the family from the rest of the people on the plantation, and clearer distinction between master and servant, mistress and maid. No great divide marks off the boundary between the upper tier of estates from those below, and no single style of living characterized the well-to-do. Some lived as gentlemen who never soiled their hands with fieldwork, but many were as adept at the ax and hoe as any of their men. The principal distinction of this ascendent class lay in the managerial nature of their daily round of duties, the need for them to keep careful accounts, and to plan ahead not only in order to maintain their good credit but to acquire stocks of necessaries for the coming year. Most importantly, they had to anticipate and provide for contingencies because of the large numbers of people dependent upon them. Many were also called upon to furnish their time and labor to the offices and duties of local government and parish, acting as justices of the peace, militia officers, and vestrymen.[32]

We are speaking, then, of a class of men who had the wherewithal to live well by the standards of their time, had they chosen to do so. Most, however, lived in a style as plain and simple as that of

[32] Many planters of the middling level also served in local offices, particularly in the earlier years. So scarce were men of education and managerial background that literacy was not a requirement to serve on the county commission. Vestries did not become established in Maryland until the royal period, 1690-1717.

their less affluent neighbors. Their preferences lay along the same lines: plain furniture and simple tableware, decent linens, some nice pieces of silver, perhaps, and good—really good—beds. Among the very richest families, there were some who lived on the level approaching that of the Wormeleys, the Fitzhughs, and the Byrds amid handsome clocks and fine furniture made by the best English craftsmen of the times; who wore elegant clothes, carried silver watches, and even sported canes. Their walls displayed portraits of the English monarchs, and their rooms held vases of fresh flowers, while velvet draperies framed their windows. This was the "formal" style as opposed to the "plain" or "country" style of their neighbors and friends; but such families were exceptional in early Maryland.

Let us introduce a few of those planters, young and old, at the very top of the economic order, for by entering their homes we can explore the range of living standards among this most affluent group, defined here to be those worth more than £450 in personal estates, exclusive of financial assets. The first two houses we will visit are those of Nicholas Wyatt and James Rigbie, of Anne Arundel County.[33] About Wyatt (died 1674) we know nothing, even though he was a man of some substance. Rigbie (died 1681) was probably a former servant. Because he held a seat in the Assembly, we might expect him to have lived more elegantly than he did. Why he chose not to do so is partly suggested by his will, which left a bequest to poor Quakers. Both Wyatt and Rigbie were among the sample of young fathers: Wyatt had one son and one daughter, Rigbie two of each. Wyatt's will mentioned two plantations, Rigbie's 1,250 acres. Both inventories valued their contents in terms of tobacco, which we will change into money at the rate of a penny per pound, 240 pence per pound sterling. To summarize:

	PPW	DR	C	C % PPW	Rms	Bldgs	Beds	Chairs	Srvts	Slaves
Wyatt	£562	£ 42	£265	47	6	3	17	42	3	2
Rigbie	409	136	79	19	6	5	13+	14	3	0

Wyatt lived in a house on his "lower" plantation, which had a hall, parlor, porch, and a staircase leading upstairs to three bedrooms. A kitchen that may have been detached from the main house had a buttery, a bedroom, and a loft. It contained the brass and

[33] Wyatt's inventory is dated April 1674 in *Testamentary Proceedings*, Liber 6, f. 212 and in *Inv. & Accts.*, Liber 2, f. 246, 263; Rigbie's is from May of 1681, ibid., Liber 7B, f. 119.

pewter ware, a still, fireplace equipment, several tables and six chairs, plus a bed. The quarter held the iron cooking pots, of which there were five, a brass kettle, more fireplace equipment, and a hand mill. All the dairy equipment lay in the milkhouse. Wyatt's estate was unusual in having a cellar with a loft, a separate structure where salt, wheat, corn, and husbandry tools were kept in addition to empty casks and some unused bricks. Three old boats and a large canoe were tied up at the landing. An "outward" plantation housed two men servants, two negro men, and a woman servant, who had two iron pots to cook with, and three beds, two of them of little value (only five shillings each), plus "old and worn" household goods worth as much as the flock bed and chest—a little more than a pound sterling.

Back at the main house, we step up onto the porch and enter through the front door into the hall with its fireplace at one end of the room. There are no beds in sight, but the couch could be pressed into that service if needed. Seven "planet pictures" decorate the walls, but there are no curtains at the window. Around the table, with its carpet covering, stand six turkey-work chairs and seven ladder chairs, so there is ample seating. A sideboard with a cloth holds the silverware, worth almost £10; a handsome chest of drawers, also covered with a cloth, and a small table and carpet complete the room's furniture. Here, too, were the owner's books. It is a spacious, well-organized room, designed for receiving company, wholly unlike most of the halls of Wyatt's neighbors and contemporaries.

The room to our left is the parlor. It too has a fireplace against the far wall, and also holds another handsome chest of drawers, plus a cupboard and eleven chairs, four of which are of the turkey-work variety. Two cushions offer additional seating on a sizable trunk that sits against another wall and contains Mrs. Wyatt's apparel. The bed with its curtains dominates the room, and under it lies a trundle bed. Together these are worth nearly £17. A small couch nearby makes up into another bed when needed, so the room can sleep five people comfortably if necessary. On the walls hang six framed pictures, and a pair of "cloths" enhance the windows. A silver caudle cup, three wine glasses, and a looking glass perch on the chest of drawers, a nest of hourglasses, and a brush lie on top of the trunk.

Two boxes, containing bed and table linen plus bolts of new cloth, are stored in the corner space under the stairs, up which we now ascend to inspect the rooms above. The chamber over the hall has a fireplace to warm it, a handsome set of curtains at the window and a "set work rug" hanging on the wall. Two chests and a trunk hold the extra linens for the three beds in the room, one of which is a trundle; the other two have curtains. Around a handsome table, covered with a carpet, stand five ladder chairs and a single joint stool. Like the rooms downstairs, this one also boasts a looking glass.

Across the landing is the chamber over the porch, without a fireplace, containing a very nice bed, a table, six stools, and three cushions. There are four small pictures that may be religious in nature, but there are no books.

On the far side of the landing lies the third bedroom, over the parlor, and it provides storage for a very extensive collection of linens. Two beds, one substantial but the other small, take up much of the floor space, but there is, in addition, a table, bench, and chair. Again, there are three pictures on the wall, and a looking glass.

Altogether the parlor and the three upstairs bedrooms contained nine beds, seventeen chairs, seven stools, and one bench, while in the hall stood one couch that could double as a bed, thirteen chairs and six stools. Each room, except for the porch chamber, held a looking glass, and all had chests, trunks, and other pieces of furniture for storing extra linens and clothing. Although there was plenty of seating in the parlor and bedrooms, these clearly served functions distinct from that of the hall, where the absence of beds, tools, and so forth lent it a formal air, into which visitors were made welcome.

No chamber pots or close stools or warming pans were found in the bedrooms, but appeared instead in the kitchen, where Wyatt's woman servant probably had carried them for cleaning. This was a big, expansive room with a large fireplace, several tables, and six chairs, besides quantities of pewter and brass. There was also a still, five painted stone jugs, five spits, an iron dripping pan, one of tin, four cleavers, a marble mortar with a pestle of lignum vitae, a half-hour glass, a cow bell, various wooden vessels, seven guns and a pistol, plus a cane and a pair of shoes. The kitchen chamber contained two beds, a chest, a barber case, and a looking glass. Up in the loft there is another bed, several wooden casks, a jack, and two casements for windows. The buttery held only some smoothing irons, a frying pan, a well bucket, a pair of bellows, and "some things more."

At Wyatt's home plantation, there were four structures: the main house with its six rooms; a kitchen with two rooms, a loft, and a buttery; a cellar with a loft; and a "quarter" without any beds, which therefore did not quarter anybody but served instead as a second kitchen. The three beds in the kitchen chamber and loft offered sleeping space for several servants on the home plantation—but just who slept in those eight beds and two couches in the main house? Since a family of four needed only three beds at most, one suspects that Wyatt either rented out lodgings or held open house.

The physical delineations of James Rigbie's house do not emerge as clearly from his inventory, but those that can be seen bear some resemblance to Wyatt's home plantation with its several outbuildings. Rigbie's hall, too, was entered by means of a door from the porch. It contained no fireplace equipment, unless the appraisers overlooked them, but there was a clock, a set of curtains, two "Barbados" hammocks, a couch bed, a chest with a tapestry coverlid, a form and table, with a writing desk on top, plus three iron-bound Dutch cases on the floor, each full of bottles. Elsewhere in the room were two looking glasses, probably small hand-held ones, two maps of Virginia and Maryland on the wall, and quantities of sheets, pillowcases, tablecloths, towels, and napkins. The "plate" is not valued in the inventory, which bears the note that both the silver and "Negro Man Anthony Leon" were bestowed by terms in Rigbie's will upon his wife and children. In the parlor there were two beds, together worth less than £8, an old cupboard with one drawer and some painted earthenware on it, an old deal chest, a small round table with its carpet, six high leather chairs, four low ones, and three flag chairs. The parlor was heated by the house's only fireplace. Upstairs there were three rooms, only two of which were used as bedrooms. One was Mrs. Rigbie's, and the inventory mentions only a table and two iron pots there, obviously omitting intentionally much of the room's contents. The other room contained a couch bed, two chests, a wicker basket, and a parcel of old bedding for servants.

Outside stood a kitchen with two rooms adjoining, a mill house with a small cog mill, a milkhouse, a workhouse, a store, and probably a small shed of some sort down at the landing. At the mulberry tree in the yard there stood a large brick fireplace with a big iron pot and a large brass kettle set into the structure, used for scalding hogs and perhaps for making soap, although the store included some good imported soap. Inside the workhouse, one found carpenters', coopers', and joiners' tools, together with two foxtraps and a rattrap. The inventory also mentions Mr. Rigbie's other plantation on Kent Island, which he farmed with a partner, plus its livestock, servants, and household goods, of which Rigbie's share came to £25.

Servants at home included a tailor and two women, one of whom was "unseasoned," and therefore newly arrived. They and the Negro man, Anthony Leon, could have slept in any number of possible places: upstairs in the main house; in the "ground chamber" adjoining the kitchen, which had three beds and a fireplace; or in the "wenches chamber," which had a bed; or in the mill house, where there was a servant's bed; or upstairs in this or another unidentified structure where there were "servants chambers" with a parcel of bedding and feathers. The "white chamber," which may have been adjacent to these, also contained three beds, one of which was quite a good feather bed worth as much as the high bed in the parlor of the main house, that is, just over £4.

In addition to thirteen beds, two parcels of servants' bedding, and two "Barbados" hammocks, there was undoubtedly another bed in Mrs. Rigbie's chamber, so there must have been at least eighteen places to sleep in any of ten or eleven rooms in buildings scattered all over the plantation. The values of the beds ranged from eight shillings for a servant's bed to £4 for the high bed in the parlor, the low bed in the "ground chamber," and the feather bed in the "white chamber."

No chairs stood in the hall, where one had to sit on the couch bed, the chest, or on the Dutch cases full of bottles, but the parlor did contain thirteen chairs, and another old one stood in the "white chamber." The only books encountered were located in the "ground chamber" adjoining the kitchen, but there may have been more in Mrs. Rigbie's room. With this same possible exception, no chamber pots or warming pans appeared in the inventory. Aside from the clock, worth £1, the hall curtains valued at £2.5, and the painted earthenware in the old cupboard in the parlor, which together with an old deal chest were worth 25 shillings, there were no indications of any decorative intentions nor of any intention to keep some room in readiness to receive guests.[34] The cooking and eating utensils were surprisingly few and described as worn and bruised. On the other hand, the large iron pot and brass kettle set into brick out by the mulberry tree in the yard were clearly designed for big chores.

[34] About one-third of those in the top decile of planter households owned nothing in the way of household adornment: no window curtains, pictures, china or other decorated earthenware, and so on.

Wyatt and Rigbie, both worth about £500 in physical personal wealth, both with children not yet of age, both living in Anne Arundel County with plantations at the waterside, illustrate the diversity in life styles displayed by the Maryland planters and their families. Rigbie's home did not match, in gentility or cultural attributes, that of Wyatt, with its books, twenty pictures, ornaments, chairs, handsome chests of drawers, expensive bed, wall hangings, wine glasses, and warming pans. Those planters who were poorer than Wyatt and Rigbie, roughly nine-tenths of all households, lived far less spaciously than either, and tended toward Rigbie's spare and unself-conscious manner. Getting a living, rather than ornamenting it, was the order of the day.

One could argue that Maryland around 1700 was still close to its frontier origins, still poor, and the Rigbies of the province still in the building stages of their careers. Former servants, as Rigbie may have been, probably felt too insecure in their economic status to waste their hard-won capital on useless objects. We would expect that men of greater means—having ampler opportunity to indulge their dreams—preferred greater comfort, more convenience, and some of the trappings of civilization in the midst of the wilderness, the better, perhaps, to clothe and enhance the authority over others that they already exercised. These are reasonable expectations and true for some men, but not for all. Take William Burgess, Esquire, for instance.[35] He died in 1687 at the age of 65, a successful merchant with a flourishing business based in Londontown in Anne Arundel County. The father of eleven children, grandfather to eight more, he had served as justice of the peace, member of the lower house of the legislature, and secretary of the provincial government. Here indeed we find the epitome of the successful man in seventeenth-century Maryland. He owned over 6,000 acres at his death, close to a 1,000 pounds sterling in personal property, plus almost £2,500 more in debts and other financial credits owing to him, while he himself owed nothing to anyone. Besides being a merchant and major office-holder, Burgess was also a successful planter, owning more than seventy cattle, nine horses, three dozen sheep and hogs, thirteen servants, and a dozen slaves.

Burgess lived well, but he, too, preferred to spread out rather than build up. His original home contained only a parlor with its fireplace and a "chamber." To these two rooms he had added, on

[35] *Inv. & Accts.*, Liber 18, f. 89. See his profile in Papenfuse et al., *Biographical Dictionary*, I, 182.

231

one side, a milkhouse to hold the dairy equipment, and on the other, a "new" room, with its own fireplace. This room contained, at his death, a bed worth only £8, half a dozen turkey-work chairs valued at just five shillings each, a small table and carpet, a looking glass, two cushions, several pieces of earthenware, a barber's case, and silverware worth £30. The closet contained some spices, apothecary wares, books, a case of knives, a pair of bellows, three tin candlesticks, a coat with gold buttons worth £4, and a scimitar and belt, valued at £2. Although rather scantily furnished, the room and closet held goods worth close to £50, but three-fifths of that sum was in precious metals.

The principal room of the house was clearly the parlor, since it contained twenty leather chairs and a clock, some pictures, and another looking glass. It also held two curtained beds, each worth only £5, plus a cupboard, two chests, a box, a case of bottles, a trunk stuffed with household linens, a dressing box, a long table, and a round one. It must have been a rather crowded room, particularly if enough people arrived to fill all twenty of those chairs.

The chamber next to the parlor was similarly crowded: four curtained beds, a cradle, four chairs, two tables, seven chests and trunks, all filled with extra linens and curtains, and a cupboard with drawers. Also in the room was a close stool with pan, a chairlike device with a hidden receptacle. The milkhouse contained the usual assortment of dairy ware, including a cheese press, plus two clothes baskets and four tubs for "powdering" meat with preservative salts. In the cellar and the cider house were stored quantities of empty barrels, while the old kitchen held copper and brass ware, five tin pudding pans, six tin dish covers, four fish plates, and a chopping block with a rack of knives. Three tables gave plenty of working space. Also in the old kitchen were two barrels of brown sugar, several hundred pounds of butter, a large chest of soap, and a box of candles, along with such miscellany as fishing lines and garden shears.

The cider house, with its supply of casks, its mill and trough, also contained horse harness, husbandry and carpentry tools, hand mills, salt, and bedding for three Negroes. Four flock beds for servants, meanwhile, were housed in the new kitchen, which held all the heavy cast-iron cook ware, together with a big copper "furnace" worth over £6 and other copper and wooden utensils.

Judge Burgess kept a store at home and one at Londontown, both filled with an assortment of imported textiles, shoes, tools, nails, and salt. He operated three other plantations, each stocked

232

with tools, livestock, and bound laborers with beds, cooking utensils, and other household goods. Clearly, the emphasis in Burgess' life lay in the pursuit of a variety of entrepreneurial activities rather than in living a life of leisure at home in a great mansion filled with paintings and fine furniture. On the other hand, Burgess' family did enjoy decent beds and plenty of linens, besides a goodly store of silver.

Contrasted with Burgess' rather plain style is the household of a man equally wealthy and equally prominent in provincial affairs, John Rousby of Calvert County, who served as clerk to the Upper House after putting in time as a member of the lower one.[36] Father of three young children, Rousby died the year before Burgess, in 1686. He owned at the time some 3,400 acres on both sides of the bay, stocked with 149 cattle, 71 hogs, 87 sheep, 30 horses, 10 servants, and an equal number of slaves. He, too, kept a store and owned a share in a ship, so that like many others of his class in Maryland, he pursued commercial as well as agricultural interests. In Rousby's case, however, the emphasis was far more on the latter than on the former.

Mr. Rousby's house had five rooms: a hall, a little hall, Mrs. Rousby's chamber, an outward chamber, and the "red" room. The inventory omitted the bed in the widow's room and there was none in the hall, but seven beds and a hammock were distributed among the other three rooms. The best was valued at £8, the others ranged from only 15 shillings to £4, but Mrs. Rousby's bed may have been worth a great deal more.

In the hall with its fireplace there stood ten leather chairs and a large "wainscot" chair with a cushioned seat, several tables and chests, two looking glasses, three maps and a landscape on the wall, a wooden clock, a glass ball, and a pair of steelyards, a portable balance with a hook attached for weighing objects. Similar furniture, with the beds, filled the other rooms, and one chest held, besides the usual assortment of linens, gloves, stockings, and shoes, two pairs of women's silk stockings, a silk gown and petticoat worth £3, a fan, and four pairs of ruffles.[37] The outward chamber had some pewter ware and a chamber pot.

The "red" room was an important one: it contained a fireplace, two "wainscotted" chests of drawers, a looking glass framed in

[36] *Inv. & Accts.*, Liber 9, f. 263.

[37] Stowed in the chests were some thirty-five pairs of shoes. The closet in the hall held nine pairs of sheep shears, two small chests, a box of drawers, three old carpets, and a clothes press.

olivewood, six Russia leather chairs, an elbow chair, a small table, and a couch. Brass andirons sat on the hearth, and a "brass" hung on the wall with three landscapes and a crucifix. More items of interest in this room include ritual wafers intended for the sacrament of Holy Communion, a parcel of glass "coffey cupps" and a chocolate pot, an ivory-hafted knife and fork set, and silverware worth £36. Sealing wax, a seal with an ivory handle, two dozen "marking letters," and two reams of paper attest Rousby's office, as almost £100 in coin may also. Riding and militia gear complete the contents.[38]

Rousby's store held the usual yardgoods, shoes, hats, and stockings, with a miscellany of hardware items for work and the house, plus 100 pounds of soap, 400 pounds of muscavado sugar, 80 gallons of rum, 20 gallons of brandy, 30,000 nails, and quantities of wheat, corn, oats, and even rye, a rarity in the Chesapeake. The kitchen held, besides the cooking ware, seven guns "fixed and unfixed," salt, tar, a dozen candlesticks and a copper lamp, and chairs, couch, and table. There were two beds in the loft along with chests of linens.

Rousby had more in the way of apparel, books, chairs, and arms than did the other three men whose inventories we have been considering: a library of books worth £20, wearing apparel valued at £15, and a watch. Wyatt, however, had far more in the way of bedding and linens. All had some decorative extras—even Rigbie, who among the four owned the least in consumption goods.

The mere passage of time increased the number of estates worth a thousand pounds or more and, thus, examples for our investigation. One that is particularly noteworthy is Richard Smith, Esquire, of Calvert County, who died in 1715.[39] Besides five working plantations, Smith also owned over 15,000 acres, a mill on St. Leonard's Creek, and Stone's Island, an accumulation of real estate rivaling those of the biggest Virginia planters of the period. Smith's farming operations were unusually scattered, but they illustrate the shifting style of commercial agriculture, which attempted to maximize returns to labor by skimming off the fertility of the soil.

Like others of his class, Smith also pursued mercantile interests. His stores contained well over £400 worth of new goods, though his only investments in shipping consisted of a small yawl worth £5

[38] Also in the room and in the closet were riding gear, a silver-plated sword and belt, five other swords, a pair of holsters with a brace of pistols, and three other pistols—all of which amounted to a substantial arsenal.

[39] *Inv. & Accts.*, Liber 36C, f. 1.

and a flatboat worth £7. For such a rich man, Smith owned very few consumption goods: his apparel came to £15, the same as Rousby's; his books were worth £5; a silver watch, some guns, and his household furnishings came to a total of only £131 compared to £1,718 in capital, a ratio of one to thirteen. Half a dozen pictures and maps decorated the walls of his seven-room house, but his two best beds were worth only £10 each, not luxurious for so wealthy a man, and the other five beds ranged in value from £1.5 to £5. The andirons in the kitchen were broken, and much of the pewter was old and worn.

Contrast Smith with Col. Henry Ridgley of Anne Arundel County, who died in 1710 possessed of total personal property worth almost exactly that of Smith's, but the ratio of his consumption goods to capital was almost one to two![40] Ridgley was an older man with grandchildren, who had held many offices of honor and profit in his time. His apparel was valued at £69, more than four times that of Smith. His silverware was worth almost £100, his library £8, and his large house was filled with china, fancy furniture, and linens. Flowers on the tables, framed maps and pictures on the walls, fine damask curtains at the windows, all lent an air of gentility and good taste to the Ridgley residence. There were five principal beds in the main house, all with rich "double" furniture, ranging in value from £20 to £25 each—more than twice the value of Smith's beds.

Many structures dotted the landscape around the Ridgley house, including a kitchen with separate chamber and pantry, a milkhouse, storehouse, two-room cellar, wash house, smokehouse, still house, barn, and quarter. The iron cooking utensils were housed in both the wash house and the quarter, not in the kitchen, while a loom sat out in the barn and eight spinning wheels were stored in the still house. The kitchen and pantry held a number of valuable pieces of pewter and brassware, a coffee mill, and two dozen large ivory-hafted knives and forks with silver ferules, plus another six silver-hafted case knives, together worth almost £9. The garden held an "arbor house," with a table and form from which to view the newly planted landscape.

Besides Ridgley's five plantations, he also owned close to a thousand acres of other real estate, and worked his land with some 32 slaves. These had the care of 126 cattle, 200 hogs, and 8 horses, but no sheep, despite the loom in the barn. In contrast to Smith, Ridgley owned no boats, not even a share in one, and the mer-

[40] Ibid., Liber 32A, f. 38; Liber 33B, f. 187.

235

chandise in his store was worth less than £140, whereas Smith's was valued at more than £400.

Let one final case illustrate the latitude of choice available to the planters with means. Maryland's richest merchant-planter was Samuel Chew of Annapolis, descendent of an early Virginia settler, himself a father and grandfather, and a Quaker.[41] Chew's estate, inventoried in 1718, shows a heavy investment in slaves and livestock: 88 slaves valued at over £2,300, 3 servants at £40, close to 350 cattle, over 500 hogs, almost 50 sheep, and a dozen horses, the value of his livestock alone totaling £880. "New goods" were worth £545, his share in the ship Charles was appraised at £160, and debts owing to Chew from others in Maryland came close to £500.

Resources tied up in agriculture were triple the value of those invested in commerce, and capital commanded five times the value of Chew's personal and household goods. These came close to £800, nevertheless, a sum that provided a great deal more in the way of luxuries than others enjoyed. When analyzed, Chew's disposition of his assets bears a strong resemblance to Ridgley's.

Planter	PPW	Consumables	Plate	Apparel, Household Items
Smith	£1907	£140	£ 2.5	£108
Ridgley	1946	550	94.0	259
Chew	5312	818	331.0	297

Chew owned a little more pewter and brass and a lot more plate than the others. Silver objects, "plate" as they called them, should be viewed as an important form of liquid savings as well as items of conspicuous consumption for the Maryland planters, since money was very scarce in the Chesapeake and there were no banks in which to keep safe an emergency fund. Chew's best bed cost £16, Ridgley's £25; but a search through the contents and values of the hall and parlor of each man's house reveals more similarities than differences in their life styles, except for Ridgley's clear predilection for decoration: pictures, flowers, fine draperies, "12 wax images in glass [and] 6 nosegay pots."

Table VI.4 presents a comparison of the contents of these two important rooms in each man's house. Chew and Ridgley stand in the extreme upper range in life styles available to the planters of early Maryland, yet theirs cannot be described as lavish when compared with contemporary West Indian or London standards.

No Marylander could rival Virginia's King Carter, ruler of "Cor-

---

[41] *Inventories*, Liber 1, f. 464. See the profile of his father in Papenfuse et al., *Biographical Dictionary*, I, 218.

TABLE VI.4

CONTENTS OF THE PRINCIPAL ROOMS OF CHEW AND RIDGLEY

Samuel Chew, 1718	Col. Henry Ridgley, 1710
Lower Lodging Room	Parlor
Bed, tea table, china, china punch bowl, lacquered punch bowl, "winn servitore," two chests of drawers, table, 8 leather chairs, one elbow chair, spring clock, looking glass, two window curtains, close stool, easy chair, 2 round stools and covers, iron dogs, hand bell, warming pan, 2 trunks, brush, household linen worth over £55, 8 doz. white [wine cups?], pewter cistern, tin ditto, spice box, two coffee mills.	Bed with rich double furniture, large trunk, escritoire, walnut table and carpet, 7 cane chairs, 4 window curtains of fine scarlet crepe, large looking glass, 29 mezzotint pictures, 18 small pictures, 12 wax images in glass, 6 nosegay pots, pair andirons, brass shovel and tongs, iron back, 3 "histories in frames," chest of drawers, walnut dressing box, 2 carpets, 26 sweet meat glasses, looking glass, dressing basket, 7 boxes, 3 trunks, 5 agate hafted knives and forks, 2 fire screens, 6 small pictures, chest of drawers, spice box, 2 cases of bottles, case, box, 23 double flute glasses, dozen china cups, 15 vials, stone jug, library of books, parcel of chinaware.
Total value less the household linens: £75.58	Total value: £67.56
[Hall]	Hall
Tables, carpet, couch, fifteen chairs, large looking glass, books, scritoire, gun, barbers' case, medicines, three cases of bottles, a ream of paper, portmanteau, trunk, lantern, andirons.	Clock, two tables, three carpets, screen, seven cane chairs, six large maps, "Queens Arms," four large chimney pieces, damask window curtains, six flower pots, six china cups, glass globe, large looking glass, pair iron dogs [andirons], iron back, brass shovel and tongs, small looking glass, chest, and three trunks.
Total £32	Total £30
Total for two rooms: £107.58	£97.56

SOURCE: *Inv. & Accts.*, Liber 32A, f. 38 for Col. Henry Ridgley; *Inventories*, Liber 1, f. 464, in Maryland probate records, in Hall of Records, Annapolis.

otoman," but neither could any other Virginian of the colonial period. When this wealthiest of all Chesapeake planters died in 1732, he possessed 300,000 acres, 1,000 slaves, and £10,000 in personal estate.[42] Insofar as records permit such comparisons, Carter's wealth outstripped even those of the Revolutionary genera-

[42] Louis B. Wright, *The First Gentlemen of Virginia: Intellectual Qualities of the Early Colonial Ruling Class* (San Marino, Cal., 1940), p. 248.

237

tion. Virginians contemporary with the planters whose inventories we have been examining—Wyatt, Burgess, or Ridgley—lived no better. Ralph Wormeley, squire of Rosegill, owned less than £3,000 sterling in personal estate when he died in 1701.[43] Rosegill, widely viewed as the most beautiful home in the colony, was only a nine-room wooden frame structure. William Byrd I left his son and heir a wooden house at Westover, built just a dozen years before his death.[44] Robert Beverly II, who married young William's sister Ursula, divided with his brothers and sisters an estate worth £5,000, with 42 slaves and 50,000 acres just about the same time the elder Byrd was building his new home.[45]

If these Virginians are representative of their colony's elite in 1700, then their standard of living may have been no different from that of their counterparts in Maryland. When one turns elsewhere among the continental colonies for similar information, we discover that New England's wealthiest class was concentrated in Boston and earned their livings as merchants. Such men did not invest heavily in slaves, land, and livestock, of course, but in ships, cargoes, and trade, and their wealth lay mainly in financial assets rather than in physical goods. For the years 1700-1719, the richest 3 percent of decedents in the probate records of the central counties of Massachusetts, all resident in Boston, were only slightly more wealthy in gross personal estate than their Maryland contemporaries, averaging slightly over £2,000 to the southerners' £1,700 sterling. Connecticut's top 3 percent could not muster half as much. Since the composition of wealth varied so greatly between the two regions, and since we do not know the value of Maryland land holdings, the relevant question to ask here is, did the richest men in New England live any better, or any worse, than those in the Chesapeake? If we measure this by the money value of their consumption goods, we find that the Maryland planters in the top 3 percent of estates averaged £264 in consumption goods, the Bostonians £233, and the Connecticut elite, £200.[46]

Remove the Chews and the Ridgleys from the computation, and

[43] Ibid., p. 191.
[44] Ibid., p. 317.
[45] Ibid., p. 287. Darrett Rutman has pointed out to me that Beverly's will distributed the estate among several children, including Robert II, which Wright apparently overlooked.
[46] Bostonians of the middling rank enjoyed a far more sophisticated life style than did their rural counterparts. The Connecticut data come from unpublished material compiled by Jackson T. Main, and the Massachusetts data from Suffolk and Hampshire counties are from my own research.

Maryland's standard of living still parallels or betters those elsewhere, which suggests two things: wealthy colonials in New England as well as in the Chesapeake lived relatively simply in the early part of the eighteenth century, compared with what was achieved in the half-century to follow; and second, Marylanders led the plain life from choice and not of necessity. One of Virginia's leading men, Robert Beverly II, had his way of life described thus by one wondering visitor in 1715: "This man lives well; but though rich, he has nothing in or about his house but what is necessary. He hath good beds . . . but no curtains; and instead of cane chairs he hath stools made of wood. He lives upon the product of his land."[47]

For the vast majority of planters, the latitude for personal expression was not so ample, and most emulated Beverly perforce. Their humble circumstances certainly were far more reminiscent of the sturdy yeoman farmer than of the planter oligarcy of Revolutionary times, but it would be a mistake to argue they had no choice. The mere act of saving, consuming less than one produces, is one of volition and provides the basis for deciding what to do with what one has saved. The plain style was shared by most Maryland planters and their families whether they liked it or not, but some had ample room for choice, and those choices can be discerned. The next chapter will take up, in more systematic fashion, the question of planter priorities.

[47] John Fontaine, "Diary," in Ann Maury, *Memoirs of a Huguenot Family* (New York, 1852), p. 265.

Chapter Seven

STANDARDS, STYLES, AND
PRIORITIES

"The new peasant gentry . . . [saw] in the thriving
town of Leicester . . . frequent visions of a less earthy
life, more comfortable, and civilized in a different
way. They were losing the homely rural culture for a
wider, more sophisticated urban culture—books, silver,
mirrors and china, carpets and curtains, cushions and
conversation."

W. G. Hoskins, *The Midland Peasant*

Implicit in the range of things the planters owned is an ordering
of priorities. At each level of personal wealth, some things were
added that poorer men did not have. Beyond bare necessities, the
planters and their families exercised choice within the confines of
what was available, or what their cultural heritage permitted them
to perceive as available and desirable. All could choose between
competing goods, even though the less affluent enjoyed a necessarily narrower range from which to do so.

Even at relatively poor levels of Maryland society, choice was
possible—choice between more investment or more consumption,
between work and leisure, between more beds or better beds, even
between frying pans and cooking pots. In the chapter on the poorer
planters and their families, we applied a selective grid over the
assortment of goods found in their living quarters and introduced
a few categories of the qualities implied by various items, such as
comfort, convenience, and civility. Let us repeat and extend that
exercise, applying a simple checkoff system for the goods among
inventoried estates at every level of wealth, from poorest to richest.
Since older men tended to have more consumption goods, on the
average, than younger men, regardless of relative wealth, we shall
here restrict the analysis to a single age group, that of the young
fathers. Because there were only a few significant changes over
time in the composition of consumption goods in Chesapeake homes,
and no trends in the average value of consumption within wealth

classes for this age, we can further simplify our analysis by disregarding time as an independent factor. We will look at the holdings, class by class, for the entire period of these items: beds, iron cooking utensils, pewter and brass ware, chairs, hand mills, books, silverware, warming pans, chamber pots, and decorative items for the house and for the individual.[1] Table VII.1 displays the proportions of estates in each wealth class with at least one of the indicator items which are arranged across the table from left to right in descending order of the overall average proportion of estates with the items in question. The first column identifies the class limits of each wealth group, whereas the second column displays the associated percentile range among all married heads of households. This provides a very rough means of generalizing from the sample to all heads of households, although such extrapolation can only be imperfect, since it does not take into account the paths of accumulation as families passed through the stages of their life cycle.

The contents of the table at once confirm the priority of beds and iron cooking pots that had already emerged in Chapter Five, in the analysis of the estates of poor married men. Pewter ware again takes a surprisingly strong third place in the hierarchy of choice disclosed in both sets of data. To dramatize these implicit priorities of the planters, the table carries a heavy black line running diagonally across it to mark off the classes in which 90 percent or more of the estates mentioned the consumption good in question. A row at the base of the table records the number of classes of young fathers' estates in which one-fourth or more owned the good. Under "brass," for instance, only one wealth class, the very poorest, showed fewer than 25 percent who owned some brass at least. In each of the nine wealth classes above the poorest, at least one-fourth of the estates possessed one or more pieces of this metal. For estates worth more than £228, almost all owned something of brass.

The first and most obvious kind of conclusion to be drawn from the table is that men with greater wealth tended to possess a greater variety of goods. Looking at the matter from another angle, one can see that the higher the value of the individual estate, the greater the probability that the inventory will mention any particular good. Thus there is a strong positive correlation between personal wealth and diversity of consumption goods.

[1] Fancy apparel could not be included in this category, since the language of most inventories does not permit a consistent basis for distinguishing between clothes for dress and clothes for work. In a sizable minority of inventories, moreover, there is no mention at all of the decedents' apparel.

241

TABLE VII.1
MARYLAND PRIORITIES AMONG CONSUMPTION GOODS, "YOUNG FATHERS"
(PROPORTION OF ESTATES IN EACH WEALTH CLASS OWNING AT LEAST ONE OF ITEM)

PPW Class	Percent of All Heads[a]	Beds	Iron Cooking Utensils	Pewter	Arms	Brass	Chairs	Hand Mills	Books[b]	Silver	Warming Pans	Pictures, Curtains	Chamber Pots	Personal Ornaments
£ 0-15		.84	.87	.48	.50	.23	.26	.10	.12	.00	.00	.00	.10	.00
16-34		.92	.92	.75	.58	.44	.28	.12	.16	.06	.07	.01	.06	.06
35-49		.91	.97	.87	.67	.48	.35	.43	.20	.10	.16	.03	.09	.07
50-71		.99	.98	.94	.80	.58	.46	.43	.31	.13	.18	.09	.11	.17
72-96		1.00	.92	.86	.80	.70	.46	.51	.33	.12	.26	.10	.06	.12
97-149		1.00	1.00	.96	.90	.82	.73	.61	.37	.32	.40	.12	.12	.22
150-228		1.00	1.00	.99	.78	.88	.80	.67	.44	.38	.38	.24	.14	.23
229-399		1.00	1.00	1.00	.87	.97	.97	.70	.52	.65	.57	.35	.34	.18
400-799		1.00	1.00	1.00	.95	.96	.98	.82	.69	.77	.69	.57	.32	.55
800-up		1.00	.96	.96	.93	.96	1.00	.84	.82	.96	.73	.90	.82	.43
Class Average		.97	.96	.88	.78	.70	.63	.53	.40	.35	.34	.24	.22	.20
Weighted Average		.965	.96	.885	.76	.68	.58	.51	.35	.28	.30	.17	.16	.17
N with at least one-fourth owning item:		10	10	10	10	9	10	8	7	5	6	3	3	2

SOURCE: Young fathers' sample, probate records of six counties, Maryland, in Hall of Records, Annapolis.

[a] Married heads of households, positively identified as such, N = 1863.
[b] Weighted by number of estates of all married heads of households falling into range of associated wealth class.
[c] Calculated directly from inventories of all married heads of households.

Equally discernible in the table are the differences among goods in the rate of acquisition from class to class. Although some articles were highly desirable but too expensive for the poor and/or middling planters, others were relatively cheap to acquire, such as chamber pots, yet planters appear to have been more or less indifferent toward them. Thus, both affordability and inclination played key roles in the patterns of consumption revealed in the young fathers' inventories, but determining which factor was paramount in the acquisition of any particular good requires knowledge of its relative cost.

Those goods that show a more or less regular progression from class to class in the proportion of households owning the item generally tend to be those with high price tags. Silverware, for instance, appears strongly correlated with the ability to buy. Although its high initial cost acted as a strong deterrent to its acquisition, for the top fifth of estates it may be viewed as almost a necessity, so universally was it held among them. Similarly, the cost of warming pans, which were generally of brass and cost about six shillings each, helped deter acquisition, but the ready availability of substitutes, such as heated bricks wrapped in blankets, meant that their convenience and usefulness did not quite so readily override their cost. The attractions held out by expensive silver, on the other hand, could not be provided by cheaper substitutes: universal liquidity, impressive durability, and symbolic social worth.

The strong correlation between relative affluence and the ownership of silverware or warming pans contrasts sharply with the relatively weak and inconsistent relationship that existed between wealth and certain other goods. Books, for instance, were not confined to the elite alone, but neither was there any widespread use of them. Not even half of those households at the three-quarter mark in Maryland's social pyramid owned books, whereas for those at the peak, books were no more highly valued than pictures on the wall or curtains at the window. Since many books were worth only a few pence, cost alone offered no critically significant deterrent to their purchase, nor were there any newspapers or magazines available to compete for readers. On the other hand, the cost of acquiring the ability to read in the first place probably played a crucial role in determining who did or who did not have books available in the home.

Most books in Maryland inventories were of a religious nature: Bibles, testaments, psalm books, psalters, catechisms, and primers made up the overwhelming majority found in planter households.

243

Only a handful of men, probably fewer than 5 percent of all free white adult males, owned reading matter other than these, such as sermons and moral treatises, or books on medicine, mathematics, history, and the law.[2]

The pattern of book ownership demonstrates quite clearly that personal wealth alone did not imply literacy, nor literacy, wealth; but this is not to deny the strong correlation between them.[3] More interesting, perhaps, is the high predictive value book ownership possessed *within* wealth classes. Of planters having similar family status and wealth, those who owned books had a higher proportion of their wealth in consumption goods than those without books. As Table VII.2 shows, the higher the level of personal wealth, the more likely a man's inventory would include any particular consumption good under investigation. However, at any level those with books placed more of their personal wealth into consumption goods, and into a greater variety of them, than did those without books. Not in the table, but pertinent to our inquiry, is the fact that ownership of books also narrowed the differences in the style and standard of living between younger planters and older ones: the mean value of consumption goods of young fathers with books fell only slightly below the mean for older men at every level of wealth.

The connection between books and other consumption goods probably arises from some factor common to both, a predisposition toward acquisition of qualitatively different things from those goods deemed necessary and desirable by all Englishmen of the period. Table VII.2 identifies four categories of consumption goods that book owners were much more likely to possess than nonowners of books: warming pans, silverware, items of household adornment (including all kinds of furnishings from window curtains to china, pictures to clocks), and things for personal adornment (such as fancy shoe buckles, silver watches, wigs, and canes). Those without books were also less likely to have some of the other things mentioned in the table, but the differences were not as great: looking glasses, chairs, and military arms, for instance. Practical objects such as hand mills were desirable to most people, once their initial cost had been taken into account.

Ownership of books, stage in the family cycle, and level of wealth explain a good deal about the differences between life styles of

[2] See Wright, *First Gentlemen of Virginia*, on the subject of books in Virginian libraries of the same period.

[3] As used here, "literacy" merely means the possession of reading matter, nothing more.

TABLE VII.2
COMPARING OWNERSHIP OF SELECTED CONSUMPTION GOODS AMONG BOOK OWNERS AND NONBOOK OWNERS, MARYLAND, 1656-1719

Selected Items	Bottom Third Score[a]			Lower Middle Score[b]			Upper Middle Score[c]			Cumulative Score
	Books	No Bks	Col.1/Col.2	Books	No Bks	Col.4/Col.5	Books	No Bks	Col.7/Col.8	Cols.3,6,9
Warming pans	24%	3%	8.0	34%	18%	1.9	53%	33%	1.6	11.5
Silverware	11	2	5.5	31	7	4.4	58	44	1.3	11.2
Household adornments	4	1	4.0	13	7	1.9	35	9	3.9	9.8
Personal adornment	2	2	0.0	26	7	3.7	32	12	2.7	6.4
Looking glasses	27	15	1.8	51	39	1.3	64	59	1.1	4.2
Chairs	37	27	1.4	64	48	1.3	89	81	1.1	3.8
Arms, armor	74	56	1.3	86	80	1.1	81	79	1.0	3.4
Chamber pots	11	6	1.8	12	8	1.5	23	26	-0.1	3.2
Spinning wheels	20	19	1.1	35	18	1.9	18	23	-0.2	2.8
Hand mills	23	24	-0.1	58	45	1.3	75	57	1.3	2.5
Wheat	4	6	-0.3	13	11	1.2	15	12	1.3	2.1

SOURCE: Young fathers' sample, probate records of six counties, Maryland, in Hall of Records, Annapolis.

[a] Bottom third consists of those with PPW £0-49.

[b] Lower middle consists of those with PPW £50-149.

[c] Upper middle consists of those with PPW £150-399.

individual Maryland planters, but their common English background imposed a particular world view of which their clothing, furniture, and houses were particular expressions. Since that view was changing, differences in life styles that cannot be explained by books, family, and wealth may represent the cutting edge of new ideas. Although the nature of the relationship between ideas, behavior, and material culture poses almost insurmountable problems of interpretation, the systematic analysis of material objects in space and time can carry us along some of the way.

The case of the missing chamber pots illustrates the difficulties that continue to impede our understanding of Maryland's case. As Table VII.2 discloses, there appears to be some relationship between relative affluence, books, and chamber pots, but no simple consistency to explain either the sparsity or the pattern of the distribution of chamber pots in Maryland households. A man was equally unlikely to own one if he possessed £20 or ten times as much, had a Bible or did not have a Bible. Planters of the middling range, between £50 and £400, were twice as likely to own silverware or a warming pan as a chamber pot, three times as likely to have a looking glass, five times as likely to use chairs.

Even among the very wealthiest households of early Maryland, as many as a fifth chose not to use these articles. Why not? Surely they offered considerable convenience, particularly on dark winter nights. Nor should the odors and nuisances of daily emptying and cleaning the pots have offended farm people, especially in an age that did not greatly value the niceties of personal privacy.[4]

The small size of the average house in early Maryland made brief trips outside less inconvenient, of course, but the probability of finding chamber pots in inventories did not improve markedly with increasing house size, as one might have supposed. In the 111 estates with room-by-room inventories, there were 28 households living in houses of three rooms or less, of which 6 owned chamber pots. Of those occupying four- or five-room houses, only 7 out of 35 room-by-room inventories listed them, the same proportion as those in the smaller houses. Even families living in houses of six rooms or more did not necessarily have them: of the 48 such households in the room-by-room inventories, 25, or more than half, apparently found no use for chamber pots.

Marylanders were not alone among English colonists in their

---

[4] The reader will recall that the members of the court of Charles II used fireplaces and room corners to relieve themselves; Stone, *Family, Sex and Marriage*, p. 159.

disinclination toward what might seem to us essential, for these objects seldom occurred in rural New England probate inventories of the same period, despite that region's colder climate, denser settlement, and perhaps slightly larger houses.[5] Limited evidence from archeological digs, furthermore, suggests that waste disposal patterns were probably the same in all the English settlements, north and south, before sometime in the middle of the eighteenth century: a fan-wise course from the front as well as the back door. No one, it appears, bothered to dig pits either for latrines or for garbage disposal.[6] People just stepped outside when nature called, and swine running loose effectively scavenged most wastes.

Some people in the colonies, north as well as south, did make use of chamber pots, however, and in Maryland they were not necessarily the same people as those who read books, kept warming pans, or hung pictures on their walls. No clearly marked boundry set apart the practices of gentility and civility from the crude and earthy manners of the old English peasant and his colonial progeny. Nor did any secular trend distinguish the yearly appearance in the inventories of such things as pictures or window curtains or chamber pots. Indeed, there were fewer chamber pots, proportionately, in the first two decades of the eighteenth century than there had been earlier, signifying, if anything, a decline in usage rather than an upswing.

Despite their relatively slight impact on our period, certain significant changes in the material culture of the English-speaking world were already well under way, portending much for the future. One of the most important of these was the adoption of tea drinking, because hot beverages required lidded containers light enough to pour with ease, cups with handles, and saucers to catch the overflow. Tea also required sweetening, preferably white sugar in its own little bowl. Thus there came into existence the material elements of a new social ritual: teapot, spoons, and dishes, all on a tray and making a pretty picture when they formed a matching ensemble. The tray sat on its own table in the midst of company gathered to sit and converse together as they sipped. With cushions and conversation, tea drinking promoted new social graces, practiced by ladies and gentlemen assembled to watch each other handle the relatively fragile table things.

Tea drinking had profound repercussions on the economy of

[5] Deetz, *Small Things Forgotten*, pp. 10, 58-61.
[6] Stanley South, *Method and Theory in Historical Archeology* (New York, 1977).

the entire western world because it stimulated demand for sugar and for new earthenware pottery that was both pretty and durable, while also less expensive than the porcelains of Dresden or China. Need for sugar fed the demand for slaves in the West Indies, and supplied huge fortunes for both planters and traders. The production of cheap but pretty chinaware stimulated the design of integrated factories for mass production and the development of large-scale marketing and distributing networks. The habit of tea drinking gradually penetrated deeper levels of society, too, and although it did not entirely replace rum and gin as the sociable drink, it exerted enough influence to enhance the health and possibly the longevity of its devotees.[7]

Tea drinking and the use of forks both began to change table manners in the colonies around 1700 or so, but their impact remained greatly limited before 1720 or later. The more genteel style of living symbolized by their use, and by the careful disposal of wastes, the tidying-up of the front yard, and the separation of sleeping quarters from the rest of the house and from outsiders— all these eventually became common practice in the seaboard settlements later in the century. Whether they came gradually or abruptly, separately or simultaneously, as a single integrated package of cultural reorientation, or as the result of a convergence of separate tendencies, only further research will discover.

Despite the increase in the incidence of tea, coffee, chocolate, and forks in the Maryland inventories, the use of other items of cultural interest did not rise uniformly before 1720. Musical instruments such as violins appeared as early as the 1680s, and three-quarters of them were recorded after 1710. In the richest county among the six in our sample, however, only eight out of some seven hundred inventories listed any musical instruments. These included a jew's-harp, eight violins, and one flute. A survey of the richest 5 percent of planters from all six counties yielded only half a dozen, mostly violins and fiddles. Only two young fathers owned any. Given this rarity, one must hesitate to speak of trends at all,

[7] Lois Green Carr, "Ceramics from the John Hicks Site, 1723-1743; The St. Mary's Town Land Community," in Ian M. G. Quimby, ed., *Ceramics in America: Winterthur Conference Report, 1972* (Charlottesville, 1973), pp. 75-102; Sheridan, *Sugar and Slaves*, pp. 27-8; N. McKendrick, "Josiah Wedgewood: An Eighteenth Century Entrepreneur in Salesmanship and Marketing Techniques," in E. M. Carus-Wilson, ed., *Essays in Economic History*, III, 353-79; Barbara and Cary Carson, "Styles and Standards of Living in Southern Maryland, 1670-1752," paper presented to the annual meeting of the Southern Historical Association, Atlanta, Georgia, November, 1976.

and emphasize the difficulties lying in wait for those who would seek signs of deeper cultural permutations in the use and design of new material artifacts.

It seems nonetheless true that mere possession of certain kinds of things indicates choices made out of needs other than those of comfort and convenience. In order to establish priorities among a people on the basis of their material possessions, one must take a step further than we have already come. The presence of a single chamber pot or warming pan demonstrates use, which is significant in itself, but the mere counting of inventories mentioning common items such as beds cannot distinguish patterns of choice among additional units of competing goods. One must count the units of all the goods and establish patterns of typicality for steps in the rank order, inferring the preferences among the planters by noting changes in the average composition of consumption goods in each wealth class compared to the one below it.

Let us examine the sequence of acquisition among beds, metal household utensils, chairs, and decedent's apparel as another step in the investigation of material priorities in early Maryland. When a family had only one bed, for instance, did it add another before, or after, acquiring its second pot or its first chair? At what point, if ever, did families opt for a better bed instead of another bed of the same quality? Did households expand their cooking equipment as fast as they added beds or chairs? Under what circumstances might personal items of adornment take precedence over additional or better household furnishings?

Chairs, for instance, can provide an instant profile of the status order among planters. In contrast to books or pictures, chairs might seem so highly utilitarian that they should have rated higher on the list than they did. As we have seen, however, chairs were not the only objects capable of providing seating, since members of the household had available to them chests, trunks, beds, and tables, as well as benches and stools. Even quite affluent planters were often content with these.[8]

---

[8] There is a marvelously Rabelaisian scene reported in a court case by witnesses of an episode that took place in the household of the notorious Major Broadnox of Kent County during the 1650s. A group of people, including the major and his wife, were seated about on a miscellany of furniture—which is why this scene is relevant to our story—and all had been distinctly affected by strong drink, when one of the men present, a neighbor of the middling class of planters, hauled off to bed in another room the not unwilling wife of his host. One of the men servants in the Broadnox household, who happened to be passing by at the time, became

The scarcity of chairs among the bottom third of households can be sufficiently explained by the already crowded nature of their small houses as well as the availability of alternative places to sit. Those who chose to own chairs, however, seem to have responded not simply to a preference in seating, but to an emphasis on formal arrangements, involving *matched* chairs. Indeed, this becomes especially evident when we count the chairs: among planters with less than £50 in personal wealth, only a third had any at all, but among those who did, the average was four apiece. Even at this level, then, those who acquired chairs bought them in groups. In the middle range of households, half had chairs, but those who did averaged six each. The richer the planter, the more chairs: a dozen in the houses of those in the £229 to £399 range, and better than three dozen in the richest estates. For the upper class of Maryland families, large numbers of chairs, grouped in matched sets, appear to have been regarded as a necessity.

Count their chairs, then, and you will be able to predict a family's position on the ladder of importance in their community. The room-by-room inventories show they were placed in the hall first, then the parlor, and finally in each of the bedrooms. Most chairs were made of one of three materials: Russia leather, the most common in the seventeenth century, was made with skins impregnated with oil distilled from birch bark; turkey-work was a heavy woven textile in multi-colored patterns and used as backing and seating on chairs framed in wood, usually oak; and cane or rush chairs had seat bottoms made of these materials, tightly woven together. These were generally of much lighter construction, using turned legs and supports. None was upholstered with springs, and all tended to be rigorously straight and squared-off in design, although the better-made light chairs of the eighteenth century became quite graceful. Homemade rush-bottomed chairs did not make

---

so delighted by the scene before him that he hurried off to the kitchen to call out several of the women there to come and share the fun. The major, meanwhile, pretended he knew nothing of it; but amid the spreading hilarity, soon felt his honor at stake and strode into the room to chastise his errant wife, now lying alone. The cuckolding neighbor, however, gallantly returned to defend the screaming woman, and so the erstwhile drinking companions set to, lumbering about in the throes of physical combat. No one was much hurt, although the neighbor later spent a miserable night in the front yard hoping to waylay his host and renew hostilities. The latter refused to show his face, and the neighbor eventually went home. Although the tale abounds in frontier rowdiness, it also documents the use of a variety of furniture for seating in the household of an important landowner and judge on the county commission; *Md.Arch.*, LIV, 116-19.

their appearance in the inventories until the 1690s, and the technique may then have been only recently introduced even in England.

Although the chairs belonging to the upper-class household might be scattered about in various rooms in the house when the appraisers came to make their rounds, they could be quickly assembled in the hall for large gatherings when necessary, since that room no longer bore its traditional burden of beds, tools, cooking equipment, and chests of linen. Many of the planters of this class served as justices of the peace, acted as merchants, landlords, and bankers to their neighbors, and frequently played host to numerous visitors. Thus the wealthy man's hall with its potential for abundant seating could be courtroom, bank, and business office as well as social center for the neighborhood.[9]

Let us turn to some of the other categories of consumption goods, and proceed with analogous inquiries. We can compare average rates of increase in the numbers and values of these goods from wealth class to wealth class, and infer from these differing rates an underlying preference order among Maryland planter families. Readers should remember, however, that we are dealing with averages based on cross-sectional data obtained from families at a single stage in the life cycle. The sources do not make us privy to the actual process of decision making itself.

Tables VII.3 and VII.4 summarize values and rates of change across wealth classes of young fathers for such selected consumption and investment goods as decedent's apparel, metal household utensils, the number of beds, family bedding, the number of chairs, farm livestock, and bound labor. The rates were calculated by dividing the average value for each good in each wealth class by the average in the wealth class below it in rank. Bedding, for instance, averaged £1.03 per estate in the poorest class and £2.19 in the next class above it, those with £16 to £34 in physical personal wealth. £2.19 divided by £1.03 yields a change of 233 percent. Each class above the poorest provides a point to compare with the others, tracing a path of relative priorities among the goods shown.

Similarly, the number of beds in the poorest class averaged 1.12, that for the richest, 11.12—almost ten times as many, although the value of bedding in the richest class proved 45 times greater. By comparing the average rates of increase from class to class for beds and bedding, it becomes clear that the *quality* of bedding took con-

---

[9] In some cases the hall may also have served as church or chapel.

TABLE VII.3
AVERAGE VALUES OR NUMBERS OF SELECTED CONSUMPTION AND INVESTMENT GOODS IN "YOUNG FATHERS'" ESTATES (£ decimals, current money≈sterling)

PPW Class	His Apparel[a]	Metal Utensils[b]	No. Beds	Family Bedding	No. Chairs	Farm Livestock	Bound Labor
£ 0-15	£ 0.95	£ 0.72	1.12	£ 1.03	0.78	£ 3.38	£ —
16-34	1.35	1.37	1.76	2.19	1.12	11.50	0.64
35-49	1.78	2.20	2.61	4.05	1.96	21.30	2.03
50-71	2.06	2.59	2.69	6.10	2.96	28.78	4.60
72-96	2.32	3.44	3.07	7.65	2.81	37.49	9.35
97-149	3.47	5.36	3.90	10.87	4.36	49.27	18.62
150-228	4.49	6.27	4.40	13.35	7.07	64.46	40.13
229-399	6.16	9.03	5.81	19.51	11.60	85.19	78.38
400-799	9.88	14.09	8.04	28.45	17.08	132.80	170.21
800-up	15.94	21.51	11.12	46.31	39.38	267.71	455.29

SOURCE: Young fathers' estates in probate records of six counties, Maryland, 1656-1719, in Hall of Records, Annapolis.
[a] Includes only those estates with inventories mentioning apparel worth 10s or more.
[b] Includes all pewter, brass, and iron household utensils.

Table VII.4
Percentage Changes between Wealth Classes of "Young Fathers" for Selected Consumption and Investment Goods, 1656-1719

PPW Class	His Apparel	Metal Utensils	No. Beds	Family Bedding	No. Chairs	Farm Livestock	Bound Labor
£ 0-15/16-34	147%	190%	157%	233%	144%	340%	— %
16-34/35-49	132	161	148	169	175	185	317
35-49/50-71	116	118	103	151	151	135	227
50-71/72-96	113	133	114	125	95	130	203
72-96/97-149	150	156	127	142	155	131	199
97-149/150-228	129	117	113	123	162	131	216
150-228/229-399	137	144	132	146	164	132	195
229-399/400-799	160	156	138	146	147	156	217
400-799/800-up	161	153	138	163	231	202	267
Average % change	138	148	130	155	158	171	230

Source: Table VII.3.

sistently greater priority over the numbers of beds, and there were no class differences in the relative strength of this preference.

The consumption goods competed with each other for the planters' resources. Between clothing, household utensils, and bedding, the last held clear precedence in monetary outlays, but the rates of increase proved remarkably similar between utensils and bedding, ahead of clothing until the richest two classes. The increase in the number of chairs, on the other hand, flattened out in the median range of the distribution of estates, after which it then ascended more steeply, with the sharpest increase marking the transition to the richest class. The number of chairs, alone among the consumption goods examined, clearly differentiated the very rich from all others.

No other class-based difference in priorities among the consumption goods emerged. The pattern resembles more a staircase of growing abundance in planter life styles than sharply defined stages. The generally high priority given the quality of bedding suggests that the people of early Maryland valued comfortable beds above other amenities. Comfort took precedence over reducing crowding or attaining privacy with more beds.

Crowding was common, by our standards. There may have been as many as four people to a bed in the poorest families. As noted in an earlier chapter, probably half of all households lived in just one or two rooms, and most of the others in houses with three to five. Many of these little homes lodged servants and family together under one roof, with some members sleeping on the floor by the hearth at night. If the pattern established in the analysis of the young fathers' sample held true for all Maryland households in our period, the children when they were grown and the servants when they were free and had the necessary resources would exercise the same preferences as their parents and masters: the soft feather bed set on a lattice of rope strung between the sides of a crude oaken bedstead. This, together with a few chests and trunks, a table and benches, made up the required complement of necessary furniture. Without these, Marylander would have felt deprived. With them, he had the luxury of choice, and added sparingly to the contents of his house.

The meagerness of material culture in the tobacco colony harkened back to rural England. Its Spartan simplicity embodied a deep distrust of the corrupting nature of "foreign" ways. Rustic spareness did not derive from aesthetic principles, as does, for example, Japanese culture, which makes much of little. The sev-

254

enteenth-century Englishman and his colonial heirs did not culti-
vate the visual arts and did not greatly value symmetry, proportion,
and orderliness in their surroundings.

The lack of visual enrichment and the scanty belongings that
satisfied the Maryland planters and their families can best be dem-
onstrated by comparison with other cultures, and a recent study
of seventeenth-century household furnishings in Friesia in the
northern Netherlands provides an unparalleled opportunity to do
so.[10] The source documents are inventories originating in Orphans'
Court proceedings, thereby drawing from a stratum of society closely
akin to our Maryland sample of young fathers. Unfortunately, most
omit monetary values so that estates cannot be arranged in a rank
order based on wealth, nor can alternative dispositions of assets be
compared on the basis of initial cost. Nevertheless, the author sorted
the estates into three groups on the basis of dairy cows: those with
none, those with fewer than ten, and those with ten or more. Men
who owned no cows proved a heterogeneous lot, including artisans
and professional men as well as poor farm laborers, so it can serve
no purpose to include them here. We will concentrate on the owners
of cows, those with fewer than ten viewed as the poorer group,
those with ten or more as the richer.

Table VII.5 presents data from two of the Friesian districts and
several time periods, showing the proportion of estates owning
beds, chairs, books, silverware, mirrors, curtains, and spinning wheels.
In addition, the table includes the average numbers of beds and
chairs in those estates with at least one bed or one chair.

All the Friesian households covered by the survey owned beds,
and most had chairs—far more than the sample of young fathers
in Maryland inventories. Those owning more cows also possessed
more beds and chairs, but the differences between the two groups
were not great: those with more cows averaged a third more chairs
and half again as many beds as did those with fewer cows. Likewise,
more of the richer class owned spinning wheels, curtains, silverware, and books than did members of the poorer class.

Also included in the table are the Maryland estimates based on
the young fathers' estates. These have been divided into three
classes based on the division into thirds of the distribution of all
married heads of households. The Friesian inventories divided
roughly two-thirds with ten or more cows, and one-third with less

[10] Jan de Vries, "Peasant Demand Patterns and Economic Development: Friesland, 1550-1750," in William Parker and Eric L. Jones, eds., *European Peasants and
Their Markets* (Princeton, 1975), pp. 205-69.

255

TABLE VII.5
COMPARISON OF CONSUMPTION GOODS IN FRIESLAND AND MARYLAND

Item	Friesland, Less than 10 Cattle	Maryland, Bottom Third[d]	Friesland, More than 10 Cattle	Maryland, Middle Third[e]	Maryland, Upper Third[f]
	1616-1686	*1656-1699*	*1616-1686*	*1656-1699*	*1656-1699*
No. chairs[a]	10.75	3.5	13.6	5.6	15.3
% with chairs	93	29	100	59	87
No. beds[a]	3.6	2.0	5.25	3.3	6.5
% with beds	100	82	100	98	100
% with books	24.5	16[b]	36	26[b]	50[b]
% with silver	33	7	42	25	75
% with spinning wheels	45	7	54	7	7
% with window curtains	41.5[c]	0	53	6	11
No. estates	25	74	43	111	79
	1711-1750	*1700-1719*	*1711-1750*	*1700-1719*	*1700-1719*
No. chairs[a]	11.5	4.9	16.7	5.8	15.0
% with chairs	90	32	95	53	92
No. beds[a]	3.1	2.1	4.6	3.1	6.3
% with beds	100	97	100	99	100
% with books	42	18[b]	56	39[b]	60[b]
% with silver	58	4	72	16	56
% with spinning wheels	79	27	95	45	37
% with window curtains	90	0	89	3	11
No. estates	23	101	24	121	120

SOURCE: Jan de Vries, "Peasant Demand Patterns and Economic Development: Friesland, 1550-1750," in William Parker and Eric L. Jones, eds., *European Peasants and Their Markets* (Princeton, 1975), pp. 205-69.

[a] Among owners only.
[b] Calculated directly from inventories of all married heads of households.
[c] 9% in 1616-1641, 74% in 1677-1686.
[d] Defined as all estates of young fathers valued at less than £50.
[e] Defined as all estates of young fathers valued £50-£149.
[f] Defined as all estates of young fathers valued at £150 or more.

than ten, so the table compares the data from the two regions first between the bottom third in each case, then, in the second part of the table, the upper two-thirds from Friesia and the upper two-thirds from Maryland, the latter separated into middle and upper segments, because only the top third of Maryland planter families lived at a scale approaching the average for the top two-thirds of Friesian dairy farmers.

The top group of Maryland planters owned almost as many chairs and as many beds as the larger dairy farmers of Friesia, and more had books and silver. The Friesians more often owned spinning wheels, and were much more inclined to hang curtains at their windows. The poor planter, on the other hand, looks very poor indeed in comparison with the lower third of Friesian estates. He had far fewer chairs, as we know, but he also possessed fewer beds, and a smaller proportion of this class had books, silver, spinning wheels, or window curtains. Except for the beds, these other articles took low priority in Maryland.

The middling third of Maryland planters did not live quite as well as the poorer dairy farmers of Friesia, although they were not far behind. Only the top stratum fared well enough to rival the peasants of the Netherlands province. They lagged behind, however, in two particular items: spinning wheels and window curtains. Upper-class Maryland women did not spin because they did not need to, whereas lower-class women could not because they worked in the fields. The failure to hang window curtains, however, must come from a difference in priorities rather than a difference of means. Among the very richest class of planters, homes sometimes did contain decorative objects, as the inventories of John Rousby, Henry Ridgley, and even the Quaker, Samuel Chew, disclosed.[11] The general lack of such articles in estates below the top 3 or 4 percent cannot be attributed to problems of initial cost, since relatively inexpensive solid linen or mixed linen and cotton materials could have served the purpose and lent some color to the otherwise drab appearance of Maryland rooms.[12] Most of these families possessed beds with curtains, after all. As an added proof that cost did not play the critical role in deterring the acquisition of decorative items, consider the stark absence of flower pots in Maryland in-

[11] See the descriptions of these planters' consumption goods in Chapter Six above.
[12] Printed calicos did not become available until later. Curtains in the inventories were seldom identified by color or material, but their value ranged from mere shillings to several pounds, and this suggests a wide variety of materials used for this purpose.

257

ventories: these were found in fewer than half a dozen homes among the young fathers' sample, and were equally rare in the room-by-room inventories. Homes affluent enough to own clocks or half a dozen fine feather beds or a few pieces of silverware did not have a single pot specifically designed for holding flowers, even though such earthen pots cost only pennies each. Even if the colonists raised food rather than flowers, there were plenty in native profusion available for the picking.[13]

That the Maryland planters and their families, including their wives, did not live as well, or show as much aesthetic sensibility, as Friesian peasants of the same period may be attributed to a time lag in English material culture itself, but one exacerbated by the prolongation of the frontier conditions in Maryland. The time to settle in on the new continent stretched over a longer period than it did in later frontier settlements in North America, partly because of the distance and the limited resources of the home base from which initial immigration took place, and partly because the New World environment was so different from the old. High death rates and a continuing imbalance in the sex ratio in the tidewater impeded family formation and shortened earning lives of the parents so that children entered adulthood with less help from them than would have been the case had they lived longer.

The depressions in the tobacco market also played a delaying role by postponing the establishment of new households, although this was an intermittent process rather than a continuing one. Particularly adverse economic conditions, however, came into play before the country had entirely shed its frontier characteristics, further inhibiting the accumulation of consumer durables such as beds and other furniture, pewter, and metal housewares and linens. New England, by contrast, was settled within a far shorter span of time by immigrant groups more generally composed of families and free individuals, rather than by poor young people burdened with contractual obligations that prevented them from retaining and investing their own earnings. Thus, the passage from frontier to mature patterns of population structure in the New World took much less time there than in the tobacco colonies to the south.

[13] See, for example, Beverly, *History*, p. 140. No flower pots appear in the room-by-room inventories transcribed from colonial Massachusetts probate records, either; the first window curtains were not mentioned until 1691, and the second set did not appear until 1716. Cummings, ed., *Rural Household Inventories*, pp. 55, 93. Research in seventeenth-century Boston probate inventories finds them much more common in city households, where they had greater functional value.

Their consumption goods must have been in greater quantity in the beginning, despite the cost of shipping them across the Atlantic. Given the struggling nature of New England agriculture, however, one suspects that farmers and their families there suffered an erosion of their standard of living over the course of the century, whereas white Marylanders who survived seasoning and servitude could look forward to some slow improvement in their circumstances.

Not poverty, then, but hindrances to family formation and the needs generated by that process explain a good deal about the relatively low level of consumption in the colony in the seventeenth century, as measured by the average value of consumption goods in the probated wealth of Maryland decedents. It does not explain the particular composition of those goods, however, which was a product of English cultural origins and manufacturing methods; yet with some few important exceptions noted above, no major changes in tastes occurred before 1720. The value and composition of household furnishings of planters in similar wealth categories and at the same stage in the life cycle had not changed at all.

It is time to address the problem of persisting cultural preferences more directly. Given some level of capital, Marylanders acquired a given set and value of consumption goods. The richer the planter, the greater the proportion of his resources invested in the production elements of his enterprise. Investment, building up the plantation, adding other plantations, acquiring more laborers—all these took priority over additional comfort, convenience, and civility in particular. In Table VII.4 one can compare the quantity of livestock and bound labor with that of bedding and chairs. The bias toward building capital becomes obvious, but additions to stocks of farm animals by natural increase formed a passive investment for the planter, whereas adding to the stock of slaves took place actively and primarily during periods of good tobacco prices.

If anything really distinguished one class from another in early Maryland, slaveholding did. The middling planters had bought servants in the seventeenth century, but those who could afford to do so bought slaves in preference to anything else after the 1680s. One suspects that, given the option, everyone would have done the same. Building up capital in the form of men, women, and children took precedence in the planter society of the early Chesapeake because the opportunity was there, and the prospect of gain overwhelmed all other concerns.

259

CONCLUSION

The growth of English settlements in the New World rested on the commercial exploitation of marketable staples. Sugar and tobacco not only built a great trading empire for the mother country, they paid for the transport of the labor force and shaped new societies based on the hoe rather than the plow. The settlers were English during the decades of founding—mainly young, mainly poor, and mainly male—and with them arrived English institutions, habits, and tastes.

The New World cooperated in the venture, but at a terrible price: the annihilation through disease of the native population, the enslavement and forced transportation of many thousands of kidnapped Africans, and for the English conquerors themselves, debilitating sicknesses and an early grave. Hard times in seventeenth-century England churned up a vast army of mobile and jobless young people whose members fed the demand for labor in the colonies. The process was mediated by an international market operating through flexible prices that, in turn, set in motion sputtering sequences of population growth in the Chesapeake and consequent expansions in its output of tobacco. The pacing of these events was not predictable, but the route itself appears in retrospect inevitable.

Supply caught up and eventually surpassed demand for the staple, putting an end to economic expansion and driving out marginal producers. The natural demographic processes at work remolded the structure of the white population so that it gradually converged toward a stable reproductive profile. These evolutionary processes had been slowed by high levels of adult mortality and periodic influxes of new male immigrants, but then accelerated by the cessation of new arrivals and the flight of freed men during the twin depressions of 1686-1696 and 1703-1715.

The transition to a family-based society in the eighteenth century, with large numbers of children, brought several significant consequences to both the social and economic structure of Chesapeake society. First, there came into being a native-born white majority that had never experienced servitude. The attitudes of this generation toward immigrants and servants must have been different from that of their parents. Second, they did not have to postpone marriage because of servitude, as their parents had. Thus they were able to see their own children grow up and help them attain full independence before they themselves died. As another conse-

260

quence of longevity, savings and reinvestment by successful fathers made their capital resources grow at a compound rate, making possible the purchase of hitherto prohibitively expensive slaves as substitutes for the vanishing supply of servants. Finally, the developing and thickening of kinship networks made possible by the intermarriages of the succeeding generations also created a self-perpetuating elite that grew strong enough to wrest away and then to monopolize the profitable and powerful political offices of the province that had formerly been given to governors' favorites.

The long-term interaction of demographic processes with those of the economy were spurred by the cessation in the growth of demand for tobacco, characterized by two prolonged depressions in its price. The consequent decline in economic opportunity for poor white men hastened the diminution in the supply of servants, particularly of healthy young men, and aggravated the overall demand for labor, which could be met by sons for many, but only by slaves for the rest.

In the beginning, the benefits of crossing the Atlantic to engage in the production of a new consumer product outweighed the risks, for many thousands of young Englishmen. Probable early death faced them at home from disease and malnutrition, perhaps even slow starvation. Why not venture all, and on a full stomach, in the colonies? Despite the hardships of their chosen lot, the reality of economic opportunity in the New World did justify their gamble if they survived. To "be for themselves," masters of their own lives, families, and fortunes was a dream within reach, but made possible only by participating in the same free market that eventually turned so cruelly against their successors.

The level of material life provided by tobacco was not impressive by our standards: small, dark, crowded houses crudely built of green wood, unpainted and unadorned, made ramshackle within a decade by cold winters and humid summers. No matter to its occupants, for it was soon time to move to more fertile ground. The bland monotony of corn, beans, and salt pork, washed down by cider, must be balanced against the double satisfaction of being one's own master and the assurance of a perennially full pot, no mean accomplishment in a preindustrial society, then or now. The loneliness of the scattered plantations carried with it the blessings of escape from close community surveillance and encouragement toward self-reliance. The degree of physical isolation, moreover, was only relative, for horses could cover with ease the gentle slopes between the rivers.

261

If churches were far apart and services only intermittent, court days were assured and well attended. Business and pleasure mixed agreeably against the backdrop of courtroom ceremony, for the reassuring functioning of the old English legal system was only mildly modified in its transplantation. The rule of law did succeed in protecting most of the weak much of the time. No warlords arose to devastate their lands, nor did any governor hold undisputed sway.

So long as the economy could expand, it was not a bad life and promised better. Even after the economy had ceased to grow, the land was so rich and the climate so mild the poorest of men could exercise some choice: move to new colonies such as the Carolinas, where the demand for labor continued strong, or to less desirable but cheaper lands closer by. There he might give up tobacco and raise livestock and wheat instead, for settlers in the new colonies needed such things to get started, New Englanders and West Indians continued to welcome them, and there were always the ships that called in growing numbers, to be provisioned from shore. The adoption of mixed farming meant only a partial retreat from involvement in the market. Without a guaranteed outlet for their surpluses, they had to hedge their bets in order to avoid losses they could not absorb and survive. Hedging in such cases meant buying less as well as selling less, and what they formerly bought, they now must make. Although they could not produce everything they had needed, wanted, and come to depend upon, they did make what they could for themselves.

Thus the expanding population of the Chesapeake tidewater spread onto cheaper lands—cheaper either because their products were less suited to the changing European market for tobacco, or because the land was less convenient to water-borne buyers. An increasing proportion of the population came to function outside the tobacco market except during periods of sharply rising prices, while those who continued to find an outlet for their staple either redoubled efforts to maintain previous levels of real income or else diversified somewhat to reduce their purchases of imported goods, which became relatively more expensive in terms of their export staple when its price fell.

Passage of time, then, brought about the coincidental maturing of both the economy and the demography of the colonial Chesapeake. It also affected the level and distribution of wealth. Wealth per head of household grew because some men who had begun with both capital and valuable kinship connections, acquired through

262

"wise" marriages to well-connected brides and widows, also lived long enough to accumulate sizable fortunes through savings and reinvestment. The rest of the adult male heads of households saw the value of their property gyrate with the fluctuating price of tobacco, for like scissors that cut both ways, the market punished as well as rewarded.

Because the poorest people moved out and the not-quite-so-poor found cheap land still abundant, the degree of inequality did not become as great as it might have otherwise, but it did increase. The causes lay in the growth of the wealth at the top of planter society, in the hands of older men and their well-endowed sons. Much of that growth was made possible by investment in a long-lived capital resource: slaves. Had there been no slaves to buy, capital accumulation in the tobacco colony could not have proceeded as rapidly as it did.

The diminution in the supply of adult male servants raised their price. This, together with the increasing financial ability of the richer planters, attracted the attention of slave traders seeking new markets for their wares. During the years of peak tobacco prices between 1697 and 1702, they delivered Africans by the boatload.

The confluence of demographic and economic processes in the upper Chesapeake, furthered by the cessation of emigration from England itself, brought about a sharp revision of the area's social structure. Not only did large-scale slavery create a new class at the bottom of Maryland society, it buttressed the fortunes of an elite at the top. By extending kinship relations on both sides of the marriage contracts, this elite established a family-based extension of local control over the political apparatus. Transfers of capital resources, especially land and slaves, endowed the sons and gave them the base from which to renew and expand family fortunes.

The relationships between class, status, and slavery need not assume in our eyes the invidious character of a dark conspiracy inspired by the unmitigated greed of a few evil men. Bemused by the successful men at the top or distracted by the plight of the servants and slaves at the bottom, we tend to overlook the roles played by the anonymous men and women of the middling sort. Nothing uncovered in the research for the present work has suggested that they subscribed to values any different from those of the men at the top. Had they commanded the means, they too would have bought slaves, and with as little regard for the moral consequences of their acts. The growth of slavery in the Chesapeake was, indeed, the result of *many* unthinking decisions.

The kinds of sources used here have emphasized the physical and material aspects of life in the tobacco colony, leading us perhaps to overstate their importance in the actual lives of the people at the time. We have dwelled at length on the economic and demographic consequences of tobacco culture and said rather little about the meaning of living with those consequences. This is the most elusive of subjects, and one better suited to the arts of the novelist than to the skills of the historian, but we can point out those factors that we believe to have been particularly important to the quality of life then.

One set of factors includes the dispersion of settlement, the lack of fixed abodes, the ramshackle buildings, and the overgrown fields. These inhibited the development of a sense of loyalty to place and undermined the potential for aesthetic consciousness that the immanence of an untouched nature might otherwise have stimulated. Neither Byrd nor Beverly ever celebrated the beauties of the Virginia spring, for instance, but chose to trumpet, instead, the rather crass promise of its abundance. Equally troubling, in its way, are the effects for community consciousness implicit in that failure to develop ties to "home." This undertow of mobility must have sapped the foundations of community identity slowly being erected by the formal and informal modes of cooperation among more settled families.

Another negative force on life in the early Chesapeake also came as a result of the universal concentration on tobacco: women working in the field rather than carrying out those household functions considered appropriate to their sex in English culture. Only about half of the white women spent truly significant portions of their days hoeing corn and tobacco, since those whose households contained many members perforce engaged in extensive activities associated with food preparation, cleaning, and care of clothing. Similarly, those living outside prime tobacco growing areas—and this was a growing proportion of the population during the eighteenth century—also spent their time indoors or in the immediate vicinity of their home. Women who were out in the fields every day, however, suffered a real loss of status and could not have entirely resisted the psychological consequences of that loss. The differences between them and the wives of middling planters were much greater than those that marked the men themselves.

The consequences of diminished status of those wives and mothers who labored at the hoe extended to the rest of the family unit, but in ways that are not clear. If lower-class women were degraded

264

in relation to other women, for instance, they may not have inspired much respect at home.

Other forces were also at work on the nature of the ties that bound together the members of the family in early Maryland. Foremost among these were the short time spans families spent together as parents died and spouses remarried, bringing in unrelated individuals to form new households in turn, thereby weakening the identities of the original core families. This process bears a superficial resemblance to the consequences of widespread divorce today as families shatter and reform. Modern parents have the awesome freedom actually to choose this separation, and then to continue their lives apart, with consequent tugs on the conflicting loyalties and emotions of their children. Chesapeake parents of the colonial era suffered no guilt in this respect, for the decision to separate families was God's, not theirs, and the parent who departed was indeed gone for good. Children of these broken marriages must have had an easier time emotionally, just as the surviving spouse did by quickly finding a new partner in order to get on with the business of everyday life. Necessity demanded it.

Historians have speculated on the effects of early death on parents and children alike. When the chance that a newborn baby would survive to adulthood was only slightly better than one out of two, did the parent armor himself or herself against probable loss by deliberately repressing affection? Did the early loss of a parent deaden the ability of the child to respond, especially when he, in turn, became a parent? Or, conversely, did impermanence make affective bonds more highly valued? Whatever the effects the frequency of death may have had on the ability of people to relate to each other, the facts are clear that life in the Chesapeake was far more uncertain than in the New England villages described by numerous studies. And the apparent niggardliness of some Massachusetts patriarchs toward their grown children is in stark contrast with the attitude of Chesapeake parents. Perhaps it was the likelihood of early death that led the Marylanders to settle their children with sufficient land and other means as early as possible in order to protect them from the threat of a greedy or spendthrift stepfather. They sought not to bind their children to them but to enable them to stand on their own feet, and to do so while still in their teens, if necessary.

Further undermining any narrow definition of the family in the Chesapeake world was the presence of other people in the household whose status or footing was not that of relative or equal. The

265

extended household of boarders, hired help, servants, and slaves was more characteristic of the frontier stage than later, but that frontier era lingered for more than half a century, perpetuating the set of relationships typical of such mixed households. Just how children and adults, free and unfree, white and black, got along together, living, as they did, at close quarters, we would like to know. The writers of moral treatises and the preachers of published sermons stressed obedience to parents and masters in old England and new, and undoubtedly these admonitions had their effect in the Chesapeake as well, if only as filtered through the minds and mouths of county leaders in the court rooms, who passed solemn judgments on the erring miscreants standing abashedly before them. Their ready resort to threats of physical punishment, if not the actual application of those means, suggests that deference within and without the family and the household rested as much on the threat of violence as on any internalized system of social control. Another, related, fact requires equal acknowledgment: there were very few killings or suspected killings reported in the court proceedings of the seventeenth century. Physical punishment or simply its threat may have been endemic, but it seldom led to the willful taking of life. If masters' hands were strengthened by the system, so also were they restrained by it.

THE goals set out at the commencement of this study were vague but all-encompassing: to describe everyday life in a tobacco colony and to understand the workings of the forces that shaped it. By tapping a documentary source of unusually broad coverage, and by applying modern methods of systematic data analysis, we were able to trace the paired paths of development, economic and demographic, and to establish the importance of the intertwining and reinforcing effects these two processes exerted on human lives. Equally important is the fact that they operated within a particular geographical region and in the context of a particular cultural and political system at a particular stage in its evolution. Given these broader constraints, the drama that unfolded in the basin of the Chesapeake followed natural lines of force. Tobacco made the drama possible, and its dark legacies continue. We wrestle with them still.

DEMOGRAPHIC EFFECTS ON WEALTH
IN EARLY MARYLAND

One can set about answering the question of whether, and to what extent, Maryland's demographic transition affected patterns of wealthholding by attempting to measure the relationship between age and wealth in the probated estates and then by estimating the numbers of dependents each wealthholder supported. Since birth records are not available for early Maryland, we must substitute indirect evidence on age for actual chronological age. Information contained in the probate records themselves can be used for this purpose. Four stages in the life cycle of adult men can be distinguished as follows: unmarried men, those married and with at least one young child, those having at least one child of age and one younger, and the men whose children were all grown or who had grandchildren. There will obviously be some overlapping of ages in categories based on relative stages of children still living, but because these stages are distinct and identifiable for approximately half of the men in the records, their use here as age surrogates seems justifiable, given the paucity of genuine birth date information.

The principal sources of data on stages of the life cycle are wills, and these are biased toward older and wealthier men, but there are clues furnished in inventories and accounts as well, such as the absence of a widow or of kin, the presence of women's or children's clothing in the inventory, references to orphans and to guardians, itemization of expenses arising from taking care of the family, schooling bills, and so forth.

Once we establish categories based on relative age as suggested by stages in the adult life cycle, we can then measure the effects of stage (that is, age) on wealth, and beyond that, ask whether average wealth within age groups grew, diminished, or merely fluctuated over time. The correlation coefficient for stage in the life cycle and wealth was estimated to be $+.32$ for GPW and $+.37$ for PPW. This means that the sum of the squared deviations from the geometric mean between age classes contributed 32 percent (or 37 percent in the case of PPW) of the sum of the squared deviations from the geometric mean of the full set of 1,942 men for whom life cycle information survives. Age or family status, then, accounted for roughly a third of the total variation around the mean, substantial evidence that alteration in the relative numbers of men in the different stages would affect the level of wealth. Table A.1 summarizes the average GPW of each of these four age groups based on stages in the life cycle.

Since age alone explains only a third of the differences between individuals, there were other factors at work, some of which undoubtedly included important distinctions in family origin, upbringing, and native ability. Transgenerational studies would provide much more light on the origins of inequality, but these require records that would permit family reconstitution as well as estimation of wealth. One further word on this subject before we return to

TABLE A.1

DETERMINING THE WEALTH OF AGE GROUPS: STAGES OF
LIFE CYCLE AND ALLOCATING UKNOWNS, SIX COUNTIES, MARYLAND
(£≈sterling)

Stage in Life Cycle	No. Estates	GPW	Index	Unknowns	No. Estates	GPW
I = single	824	£ 54	100	Married	851	£152
II = young children	684	204	378	No info.	903	81
III = older children	234	267	494			
IV = grown children	200	397	735			
Total	1942	£168			1754	£115

Allocating 851 married unknowns—II, III, IV
Allocating 903 other unknowns—I, II, III, IV

Expanded Age Classes with unknowns allocated

I = single	1253	£ 64	100			
II = young children	1403	161	252			
III = older children	562	185	289			
IV = grown children	481	238	372			
Total	3696	£158				

SOURCE: Probated estates of six counties, Maryland, in Hall of Records, Annapolis.

measuring age effects on the level and distribution of wealth: men supplemented their earnings from farming in a variety of ways in the colonial period, according to the opportunities afforded by the local economy, which were, in turn, dependent not only on local resources and technology but on the degree of development in the past, the density of population, the relative freedom of access to pursue these opportunities, and the nature of the relationship between the local economy and the larger world beyond. Few people specialized in a single occupation other than doctors and ministers, except for those who farmed and only farmed. Even among these, one could distinguish between those who specialized entirely on a market crop and those who supplemented their earnings from such a crop by raising their own food and producing their own textile fibers. Thus, occupation may or may not prove to be a useful designation in measuring the effects of various factors on the determination of individual wealth. What we would really like to know are the sources of income and their relative importance, and it is only to the extent that occupational designation identifies these properly that such labels prove useful.

Returning to the problems raised by Maryland's changing population for interpreting the probate evidence on wealthholding, we must note again that the fact that the sources on which age class assignments were made are themselves heavily biased toward the wealthier planters. As a result, the sample data overstate the wealth differences between unmarried and married men, and between younger and older heads of households. Several corrections are in order, as Table A.1 shows. Married men of otherwise unknown family status owned about £100 less, on the average, than married men of known status, so these had to be allocated into the three categories according to some rule in order to correct for the wealth bias inherent in the sources. I chose to do so by allocating them according to the proportions prevailing among the men whose status was known: N = 851, so 61.2 percent were allocated to class II, 20.9 percent to class III, and 17.9 percent to class IV, each class receiving its due proportion of 851 men whose average wealth was £152. Thus, the allocation procedure resulted in larger numbers and lowered mean wealth for each of these three age classes. There remained to be allocated those for whom we have neither data on marital status nor stage in the life cycle. These numbered 903, with an average wealth of £81, of whom 42.4 percent were assumed to be unmarried, because that was their proportion among the 1,942 whose family status was known. This allocation expanded the age class of unmarried men to 1,253 in number, and raised their average wealth to £64. There still remained 520 men who were presumably married and had to be allocated to classes II, III, and IV, which I did by following the same proportions as the preceding allocation of married men: 61.2 percent, 20.9 percent and 17.9 percent, respectively.

After completing the allocations, the new class sizes are as follows:

Class I: N = 824 + 383 = 1,207
Class II: N = 684 + 521 + 318 = 1,523
Class III: N = 234 + 178 + 109 = 521
Class IV: N = 200 + 152 + 93 = 445

A grand total of 3,696 estates, constituting all the adult males encountered in the probate records of the six counties, has been subsumed into one or another of these four classes based on relative age. Doing so altered the average wealth of each age class. For unmarried men, the mean rose from £54 to £64, whereas for married men, mean wealth fell: from £204 to £161 for class II (the "young fathers"), from £267 to £185 for class III (fathers who had at least one grown child and one underage), from £397 to £238 for the oldest group, class IV. In the revised figures, the wealth of the oldest averaged only four times as much as that of the youngest (£238/£64 = 3.72), compared to a difference of seven times in the uncorrected data.

The wealth of each age group fluctuated with the phases of the tobacco price cycle, just as the relative proportion of estates altered as a result of the demographic processes at work in the living population. When we wish to isolate purely economic changes in wealthholding, we have to control the demographic effects by freezing the relative proportions contributed to each time period's set of estates. Thus by holding constant the age structure, we can recompute distributional measures for each period and attribute these to nondemographic determinants. For instance, in the text of Chapter Two, mean GPW grew from £108 in 1656-1683 to £167 in 1713-1719 in the unadjusted estates of the six counties. By estimating mean wealth of each age group in each time period, and multiplying that mean by *fixed* proportions for each age group, an adjusted mean resulted, one that did not grow from period to period but that fluctuated:

270

Years	Mean GPW, Unadjusted for Age Distribution	Mean GPW, Using a Fixed Age Distribution
1656-1683	£108	£108
1684-1696	125	95
1697-1704	143	116
1705-1712	162	112
1713-1719	167	118

The conclusion one draws from the reweighting of age class means is that the rising level of GPW observed in the inventories is almost entirely due to the effect of larger numbers of older men in the probated estates.

If we transform age class means into multiples of that for the youngest group, we can also construct a simple index of the effect of age on wealth in early Maryland, and compare that index with those using similar data from other times and places. Table A.2 translates stages into age classes for this purpose, then transforms the mean wealth of each into an index based on the relative wealth of the youngest group. Finally, it then compares this index with similarly derived ones for Revolutionary Connecticut, the thirteen colonies in 1774, and the United States in 1870 and 1963. Note that the use of this indexing system avoids concerns with differences in currency or price levels.

Since colonial New Englanders lived considerably longer, on the average, than did tidewater planters, one can observe there a "post-retirement" effect on wealthholding, a lowering of savings among the Connecticut men over age 70. For the thirteen colonies as a whole, on the eve of the Revolution, total wealth (including land in the study on which these data are based) averages for each age class yield a profile similar to those for personal wealth among the Maryland planters three-quarters of a century earlier. A hundred years after the Revolution, the age-wealth curve had grown much steeper, and it shows no sign of leveling in our own times. Interesting to note is that the 1870 profiles show no retirement effects, whereas in 1963 the curve flattens out for the older age group.

Placing the relationship between relative age and wealth into a comparative perspective, as Table A.2 has done, permits us to say some things not only about early Maryland but also about trends in the country as a whole. The higher the average difference in

271

TABLE A.2
RELATIVE WEALTH AND AGE IN EARLY MARYLAND, REVOLUTIONARY CONNECTICUT, THIRTEEN COLONIES, AND THE UNITED STATES IN 1870 AND 1963 (Wealth of youngest adults = 100)

Stage in Life Cycle	Maryland c. 1700	Age	Revolutionary Connecticut	Age	Thirteen Colonies 1774	Age	United States 1870	Age	United States 1963
I. single	100	20-29	100	21-25	100	20-34	100	20-34	100
II. young children	252	30-39	173	26-44	213	35-44	270	35-44	254
		40-49	195						
III. older children	289	50-59	207	45+	244	45-54	450	45-54	354
IV. grown children	372	60-69	250			55-64	495	55-64	500
		70+	183			65+	552	65+	500

SOURCES: Probated estates of six counties, Maryland, in Hall of Records, Annapolis; Jackson T. Main, *Connecticut Society in the Era of the American Revolution* (Hartford, 1977); Alice Hanson Jones, *American Colonial Wealth*, III (New York, 1977); Lee Soltow, *Men and Wealth* (New Haven, 1975).

NOTE: Total wealth includes land for all data except those from Maryland, which include physical personal wealth only.

wealth between age groups, for instance, the higher the current rate of accumulation in the economy and, therefore, the higher income must have been relative to the cost of living. The nine-teenth- and twentieth-century figures, therefore, suggest a faster rate of growth and savings than existed in the eighteenth century.

When we look at the differences between particular age groups, although the imprecision and inconsistency of class boundaries makes the data difficult to compare directly, we see greater evidence in the earlier period of a pause in accumulation between young fathers and those who have children just coming of age than we find in later data. The sharpness of that pause can probably be attributed to greater costs of getting children started on their own as farmers than as skilled workers or independent businessmen in later pe-riods. Once this fundamental duty has been fulfilled, the head of the household is free to save for himself and posterity again. The differences between the oldest group and that just younger, then, might offer a possible measure of the degree of patriarchal control over assets. If that difference does in fact represent the father's greater or lesser willingness to give his assets to his children before he dies, the fathers of the nineteenth century appear to have been more conservative, or patriarchal, in the matter than their colonial predecessors.

MARYLAND CURRENCY AND PRICE
FLUCTUATIONS

The appraisers' values listed in probate inventories were not prices determined by the market but guesses of what a forced sale at auction would bring. With the exception of livestock and crops, most such goods were used and not, therefore, in "store" condition. Even cloth yardage that had never been cut eventually suffered from the dampness, so that new goods kept in storage might also be discounted in value by the appraisers. Their guesses, however, reflected local conditions and expectations about the economy, particularly what tobacco would bring, and can be interpreted, therefore, as an imperfect response to such expectations. The course of inventory values over time probably resembles a similar profile in commodity prices and offers a reasonably firm basis on which to discuss the fortunes of both the economy and of its human participants.

The currency in which the inventory values were expressed was originally pounds of tobacco, but this was replaced by money of the British system in 1683. Tobacco continued to be the common medium of debt, but its values in the accounts of administration are generally those set by the courts, not those of the marketplace.

Prices of individual commodities moved at their own individual rhythms according to local conditions of supply and demand, but the paramount source of fluctuations in the general level of prices of domestically produced goods was the state of the market for tobacco. All other things being equal, a rise in the market drew in more resources with which to produce the next crop, since the size of the existing crop could not be altered without greatly lowering its quality. (Portions of the plant not normally used might be added illegally to the hogshead to enhance its weight.) Additional resources attracted into raising tobacco when the price went up included labor as well as land. More mouths and more operating units in turn raised the demand for livestock and food crops which, being in fixed supply in the short run, tended to raise prices on these goods as well. Long-term trends in these prices, however,

274

tended downward in an expanding economy until they just matched replacement costs, so short-run and long-run movements could either conflict with or reinforce each other, depending on circumstances.

Since the provincial assembly raised the value of silver coins in 1708 to conform to Parliament's decree, the official rate of exchange between Maryland currency and British sterling rose to 133.33 : 100.00. The effect of this act on inventory prices appears to have been quite negligible. A careful analysis of selected commodities as set forth in the accompanying tables demonstrates that the upward drift in tobacco, slave, and metals' prices was substantially counteracted by the continuing slide in the prices of cattle and corn. Note that the prices of various commodities did not move in unison: cattle and corn crested in 1707-1708 and troughed in 1716-1717. Tobacco, pewter, and pot iron began to rise in 1713, slaves and plate not until 1717. All, however, rose sharply in 1718.

Because the composition of estate assets varied significantly with the level of wealth, one must design a price index that weights the prices of commodity groups according to their proportion in estate inventories at separate levels. In the period 1713-1719, the proportion of gross personal wealth in livestock, for instance, varied from 44 percent in the class £50 to £71 to just 13 percent for the richest group. Estates of £150 and over placed a third of their assets into bound labor, whereas those under £72 owned virtually none at all during these years. It would be highly inappropriate, therefore, to load a summary index for estate wealth with the rise in the price of slaves, and then apply a deflator based on this index against the mean wealth of the bottom 30 percent or even of the next 50 percent of estates, since their value principally affected the mean of only the top fifth of all estates in this period.

The commodities selected for constructing the price index of probate wealth are: cow-and-calf, barrel of corn, bushel of wheat, pounds of pewter, pounds of pot iron, ounces of silver, "best" Negro man, and, of course, tobacco by the pound. These items appear often enough and are reasonably consistent in quality to afford some confidence in their levels or averages over time. If any qualifying adjective accompanied the value of an observation in an inventory, such as "old," "worn," "sick," "good-for-nothing," "trash," and so forth, that price did not enter into the calculation of the mean for that county and that year. Appraisal practices did vary, and not just by county, so that some inventories offer a very fine and careful breakdown of assets while others group them indiscriminately, precluding price data collection. Most provoking to the researcher are teasers that promise this information and then snatch it away: "Negro man age 25 and thirty bushels of wheat, £29," or "two cows with calves by their side, three steers age three years, two heifers, and a bull, three yearlings, and a yoke of steers, five years old, all £17." When inventories offer "two negroes, £25" or "six head of cattle, £10," these are not included in the calculations of prices because of the variation of quality within categories.

Gathering prices on "best Negro man" however, presented another kind of problem. A very large proportion of those inventories that included slaves among the listed assets and also offered information of their ages and sex did not have this category of slave. The overwhelming majority of planters (80 percent) did not own any slaves at all, and of those who did and whose human chattels are described, most did not own a healthy young male black simply because they could not afford one. Unfortunately, then, price observations on the "best Negro man" come primarily from estates of the richest planters, and an index based on them is inappropriate for estates in the lower strata. One cannot assume without testing that alterations in the general level of slave prices were of the same magnitude as those of the highest quality, and so an attempt was made to compare the two sets of slave prices.

Excluding the sick and the children from our observations, the average value of "slaves" was below £17 before 1683, rose to just under £18 in the next decade, then jumped to the level at which it stayed, £21 to £22, right through the year 1717. Only in the last two years of the study, 1718-1719, did this average price reach £25. This jump was probably caused more by a general rise in the price level than to changes in the makeup of the adult slave population. By comparison, the increase in the value of healthy young adult male slaves was from £30 about 1700 to £40 in the years 1718-1719 (1.33 to 1.00, the same as the change in the official exchange rate), while the rise in the level of "slave" prices was only from 22.0 in 1694-1717 to 24.9 in 1718-1719 (1.13 to 1.00). The appropriate deflator for labor costs for the majority of estates, therefore, for the study period 1713-1719 as compared to 1705-1712 is only $1.00/1.03 = 0.97$.

Mild increases in the average value of household metals during the years after 1713 were offset by decreases in the value of livestock, whereas crops other than tobacco showed no tendency at all. Prices of tobacco and slaves both experienced a boom very late, but significantly higher prices appear in only a handful of estate

276

inventories, reflecting either the conservative tendencies of appraisers or their confusion about the actual state of the currency. The values in the inventories, then, remained reasonably consistent over time, even in the last few years of this study, and for that reason I did not undertake the difficult task of applying class weights. Summary tables on the composition of personal wealth and of prices follow.

TABLE B.1
PRICES OF INDICATOR COMMODITIES IN INVENTORIES BY COUNTY, 1705-1719

County	Cow/ Calf	Barrel Corn	Bushel Wheat	Pounds Pewter	Pounds Pot Iron	Ounces Plate	Best Negro Man	Pounds Tobacco
Anne Arundel	£2.62	s.8.16	s.3.44	s.8.27	d.2.94	s.5.07	£30.43	d.1.07
Baltimore	2.40	7.82	3.48	8.79	2.98	5.23	28.13	1.00
Calvert	2.29	8.01	3.49	7.12	2.48	5.15	30.41	1.02
Charles	2.02	7.79	2.92	9.01	3.02	4.93	28.15	1.11
Kent	2.30	7.91	3.17	9.69	2.87	5.00	29.41	0.98
Somerset	1.46	7.00	3.21	9.69	3.55	5.13	29.42	0.79

SOURCE: Probate records of six counties, Maryland, in Hall of Records, Annapolis, Maryland.

TABLE B.2

CHANGES IN PRICES OF INDICATOR COMMODITIES BY COUNTY, 1705-1712, 1713-1719

(1705-1712 = 1.00)

County	Cow/ Calf	Barrel Corn	Bushel Wheat	Pounds Pewter	Pounds Pot Iron	Ounces Plate	Best Negro Man	Pounds Tobacco
Anne Arundel	0.81	1.01	0.93	1.09	1.11	1.12	1.08	1.22
Baltimore	0.86	1.04	1.13	1.10	1.32	1.10	1.10	1.00
Calvert	0.81	0.92	1.00	1.04	1.22	1.11	1.04	1.09
Charles	0.90	0.95	0.94	1.05	a	1.12	1.03	1.33
Kent	0.88	1.05	0.82	1.18	0.98	a	1.03	1.00
Somerset	0.99	1.07	0.99	1.02	1.07	1.12	1.14	1.14
Weighted Average[b]	0.90	1.00	0.90	1.07	1.13	1.11	1.08	1.16

SOURCE: Probate records of six counties, Maryland, in Hall of Records, Annapolis, Maryland.

[a] Insufficient data.

[b] Weighted by proportion of estates in 1713-1719 contributed by each county: Anne Arundel, .181; Baltimore .107; Calvert .138; Charles .229; Kent, .108; Somerset, .238.

Table B.3
Composition of Personal Wealth by Classes in 1713-1719
Six Counties in Maryland (percent)

PPW	Livestock	Labor	Crops	New Goods	Debts Receivable	Cash	Consumption	Other	Total	N
£ 0-15	29	00	13	00	18	00	37	3	100	151
16-34	41	01	10	00	12	00	34	2	100	165
35-49	40	05	08	00	13	00	31	3	100	96
50-71	44	02	09	02	04	01	36	2	100	69
72-96	39	08	07	02	09	03	31	1	100	58
97-149	32	14	09	03	09	02	28	3	100	64
150-228	25	27	10	02	10	02	23	1	100	55
229-399	22	30	06	04	10	01	22	5	100	53
400-799	18	36	08	04	10	01	21	2	100	26
800-up	13	27	06	11	22	02	14	5	100	29
										766

Source: Probate records of six counties, Maryland, in Hall of Records, Annapolis, Maryland.

TABLE B.4
DERIVATION OF PRICE DEFLATORS: STEP ONE

Asset Group	Indicator Commodity	Price Index*
Livestock, other	Cow-and-calf	0.90
Labor	below £150, x̄£ adult slaves	1.03
	£150+, x̄£ best Negro man	1.08
Crop	1/3 bbl corn, 2/3 tobacco	1.11
New goods	silver plate	1.11
Debts receivable, cash	silver plate	1.11
Consumption goods	silver plate	1.11

SOURCE: Probate records of six counties, Maryland, in Hall of Records, Annapolis, Maryland.

* Based on prices 1705-1712/1713-1719.

TABLE B.5
DERIVATION OF PRICE DEFLATORS: STEP TWO

PPW	% N, 1713-1719	Weighted Price Index[a]	Deflator
£ 0-15	20.05	1.04	.96
16-34	21.91	1.02	.98
35-49	10.89	1.01	.99
50-71	9.16	1.01	.99
72-96	7.84	1.01	.99
97-149	8.50	1.02	.98
150-228	7.30	1.05	.95
229-399	7.04	1.05	.95
400-799	3.45	1.06	.94
800-up	3.85	1.07	.93
Total	99.99		
Composite			.97[b]

SOURCE: Probate records of six counties, Maryland, in Hall of Records, Annapolis, Maryland.

[a] For each stratum, multiply proportion of GPW in each asset group (Table B.3) by the price index of its indicator commodity, and add results to get weighted price index for all assets of groups owned by estates in stratum.

[b] Weighted by proportion of N in each stratum.

PROBATE RECORDS AS A SOURCE
FOR HISTORICAL INVESTIGATION

The great mass of early Maryland probate records offers a singular body of evidence on what happened to those who came to one area of the Chesapeake and who survived both their seasoning and their servitude. It behooves us, then, to understand how the records were prepared and for what purposes.

The primary function of the English court system was enforcement of contracts, including the timely liquidation of private debts. Courts dealing with testamentary proceedings facilitated this process and also protected the rights of legitimate heirs. The records of courts designated as such are legal documents assembled and preserved for the purpose of ensuring an orderly transfer of property between donor and recipient, and between debtor and creditor. Executors of creditor estates and creditors of debtor estates relied on the probate process to collect their debts; no such self-interest motivated the operation by the government of orphans' courts, however. These functioned at the behest of all free adults who feared what might befall their children should they die young.

Driven by the need to oversee a minor's inheritance through the suspect hands of stepfather or guardian and the need to settle debts to and from deceased freemen, the probate courts generated lists of assets and liabilities, described and valued in local currency, and accounts of their management and disposal, all signed, witnessed, and sealed in formal and orderly fashion. Men of little property and less debt did not appear as often in the records as their numbers warranted, whereas those with both the means and the foresight to keep their wills and estates clear of complication and encumbrances might also have escaped the probate process. On the whole, however, the early records appear to have covered most of the spectrum of deceased freemen, and in a consistent fashion, as the proportional makeup of these freemen changed over time, shifting from a preponderance of foreign-born young bachelors to one of native-born fathers and grandfathers.[1]

---

[1] Like most human institutions, the county probate courts of Maryland underwent some modification over the course of time. The estate materials, therefore, are not

Men who died in any one year or decade did not come proportionately from all age groups, because the risk of dying advances with age, even in the disease-laden environment of seventeenth-century tidewater Maryland. The probate records, therefore, distort the picture of wealthholding among the living population from which they drew—more from older and richer, and less from younger and poorer age groups. The degree of distortion, however, depends on the relationship between age and wealth accumulation as well as on the disparities in the age profiles among the two populations. That relationship can be measured and adjusted for to provide comparability in the records over time and place.

Real estate did not enter into the Maryland inventories of property, with the result that the records are seriously deficient in providing us with measures of wealth, but wills often furnish some description of the lands owned by the deceased, at least in terms of acres and plantations. In the absence of adequate price information, however, one cannot estimate the value of individual holdings. A further problem is that many men left no wills, so their acreages, or the lack of them, must be tracked through deeds, where these exist, or otherwise estimated. Attempts to estimate holdings by means of regressions yielded results with intolerably wide margins of error, and efforts along these lines were therefore abandoned.

The values of personal property appearing in the inventories

---

strictly comparable. Not only did counties change their borders but the processing of records altered, as well. The ratio of accounts of administration to estate inventories rose steadily in all of the counties, while the legal requirements dealing with their handling were modified by the new royal governors. The signatures of major creditors appear on inventories dating to the earliest years of the eighteenth century, a matter bringing joy to the hearts of genealogists as well as historians. These signatures greatly increase our confidence in the coverage and accuracy of the appraisers' efforts.

The most obvious alteration in the probate process was the shift from tobacco as the money of account to pounds, shillings, and pence in the British system. However, tobacco continued to be used as money in Maryland: most debts were made in terms of it, taxes were collected in it, and one suspects that appraisers' efforts involved mental division in order to shift from the usual system of valuation to that demanded by the courts.

The rate of exchange between current money and sterling stayed more or less at par despite the act by Parliament in 1708 that set the official rate of exchange between the colonies and the mother country at 133.33 : 100.00, and Maryland's legislature dutifully passed laws in compliance. The appendix on prices treats the problems presented by changing rates and shifting commodity prices. See Curtis Nettels, *The Money Supply of the American Colonies before 1720* (1934, reprinted New York, 1969), pp. 242-49.

and accounts are expressed either in tobacco, current money, or sterling. I have translated tobacco into current money at the rate of a penny per pound, which greatly stabilizes the data base and offers greater comparability over time. Although the precise relationship between current money and sterling fluctuated slightly until about 1713, they have been treated as equivalent throughout the present work. The only period of concern is that of the final years of this study, 1714-1719, when rising tobacco prices and a presumably inflated exchange between current money and sterling occurred. Prices of major commodities in individual counties during these years are reported in Appendix B, and their relative stability for capital goods persuaded me to leave unadjusted figures relating to these and to personal wealth in general, while deflating those for consumption goods.

Values of individual commodities fluctuated in accordance with a variety of causes, and resembles somewhat the optical effects one encounters in the undersea world, where relative positions of things are in continual motion, yet the level itself may not rise or fall. The inventory values are merely guesses, and rather conservative ones, on the part of the appraisers of what the items might bring in a forced sale. For this reason, as well as for unidentified differences in the quality or condition of the goods themselves, valuations of assets vary from inventory to inventory, from year to year, and even from county to county. Inventory values for standard items in Somerset County, for instance, were markedly below those of other counties, even of nearby Kent.

Appraisers did not include in their lists everything they saw. The clothing and personal effects of the decedent's wife, children, and servants were excluded, as were dogs, cats, and other pets. Many inventories omit things that were clearly necessary to housekeeping, either through carelessness on the part of the appraisers or because of deliberate oversight. In the case of poor families, one suspects a benevolent conspiracy at work to protect the widow and her brood from the grasping reach of creditors. The courts carefully instructed the appraisers and the administrator to include everything in the inventory, and began regularizing such practices by allowing a proportion of the household goods to be deducted in the account for housekeeping, notwithstanding any claims against the estate that remained unsatisfied.

Other exclusions permitted by law from inventories of estates were gifts made by the decedent before he died, such as his clothing,

284

though legacies and bequests made in his will remained part of the estate until settlement. Any property belonging to his widow in her own right also would not appear among his assets. Women who married a second time owning such property often exacted an agreement from their second husbands to permit such exclusion in return for not claiming their widow's thirds, which was their right under the law. Thus the children and heirs of both found assurance that their parents' marriage would not deprive them of their expectations.

The effect of all these exclusions and omissions reduced the gross value of estates, but the claims of creditors kept such practices within strict bounds, and they averaged out over the majority of cases. More serious than any of these rather incidental omissions was the frequent failure of administrators to complete their tasks by bringing in all accounts of debts received and paid. Many of the richest men in Maryland engaged in trade, with a large backlog of unsettled accounts. Yet one often searches the records in vain for a full accounting of these, and as a consequence the gross personal wealth of such men remains understated to some unknown degree.

The set of probate records serving as the primary data source for the present study constitute a complete collection of all records identified directly or indirectly as originating from six tidewater counties of colonial Maryland during the years 1656 through 1719. Individual notes were made on all inventories and accounts from these counties and then assembled into dockets pertaining to the estates of all adult male decedents so encountered. Estates were dated by the earliest date in the records associated with the individual decedent. Linking records by means of decedents' names occasionally gets muddled by the problem of duplicate names, and the general absence of parish records for this period makes impossible any certainty about the identities of some of these individuals.

The six counties selected for the study draw from all areas fronting on the Chesapeake: on the western shore, Baltimore lies in the north, Anne Arundel just to the south, then Calvert, and finally Charles on the Potomac. Across the bay, on the eastern shore, Kent County is opposite southern Baltimore and northern Anne Arundel, while seventeenth-century Somerset covered the entire peninsula north of Virginia, on both sides of the spine of hills running down it, and north to the border of Talbot County.

Boundary adjustments made by the provincial legislature altered the size and location of some of the counties. Kent County's boundaries were rearranged three times in the course of a single decade, which probably altered the population base of that county's probate records in an important way during that period. Calvert County was shorn of its western frontier when Prince George's County was founded in 1692, and its borders with Charles were realigned at the same time. The principal effect on the probate records originating from this county was to reduce markedly its contribution in numbers; its character did not alter significantly.[2]

The following tables describe the full set and various subsets of the probated estates forming the basis for this book.[3]

TECHNICAL NOTE ON THE USE OF GPW AND PPW SETS OF RECORDS

For 166 estates, there were accounts but no inventories, and there is some evidence to believe that many of these are actually partial accounts, mere fragments of the original estate values involved. The mean gross personal wealth of these estates lies well below the mean of all inventoried estates, being valued at roughly a quarter of the mean value, but the effect on the mean for all estates is relatively small in any one time period with the exception of 1705-1712, when there were some 44 such estates and their values averaged only 16 percent of the mean for all inventoried estates in this period. Although these 166 estates were included in the per capita wealth estimates given in Chapter Three, they are excluded from all analyses dealing with the composition of wealth.

[2] The legislative acts establishing the system of inheritance in Maryland will be found in *Md.Arch.*, I, 64, 108, 155-57. In the same volume, pp. 533-34, one finds the legislation that first defined slavery as a lifetime condition, as distinguished from servitude and other forms of unfree status. A useful summary of seventeenth-century legislation on both these subjects is in *The Laws of the Province of Maryland . . . to the Year 1719* (Philadelphia, 1718), reprinted with an editorial note by John D. Cusing (Wilmington, Del., 1978).

[3] Edward B. Mathews, *The Counties of Maryland, Their Origin, Boundaries, and Election Districts* (Baltimore, 1907) is the authority. For the six counties used in the present study, probated estates of their residents numbered 3,699, only 3,533 of which included inventories. Hand tallies of estates without accounts of administration revealed that, on the average, the probability of encountering these rose with relative wealth and over time, but varied from county to county. The rate of accounts registered by upper wealth groups in Charles and Somerset fell substantially below the rates achieved by the other counties, whereas the poorest estates in Baltimore and Kent counties were much less likely to have accounts than those elsewhere. Somerset County proved most erratic overall.

Year	No. All	No. with Inventory	No. without Inventory	% All	x̄ GPW with Inventory	x̄ GPW without Inventory
1656-1683	661	640	21	3	£110	£78$^{1}/_{2}$
1684-1696	753	728	25	3	131$^{1}/_{2}$	56
1697-1704	716	678	38	5	149	74
1705-1712	741	697	44	6	166	49
1713-1719	828	790	38	5	172	64
Totals	3699	3533	166	4	147	63

TABLE C.1
NUMBERS OF INVENTORIED ESTATES IN SIX COUNTIES,
MARYLAND, BY WEALTH AND BY TIME
(£ current money≈sterling)

PPW	1656-1683	1684-1696	1697-1704	1705-1712	1713-1719	Total
£ 0-15	141	142	125	124	151	683
16-34	131	148	125	144	165	713
35-49	86	82	87	82	96	433
50-71	65	89	52	74	69	349
72-96	46	55	55	52	58	266
97-149	62	67	63	60	64	316
150-228	47	49	55	46	55	252
229-399	37	53	51	41	53	235
400-799	12	18	40	33	26	129
800-up	2	11	12	24	29	78
Total	629	714	665	680	766	3454

SOURCE FOR ALL TABLES IN APPENDIX C: Probate records of six counties, Maryland, in Hall of Records, Annapolis, Maryland.

TABLE C.2
DISTRIBUTION OF INVENTORIED ESTATES BY PERSONAL WEALTH,
Six Counties, Maryland, 1657-1719

PPW	All Estates	Heads of Households	Young Fathers	Room by Room
£ 0-49	52.95%	34.5%	28.8%	4.5%
50-149	26.95	34.5	38.1	14.3
150-799	17.8	27.1	30.0	55.3
800-up	2.3	3.9	3.1	25.9
Total	100.0%	100.0%	100.0%	100.0%
Nos.	3454	1863	604	111

TABLE C.3
DISTRIBUTION OF INVENTORIED ESTATES, HEADS OF HOUSEHOLDS*

PPW	1656-1683	1684-1696	1697-1704	1705-1712	1713-1719	Total
£ 0-15	16	22	29	20	26	113
16-34	44	57	51	55	74	281
35-49	50	38	50	47	63	248
50-71	35	53	36	53	48	225
72-96	25	32	37	44	41	179
97-149	37	53	43	54	52	179
150-228	31	45	42	42	44	204
229-399	32	44	38	32	41	187
400-799	9	16	31	33	25	114
800-up	2	11	10	23	27	73
Total	281	371	367	403	441	1863

* Includes only those positively identified as married.

TABLE C.4
DISTRIBUTION OF "YOUNG FATHERS'" ESTATES BY WEALTH CLASS
(£PPW≈sterling)

PPW	1656-1683	1684-1696	1697-1704	1705-1712	1713-1719	All	%
£ 0-15	6	6	9	2	8	31	5
16-34	17	15	16	9	16	73	12
35-49	17	13	13	14	13	70	12
50-71	18	21	15	16	12	82	14
72-96	15	17	9	13	13	67	11
97-149	19	20	14	21	7	81	13
150-228	18	18	21	7	9	73	12
229-399	14	11	18	10	10	63	10
400-799	7	7	11	12	8	45	7
800-up	2	2	4	6	5	19	3
Total	133	130	130	110	101	604	99

TABLE C.5
GEOGRAPHICAL DISTRIBUTION OF MARRIED MEN BELOW £50 PPW

County	1656-1683	1684-1696	1697-1704	1705-1712	1713-1719	Total
Anne Arundel	9	4	4	10	9	36
Baltimore	4	5	7	11	8	35
Calvert	6	9	13	5	1	34
Charles	5	5	23	14	13	60
Kent	2	3	3	7	4	19
Somerset	1	7	8	13	26	55
Totals	27	33	58	60	61	239

TABLE C.6
GEOGRAPHICAL DISTRIBUTION OF "YOUNG FATHERS'" ESTATES

County	1656-1683	1684-1696	1697-1704	1705-1712	1713-1719	Total
Anne Arundel	33	33	37	15	20	138
Baltimore	14	12	20	17	10	73
Calvert	44	40	27	12	16	139
Charles	19	15	19	21	20	94
Kent	16	8	9	25	13	71
Somerset	7	22	18	20	22	89
Totals	133	130	130	110	101	604

TABLE C.7
DISTRIBUTION OF ROOM-BY-ROOM INVENTORIES BY COUNTY AND TIME

County	1656-1683	1684-1696	1697-1704	1705-1712	1713-1719	Total
Anne Arundel	12	4	5	4	3	28
Baltimore	1	0	0	1	1	3
Calvert	8	15	4	6	9	42
Charles	0	5	2	3	1	11
Kent	1	2	0	6	0	9
Somerset	2	6	2	5	3	18
Total	24	32	13	25	17	111

TABLE C.8
DISTRIBUTION OF ROOM-BY-ROOM INVENTORIES BY WEALTH CLASS AND TIME

PPW	1656-1683	1684-1696	1697-1704	1705-1712	1713-1719	Total
£ 0-49	2	1	1	1	0	5
50-149	7	3	1	1	4	16
150-799	14	22	8	13	4	61
800-up	1	6	3	10	9	29
Total	24	32	13	25	17	111

TABLE C.9
NUMBERS OF ESTATES IN EACH STAGE OF THE LIFE CYCLE

Stage in Life Cycle	1656-1683	1684-1696	1697-1704	1705-1712	1713-1719	Total
?	230	210	176	134	153	903
1	144	154	142	175	210	825
9	48	72	108	124	130	482
2	42	39	27	41	43	192
0	13	36	22	28	22	121
3	144	147	143	125	126	685
7	8	17	24	25	21	95
4	19	46	35	42	58	200
5	8	16	22	24	35	105
8	2	7	5	12	9	35
6	3	9	12	11	21	56
Total	661	753	716	741	828	3699

KEY:
0 = children of uncertain age
1 = single
2 = married, no children in will
3 = married, all children under age
4 = married, oldest child of age, youngest child a minor
5 = married, all children grown, grandchildren
6 = married, at least one child of age, no other information
7 = married, all children grown
8 = married, grandchildren, but young children still at home
9 = married, no other information
? = unknown

TABLE C.10
PROPORTION OF ESTATES IN STAGES OF LIFE CYCLE

Stage	1656-1683	1684-1696	1697-1704	1705-1712	1713-1719
			Knowns Only		
Single	.33	.30	.28	.29$^{1}/_{2}$	.32
Young children	.53	.43	.42	.37	.32
Older children	.08	.17	.14	.17$^{1}/_{2}$	.20
Grown children	.06	.10	.16	.16	.16
			After Allocating Unknowns		
Single	.57	.29	.27	.29	.31
Young children	.34	.43	.43	.37	.32
Older children	.05	.17	.14	.18	.20
Grown children	.04	.11	.16	.16	.17

TABLE C.11
AVERAGE £GPW OF ESTATES IN EACH STAGE OF THE LIFE CYCLE
(current money of Maryland≈sterling)

Stage in Life Cycle	1656-1683	1684-1696	1697-1704	1705-1712	1713-1719	Average
?	£ 83	£ 66	£ 77	£ 99	£ 90	£ 81
1	60	54	86	39	42	54
9	99	122	101	85	130	108
2	118	198	348	296	230	230
0	261	116	117	354	176	198
3	177	177	198	225	251	204
7	80	225	403	266	260	278
4	142	265	223	271	231	237
5	211	178	256	640	788	506
8	96	874	282	319	426	376
6	175	319	127	359	177	225
Average	109	129	145	159	167	143

KEY:
0 = children of uncertain age
1 = single
2 = married, no children in will
3 = married, all children under age
4 = married, oldest child of age, youngest child a minor
5 = married, all children grown, grandchildren
6 = married, at least one child of age, no other information
7 = married, all children grown
8 = married, grandchildren, but young children still at home
9 = married, no other information
? = unknown

GLOSSARY OF ROOM NAMES IN MARYLAND INVENTORIES, 1660-1719

(percents indicate frequency of occurrence in room-by-room inventories)

buttery: 6 percent, used primarily for storage of dairy vessels, secondarily for brewing utensils.

cellar: 22 percent, used primarily for storage of beverages and other provisions, not always below ground or beneath other structures.

chamber: 82 percent, usually bedroom upstairs in houses with second story, occasionally on ground floor.

closet: 23 percent, used for storage and for reading; only in top quintile of general distribution, occurs both upstairs and downstairs, sometimes used as study.

garret: 4 percent, storage only, not in smaller houses of lower class; no trend.

hall: 68 percent, principally for dining and other activities, but changed over time, since half were used for sleeping in period before 1700, only a fifth thereafter; also slight decline in numbers. Similar to "outer room" in functions.

inner room: 20 percent, principally for sleeping, occasionaly for dining; no class difference; general increase in numbers.

kitchen: 71 percent, primarily for cooking, secondarily for other work tasks such as grinding. Few with beds; no class difference; increase in numbers.

loft: 17 percent, primarily for sleeping and storage; little class difference, but decline in usage over time.

milkhouse: 32 percent, primarily for dairying and storage, only secondarily for cooking, occasionally for sleeping. Not in lower class; increased in numbers among richest estates after 1700, declined elsewhere.

nursery: 3 percent, bedrooms, presumably for children, confined to upper classes entirely; occurred especially after 1700.

outer room: 18 percent, similar to hall but used more often for sleeping than hall, and usage more frequent among lower class. No change in numbers or usage over time.

parlor: 25 percent, primarily for sleeping, secondarily for dining. Although

293

not found in lower class, not confined to richest strata; general increase in numbers over time.

porch: 27 percent, appendage to front of house, particularly to protect front door; extended to second floor, which was generally walled over and used for storage, and more often found on larger houses than smaller ones. Decline in use among middle range of estates, expansion among the richest.

quarters: 31 percent, confined primarily to upper third of distribution, referred to separate building or work site, housing servants and/or slaves. Cooking utensils found in three-fifths of them, more likely among those belonging to the richest estates; declined in numbers over time, as other outbuildings with specialized functions made their appearance.

shed: 11 percent, one-story extension, usually lateral, often attached to the kitchen and used as a milkhouse. A third had beds in them before 1700; after that, all had beds.

store: 34 percent, used as storage for new goods, including hardware items, soap, and textiles. Confined to upper strata, some attached to the main house, but most separate buildings and without heating facilities.

study: 4 percent, not in lower class but not confined to richest strata; contain books, and occasionally a desk and writing materials.

GLOSSARY OF ROOM NAMES IN ENGLISH FARMHOUSES, SIXTEENTH AND SEVENTEENTH CENTURIES

buttery: a cool storage place, which may have been used for food currently being consumed, but primarily for drink (beer). Also a storage place for pots and pans not in use, especially in houses that had no kitchen and where cooking was done in the hall.

cellar: storage, usually below ground.

chamber: regional differences; in south, ground-floor room used for sleeping (replaced elsewhere by "parlour"); in north, usually, but not always, upstairs; in southwest: upstairs room for sleeping.

cheese house: usually an outbuilding, for storing cheese for ripening.

closet: invariably upstairs, a small room without a window.

cockloft: alternative name for garret, used for storage, over the hall or over the chambers, up against the roof.

dairy: alternative of milkhouse, used in Essex, Suffolk, and Norfolk, and west of the limestone belt.

dish house: variation on buttery.

drink house: same as dish house.

firehouse: where the hearth was; variation of hall.

fire room: same as firehouse.

garret: roof space.

hall: the living room, also "hall house"; replaced "house."

kitchen: complex, not always for cooking. Provided room for growing amount of equipment needed for baking, brewing, salting bacon, and making butter and cheese.

loft: roof space, no fixed access.

milkhouse: standard term in eastern and southern parts of England for dairy.

parlour: always ground floor, at superior end of hall, not always with a bed in it.

room: very rare except in East Anglia.

wash house: principally Kent: water supply.

BIBLIOGRAPHY

PRIMARY SOURCES

Manuscript Materials in Hall of Records, Annapolis:

Inventories and Accounts
Inventories
Accounts
Testamentary Proceedings
Will Books
Baltimore County Court Proceedings and Land Records
Charles County Inventories and Accounts
Kent County Inventories

Published Works

Archives of Maryland. Edited by William Hand Browne, et al. 72 vols. to date. Baltimore, 1883- .

Calendar of State Papers, Colonial Series, America and West Indies. Edited by W. Noel Sainsbury, et al. 43 vols. to date. London, 1860- .

Calvert Papers. Maryland Historical Society. Baltimore, 1889-1899.

Hartsook, Elizabeth, and Gust Skordas. *Land Office and Prerogative Court Records of Colonial Maryland.* Hall of Records Commission Publication No. 4. Annapolis, 1946.

The Statutes at Large, Being a Collection of All the Laws of Virginia. Edited by W. W. Hening. 13 vols. 1809-1823.

The Laws of the Province of Maryland, Collected into One Volume, by Order of the Governour and Assembly of the Said Province . . . to the Year 1719. Philadelphia, 1718; reprinted with an editorial note by John D. Cusing, Wilmington, Del., 1978.

Court Records of Prince Georges County, Maryland 1696-1699. Edited by Joseph H. Smith and Philip A. Crowl. American Legal Records, Vol. 9. Washington, D.C., 1964.

United States Bureau of the Census. *Historical Statistics of the United States, Colonial Times to 1970.* Bicentennial ed. 2 parts. Washington, D.C., 1975.

United States Department of Agriculture, Soil Conservation Service in cooperation with Maryland Agricultural Experiment Station. *Soil Survey of Anne Arundel County, Maryland.* Washington, D.C., 1973.

————. *Soil Survey of Calvert County, Maryland.* Washington, D.C., 1971.

————. *Soil Survey of Charles County, Maryland.* Washington, D.C., 1974.

————. *Soil Survey of Worcester County, Maryland.* Washington, D.C., 1973.

Billings, Warren M., ed. *The Old Dominion in the Seventeenth Century: A Documentary History of Virginia, 1606-1689.* Chapel Hill, 1975.

Brock, R. A., ed. *Alexander Spotswood, The Official Letters, 1710-1722.* 2 vols. Richmond, Va., 1882-1885.

Cummings, Abbott Lowell, ed. *Rural Household Inventories: Establishing the Names, Uses and Furnishings of Rooms in the Colonial New England Home, 1675-1775.* Boston, 1964.

Force, Peter. *Tracts and Other Papers, Relating Principally to the Origin, Settlement, and Progress of the Colonies in North America, from the Discovery of the Country to the Year 1776.* 4 vols. Washington, D.C., 1837-1846; reprinted Gloucester, Mass., 1963.

Hall, Clayton Coleman, ed. *Narratives of Early Maryland, 1633-84.* New York, 1910; reprinted New York, 1946.

Papenfuse, Edward C., Alan F. Day, David W. Jordon, and Gregory A. Stiverson. *A Biographical Dictionary of the Maryland Legislature, 1635-1789.* Vol. 1. A-H. Baltimore, 1979.

Beverly, Robert. *The History and Present State of Virginia.* Edited by Louis B. Wright. Charlottesville, 1947.

Bordley, John Beale. *A Summary View of the Courses of Crops, in the Husbandry of England and Maryland.* Philadelphia, 1789.

Byrd, William. *The Great American Gentleman: The Secret Diary of William Byrd of Westover, 1709-1712.* Edited by Louis B. Wright and Marion Tinling. New York, 1963.

———. *The Prose Works of William Byrd of Westover.* Edited by Louis B. Wright. Cambridge, Mass., 1966.

C. T. *An Advice How to Plant Tobacco in England and How to Bring It to Colour and Perfection, to Whom It May Be Profitable, and to Whom Harmfull.* London, 1615.

Carter, Robert. *The Letters of Robert Carter, 1720-1727.* Edited by Louis B. Wright. Chapel Hill, 1940.

Carver, Jonathan. *A Treatise on the Culture of the Tobacco Plant: with the Manner in Which It Is Usually Cured. Adapted to Northern Climates, and Designed for the Use of the Landholders of Great Britain.* London, 1779.

Cook, Ebenezer. *The Sot-Weed Factor: Or, a Voyage to Maryland. A Satyr.* London, 1708.

Child, Sir Josiah. *A New Discourse of Trade.* 1668; London, 1718.

Clayton, John. *The Reverend John Clayton, a Parson with a Scientific Mind: His Scientific Writings and Other Related Papers.* Edited by Edmund and Dorothy Smith Berkeley. Virginia Historical Society, *Documents,* VI. Charlottesville, 1965.

Dankers, Jaspar and Peter Sluyter. *Journal of a Voyage to New York and a Tour in Several of the American Colonies in 1679-80 by Jaspar Dankers and Peter Sluyter of Wieward in Friesland.* Translated by Henry C. Murphy. Brooklyn, 1867.

De Vries, David. *David Peterson de Vries, Voyages from Holland to America, 1632-1644.* Translated and edited by Henry C. Murphy. New York, 1857.

Doddridge, Joseph. *Notes on the Settlements and Indian Wars of the Western Parts of Virginia and Pennsylvania from 1763 to 1783, Inclusive, Together with a Review of the State of Society and Manners of the First Settlers of the Western Country.* 1824; Pittsburgh, 1912.

Durand, Monsieur. *A Frenchman in Virginia: Being the Memoirs of a Huguenot Refugee in 1686.* Translated and edited by Fairfax Harrison. N.p., 1923.

Fitzhugh, William. *Letters and Other Documents, 1676-1701.* Edited by Richard B. Davis. Charlottesville, 1963.

Fontaine, John. "Travel Diary, December 1714 to December 1718, a Journey from England to America." In Ann Maury, ed. *Memoirs of a Huguenot Family.* New York, 1852.

Harrower, John. *The Journal of John Harrower, an Indentured Servant in the Colony of Virginia, 1773-1776.* Edited by Edward Miles Riley. Colonial Williamsburg, 1963.

Hartwell, Henry; James Blair; and Edward Chilton. *The Present State of Virginia, and the College.* Edited by Hunter Dickinson Farish. Colonial Williamsburg, 1940, 1964.

Herndon, G. Melvin. *William Tatham and the Culture of Tobacco. Including a Facsimile Reprint of an Historical and Practical Essay on the Culture and Commerce of Tobacco by William Tatham.* Coral Gables, Florida, 1969.

Herrman, Augustin. *Virginia and Maryland . . . Surveyed and Exactly Drawn.* London, 1673.

Jefferson, Thomas. *Notes on the State of Virginia, 1781.* Edited by William Peden. Chapel Hill, 1955.

Jones, Hugh. "Maryland in 1699; A Letter from the Reverend Hugh Jones." Edited by Michael Kammen. *Journal of Southern History,* XXIX (1963), 362-72.

Jones, Hugh II. *The Present State of Virginia from Whence is Inferred a Short View of Maryland and North Carolina.* Edited with introduction by Richard L. Morton. Chapel Hill, 1956.

Josselyn, John. "Account of Two Voyages to New England." In *Massachusetts Historical Collections,* III. Boston, 1798, pp. 311-54.

Lawson, John. *A New Voyage to Carolina.* London, 1709. Readex Microprint.

Markham, Gervaise. *Country Contentments . . . The English Housewife: Containing the Inward and Outward Vertues Which Ought to be in a Compleate Woman: as Her Phisicke, Cookery, Banqueting-Stuffe, Distillation, Perfumes, Wooll, Hemp, Flaxe, Dairies, Brewing, Baking, and All Other Things Belonging to an Household.* London, 1615; reprinted New York, 1973.

"Narrative of a Voyage to Maryland, 1705-1706." *American Historical Review,* XII (1907), pp. 327-40.

Parr, Charles McKew, ed. *The Voyages of David De Vries, Navigator and Adventurer.* New York, 1969.

Randolph, Mary. *Virginia Housewife.* Philadelphia, 1855.

Taylor, John. *Arator.* 1813; Baltimore, 1817.

SECONDARY SOURCES

Alpert, Jonathan L. "The Origins of Slavery in the United States—The Maryland Precedent." *American Journal of Legal History,* XIV (1970), 189-221.

Anderson, Terry L. and Robert Paul Thomas. "The Growth of Population and Labor Force in the 17th-Century Chesapeake." *Explorations in Economic History,* XV (1978), 290-312.

Andrews, Charles M. *The Colonial Period of American History.* IV: *England's Commercial and Colonial Policy.* New Haven, 1938.

Appleby, Joyce Oldham. *Economic Thought and Ideology in Seventeenth-Century England.* Princeton, 1978.

Barley, M. W. *The English Farmhouse and Cottage.* London, 1961. "Farmhouses and Cottages, 1550-1725." *Economic History Review,* VII (1955), 291-306.

———. "Glossary of Names for Rooms in Houses of the Sixteenth and Seventeenth Centuries." In I. D. Foster and J. Alcock, eds. *Culture and Environment.* London, 1963, pp. 483-95.

Barrow, Thomas C. *Trade and Empire: The British Customs Service in Colonial America, 1660-1775.* Cambridge, Mass., 1967.

Batie, Robert Carlyle. "Why Sugar? Economic Cycles and the Changing of Staples on the English and French Antilles, 1624-54." *Journal of Caribbean History,* VIII (1976), 1-41.

Beer, George Louis. *The Old Colonial System, 1660-1754.* Part 1. *The Establishment of the System, 1660-1688.* New York, 1912.

———. *The Origins of the British Colonial System, 1578-1660.* New York, 1908.

Bowler, Clara Ann. "Carted Whores and White Shrouded Apologies: Slander in the County Courts of Seventeenth-Century Virginia." *Virginia Magazine of History and Biography,* LXXXV (1977), 411-26.

Bridenbaugh, Carl. *Vexed and Troubled Englishmen, 1590-1642.* New York, 1968.

Bronfenbrenner, Martin B. *Income Distribution Theory.* Chicago, 1972.

Brown, John Hull. *Early American Beverages.* Rutland, Vt., 1966.

Bruce, Philip A. *Economic History of Virginia in the Seventeenth Century.* 2 vols. New York, 1895.

Brunskill, R. W. *Illustrated Handbook of Vernacular Architecture.* London, 1970.

Buck, Philip W. *The Politics of Mercantilism.* New York, 1942.

Campbell, Mildred. "Social Origins of Some Early Americans." In James Morton Smith, ed. *Seventeenth-Century America: Essays in Colonial History.* Chapel Hill, 1959. Pp. 63-89.

300

Carr, Lois Green. "Ceramics from the John Hicks Site, 1723-1743; The St. Mary's Town Land Community." In Ian M. G. Quimby, ed. *Ceramics in America: Winterthur Conference Report, 1972.* Charlottesville, 1973.

———. "County Government in Maryland, 1684-1709." Ph.D. dissertation, Harvard University, 1968.

———. "The Foundations of Social Order: Local Government in Colonial Maryland." In Bruce C. Daniels, ed. *Essays in the Structure of Local Government in the American Colonies.* Middletown, Conn., 1978, pp. 72-110.

———. " 'The Metropolis of Maryland': A Comment on Town Development along the Tobacco Coast." *Maryland Historical Magazine,* LXIX (1974), 124-45.

———, and David William Jordan. *Maryland's Revolution of Government, 1689-1692.* Ithaca, 1974.

———, and Lorena S. Walsh. "Inventories and the Analysis of Wealth and Consumption Patterns in St. Mary's County, Maryland, 1658-1777." *The Newberry Papers in Family and Community History.* Chicago, 1978.

———. "Inventories and the Analysis of Wealth and Consumption Patterns in St. Mary's County, Maryland, 1658-1777." *Historical Methods,* XIII (1980), 81-104.

———. "The Planter's Wife: The Experience of White Women in Seventeenth-Century Maryland." *William and Mary Quarterly,* 3d. ser. XXXIV (1977), 542-71.

Carson, Barbara and Cary. "Styles and Standards of Living in Southern Maryland, 1670-1752." Paper presented to the annual meeting of the Southern Historical Association, Atlanta, 1976.

Carson, Cary. "The 'Virginia House' in Maryland." *Maryland Historical Magazine,* LXIX (1974), 185-96.

Carson, Cary, Norman F. Barka, William M. Kelso, Garry Wheeler Stone, and Dell Upton. "Impermanent Architecture in the Southern American Colonies." *Winterthur Portfolio,* XVI (1981), 135-96.

Clemens, Paul G. E. *The Atlantic Economy and Colonial Maryland's Eastern Shore: From Tobacco to Grain.* Ithaca, 1980.

Coleman, D. C. *The Economy of England, 1450-1750.* New York, 1977.

———. "Labour in the English Economy of the Seventeenth Century." *Economic History Review,* 2d ser. VIII (1956), 280-95.

Copeland, Peter. *Working Dress in Colonial and Revolutionary America.* Westport, Conn., 1977.

Cornwall, J. "Migration in England, 1660-1730." *Past and Present,* LXXXIII (1979), 57-90.

Craven, Avery Odelle. *Soil Exhaustion as a Factor in the Agricultural History of Virginia and Maryland, 1606-1860.* Urbana, Ill., 1926; reprint Gloucester, Mass., 1965.

Craven, Wesley Frank. *Red, White, and Black: The Seventeenth-Century Virginian.* Charlottesville, 1971.

Cunningham, William. *Growth of English Industry and Commerce*. 3 vols. Cambridge, 1921-1927.

Cunnington, C. Willett and Phillis Cunnington. *Handbook of English Costume in the 17th Century*. Boston, 1972.

————. *The History of Underclothes*. London, 1951.

Davies, K. G. *The Royal African Company*. London, 1957.

Deetz, James. *In Small Things Forgotten*. Boston, 1972.

Demos, John. "Families in Colonial Bristol, Rhode Island: An Exercise in Historical Demography." *William and Mary Quarterly*, 3d ser. XXV (1968), 40-57.

de Vries, Jan. "Peasant Demand Patterns and Economic Development: Friesland, 1500-1750." In William Parker and Eric L. Jones, eds. *European Peasants and Their Markets*. Princeton, 1975, pp. 205-69.

Dollar, Charles M. and Richard J. Jensen. *Historian's Guide to Statistics: Quantitative Analysis and Historical Research*. New York, 1971.

Domar, Evsey D. "The Causes of Slavery or Serfdom: A Hypothesis." *Journal of Economic History*, XXX (1970), 18-32.

Dow, George. *Everyday Life in the Massachusetts Bay Colony*. New York, 1935; reprint New York, 1967.

Drummond, Jack Cecil, and Anne Wilbraham. *The Englishman's Food: A History of Five Centuries of English Diet*. London, 1939.

Dunn, Richard S. "The Barbados Census of 1680: Profile of the Richest Colony in America." *William and Mary Quarterly*, 3d ser. XXVI (1969), 3-30.

————. *Sugar and Slaves: The Rise of the English Planter Class in the English West Indies, 1624-1713*. Chapel Hill, 1972.

Earle, Alice Morse. *Colonial Dames and Good Wives*. Boston and New York, 1896.

————. *Two Centuries of Costume*. 2 vols. Boston, 1903.

Earle, Carville V. *The Evolution of a Tidewater Settlement System: All Hallow's Parish, Maryland, 1650-1783*. Chicago, 1975.

Ernst, Joseph A., and H. Roy Merrens. " 'Camden's turrets pierce the skies!': The Urban Process in the Southern Colonies during the Eighteenth Century." *William and Mary Quarterly*, 3d ser. XXX (1973), 549-74.

Farnie, D. A. "The Commercial Empire of the Atlantic, 1607-1783." *Economic History Review*, 2d ser. XV (1962), 205-18.

Flaherty, David H. *Privacy in Colonial New England*. Charlottesville, 1972.

Fleisig, Heywood. "Slavery, the Supply of Agricultural Labor, and the Industrialization of the South." *Journal of Economic History*, XXXVI (1976), 572-97.

Fogel, Robert William and Stanley L. Engerman. *Time on the Cross: The Economics of American Negro Slavery*. 2 vols. Boston, 1974.

Forman, Henry C. *Early Manor and Plantation Houses of Maryland*. Easton, Md., 1934.

————. *Maryland Architecture: A Short History from 1634 through the Civil War.* Cambridge, Md., 1968.

————. *Old Buildings, Gardens, and Furniture in Tidewater Maryland.* Cambridge, Md., 1967.

————. *Tidewater Maryland Architecture and Gardens: a Sequel to Early Manor and Plantation Houses of Maryland.* New York, 1956.

————. *Virginia Architecture in the Seventeenth Century.* Williamsburg, Va., 1957.

Galenson, David. "British Servants and the Colonial Indenture System in the Eighteenth Century." *Journal of Southern History,* XLIV (1978), 41-66.

————. "Immigration and the Colonial Labor System: An Analysis of the Length of Indenture." *Explorations in Economic History,* XIV (1977), 36-77.

————. " 'Middling People' or 'Common Sort'?: The Social Origins of Some Early Americans Reexamined." With a "Rebuttal" by Mildred Campbell. *William and Mary Quarterly,* 3d ser. XXXV (1978), 499-540.

————. "The Slave Trade to the English West Indies, 1673-1724." *Economic History Review,* 2d ser. XXXII (1979), 241-49.

————, and Russell R. Menard. "Approaches to the Analysis of Economic Growth in Colonial British America." *Historical Methods,* XIII (1980), 3-18.

Gallman, J. M. "Determinants of the Age at First Marriage in Colonial North Carolina." *William and Mary Quarterly,* 3d ser., forthcoming.

————. "Mortality among White Males in Colonial North Carolina." *Social Science History,* IV (1980), 295-316.

Gemery, Henry A. "Emigration from the British Isles to the New World, 1630-1700: Inferences from Colonial Populations." *Research in Economic History,* V (1980), 179-232.

Gill, Harold B. Jr. "Cereal Grains in Colonial Virginia." Report prepared for Colonial Williamsburg Foundation, Inc. October 1974.

————. "Tobacco Culture in Colonial Virginia. A Preliminary Report." Prepared for Colonial Williamsburg Foundation, Inc. April 1972.

————, and George M. Curtis III. "Virginia's Colonial Probate Policies and the Preconditions for Economic History." *Virginia Magazine of History and Biography,* LXXXVII (1979), 68-73.

Glass, D. V., and D.E.C. Eversley, eds. *Population in History: Essays in Historical Demography.* Chicago, 1965.

Glassie, Henry H. *Folk Housing in Middle Virginia.* Philadelphia, 1975.

————. *Pattern in the Material Folk Culture of the Eastern United States.* Philadelphia, 1968.

Gray, Lewis C. *History of Agriculture in the Southern United States to 1860.* 2 vols. Washington, D.C., 1932.

————. "The Market Surplus Problems of Colonial Tobacco." *Agricultural History,* II (1928), 1-34.

Greven, Philip J. Jr. *Four Generations: Population, Land and Family in Colonial Andover, Massachusetts*. Ithaca, 1970.

Harper, Lawrence A. *The English Navigation Laws: A Seventeenth-Century Experiment in Social Engineering*. New York, 1939.

Harris, Marshall. *Origin of the Land Tenure System in the United States*. Ames, Iowa, 1953.

Harris, P.M.G. "Integrating Interpretations of Local and Regionwide Changes in the Study of Economic Development and Demographic Growth in the Colonial Chesapeake, 1630-1775." In *Working Papers from the Regional Economic History Research Center*, I (1978), 35-71.

Hecht, Irene W.D. "The Virginia Muster of 1624/5 as a Source for Demographic History." *William and Mary Quarterly*, 3d ser. XXX (1973), 65-92.

Hecksher, Eli F. *Mercantilism*. 2d. ed. 2 vols. London, 1955.

Hemphill, John M. "Virginia and the English Commercial System, 1689-1733: Studies in the Development and Fluctuations of a Colonial Economy under Imperial Control." Ph.D. dissertation, Princeton University, 1964.

Hicks, Marjorie, comp. *Clothing for Ladies and Gentlemen of Higher and Lower Standing: A Working Pamphlet to Aid the Imitation of New England Citizens of the Eighteenth Century*. Washington, D.C., 1976.

Hilliard, Sam. *Hogmeat and Hoecakes: Food Supply in the Old South, 1840-1860*. Carbondale, Ill., 1972.

Hole, Christine. *The English Housewife in the Seventeenth Century*. London, 1953.

Holliday, Carl. *Woman's Life in Colonial Days*. Boston, 1922.

Hoskins, W. G. "Harvest Fluctuations, 1620-1759." *Agricultural History Review*, XVI (1968), 15-31.

———. *The Midland Peasant*. London and New York, 1965.

———. "The Rebuilding of Rural England, 1570-1640." *Past and Present*, IV (1953), 44-59.

Hranacky, William Jack. "A Paleodemographic Study of Prehistoric Virginia Skeletons." *Quarterly Bulletin of the Archeological Society of Virginia*, XXX (1975), 1-17.

Jonas, Manfred. "Wages in Early Colonial Maryland." *Maryland Historical Magazine*, II (1956), 27-28.

Jones, Alice Hanson. *Wealth of a Nation to Be*. New York, 1980.

Kammen, Michael. *Empire and Interest: The American Colonies and the Politics of Mercantilism*. New York, 1970.

Karinen, Arthur E. "Numerical and Distributional Aspects of Maryland Population 1631-1840." *Maryland Historical Magazine*, LIV (1959), 365-407; LX (1965), 139-59.

Kerridge, E. "The Movement of Rent, 1540-1640." *Economic History Review*, 2d ser. VI (1953), 16-34.

Kiple, Kenneth F. and Virginia H. "Black Yellow Fever Immunities, Innate and Acquired, as Revealed in the American South." *Social Science History*, I (1977), 419-36.

Kulikoff, Allan. "The Origins of Afro-American Society in Tidewater Maryland and Virginia, 1700 to 1790." *William and Mary Quarterly*, 3d ser. XXXV (1978), 226-59.

————. "A 'Prolifick' People: Black Population Growth in the Chesapeake Colonies, 1700-1790." *Southern Studies*, XVI (1977), 391-428.

Kupp, Jan. "Dutch Notarial Acts Relating to the Tobacco Trade of Virginia, 1608-1653." *William and Mary Quarterly*, 3d ser. XXX (1973), 653-55.

Land, Aubrey C. *The Dulaneys of Maryland: Daniel Dulany the Elder (1685-1753) and Daniel Dulany the Younger (1722-1797)*. Baltimore, 1955.

————. "Economic Base and Social Structure: The Northern Chesapeake in the Eighteenth Century." *Journal of Economic History*, XXV (1965), 639-54.

————, Lois Green Carr, and Edward C. Papenfuse, eds. *Law, Society, and Politics in Early Maryland*. Baltimore, 1977.

Lemon, James T. *The Best Poor Man's Country: A Geographical Study of Early Southeastern Pennsylvania*. Baltimore, 1972.

Leonard, Sister Joan de Lourdes. "Operation Checkmate: The Birth and Death of a Virginia Blueprint for Progress, 1600-1676." *William and Mary Quarterly*, 3d ser. XXIV (1967), 44-74.

Lockridge, Kenneth A. "The Population of Dedham, Massachusetts, 1636-1736." *Economic History Review*, 2d ser. XIX (1966), 318-44.

Machin, R. "The Great Rebuilding: A Reassessment." *Past and Present*, LXXVII (1977), 33-56.

Main, Gloria L. "The Correction of Biases in Colonial American Probate Records." *Historical Methods Newsletter*, VIII (1974), 10-28.

————. "Inequality in Early America: The Evidence from Probate Records of Massachusetts and Maryland." *Journal of Interdisciplinary History*, VII (1977), 559-81.

————. "Probate Records as a Source for Early American History." *William and Mary Quarterly*, 3d ser. XXXII (1975), 88-99.

Main, Jackson Turner. *Connecticut Society in the Era of the American Revolution*. Hartford, Conn., 1977.

————. "The Distribution of Property in Post-Revolutionary Virginia." *Mississippi Valley Historical Review*, XLI (1954), 241-58.

————. "The One Hundred." *William and Mary Quarterly*, 3d ser. XI (1954), 354-84.

Mathews, Edward Bennett. *The Counties of Maryland: Their Origin, Boundaries, and Election Districts*. Maryland Geological Survey, VI. Baltimore, 1907.

————. *The Maps and Map-Makers of Maryland*. Baltimore, 1898.

McCusker, John J. *Money and Exchange in Europe and America, 1600-1775: A Handbook.* Chapel Hill, 1978.

————, and Russell R. Menard. "The Economy of British America, 1607-1790: Needs and Opportunities for Study." Paper Prepared for a Conference on the Economy of British America at Williamsburg, Virginia, October 9-10, 1980.

Menard, Russell R. "British Migration to the Chesapeake Colonies in the Seventeenth Century." Paper presented to the Economic History Workshop, Department of Economics, University of Chicago, February 29, 1980.

————. "The Demography of Somerset County, Maryland: a Preliminary Report." Paper presented at the Stony Brook Conference on Social History, June 1975.

————. "Economy and Society in Early Colonial Maryland." Ph.D. Dissertation, University of Iowa, 1974.

————. "Farm Prices of Maryland Tobacco, 1659-1710." *Maryland Historical Magazine,* LXVIII (1973), 80-85.

————. "Five Maryland Censuses, 1700 to 1712: A Note on the Quality of the Quantities." *William and Mary Quarterly,* 3d ser. XXXVII (1980), 616-26.

————. "From Servant to Freeholder: Status Mobility and Property Accumulation in Seventeenth-Century Maryland." *William and Mary Quarterly,* 3d ser. XXX (1973), 37-64.

————. "From Servants to Slaves: The Transformation of the Chesapeake Labor System." *Southern Studies,* XVI (1977), 355-90.

————. "The Growth of Population in Early Colonial Maryland, 1631-1712." Report prepared for the St. Mary's City Commission, April 1972.

————. "The Maryland Slave Population, 1658 to 1730: A Demographic Profile of Blacks in Four Counties." *William and Mary Quarterly,* 3d ser. XXXII (1975), 29-54.

————. "A Note on Chesapeake Tobacco Prices, 1618-1660." *Virginia Magazine of History and Biography,* LXXIV (1976), 401-10.

————. "The Tobacco Industry in the Chesapeake Colonies, 1617-1730: an Interpretation." *Research in Economic History,* V (1980), 109-77.

————. "Why African Slavery? Free Land, Plantation Agriculture, and the Supply of Labor in the Growth of British-American Slave Societies." Paper presented at the Conference on New World Slavery: Comparative Perspectives, Rutgers University, Newark, N.J., May 1980.

————, P.M.G. Harris, and Lois Green Carr. "Opportunity and Inequality: The Distribution of Wealth on the Lower Western Shore of Maryland, 1638-1705." *Maryland Historical Magazine,* LXIX (1974), 169-84.

Middleton, Arthur Pierce. *Tobacco Coast: A Maritime History of Chesapeake Bay in the Colonial Era.* Newport News, 1953.

Montell, William Lynwood, and Michael Lynn Morse. *Kentucky Folk Architecture*. Lexington, Ky., 1976.

Morgan, Edmund S. *American Slavery, American Freedom: The Ordeal of Colonial Virginia*. New York, 1975.

———. "Slavery and Freedom: The American Paradox." *Journal of American History*, LIX (1972), 5-29.

Morris, Richard B. *Government and Labor in Early America*. New York, 1946.

Morriss, Margaret. *Colonial Trade of Maryland, 1689-1715*. Baltimore, 1914.

Nettels, Curtis P. "British Mercantilism and Economic Development of the Thirteen Colonies." *Journal of Economic History*, XII (1952), 105-14.

———. *The Money Supply of the American Colonies before 1720*. 1934; reprinted New York, 1967.

Noel-Hume, Ivor. *A Guide to Artifacts of Colonial America*. New York, 1970.

Norton, Susan L. "Population Growth in Colonial America: A Study of Ipswich, Massachusetts." *Population Studies*, XXV (1971), 433-52.

Owings, Donnell M. *His Lordship's Patronage: Offices of Profit in Colonial Maryland*. Baltimore, 1953.

Papenfuse, Edward C., Jr. "Planter Behavior and Economic Opportunity in a Staple Economy." *Agricultural History*, XLVI (1972), 297-311.

Pearsall, Marion. "Cultures of the American South." *Anthropological Quarterly*, XXXIX (1966), 128-41.

Phelps Brown, E. H., and S. V. Hopkins. "Seven Centuries of the Prices of Consumables Compared with Builders' Wage-Rates." *Economica*, XXIII (1956), 296-314.

Phipps, Frances. *Colonial Kitchens, Their Furnishings, and Their Gardens*. Hawthorne, N.Y., 1972.

Pillsbury, Richard and Andrew Kardos. *A Field Guide to the Folk Architecture of the Northeastern United States*. Hanover, N.H., n.d.

Porter, Frank W. "A Century of Accomodation: The Nanticoke Indians in Colonial Maryland." *Maryland Historical Magazine*, LXXIV (1979), 175-92.

Price, Jacob. "The Economic Growth of the Chesapeake and the European Market, 1697-1775." *Journal of Economic History*, XXIV (1964), 496-511.

———. "The Rise of Glasgow in the Chesapeake Tobacco Trade, 1707-1775." *William and Mary Quarterly*, 3d ser. XI (1954), 179-99.

———. *France and the Chesapeake: A History of the French Tobacco Monopoly, 1674-1791, and of Its Relationship to the British American Tobacco Trades*. 2 vols. Ann Arbor, 1973.

———. *The Tobacco Adventure to Russia: Enterprise, Politics, and Diplomacy in the Quest for a Northern Market for English Colonial Tobacco, 1676-1722*. In *Transactions of the American Philosophical Society*, New ser. LI, part 1 (1961).

Rainbolt, John C. "The Absence of Towns in Seventeenth-Century Virginia." *Journal of Southern History*, XXXV (1969), 343-60.

Rainbolt, John C. "The Alteration in the Relationship between Leadership and Constituents in Virginia, 1660 to 1720." *William and Mary Quarterly*, 3d ser. XXVII (1970), 411-34.

———. *From Prescription to Persuasion: Manipulation of the Seventeenth-Century Virginia Economy*. Port Washington, N.Y., 1974.

Rees, J[ames] F. "Mercantilism and the Colonies." In *The Old Empire from the Beginning to 1781*, Vol. 1 of *Cambridge History of the British Empire*. Edited by J[ohn] Holland Rose et al. Cambridge, 1929, pp. 561-602.

Reps, John W. *Tidewater Towns: City Planning in Colonial Virginia and Maryland*. Colonial Williamsburg, 1972.

Roeber, A. G. "Authority, Law, and Customs: The Ritual of Court Day in Tidewater Virginia, 1720-1750." *William and Mary Quarterly*, 3d ser. XXXVII (1980), 29-52.

Russell, John H. *The Free Negro in Virginia, 1619-1865*. 1913; reprinted New York, 1967.

Rutman, Darrett B. "The Social Web: A Prospectus for the Study of Early American Community." In William L. O'Neill, ed. *Insights and Parallels: Problems and Issues of American Social Study*. Minneapolis, 1973, pp. 57-123.

———, and Anita H. Rutman. "Of Agues and Fevers: Malaria in the Early Chesapeake." *William and Mary Quarterly*, 3d ser. XXXIII (1976), 31-60.

———. " 'More True and Perfect Lists': The Reconstruction of Censuses for Middlesex County, Virginia, 1668-1704." *Virginia Magazine of History and Biography*, LXXXVIII (1980), 37-74.

Rutman, Darrett B., Charles Wetherell, and Anita H. Rutman. "Rhythms of Life: Black and White Seasonality in the Early Chesapeake." *Journal of Interdisciplinary History*, XI (1980), 29-53.

Scharf, J. Thomas. *History of Maryland from the Earliest Period to the Present Day*. 3 vols. 1879; reprinted Hatboro, Pa., 1967.

Schlebecker, John. *Agricultural Implements and Machines in the Collection of the National Museum of History and Technology*. Washington, D.C., 1972.

Schmidt, Albert J. "Applying Old World Habits to the New Life in South Carolina at the Turn of the Eighteenth Century." *Huntington Library Quarterly*, XXV (1961-1962), 51-59.

Schumpeter, Elizabeth B. "English Prices and Public Finance, 1660-1682." *Review of Economics and Statistics*, XX (1938), 21-37.

Seebohm, M. E. *The Evolution of the English Farm*. London, 1927.

Semmes, Raphael. *Crime and Punishment in Early Maryland*. Baltimore, 1938.

Sheridan, Richard B. *Sugar and Slavery: An Economic History of the British West Indies, 1623-1775*. St. Lawrence, Barbados, 1974.

Shurtleff, Harold R. *The Log Cabin Myth: A Study of the Early Dwellings of the English Colonists in North America*. Cambridge, Mass., 1939.

Slicher Van Bath, B. H. *The Agrarian History of Western Europe, A.D. 500-1850*. Translated by Olive Ordish. London, 1963.

Sloane, Eric. *A Museum of Early American Tools*. New York, 1964.

Smith, Abbot Emerson. *Colonists in Bondage: White Servitude and Convict Labor in America, 1607-1776*. Chapel Hill, 1947.

Smith, Daniel Blake. "Mortality and Family in the Colonial Chesapeake." *Journal of Interdisciplinary History*, VIII (1978), 403-27.

Smith, Daniel Scott. "The Demographic History of Colonial New England." *Journal of Economic History*, XXXII (1972), 165-83.

————. "The Estimation of Early American Historical Demographers: Two Steps Forward, One Step Back, What Steps in the Future." *Historical Methods*, XII (1979), 24-38.

————. "Parental Power and Marriage Patterns: An Analysis of Historical Trends in Hingham, Massachusetts." *Journal of Marriage and the Family*, XXXV (1973), 419-28.

Smith, J. T. "The Evolution of the English Peasant House to the Late Seventeenth Century: The Evidence of Buildings." *Journal of British Archeological Association*, 3d ser. XXXIII (1970), 122-27.

Sosin, Jack M. *English America and the Restoration Monarchy of Charles II: Transatlantic Politics, Commerce, and Kinship*. Lincoln, Neb., 1980.

Souden, David. " 'Rogues, Whores, and Vagabonds' ": Indentured Servant Emigrants to North America, and the Case of Mid-Seventeenth Century Bristol." *Social History*, III (1978).

South, Stanley. *Method and Theory in Historical Archeology*. New York, 1977.

Spruill, Julia Cherry. *Women's Life and Work in the Southern Colonies*. 1938; reprinted New York, 1972.

Stein, Charles Francis. *A History of Calvert County, Maryland*. Baltimore, 1960.

Steiner, Bernard C. *The Institutions and Civil Government of Maryland*. Boston, 1899.

Stiverson, Gregory A., and Patrick H. Butler III, eds. "Virginia in 1732: The Travel Journal of William Hugh Grove." *Virginia Magazine of History and Biography*, LXXXV (1977), 18-44.

Stone, Garry Wheeler. "St. John's: Archeological Questions and Answers." *Maryland Historical Magazine*, LXIX (1974), 146-68.

Stone, Lawrence. *Family, Sex and Marriage in England, 1500-1800*. New York, 1977.

Supple, Barry E. *Commercial Crisis and Change in England, 1600-1642*. Cambridge, 1959.

Tate, Thad W., and David L. Ammerman, eds. *The Chesapeake in the Seventeenth Century: Essays on Anglo-American Society*. Chapel Hill, 1979.

Thirsk, Joan, ed. *The Agrarian History of England and Wales, IV, 1500-1640*. Cambridge, 1967.

————. "Seventeenth-Century Agriculture and Social Change." *Agricultural History Review*, XVIII (1970), *Supplement*, 167-77.

Thompson, Tommy R. "Debtors, Creditors, and the General Assembly in Colonial Maryland." *Maryland Historical Magazine*, LXXII (1977), 59-77.

309

Tryon, Rolla M. *Household Manufactures in the United States, 1640-1860.* Chicago, 1917; reprinted New York, 1966.

Van Wagenen, Jared, Jr. *The Golden Age of Homespun.* Ithaca, 1953.

Viner, Jacob. *Studies in the Theory of International Trade.* New York, 1937.

Vinovskis, Maris A. "Mortality Rates and Trends in Massachusetts before 1860." *Journal of Economic History,* XXXII (1972), 184-213.

Walsh, Lorena Seeback. "Charles County, Maryland, 1658-1705: A Study of Chesapeake Social and Political Structure." Ph.D. dissertation, Michigan State University, 1977.

———, and Russell R. Menard. "Death in the Chesapeake: Two Life Tables for Men in Early Colonial Maryland." *Maryland Historical Magazine,* LIX (1974), 211-27.

Walsh, Richard, and William Lloyd Fox, eds. *Maryland: A History, 1632-1974.* Baltimore, 1974.

Warfield, J. D. *The Founders of Anne Arundel and Howard Counties, Maryland.* 1905; reprinted Baltimore, 1967.

Weatherwax, Paul. *Indian Corn in Old America.* New York, 1954.

Wertenbaker, Thomas Jefferson. *Planters of Colonial Virginia.* Princeton, 1922.

Weslager, C. A. *The Log Cabin in America: From Pioneer Days to the Present.* New Brunswick, N.J., 1969.

Wiecek, William M. "The Statutory Law of Slavery and Race in the Thirteen Mainland Colonies of British America." *William and Mary Quarterly,* 3d ser. XXXIV (1977), 258-80.

Wilson, Charles. *Mercantilism.* London, 1958.

Wood, Peter H. *Black Majority: Negroes in Colonial South Carolina from 1670 through the Stono Rebellion.* New York, 1974.

Wright, James M. *The Free Negro in Maryland, 1634-1860. Studies in History, Economics and Public Law,* XCVII, No. 3. New York, 1921.

Wright, Louis B. *The First Gentlemen of Virginia: Intellectual Qualities of the Early Colonial Ruling Class.* San Marino, Cal., 1940.

Wycoff, Vertress J. "Land Prices in Seventeenth-Century Maryland." *American Economic Review,* XXVIII (1938), 81-88.

———. "The Sizes of Plantations in Seventeenth-Century Maryland." *Maryland Historical Magazine,* XXXII (1937), 331-39.

———. *Tobacco Regulation in Colonial Maryland.* Baltimore, 1936.

INDEX

311

Deane, John, 120
death: average age at, 14; rates, 258
debts, 43, 58, 70; payable, 86; receivable, 50-52, 81, 86, 87, 90, 226
decorative effects, 157
Delty, George, 167
demographic transition in Maryland, 85, 92
demography, works in, 13
Dennis, Dommack, 223, 224
Dent, Col. William, 135
Denton, Thomas, 178
depressions, economic, 6, 7, 17, 21, 164, 258, 260
desk, 229
Diddy (Negro), 134
Diggs, Col. William, 107
dining room, 165
dish covers, 232
dish house, 163
distiller, 82
diversification, economic, 58, 72, 78, 86
division of labor between the sexes, 175, 179, 180
doctor, 82
dogs, 136, 171
domestic manufactures, *see* home manufactures
doublet and hose, 188
dower rights, 172
DR, *see* debts receivable
drams, 198, 212, 213
draperies, 226
drawers (apparel), 186-188
dressing basket, 237
dressing box, 232
Drewry, William, 211
drinking pot, 222-224
drinking vessel, 171, 190
dripping pan, 223, 224, 228
duck, 208, 209
Durand, of Dauphine, 115, 144, 151, 192
dutch cases (of glass bottles), 229
dysentery, 13, 136

Earl, William, 118
earthen pans, 83

earthenware, 169-172, 176, 223-225, 229, 230, 232, 248
East Midlands (England), 149
eating, 169, 175, 181, 191
economic development: colonies, 5, 7, 8; growth, 53-54
eggs, 208, 209
Ellery, Hugh, 213
employment, in England, 24
England (also Britain and Great Britain), 18, 21, 22, 24, 28, 153, 251, 266
English, 246, 254, 258-260, 262; culture, 264; goods imported into the colonies, 69-72; immigrants, 9, 10
epidemic diseases, 12
Erickson, John, 179
Essex County, Massachusetts, 153, 154
estuaries, pollution of, 136
Evans, Lewis, 117
export staples: tobacco and sugar, 5

factories, 248
fallow, 41
families, composition of, 157
family connections, 80
family formation, 258; among blacks, 127
family relationships, 86
family size in New England, 157
family ties, nature of, in Chesapeake, 264
fans, 207, 233
farmers in England, 10
farmhouses, 142, 147, 153; in England, 163
farm laborers in England, 10, 155
farm technology in seventeenth century, 68
feathers, 215, 224
Fenix, William, 121
fertilizer (dung), 31, 41
fieldwork, 108, 112, 177, 178, 180
financial credits, 87
fire room, 163
fire screen, 237
firehouse, 163
fireplace, 167, 191, 223, 227-233

livestock, 60, 62, 67, 68, 83, 87, 88, 90,
 208, 230, 233, 236, 238, 251-253,
 259, 262
living conditions, of wealth classes
 compared, 225
"Locust Thicket" (Quarter), 133
Loe (Lee?), Richard, 188
loft, 142, 161, 162, 164, 168, 226-229,
 234
log cabins, 143, 150
London, England, 236; merchant firms
 of, 58
Londontown, Anne Arundel County,
 211, 231
longevity, 13
looking glasses, 169, 170, 174, 175,
 208, 222-224, 227-229, 232, 233,
 237, 240, 244-246, 255
looms, 51, 73, 109, 164, 235
Loyler, James, 116
LV (livestock), 88, 89

Magruder, Alexander, 125
Maine, Robert, 121, 122, 150
malaria, 6, 13, 111, 136, 137
Malone, Edward, 133, 134
malt, 161
mantle, fireplace, 222
maps, 229, 233, 235
markets: in colonies, for English
 goods, 4; domestic, 42
Markham, Gervaise, 175, 181
Markham, Richard, 107
"marking letters," 234
marriage, average age at: men, 14;
 women, 15
marriageable women, scarcity of, 109
marriages, duration of, 15
married heads of households, 170
Martin, Robert, 179
Maryland Assembly, 38, 82, 173, 226;
 census of 1704, 93; economy, dependent on tobacco, 5; founded, 6
mass production, 248
Massachusetts, 12, 217, 238, 265
Matapan River, 30
material culture, 247, 254, 258
material life, 261
material standard of living, 155

mathematics, 244
Mattawoman Creek, 135
meat, 190, 191, 195, 200, 202, 203,
 208; estimating consumption of,
 203-204
medicines, 237
Menard, Russell R., 7, 23
mercantile investments, 87
mercantilism, English, 3
merchant-planters, 90, 236
merchants, 79, 82, 231, 238, 251
Middle Colonies, 94, 95
Middlesex County, Virginia, 136
militia, 82, 225, 234
milk, 83, 171, 192, 195, 199, 200, 205,
 208
milk room, 219
milk trays, 223
milkhouse, 83, 142, 160, 161, 163,
 164, 166, 222, 227, 229, 232, 235
mill, 133
mill house, 163, 193, 229
millers, 77, 78, 84, 108
milling, 87
millstones, 193, 195
Mingo (Negro), 125
mirrors, *see* looking glasses
mobility, 92
Model T, 45
molasses, 122, 198, 205, 208, 221
Moll (Negro girl), 134
Moloney, Loling, 211
moral treatises, 244
Morgan, Edmund S., 197
Morgan, Mistress, 212
mortality, 137, 197, 260; adult, 6, 12,
 15; race differences, 136-137; rates
 of, 91, 99
"mortar boys," 194
mortars, 109, 111, 163, 169, 192, 193,
 222, 228
muffs, 207
mulattoes, 127, 187
Mungoe (free Negro), 123
musical instruments, 248
mutton, 195, 208, 209

nails, 70, 182, 234
nakedness, 184

pillowcases, 229
pipe smoking, 22
pistols, 228
"plain" style, 226, 231, 239
plantations, layouts of, 140, 148, 215
planter oligarchy, 239
plate, *see* silver
Plater, George, 133, 134, 135
Plowden, Edmund, 144
plows, 74, 75, 76, 77, 200, 260
pneumonia, 13
pone, 192, 195, 199, 205. *See also* corn
"poor married men" sample, 67
Popes Creek, 134
population: of Maryland, 6; of Virginia and Maryland, 18, 19
population, black, conditions for natural growth, 125-126
population, Chesapeake colonies: composition, 19; density, 269; dispersal, 42, 44; fertility, 13; growth, 12, 15, 16, 24, 100, 123, 260
population growth in England, 10
population growth in older colonies after 1700, 11
porch, 161, 226, 227
pork, 21, 66, 69, 192, 196, 200, 202–204, 209, 261
porridge, 220
porringers, 224
Port Tobacco Creek, 130, 131
portmanteau, 237
Portobacco, 135
Portugal, 198
posture, 190
pot racks, 224
potatoes (sweet), 195–197, 204, 221
pothooks, 182
Potomac River, 28, 30, 81, 130, 285
pots, 169, 170, 174, 176, 191, 220, 224, 227, 229, 230, 240; cast iron, 168; iron, 172, 182
poultry, 83, 177
powder (gun), 223
powdering tubs, 232
PPW (physical personal wealth), 51–54, 57, 59, 60, 74–77, 80, 81, 84, 152, 154, 158, 219, 226, 236, 242, 252, 253, 267, 268, 286, 288, 289

prenuptial agreements, 172
prices: in inventories, *see* Appendix B; of farm crops in England, 10; of food in England, 11; of servants and slaves, 101-102; of sugar, 11; of tobacco, *see* tobacco
primers, 243
Prince George's County, 107, 286
priorities, planter, 7, 166, 168, 239, 240, 249, 254, 256
privacy, 157, 246, 254
privateers, French, 22
Privy Council, 148
probate records, Maryland, 7, 16, 48, 49, 91. *See also* Appendix C.
probate records, York County, Virginia, 102
propertyless, 101; in England, 115
Proprietor, of Maryland, 79
Protestants, 130
Provincial Court, 173
psalm books, 243
psalters, 243
pudding pans, 232
pumpkins, 197, 198
punch bowl, 237
punishment, 266
Puritans, 6, 184
Pye, Col. Edward, 107

Quakers, 6, 79, 85, 138, 226, 236, 257; missionaries, 45
quarters, 152, 153, 161–164, 217, 223, 227, 229, 235; at home, 128; housekeeping equipment, 133, 134; material conditions, 133; outlying, 128
Queen Anne's County, 104
"Queens Arms," 237
quilts, 215
quince drink, 197
quinces, 198
quoifs, 207

"R. G.," 137
Raby, John, 180
race relations, 130, 134, 137–139
Rains, John, 122
Rappahannock River, 28, 81
raspberries, 208

Library of Congress Cataloging in Publication Data

Main, Gloria L. (Gloria Lund), 1933-
Tobacco colony.

Bibliography: p.
Includes index.
1. Tobacco industry—Maryland—History.
2. Maryland—History—Colonial period, ca. 1600-
1775. 3. Maryland—Economic conditions.
4. Plantations—Maryland—History. I. Title.
HD9137.M3M34 1982 338.1'7371'0952 82-47603
ISBN 0-691-04693-X   AACR2